WORLD® AIR POWER
JOURNAL

Aerospace Publishing Ltd
AIRtime Publishing Inc.

Published quarterly by
Aerospace Publishing Ltd
179 Dalling Road
London W6 0ES
UK

Copyright © Aerospace Publishing Ltd
Cutaway drawings copyright
© Mike Badrocke/Aviagraphica

ISSN 0959-7050
Aerospace ISBN 1 86184 006 3
(softback)
1 86184 007 1
(hardback)
Airtime ISBN   1-880588-07-2
(hardback)

Published under licence in USA and
Canada by AIRtime Publishing Inc.,
USA

Editorial Offices:
WORLD AIR POWER JOURNAL
Aerospace Publishing Ltd
3A Brackenbury Road
London   W6 0BE   UK
E-mail: info@aerospacepbl.co.uk

Publisher: Stan Morse
Managing Editor: David Donald

Editors: Robert Hewson
    E-mail: rob@aerospacepbl.co.uk

    David Donald
    E-mail: dave@aerospacepbl.co.uk

Sub Editor: Karen Leverington

Editorial Assistant: Tim Senior

Origination by Chroma Graphics
Printed in Italy by Officine Grafiche
    de Agostini

Correspondents:
General military: Jon Lake
USA Washington: Robert F. Dorr
USA Southwest: Randy Jolly
Europe: John Fricker
Russia/CIS: Yefim Gordon
Asia: Pushpindar Singh
Canada: Jeff Rankin-Lowe
Argentina: Jorge Nunez Padin
Chile: Patrick Laureau

The editorial team at *World Air Power Journal* can
now be contacted, via E-mail, on the individual
addresses opposite. General queries should be
addressed to info@aerospacepbl.co.uk

The authors and publishers gratefully acknowledge
the assistance given by the following people:

The Patuxent River PA team, Lt Brenda Malone,
CINFO, Mike Maurs, AIRLANT, Jeoff Binder,
CINCLANT, Lt Col Bob Edgerton, USIA and
Rod Frances, US Embassy, London for their help
with the Patuxent River briefing.

Mr Tim Lewis/DCPRO Strike Command, Sqn Ldr
(Retd) Ed Bulpett/CRO Marham, Wg Cdr David
Bruce/MoD Recce 1, Wg Cdr Dick Garwood/OC
No. II(AC) Sqn, Sqn Ldr Andy Tucker/No. II(AC)
Sqn, Sqn Ldr Mark Knight/No. II(AC) Sqn, Sqn
Ldr Brian Cole/No. 39 (1PRU) Sqn and Mrs.
Shirley Grainger/W. Vinten Ltd for their assistance
and patience during the preparation of the Marham
Reconnaissance Wing article.

Irv Waaland, John Cashen, Alan Brown, Paul
Kaminski, Ed Smith, Lieutenant Gina Quirk
(Whiteman PA) for their assistance with the B-2
article. Credit is also due to James Clerk Maxwell,
without whom none of it would have been
possible. Thanks also go out to Tony Chong, Craig
Kaston and Robert F. Dorr.

Captain 'Bo' H.C. Norton, Commanders John
Flynn, Phil Winters, Ray Aguilar, Carl Mayabb,
Lieutenant Commanders Bob Galloway, Hal
Pittman, Dave Wells, Jeff Dodd, Mike Norman,
Will Oxx, Ralph Merg, Horst Brauchler,
Lieutenants Brenda Malone, Pete Kaczanowski,
JOC Boydston, AOC(AW) Mark Williams, AW1
Keith Watkins, Lieutenant JG Wendy Snyder,
Sandy Miller, and the many others that helped with
the P-3 Orion feature.

Mel French, Skip Howse, Charles Kaman, David
Long, Ken Nasshan, Loring B. 'Nick' Nichols;
David G. Jussaume and John Shelanskas at Kaman;
Wade Burchell, Tim Kempf and J. R. Simonds at
HSL-94, for their help with the Super Seasprite
feature. Other valuable assistance was provided by,
A. D. 'Dave' Baker, Mike Benolkin, Rick Burgess,
Tony Chong, Steve Czerviski, John Gresham,
Craig Kaston, Jim McGuire, Norman Polmar,
Skip Robinson, Eric Scheie.

World Air Power Journal is a
registered trademark in the
United States of America of
AIRtime Publishing Inc.

World Air Power Journal is
published quarterly and is
available by subscription and
from many fine book and hobby
stores.

**SUBSCRIPTION AND BACK
NUMBERS:**

UK and World (except USA and
Canada) write to:
**Aerospace Publishing Ltd
FREEPOST
PO Box 2822
London
W6 0BR
UK**

**(No stamp required if posted in
the UK)**

USA and Canada, write to:
**AIRtime Publishing Inc.
Subscription Dept
10 Bay Street
Westport
CT 06880, USA
(203) 838-7979
Toll-free order number in USA:
1 800 359-3003**

Prevailing subscription rates are
as follows:
Softbound edition for 1 year:
    $59.95
Softbound edition for 2 years:
    $112.00
Softbound back numbers
(subject to availability) are
$16.00 each, plus shipping and
handling. All rates are for
delivery within mainland USA,
Alaska and Hawaii. Canadian
and overseas prices available
upon request. American Express,
Discover Card, MasterCard and
Visa accepted. When ordering
please include card number,
expiration date and signature.

**U.S. Publisher:
    Mel Williams
Subscriptions Director:
    Linda DeAngelis
Charter Member Services
Manager:
    Janie Munro
Retail Sales Director: Jill Brooks
Shipping Manager: E. Rex Anku**

WORLD
AIR POWER

J O U R N A L

CONTENTS

Volume 31   Winter 1997

International

BAe joins Lockheed Martin in JSF programme

British Aerospace indecision over which of the two short-listed US groups it should join for the US Joint Strike Fighter programme (worth a potential $100 billion) was resolved in June 1997, after more than seven months of discussions with both groups, when it opted for membership of the Lockheed Martin team as a sub-contractor. With a 10 per cent partnership in the programme, the UK government and industry have already invested some $200 million in initial JSF development, and BAe was previously involved with McDonnell Douglas and Northrop Grumman in their unsuccessful JSF submission.

As BAe's long-standing partner in the AV-8 and T-45 programmes, MDC is now teamed with the Boeing group for its X-32 JSF submission; Northrop Grumman has transferred to Lockheed Martin, and each team is contracted to produce and fly two concept demonstration prototypes. Northrop Grumman is also teamed with Hughes and Texas Instruments for weapons and infra-red systems, as sub-contractor to Boeing for its JSF project. As a full technology partner the UK's share is promised to be substantial in size and technical content.

BAe chief executive Sir Richard Evans said that the UK group was looking forward to making a significant contribution to JSF, particularly in systems integration, low-cost design and manufacture, and short take-off and vertical landing (STOVL) technologies. BAe's participation would ensure its application of an in-depth understanding of the RN requirements (for 64 STOVL JSF versions).

Two more European nations have joined the UK in JSF participation, although on a much more modest scale. The Netherlands and Norway, soon to be joined by Denmark, have become limited co-operative partners in JSF concept demonstration, which for $10 million each ensures five-year participation in definition and validation of JSF operational requirements. Canada and Israel are expected to join the programme later on a similar basis.

Lockheed Martin has completed its initial design review and finalised configurations for the two X-35 technology demonstrators funded from its $718.8 million JSF contract. Its basic Configuration 220 will include two closely-related variants with a span of 33 ft (10 m), fuselage length of 50.8 ft (15.5 m), and wing area of 450 sq ft (41.8 m²), comprising the USAF's Model 220A, plus the STOVL 220B for the USMC and RN. For carrier operation, the USN's Model 220C has a larger wing of 540 sq ft (50.1 m²) area, with folding tip-sections (also on the RN version), plus a bigger tail and control surfaces. The Model 220B achieves STOVL capability from an Allison lift-fan behind the cockpit, shaft-driven when required from the Pratt & Whitney F119-SE611 turbofan, fitted with a Yak-141-type three-bearing thrust-vectoring nozzle.

Detailed design has now started of the JSF concept demonstration aircraft, for roll-out in 1999. The selected finalist will move to the demonstration and validation stages in early 2001, for planned service entry in 2008. Apart from at least 2,852 JSFs for USAF, USN and USMC procurement, export sales could add another 2,000 aircraft to the programme.

Germany shuffles closer to Eurofighter decision

As the largest Eurofighter partner after Britain, Germany has requirements for 180 EF 2000s costing DM22.57 billion (around $14 billion), including long-term logistic support and operating costs, against the RAF's 232. Bonn's matching commitment to the production investment phase declared by Britain last year, and now endorsed by Italy and Spain, has been delayed by public spending restrictions required to meet convergency criteria for European Monetary Union by its planned deadline of 1 January 1999.

These restrictions limited the 1998 defence budget to DM46.2 billion, instead of the planned DM47 billion, and long-term EF 2000 funding to DM21 billion. On 11 July 1997, during its last sitting before summer recess, the German cabinet approved spending DM850 million ($500 million) on the EF2000 for the 1998 budget plan, which now totals some DM46.8 billion. However, this must receive parliamentary approval when the Bundestag reconvenes in September. Separate votes will be taken to approve the defence budget and EF2000 funding, specifically.

Germany's political parties are split into vehemently pro- and anti-EF2000 groups, but the majority of Chancellor Kohl's ruling coalition support the project. The financial deal for Eurofighter also involves a transfer of DM1.2 billion in funding to Daimler-Benz Aerospace (DASA), as part of the EF2000 pre-production monies, allocated in the 1997 budget. Still to be resolved is the question of whether the government can redirect DM250 million in (early) repayments for Airbus costs, to DASA, for use on Eurofighter instead. This issue was deliberately dropped from the 11 July meeting to ensure that basic EF2000 funding was approved.

After the cabinet decision was announced, the British Defence Secretary Mr George Brown said, "I am delighted the German government has approved production funding for Eurofighter. This is excellent news for the air forces of the partner nations…and the European aerospace industry." A DASA spokesman said "we are very satisfied with the government's decision, (but) nothing in politics is absolutely certain."

Technically, Eurofighter is making better progress. DASA's first development aircraft (DA.1) began flying its primary sensor, the new ECR-90 radar, in February 1997, and was joined in the summer by BAe's similarly-equipped DA.4 two-seat prototype. Having flown since January 1993, in a BAC One-Eleven trials aircraft, the ECR-90 performed "perfectly" in DA.1, meeting all specified maturity requirements in its first five sorties.

At Warton, BAe's DA.2 resumed flight development in June with a spin-recovery parachute tail gantry for high-Alpha carefree handling trials. This was a precautionary installation for AoA exploration beyond 25°, since DA.2 will not be intentionally spun, and its automatic flight-control system is programmed to prevent unscheduled departures from any flight attitude. DA.1 and DA.2 still fly with their interim RB.199 turbofans, but in 1998 they will receive definitive Eurojet EJ200s, which are performing well in the remaining Eurofighter fleet. An omni-directional thrust-vectoring nozzle with 20° all-round deflection is also being developed for the EJ200 by Spain's Industria de Turbo Propulsores (ITP), and will start bench-running in early 1998. Wit h four hydraulic actuators, it also offers 2 per cent more take-off thrust and a 7 per cent increase in supersonic cruise, and will fly in an EF 2000 in 2001.

Alenia's DA.7, employed on performance and weapons integration, was flown at the Paris air show alongside the second two-seat Eurofighter, CASA's DA.6, used for avionics and systems trials. Italy is buying 130 EF 2000s and Spain 87, increasing overall programme totals to 629 aircraft. Regarded by Eurofighter as "hugely underestimated" and having world-beating potential, the EF 2000 is now being marketed through a major export campaign. Apart from its short-listing in Norway and the UAE, Australia and South Korea are evaluating it on the claimed basis of BVR combat capabilities "very close" to the more costly Lockheed Martin F-22A, with greater air-to-ground flexibility.

Above: Eurofighter took the opportunity of the Paris air show in June 1997 to show off single- and two-seat EF2000s together. The single-seat Italian aircraft (DA.7) was partnered by the Spanish two-seater (DA.6). All seven development airframes are now flying in the test programme.

The Aero L-159 ALCA (Advanced Light Combat Aircraft) was rolled out at Vodochody on 12 June 1997. On the same day the Czech government announced an order for 72 of the type. The first prototype is a two-seater, to be followed by the production-standard single-seater.

Europe

AUSTRIA:

Gripen evaluation completed

A pre-evaluation team from the Austrian Air Defence (ÖeLk) Forces completed a nine-flight evaluation of the JAS 39 Gripen in March at the Saab factory airfield of Linköping. All flights were made in the front cockpit of a JAS 39B combat trainer, and the Austrian team also logged around 50 hours in flight and tactical simulators at Linköping. Similar evaluations have been made by ÖeLk teams of the F-16C/D and F/A-18C/D in the US, and of the MiG-29 and Mirage 2000-5, to replace Saab Drakens with up to 30 new fighters for service early next century. A decision is expected in 1998.

BELGIUM:

Sea King upgrade

Five FAeB Westland Sea King Mk 48s of No. 40 Squadron are undergoing a further upgrade by the manufacturers, incorporating installation of Smiths Newmark SN500 automatic flight control system.

BULGARIA:

MiG ATs and more MiG-29s ordered

An evaluation order from the Bulgarian air force for two MiG ATs, recently announced by the MIG MAPO group, appears to be the first export contract for this new advanced trainer, now in limited production for the Russian air force. The order is part of a procurement package which also includes 14 MiG-29SM fighters, costing some $450 million in all, partly funded by Russian trade debts. With upgraded N-019ME radar, a 3-tonne increase in weapon load, and PGM capability, the multi-role MiG-29SMs will supplement 18 earlier 'Fulcrum' fighters and four two-seat MiG-29UBs already operated by Bulgaria.

CZECH REPUBLIC:

L-159 contract approved

Funding was finally approved in Prague in June for the long-awaited Krna23 billion ($717 million) Czech air force order for 72 Aero L-159 light ground-attack fighters. The first of the renamed advanced light combat aircraft (ALCA) – an L-159T two-seat dual-control version without combat equipment – was rolled out at the Aero Vodochody factory on 12 June. However, the order will mainly comprise single-seat L-159s with Boeing North American/GEC-Marconi/AlliedSignal/Vinten nav/attack avionics and FIAR Grifo-L radar for light close-support and air defence roles.

Similarly powered by a 6,300-lb (28.02-kN) AlliedSignal/AIDC F124-GA-100 turbofan, the first single-seat prototype L-159 with a full avionics fit will start flight development in 1998. Czech air force deliveries are due between 1999 and 2002, and will include some L-159Ts with full systems for combat missions and lead-in fighter training. A Boeing-led team, including McDonnell Douglas and CSA Czech Airlines, is buying a 34-40 per cent interest in newly-privatised Aero Vodochody to boost its currently precarious financial situation, reflected by only 12 L-39 deliveries in 1996.

Although the Czechs issued requests for tenders for 24 new combat aircraft in April, funding is now not expected for about four years, and initial interest is in leasing one two-seat and six new or surplus single-seat fighters. The US has offered F-16s and F/A-18s, but the Czechs are also evaluating the Gripen and Mirage 2000-5. Offers from the US Office of Defense Co-operation have included the lease of seven F-16s or F/A-18s for $108 million and $172 million, respectively.

DENMARK:

More F-16s acquired

Accident attrition from original deliveries has necessitated the acquisition of four ex-USAF F-16s from AMARC storage. They were shipped to Denmark in February 1997, to maintain the RDAF's target participation of 61 F-16s in the European/US MLU programme now in progress. At least three more surplus F-16s are expected to be sought by the RDAF from the US.

FRANCE:

Rafale production contracts

Initial production orders for the Dassault Rafale, originally planned for November 1995 and having funding allocations in successive military budgets since 1993, were finally placed by

the French government in May, for initial deliveries in 1999. DGA armament agency contracts for the first 13 production Rafales followed a cost reduction programme which pared about 10 per cent off original estimates, although apparently involved further delays in deliveries.

Ten Rafale Ms have now been ordered for Aéronavale operational service from the new aircraft-carrier *Charles de Gaulle* from 2002, and three multi-role Rafale Cs for the Armée de l'Air, with a target service date of 2005. Follow-on multi-year procurement is sought of 48 more Rafales costing FF14.5 billion ($2.48 billion, or a programme unit cost of $51.6 million), including 10 Rafale Cs for early delivery to the AA, which the French industry hopes will make some Rafales available for early export orders.

The four prototypes, comprising a two-seat Rafale B combat trainer, a single-seat Rafale C and two navalised Rafale Ms, had accumulated more than 3,500 test flights without incident by mid-1997.

Transport reinforcements

Following earlier deliveries of 12 Lockheed C-130Hs to ET 61 at Orléans from 1988, two similar aircraft formerly operated by Zaïre have recently been acquired the French air

Right: The Irish Air Corps had two celebrations in 1997. The first commemorated 25 years of Cessna FR 172H/K operations, the type being first taken on charge by the Basic Flying Training School in 1972, replacing Chipmunks. The Cessnas now serve as part of the Army Co-Op Squadron, based at Gormanstown. This aircraft was specially marked for the occasion. More importantly, the IAC celebrated its 75th anniversary at Casement Aerodrome, Baldonnel, on 6 July.

Left: Wearing special markings, this Danish F-16B is the first for that nation to emerge from the MLU programme at Fort Worth.

Below: In June 1997 the French aircraft-carrier Clemenceau embarked on its final cruise before decommissioning on 1 October. Among the air group were the Alizé patrollers of 6F, wearing farewell markings for sister unit 4F which disbanded this year. 4 Flottille will be the first operator of the E-2C.

Above: This KC-135A is seen at Davis-Monthan AFB before preparing to fly to Wichita. There, Boeing is re-engining the aircraft with CFM56 turbofans prior to delivery to the Armée de l'Air as a C-135FR.

force. This service also took delivery in mid-1997 of the first of an additional seven CN.235Ms ordered from CASA for $100 million in 1996 to supplement eight delivered from early 1991.

Naval surveillance order

Four second-hand Dassault Falcon 50s are being converted by Dassault and Thomson-CSF through an Aéronavale contract for SAR and maritime surveillance roles. They will supplement five special-mission Aéronavale Falcon 20H Gardian versions operated since 1982 on SAR and exclusive economic zone surveillance around France and its overseas territories. The Thomson-CSF mission equipment package will include Ocean Master search radar, a Chlio FLIR, and communications systems. Up to eight 25-person inflatable life-rafts will also be carried for dropping through a cabin floor hatch.

GREECE:

Second batch of F-16s

Formal acceptance took place in late May at Fort Worth of the first of 32 Block 50D F-16CGs and eight F-16DG combat trainers ordered by Hellenic Military Aviation (EPA). They follow the first batch of 40 Block 30 F-16CG/DGs delivered to Greece from late 1988, but are powered by GE F110-129 IPE turbofans uprated to 29,588 lb (131.62 kN), instead of the original 28,984-lb (128.93-kN) F110-100s. The EPA is also buying 16 LANTIRN pods and 24 associated navigation pods, and procurement is planned of another 50 F-16s.

HUNGARY:

Fighter replacements deferred

While the Hungarian air force is continuing to evaluate Western fighters to replace its Soviet-supplied combat aircraft, it has withdrawn about 40 aircraft, including all its MiG-23s and Su-22M-3s, plus a squadron of MiG-21s, to reserve status for cost reason. Its first-line strength now comprises only 22 MiG-21bis and 28 MiG-29As.

Hungary was the first country to show firm interest in the JAS 39, with an MoU for flight and technical evaluation, recently completed in Sweden, and possible purchase of 30 NATO-compatible Gripens costing some $1 billion, signed with Saab in late 1995. This also included a sub-contract with Danubian Aircraft in Budapest for Gripen tailcone fittings, with proposals for more extensive work and industrial offsets from a Hungarian order.

Hungary has since widened its MiG-21MF/MiG-23MF replacement evaluation to include the F-16, F/A-18 and Mirage 2000-5. In mid-1996, however, its government deferred formal tenders for its new fighters until after crucial meetings in July 1997 on NATO membership, with selection planned in 1998. Meanwhile, Saab-

Above: In late 1996 the Armée de l'Air replaced its Mirage 2000C detachment in Saudi Arabia with Mirage F1CRs from ER 01/033 and 02/033. This example is seen at Prince Sultan AB, Al Kharj, carrying an ASTAC Elint pod and Phimat chaff/flare pod.

Below: The Kongelige Norsk Luftforsvaret (Royal Norwegian air force) uses the diminutive Saab MFI-15 for flight screening with the Primary Flying School at Trondheim-Vaernes. Most are in this yellow scheme but at least one is in all-over dark green.

BAe Gripen AB recently opened a new office in Budapest, and Sweden's Wallenburg Electrolux group inaugurated a new refrigerator factory in Hungary through its offsets programme.

Second Western missile order

Having been the first Western company to sell missiles to a former Eastern bloc country with a 1996 contract from Romania for Magic 2 close-combat AAMs, MATRA BAe Dynamics has now received a $100 million contract from Hungary for 'several hundred' Mistral short-range air defence missiles.

ITALY:

Starfighter upgrades reduced

Cut-backs in Alenia's further upgrade of Italian air force (AMI) F-104S/ASA Starfighters from 108 to 64, because of budget economies and the lease of 24 RAF Tornado F.Mk 3s, will reduce AMI squadrons equipped with Starfighters from eight to six. Completion was scheduled for July 1997 of the first of 49 single-seat versions being rewired and fitted with new TACAN, communications and integrated GPS/INS systems to F-104S/ASAM (Modificato) standards, which are also

being incorporated in 15 two-seat TF-104G combat trainers.

Some upgrade work is being done on the Starfighters' hydraulic system, and by Fiat Avio on the GE J79 turbojet, to equip five AMI air defence squadrons (9°, 10°, 18°, 22° and 23° Gruppi), each with 10 aircraft, plus the OCU. The latter unit, the 20° Gruppo of the 4° Stormo at Grosseto, was the first to receive the F-104S/ASAM, plus most of the TF-104Gs, for operation until replaced by EF2000.

NETHERLANDS:

MLU equipment selection

Orders totalling $90 million for 60 GEC-Marconi Atlantic navigation pods and 10 Lockheed Martin Sharpshooter targeting pods, for delivery between 1999-2001, have been placed by the Dutch government to equip its 136 F-16A/Bs undergoing MLU.

POLAND:

New fighter requirements

With over 300 Soviet-supplied combat aircraft in service, Poland's pending requests for proposals for 100-140 new fighters between 1999-2008 are among the largest in Eastern Europe. Saab-BAe offset offers for JAS 39 Gripen

procurement include final assembly by PZL Mielec, and of its Volvo RM12 engine at Rzeszow, plus interim lease of a squadron of multi-role AJS 37 Viggens. Parallel bids are also being made of new or surplus F-16s, F/A-18s and Mirage 2000-5s.

ROMANIA:

Upgraded Lancers enter service

Following modifications by Aerostar and Elbit, initial deliveries of 11 single-seat and one two-seat upgraded MiG-21s have equipped the Romanian air force's first ground-attack squadron of upgraded MiG-21 Lancer fighters at Bacau. Seventy-five MiG-21MFs, plus 10 MiG-21UMs, are being modernised there with digital Elbit avionics, including Elta's EL/M-2001-B range-only radar, to launch PGMs for close-support roles. Similar avionics, but with Elta EL/M-2032 multi-mode radar, are being fitted to 25 more MiG-21MFs, including the prototype flown in the Paris air show, to operate with Rafael Python 3 and R-73 AAMs for air defence missions. Some 40 of Romania's 110 upgraded MiG-21s will be delivered by the end of 1997.

Elbit's ground-attack Lancer avionics have also been installed in a lead-in fighter trainer version of the IAR-99 Soim, shown in Paris for the first time in June. With a HUD, colour and monochrome cockpit displays, HOTAS and GPS/INS, the upgraded IAR-99 retains the original Viper Mk 632-41M turbojet, and made its first flight only on 22 May 1997. Over 20 of the earlier IAR-99s are now operated by the Romanian air force.

Brasov/Super Cobra purchase finalised

Acquisition by Bell Helicopter Textron of a 70 per cent shareholding in Romania's IAR SA Brasov helicopter production company accompanied the Bucharest government's long-discussed $1.4 billion contract for 96 AH-1W Super Cobras. Powered by twin GE T700-401 turboshaft engines, most will be licence-built by Brasov, which will also share in other Bell AH-1W production.

In Romanian service, the AH-1Ws will be renamed the AH-1RO Dracula, and will be equipped with an Elbit SOCAT avionics and weapons suite. This will be sub-contracted to Israel's Elbit Systems Romanian subsidiary, owned jointly by Aerostar SA at Bacau, to provide similar capabilities to the new IAI Tamam/Kollsman Night Targeting System (NTS) in 195 US Marine Corps AH-1Ws. In addition to monochrome cockpit and moving map displays, and GPS/INS, it will include FLIR and laser.

Hitherto, Brasov has been mainly involved with Eurocopter France in licence-building Alouette and Puma helicopters. It is just starting a seven-year upgrade of the 24 licence-built IAR-330L Pumas operated by the

Military Aviation Review

The HAF accepted the first of its 40 new F-16 Block 50s on 22 May 1997 at Fort Worth. Unlike USAF Block 50s, the Greek aircraft have brake parachute fairings and F-16ADF-style IFF antennas forward of the cockpit. They are powered by the General Electric F110-GE-129. Deliveries will be made to 347 Mira (ex-A-7) at Larissa, and 349 Mira (currently with F-5s) which will transfer to Nea Ankhialos.

Romanian forces, through a $100 million contract which also involves installation of Elbit's SOCAT anti-tank optronic search and combat system package.

More C-130s sought

Having taken delivery in 1996 of four C-130B Hercules, as the first ex-Warsaw Pact Central European country to acquire US surplus military equipment, Romania is planning to acquire five more of these tactical transports. They would also be delivered through the Pentagon's Excess Defense Articles (EDA) transfer programme, and several would be equipped for AEW and aerial tanker roles.

US UAVs ordered

The Romanian government has ordered an AAI Corporation Shadow 600 twin-boom piston-engined UAV system from the US United Industrial Corporation, for delivery within one year. In addition to six UAVs and support equipment, the $20 million Defence Export Loan Guarantee finance programme will also include an AAI Moving Target Simulator close-range air defence training system.

RUSSIA:

Governments support YakAEM-130 consortium

Aermacchi, Yakovlev and Povazske Strojarnye have put together a formal consortium, backed by funding from the Italian, Russian and Slovakian governments, to develop, produce and market the YakAEM-130 advanced trainer. At a Paris press conference held by Russia's Rosvoorouzhenie arms export organisation, Aermacchi president George Brazelli said that 180 billion lire ($106 million) had been included in a 1995 Italian aerospace industry five-year technology plan for the programme, to further Aermacchi leadership attempts in world trainer markets. Yakovlev chairman and general designer Alexandr Dondukov quoted 1997 Russian YakAEM-130 allocations as totalling 30 billion roubles ($5.2 million). As with the MiG AT, 10 YakAEM-130s had been ordered for Russian air force evaluation.

According to Pavel Ando, managing director of Povazske Strojarnye responsible for the YakAEM-130's DV-2S turbofan, Slovakia's contribution is currently Kr260 million ($7.7 million). Construction is being undertaken by

The Hellenic air force is adopting a new three-tone 'Ghost' scheme for its air defence-tasked F-4E Phantoms, the work being performed by HAI. This example flies with 337 MPK at Larissa.

the Sokol Production Enterprise in Nizhni Novgorod, where the first series aircraft will fly next year. This will be slightly smaller and lighter than the two Yak-130D prototypes, for a better power/weight ratio and improved performance.

Other changes will include revised cockpit avionics, instrumentation and layout, involving three MFDs and a HUD, that is based on the Aermacchi MB-339D and developed by Alenia and Finmeccanica. Minor aerodynamic improvements are also planned, perhaps involving winglet changes, or possibly even their removal.

Meanwhile, several hundred Aero L-39C trainers from 2,094 delivered to the former Soviet air forces are to be upgraded with new avionics and cockpit equipment by the Myasischchev Design Bureau in Moscow, to extend their service until replaced by the MiG-AT or YakAEM-130 in about 2010.

LFI supersedes MiG 1.42

Several contenders now appear to be emerging for Russia's less ambitious and lower-cost next-generation combat aircraft requirement, known as the LFI, or lightweight fighter – with MiG's 1-42/1-44 advanced fighter project now all but abandoned. The LFI has been linked with continuing development by the MAPO group of the upgraded MiG-29M (proposed as the MiG-33 for export), as the projected MiG-35. In addition to a new digitised avionics and cockpit MFDs, plus a fly-by-wire flight-control system, the MiG-35 is believed to have a new wing, with more leading-edge sweep, taper and a cranked trailing edge. It may also have destabilising canard foreplanes and three-dimensional thrust-vectoring control (TVC) for its RD-33 turbofans. TVC flight-testing is due to start in a modified MiG-29 next year.

Russia's Phazotron group is proposing its new RP-35 electronically-scanned phased-array fire-control system with a NIIP antenna for the MiG-35, which will account for much of the equivalent of some $500 million to be spent by VPK MAPO on R&D over the next couple of years. Standard MiG-29 sales are continuing, with 10 deliveries to Slovakia in 1996, an imminent $450 million contract for 14 more for Bulgaria, and a second batch of 18 for Malaysia. Production of 40 MiG-29s is planned for 1997.

As the sole producer of two-seat MiG-29Bs, the Sokol factory at Nizhni Novgorod is planning an upgrade programme with Phazotron to add an advanced NO10 Zhuk radar with new data and signal processors, plus other changes, to existing 'Fulcrum-Bs' to achieve a full multi-role capability for combat or operational training. Additional options include such NATO-compatible avionics as Trimble 2000 GPS, TACAN, Cossor Electronics IFF 4700/4800 (Mk XII), and IFR nav/com equipment.

Sukhoi and LFI

Sukhoi's S-32 design studies were originally thought to be associated with the LFI requirement, but a single-seat redesign of the S-54 two-seat combat-trainer/light ground-attack project shown in model form in Paris appears to be aimed at the fifth-generation combat aircraft market. Powered by a Saturn/Lyul'ka AL-31F or AL-41F turbofan with a ventral ramp intake and apparently vectored-thrust, the new S-54 employs the 'unstable integral tandem triplane' layout of the Su-27 series, with canards, stabilators and forward-set twin vertical fins, but is probably about half their design take-off weight. It also has a forward-set cockpit, with a frameless bubble

canopy, and was shown by Phazotron as using a new X-band Sokol phased-array radar with electronic scanning.

In a further move towards the long drawn-out Russian aerospace industry rationalisation, the Sukhoi and Beriev Design Bureaux (OKBs) have combined with three production centres to form a new Aviation Military Industrial Complex, known as AVPK Sukhoi or AviaComp for short. The factories concerned, with their current production programmes, comprise the Irkutsk Aviation Production Association (IAPO) – Su-27UB, Su-30K/MK/MKI, and Be-200 twin-turbofan amphibian; the Komsomolsk-na-Amur APA (KNAAPO) – Su-27, Su-27K (Su-33), Su-27M (Su-35), Su-37, S-80 twin turboprop transport, and Be-103 light amphibian; and Novosibirsk APA – Su-27IB (Su-32FN, Su-34), and Antonov An-38.

Two other factories producing Sukhoi Su-25s and not currently included in the new consortium comprise the Ulan Ude Aviation Plant joint-stock company (JSC) in Russia and the Saturn facility in Georgia. Su-25 production was halted at Saturn, where 12 upgraded Su-25Ts built from Russian funding in 1990-92 remain undelivered because of political differences with Russia. Another 18 Su-25s completed in Georgia for national use still await delivery of their Russian nav/attack systems.

SLOVENIA:

Attack helicopters sought

As the first country from the former Yugoslav federation to seek US military equipment, Slovenia has been discussing with the Pentagon and Bell Helicopter Textron the possible

Military Aviation Review

Left: Old rivals came face to face during Exercise Rhino-Drawsko in Poland in April 1997, when Dutch THG AH-64A Apaches operated in concert with Polish Mi-24Vs of the 56 PSB.

The 'Russian Knights' display team has adopted new colours for its Su-27s, replacing the original tactical camouflage background (on right-hand aircraft) with a bright blue. The troubled team suffered another mishap at the Bratislava air show in June 1997 when an aircraft landed with its undercarriage up.

purchase of 12 AH-1Ws, armed with TOW 2A anti-tank missiles. Considerable Congressional resistance is expected to supplying arms to a currently politically volatile region.

SPAIN:

Stretched CN.235 proposals

CASA is working on a major stretch of its CN.235 tactical transport, apparently independently of IPTN as its partner in this originally joint project. Now in the detailed design stage, the proposed C-295 would combine a 9.8-ft (3-m) fuselage stretch with Pratt & Whitney Canada PW127G turboprops rated at 2,750 shp (2051 kW), and a payload increase of 8,157 lb (3707 kg) to 21,385 lb (9720 kg). This private venture is aimed at Spanish air force needs, but is also firmly directed at prospective customers, such as Australia.

Turbo Pillan interest

Another Spanish air force (EdA) requirement is taking shape for a turboprop basic trainer to supplement the ENAER T-35C Pillans (E.26 Tamiz) at the San Javier Air Academy. The Allison 250-engined T-35DT Turbo Pillan is reportedly favoured for this requirement.

SWEDEN:

Batch three Gripens

Cabinet approval was announced in June for the third production batch of 64 JAS 39 Gripen multi-role fighters, including another 14 two-seat JAS 39B combat trainers, to re-equip four more

Swedish air force squadrons between 2003-2007, to cost SK28 billion ($3.6 billion). This represents an apparent programme unit cost of around $56.25 million, although it also includes funding for JAS 39 technology upgrades.

Among them will be improvements to the Gripen's GE/Volvo F404/RM12 turbofan, including full-authority digital engine control (FADEC); turbine upgrades from third-generation monocrystal blades; and an F414-type radial augmentor. Other upgrades could include an enhanced Ericsson radar with an azimuth-gimballed active electronically-scanned array antenna (AESA), IRST, new defensive EW sub-systems, new air-defence missiles and, for the longer term, the possible addition of thrust-vectoring. Batch three Gripens will be delivered with colour Ericsson/Saab MFDs, and probably modified Sundstrand T46C/APS1000 auxiliary power turbines replacing current Microturbo APUs.

All 30 first-batch Gripens are now in service, with second-batch deliveries of 110, including 14 JAS 39Bs, following since December 1996 at about 18 per year.

Gripen export sales are now being sought with British Aerospace, following a 1995 joint-venture agreement involving shared marketing investment, revenue and profits. For export, the Gripen will incorporate several modifications, including an inflight refuelling system with a retractable probe, onboard oxygen generation, NATO standard weapons pylons, and NATO-compatible nav/com avionics and IFF.

Besides marketing, modification and support, the JAS/BAe joint-venture agreement includes British manufacture of over 30 per cent of any export Gripens, plus full backing by the UK

MoD's Defence Export Services Organisation. Up to 40 countries have been targeted as potential Gripen customers, with Austria, Chile and perhaps Brazil offering the best short-term prospects.

Sk 60 transfer proposals

Defence liaison plans between Sweden and Estonia, Latvia and Lithuania have included discussions concerning the possible transfer of about 30 surplus Saab Sk 60 trainers to these Baltic states for a joint training programme.

TURKEY:

Attack helicopter RFPs

Following the Turkish government's late 1996 cancellation of an order for 10 Bell AH-1Ws because of objections raised by the US Congress concerning their possible use against separatist Kurds, requests for proposals were issued in May from Ankara for possible alternatives for Turkish Army Aviation (TKUK). They went to Agusta, Denel, Eurocopter and Mil, and although Bell, Boeing, McDonnell Helicopters and Sikorsky were also included, the Turkish government warned that it was not prepared to accept any end-use restrictions. Initial procurement of a small batch of the selected attack helicopter is planned to be followed by licensed production in Turkey of up to 145 additional examples.

One of the TKUK's 10 Bell AH-1W Super Cobras was shot down by an SA-7 during operations against separatist Kurdistan forces in northern Iraq on 18 May, killing the crew. Although the TKUK also operates 28 Bell AH-1Ps, the loss on 4 June of one of the 20 recently delivered Turkish army AS 532 Cougar Mk 1 transport helicopters, with 11 military personnel on board, to another Kurdish SA-7 in the same area gave additional urgency to TKUK requirements for more rotary-

wing gunships. One possibility being discussed with MIG MAPO is reportedly procurement and licensed production by Turkey of the Kamov Ka-50.

Popeye acquisition plans

The $632 million six-year upgrade by the Lahav division of Israel Aircraft Industries of 54 Turkish air force (THK) MDC F-4Es to Phantom 2000 standard includes at least $25 million for up to 50 Rafael Popeye (3,000-lb/1360-kg) stand-off missiles. They are similar to the AGM-142A Have Nap version produced jointly with Lockheed Martin Electronics & Missiles for the USAF, and can deliver an 800-lb (363-kg) warhead over ranges of nearly 50 nm (58 miles; 93 km). Agreement has also been reached in Turkey through a $150 million contract for local production of the smaller (2,450-lb/1111-kg) Popeye 2 for THK F-16s.

UKRAINE:

An-70 progress

First flight of the second prototype 133-tonne Antonov An-70 propfan heavy transport, totalling 26 minutes, took place from the factory airfield at Gostomel, in Kiev, on 24 April 1997. The first prototype crashed on 10 February 1995, on its fourth test sortie, when its escorting An-72 collided with its vertical tail. Emphasising the project's continuation as a joint one with Russia, the co-pilot in the test crew with Antonov chief test pilot A. V. Galunenko was A. V. Adnonov of the Russian air force (VVS). Russian prime minister Viktor Chernomirdin visited Kiev in June and made a visit to the Antonov OKB specifically to accent Moscow's full commitment to and support for the An-70 programme.

UNITED KINGDOM:

Production Tornado GR.Mk 4 joins flight test programme

The first of 142 RAF Tornado GR.Mk 1s to be given a full-scale mid-life upgrade to GR.Mk 4 standards to meet the MoD's SR(A) 417 requirement made its initial 39-minute flight at BAe's Warton facility on 4 April. Following the development contract signed with Panavia in March 1989, flight trials with three early production Tornados (XZ631, ZD708 and ZG773) with the upgrade changes started at Warton on 29 May 1993.

Modification of the first RAF version (build number BT51, ZG750) followed its arrival at Warton on 1 April 1996. To minimise programme costs, this excluded the planned addition of the GEC-Marconi Avionics SPARTAN passive terrain-referenced navigation and terrain-following systems, plus a covert radar altimeter. As prime sub-contractor, GMAv supplied a digital map generator, an MFD cockpit and wide-angle HUDs, cockpit symbol generator, GPS, computer loading system, and video/audio recorders.

Other changes include improved onboard defensive systems, and an enhanced stores management system for use with precision-guided munitions, via a TIALD pod. They are linked by a 1553B databus, and integrated with a FLIR system in a second fairing under the nose, with HUD imaging presentation, and NVGs. The GR.Mk 4's port FLIR fairing matches that to starboard that houses the GR.Mk 1's laser-ranger optics.

GR.Mk 4 deliveries to combat units will start in 1998, and all 142 are due for completion by 2002. BAe has also received a recent contract to convert two GR.Mk 1s to GR.Mk 1A standard, with sideways-looking infra-red and Vinten Linescan 4000 surveillance systems, supplementing 30 GR.Mk 1As previously delivered for tactical reconnaissance. All GR.Mk 1As are scheduled for similar upgrading to GR.Mk 4A standards, including a new long-range electro-optical reconnaissance pod under development for the MoD's SR(A) 1368 requirement.

Above: On 13 June 1997 the Pumas of the RAF's No. 33 Squadron transferred en masse from RAF Odiham to a new home at RAF Benson. Four of the aircraft still wore large Union Jack markings, having just returned from Operation Determinant UN peacekeeping operations in Zaïre.

Right: Among the war spoils brought back from Iraq by US forces after Desert Storm was this Bell 214ST. Iraq purchased 45 during the 1980s.

First helmet-mounted sights for Jaguar and EF 2000

GEC-Marconi Avionics recently received its first MoD production orders from RAF Logistics Command for helmet-mounted sighting systems (HMSS) to equip upgraded Jaguar strike-fighters. A parallel £28.5 million development contract was also received for similar equipment from BAe Military Aircraft at Warton from the Eurofighter consortium.

Both contracts involve joint programmes; that for the Jaguars is undertaken by GMAv's Mission Avionics Division in conjunction with Honeywell Military Avionics in the US, and the UK's Defence Evaluation and Research Agency (DERA) at Farnborough. The two companies have previously worked on several integrated helmet programmes, and the new HMSS uses GMAv's Alpha sight and Honeywell's Advanced Metal-Tolerant Tracking (AMTT) system mounted on the RAF's current Mk 10B protective helmet.

Apart from development and supply of pre-production systems for flight trials in 1997, the RAF contract includes an option for 20 HMS systems for 1998 delivery. Jaguar HMSS integration represents a further stage in the upgrade of 40 of these veteran strike-fighters, now being equipped with new Mil Std 1553B avionics.

GMAv's HMSS contract for the Eurofighter is shared with the Finmeccanica group in Italy and will incorporate advanced technologies in fully-

integrated binocular, day and night display helmets, with added night-vision capability. The visor display will be linked with the EF 2000's IRST system, and will also allow the launch of new air-to-air missiles at very high off-boresight angles.

Compensation sought for C-130J delays

Following expected delays of at least a year in deliveries of the first of 25 RAF C-130J Hercules, the UK government – as lead customer for the Hercules 2 – is seeking contractual penalties against Lockheed Martin of up to an estimated £40 million. Extra RAF expenses incurred are likely to include costs relating to major overhauls by Marshall Aerospace to extend the operating lives of at least five C-130Ks, due for replacement by the first C-130Js.

Lockheed Martin Aeronautical Systems president Bill Bullock has acknowledged that negotiations on the penalty clauses in the UK's £1.1 billion C-130J contract were in progress, and that no firm delivery date had been quoted by mid-1997. US certification and first deliveries of the RAF's first Hercules 2 – initially all stretched C-130J-30s – were originally due in late 1996, after tactical trials and clearance at DERA's Boscombe Down facility, to start replacing its 60 or so C-130Ks. Initial delays reportedly resulted from problems with the C-130J's new flat-panel liquid-crystal cockpit displays, resulting in a change in contractors from Litton Systems Canada to ADC in Atlanta, GA for their supply and integration.

More fundamental problems in C-130J flight development and certification relate to low-speed handling and stall characteristics, ensuing mainly from the new Allison AE2100D3

Left: Photographed during a visit to RAF Brize Norton is the Saudi government Airbus A340 (HZ-114). The aircraft has been fitted with a comprehensive suite of communications equipment.

powerplant installation and Dowty six-bladed propellers. They provide extra forward airframe area and wing airflow interaction which have a destabilising effect at low airspeeds and high angles of attack.

Since aerodynamic solutions to these problems proved complex and time-consuming, servo-actuated stick-pusher stall protection in an augmented flight-control system was developed for initial FAA certification. Fine-tuning and flight testing of the final FCS software was in progress earlier in 1997, to achieve FAA and military clearances by late summer. Clearance was also included of the new HUD, which has proved outstanding, to gain FAA approval for the first time as primary flight instrumentation.

Three RAF C-130J-30s and two short-fuselaged USAF C-130Js were employed on initial flight development, backed by another RAF and USAF example, plus the first -30 for the RAAF. It made its initial flight in mid-April, from low-rate production. Firm orders or commitments in mid-1997 totalled 25 for the RAF, 21 for the USAF and 12 for the RAAF, while

Below: The 21st FS 'Gamblers' has recently been established at Luke AFB within the 56th FW to train Taiwanese pilots destined for the F-16. Although operated in USAF colours, the aircraft are owned by Taiwan and are to the same Block 20 standards as the operational aircraft. They have brake 'chute housings, ADF-style IFF aerials and extra chaff/flare dispensers. The F-16Bs such as this example have ASHM (aft seat HUD monitor) fitted (à la F-16D Block 40).

Above: For primary training the JMSDF uses the Fuji T-5, a refined version of the KM-2 with an Allison 250-B17D turboprop. An 11-year procurement programme begun in 1986 has resulted in a total order of 36, all of which serve with 201 Kyoiko Kokutai of the Ozuki air training group.

a $1.2 billion contract for 18 Hercules 2s was awaiting final parliamentary clearance in Italy. The Royal Norwegian air force, which has operated six C-130Hs since 1969, was forecast by Bullock to be the next customer, for probable replacement on a one-for-one basis.

FMRAAM is BVRAAM

Delays of at least 12 months were announced in May in the MoD's SR(A) 1239 requirement programme for a future medium-range air-to-air missile, which was also renamed from FMRAAM to BVRAAM (beyond visual-range air-to-air missile). This was possibly to avoid identification with the Hughes (UK) Ltd next-generation FMRAAM submission, shortlisted with the European Meteor project headed by MATRA BAe Dynamics, on which a decision had been expected before the end of 1997.

An MoD spokesman said in May that further work was needed to reduce technical risk in performance and time-scale before a BVRAAM development and production contract could be placed. The Defence Ministry therefore intended to place 12-month £5 million project definition and risk-reduction contracts in July with both MATRA BAe and Hughes for their respective BVRAAM solutions, to ensure that Eurofighter entered operational service with the most cost-effective equipment available. Both BVRAAM proposals employ ramjet propulsion to achieve the required range and manoeuvrability requirements, and will supplement MATRA BAeD's ASRAAM for the EF 2000's close-combat engagements.

Helicopter unit changes

Recent changes in the RAF's support helicopter forces have included disbandment on March 31 of No. 60 Squadron at Benson, and the withdrawal of its nine Westland Wessex HC.Mk 2s. Some equip the RAF's two remaining long-term Wessex units, comprising No. 72 Sqn, with an

establishment of 15 (now reinforced by No. 18 Squadron's five Westland/Aérospatiale Puma HC.Mk 1s from Laarbruch) at Aldergrove, in Northern Ireland, and No. 84 Sqn, operating four from Akrotiri, in Cyprus. Others will remain in reserve, since the sturdy Wessex is committed to continuing RAF operation until 2002.

General Cesar Borucki, commanding the Uruguayan air force (FAU), took formal delivery of the six Westland Wessex HC.Mk 2s formerly operated by No. 28 Squadron, RAF, after their farewell fly-past from Kai Tak, in Hong Kong, on 3 June. The RAF Wessex squadron was among the last British service units withdrawn from the former Crown Colony, following its transfer to China on 30 June. No. 28 Squadron's formal disbandment was scheduled for 16 August in the UK, pending reformation at Benson around 2000 as the first RAF EH101 Merlin transport helicopter unit.

'C' Flight of No. 22 Squadron began replacing its remaining Wessex helicopters with Sea King HAR.Mk 3s at RAF Valley, in Anglesey, North Wales. This follows entry into RAF service of the first of six new Westland Sea King HAR.Mk 3A SAR helicopters on 12 May, with 'A' Flight of the same squadron at Chivenor, in North Devon. Its HAR.Mk 3s went to Valley, while 'B' Flight of No. 22 Squadron will operate the other three Sea King HAR.Mk 3As on SAR roles from RAF Wattisham, in Suffolk. New avionics in the Sea King 3A include a Racal RNAV2 satellite-navigation computer and Doppler 91 nav radar, Thomson Thorn ARI5955/2 search radar, Smiths-Newmark SN500 three-axis automatic flight-control system, and new US nav/com equipment.

Twelve Puma HC.Mk 1s of No. 33 Squadron transferred from Odiham to RAF Benson in June, to make room for the six heavy-lift Boeing Chinook HC.Mk 2s of No. 18 Squadron, which then arrived from Laarbruch, from

RAF Germany. All RAF Chinooks, from Nos 7, 18 and 27 (Reserve) Sqns, are now Odiham-based, and no helicopter units remain in Germany.

Middle East

BAHRAIN:

F-16 follow-up order

Negotiations were reportedly nearing finalisation in June 1997 by the Bahrain Amiri air force with the USA for the acquisition of a second batch of 10-12 F-16C/Ds or 20 refurbished ex-USAF F-16A/Bs.

IRAN:

Eastern weapons acquired

Chinese CPMIEC C-801 anti-ship missiles were launched from Iranian F-4E Phantoms in two operational trials on 3 and 6 June, according to US intelligence sources. With an operating range of up to 27 nm (31 miles; 50 km), the C-801 has a launch weight of 1,796 lb (815 kg), including a 363-lb (165-kg) warhead, and its use represents a new capability for IRIAF F-4s.

US intelligence has also reported details of proposed arms sales to Iran by private factions in Russia as including T-72 tanks and Mi-17 helicopters, as well as planned shipments of 500 Igla-1M (SA-16 'Gimlet') advanced shoulder-launched IR-homing SAMs. With capabilities similar to the US Stinger, the SA-16 can intercept high-speed targets flying at between 30 and 11,500 ft (9 and 3500 m), over ranges of up to 2.7 nm (3.1 miles; 5 km), and the US is concerned that some may be transferred to the Iranian-backed Hizbollah terrorist group for use against Israeli or American military and civil aircraft.

First RN Merlin delivered

Formal delivery of the first of 44 EH101 Merlin HAS.Mk 1s to the Royal Navy took place at GKN Westland's Yeovil factory on 27 May. The RN's first Merlins are expected to go to Boscombe Down for service clearance, before equipping an RN working-up squadron. Submission of a modified version of the Merlin is expected for the RN's Staff Target (Sea) 6845 requirement for a Sea King HC.Mk 4 assault helicopter successor.

More Starstreaks

Shorts Missiles Systems has received a further MoD contract for 1,000 Starstreak air defence missiles for the British army, increasing its total orders to over 7,000. Phase II testing of Starstreak in air-to-air roles from the AH-64 is now continuing through a joint UK/US programme. Phase I AAM tests completed in late 1996 included six successful launches from Apache pylons. Current tests involve integration of Starstreak's laser guidance with the AH-64's TADS and own guidance systems systems.

IRAQ:

Air force reconstituted

The Iraqi air force is estimated by General Binford Peay, C-in-C of the US Central Command, to have a current operating strength of some 300 aircraft. They include MiG-23 all-weather fighters, which recently began training in night operations.

ISRAEL:

AWACS agreement with Russia

Following its search for an Ilyushin Il-76 to modify with Elta surveillance radar and electronics for a Chinese AWACS requirement, Israel Aircraft Industries reached agreement in June with Russia's Taganrog Aviation Complex and the Rosvooruzhenie arms export agency for the joint development of a redesigned Beriev A-50 'Mainstay'. Apart from its dorsal-mounted Elta radar, to be installed and integrated in Taganrog, this would retain much of the original Russian mission avionics upgraded in the current A-50U, and would become available for export within two or three years.

More Black Hawks sought

Recent Pentagon notifications to Congress have included the proposed FMS supply to Israel's defence forces of 15 more Sikorsky UH-60L Black Hawk transport helicopters, plus four spare General Electric T700 turboshaft engines, costing some $200 million.

UNITED ARAB EMIRATES:

Helicopter requirements

Follow-up orders worth over $26 million for seven helicopters for its armed forces were being planned earlier this year by the UAE. Already a long-term Eurocopter customer, the UAE has a requirement for five SA 342L Gazelle light helicopters, with options on another five, to supplement survivors of a dozen similar types bought by Abu Dhabi in 1979. The Gazelle has been out of full-scale production for some time, but Eurocopter France retains the capability to build some for special orders, as was done for China, which bought eight about three years ago. The UAE also plans to buy two Eurocopter AS 565UA Panther utility helicopters, with options on two more, to supplement 1995 deliveries of seven.

Far East

BRUNEI:

Equipment news

Negotiations were nearing finalisation earlier this year with British Aerospace for Brunei's long-awaited Hawk order, believed to comprise four Hawk 100s and six single-seat Hawk 200s. Delivery recently started to the Royal Brunei air force of the four Sikorsky UH-60Ls ordered in 1995. All four are scheduled to arrive before the end of 1997.

CHINA:

Status of AF/PLA

An up-beat account of Air Force of the People's Liberation Army (AF/PLA) capabilities was recently given by its commander-in-chief, Lieutenant General Liu Shunyao, on assuming his new post. They included, he said, the ability to fight both defensive and offensive high-technology battles, plus development of new weapons and electronic warfare systems, advanced AEW aircraft, and various missiles. He gave no details of AF/PLA combat aircraft imports and national development, although Russian sources have indicated that China's $1.2 billion Sukhoi Su-27 licensed production programme will cover up to 200 aircraft, with output increasing to 50 aircraft per year, over a five-year period.

Three of the initial 50 'Flanker' air superiority fighters (36 Su-27SKs and 14 two-seat Su-27UBKs costing $1.7 billion) delivered to the AF/PLA in 1992-96 were reportedly completely destroyed on the ground in April, when their Fujian base was swept by a typhoon. Another 14 Su-27s suffered various degrees of damage, but are apparently repairable. AF/PLA orders for a third batch of 55 Su-27s from KNAAPO's Komsomolsk factory in Russia were being finalised in mid-1997.

A long-awaited AF/PLA order for the Nanchang K-8 Karakoram 8 jet trainer appears to have materialised from a Chinese contract with the Progress/Motor Sich engine group at Zaporozhye in Ukraine for an initial batch of 30 3,792-lb (16.87-kN) AI-25TLK turbofans as the selected powerplants. Developed and produced jointly with Pakistan's Kamra Aeronautical Complex, current production K-8s delivered to the PAF have AlliedSignal TFE731-2A-2A turbofans and US avionics, which have been rejected as hard-currency options for those required by China.

INDONESIA:

Hawk deliveries completed

Delivery of the eight two-seat BAe Hawk 100 lead-in fighter trainers and 16 single-seat Hawk 200 interceptor/ground-attack fighters ordered by the Indonesian air force (TNI/AU) in 1992 was completed earlier in 1997 to No. 12 Sqn at Pekanbaru air base in Sumatra. Four of its Hawk 100s used to train crews for the second TNI/AU operational Hawk squadron, No. 1, will be transferred to this unit when it re-equips by 2000 at Subadio air base, in West Kalimantan, with the second batch of 16 Hawk 200s ordered in mid-1996.

New Zealand has introduced this new grey scheme to its P-3K fleet (below). The aircraft fly with No. 5 Sqn at Whenuapai, and continue to carry the large albatross badge on the fin, albeit in toned-down form. At Ohakea a No. 75 Sqn A-4K Kahu (right) has been tested with this very low-visibility scheme, the markings being presented in a shade of green barely lighter than the base camouflage.

This Hawk Mk 108 wears the colours devised for the Malaysian 'Panji Wira' aerobatic team. Two Mk 108s and four Mk 208s have been assigned to the team but, following the loss of one aircraft in June 1996 and other technical difficulties, the inauguration of the team has been postponed.

Non-US fighters sought

Continued US criticism of Jakarta's human rights infringements has resulted in abandonment of TNI/AU plans to acquire nine of the 28 Block 15OCU F-16A/Bs built for the Pakistan air force and embargoed by the US. The TNI/AU has therefore begun studying possible alternatives, which have included the MiG-29 and Su-27 series, as well as the Mirage 2000-5.

JAPAN:

F-2 delays cause JASDF reorganisation

Delays of up to three years in production of the Mitsubishi F-2 have resulted in the JASDF having to form an eighth squadron with F-15J fighters – one more than originally planned. The unit concerned is the 306th Air Squadron in the 6th Air Wing at Komatsu air base, in central Japan, which re-equipped with F-15Js from F-4EJ Kais.

In turn, the 306th Squadron F-4EJ Kais have been passed to the 8th Air Squadron of the 3rd Air Wing at Misawa, to replace its Mitsubishi F-1s, leaving only two JASDF F-1 squadrons awaiting re-equipment at Misawa and Tsuiki. Mitsubishi's F-15J production is just ending, apparently with no plans to extend JASDF procurement beyond the originally planned 213 aircraft, including 47 two-seat F-15DJs. By 2000, the JASDF plans to operate 357 combat aircraft – only three fewer than at present – comprising (with current totals in parentheses), 197 (192) F-15J/DJs, 104 (109) F-4EJs, 37 (59) F-1s and 19 (0) F-2s. The first three F-2s will enter JASDF service in 1999.

REPUBLIC OF KOREA:

Supersonic trainer team

Daimler-Benz Aerospace is planning a joint launch, with the RoK's Hyundai group and Denel in South Africa, of a 12-month project definition study of a stealthy supersonic tandem trainer/light combat aircraft designated AT-2000.

The AT-2000 would employ a single Eurojet EJ200 or similar turbofan, flat-rated to about 17,000 lb (75.62 kN) with a maximum take-off weight of around 16,800 lb (7620 kg) from extensive use of composites. This would result in a thrust/weight ratio of around unity for take-off, and a maximum speed of around Mach 1.5. Basic design work and wind-tunnel tests of the AT-2000 should end by mid-1998, with initial deliveries planned to follow by 2005.

Both single- and two-seat AT-2000s are envisaged, with modular equipment, avionics and nav/attack systems, including radar, tailored for advanced or lead-in fighter training, air defence,

ground attack and reconnaissance, as required. Funding will be sought to meet RoKAF requirements for up to 250, plus up to 80 or more for South Africa, from joint production and assembly, while the AT-2000 is also being offered to Germany as an Alpha Jet replacement.

New naval Lynx order

A $337 million contract has been signed by the RoK navy for 13 Westland Super Lynx ASW helicopters, effectively doubling original procurement of 12 Mk 99s operated by No. 627 Squadron since late 1989. Two have been lost in service, and the new order includes an attrition replacement, plus upgrades for the remainder with new mission system avionics to latest Super Lynx standards.

RoK Navy Caravan IIs

Recent RoKN aircraft acquisitions have also included five Reims Aviation F406 Caravan II twin-turboprop light transports, costing $25 million. They will tow targets for naval gunnery practice, and perform general utility roles. The RoKN has also been the purchaser of a second batch of P-3C maritime patrol aircraft, and the RoKAF is interested in special-mission MC-130J Hercules 2s, as well as allocating funding for 20 C-130J transport versions.

MALAYSIA:

Helicopter developments

Following the recent conclusion of an industrial co-operation, possible joint weapons production, and defence agreements between Malaysia and

South Africa, plus competitive evaluation, the Malaysian Defence Ministry has confirmed proposals to buy eight Denel CSH-2 Rooivalks costing some $350 million. This could also involve local assembly of Denel's Oryx development of the SA 330 Puma to replace the RMAF's 30 or so remaining Sikorsky S-61A-4 Nuri transport helicopters, although upgrades are planned for them to continue operating until about 2012. In 1998 two Sikorsky S-70As, configured for VIP transport, will be delivered and further examples may follow.

The Royal Malaysian navy is also seeking to replace its Westland Wasps with up to six new frigate-operated helicopters from such types as the AS 565SA Panther, SH-2G, S-70B and Super Lynx.

PAPUA NEW GUINEA:

Clandestine arms deliveries

Early 1997 reports concerning South African mercenary activity to support the PNG government against rebel army forces included their acquisition of at least two Mil Mi-24 gunships, among $30 million worth of CIS military equipment. Two more Mi-24s and two Mi-17 transports, plus tons of weapons and ammunition, en route to PNG in an An-124, were impounded in Australia when it was forced to land at Tindal air base in late March.

PHILIPPINES:

Combat aircraft requirements narrowed

The Philippine air force issued requests for proposals for 18 single-seat and six two-seat advanced combat aircraft by 30 May, with submissions expected for the Mirage 2000-5, Kfir 2000, F-16C/D, F/A-18C/D, MiG-29 and JAS 39 Gripen, but economies in the 15-year Peso164.5 billion ($6.23 billion) defence modernisation budget seem likely to price most of those types beyond consideration.

Earlier in 1997, Philippine armed forces chief of staff General Arnulfo Acedera indicated a preference for the multi-role Hornet, armed with the AIM-120, and the lease of surplus US F/A-18C/Ds pending deliveries of new aircraft. More recently, interest has reportedly switched to the 23 A-4KU and two-seat TA-4KU Skyhawks in storage in Kuwait since their 1992-93 replacement by Hornets.

The defence modernisation programme also included allocations of $200 million for 36 lead-in fighter

UN peacekeeping operations in the Republic of Congo have allowed a rare glimpse of the military aircraft based at Maya-Maya Airport, just outside Brazzaville. Shown above is a line of MiG-21/21UMs received in 1986 and still in good condition, having been kept in a hangar.

trainers with secondary combat capabilities, for which surplus F-5E/Fs are being sought. Prime candidates might be 24 Canadian two-seat CF-5Ds now offered together with 36 unmodified CF-5s for disposal by Bristol Aerospace. PhilAF F-5 procurement discussions have extended to South Korea, Taiwan and Saudi Arabia. Funding is further included in the long-term defence plan for 12 new ground-attack and six maritime patrol aircraft.

SINGAPORE:

More Chinooks required

A second batch of six Boeing CH-47D Chinooks is being sought by the Republic of Singapore air force, following six being delivered from a 1994 order. They are operated on long-term training roles alongside US Army aviation units at Grand Prairie, Texas, and the second batch, for which lease/purchase terms are being sought, is required for use in Singapore.

TAIWAN:

Last Starfighters retired

Deliveries of 48 Mirage 2000-5Eis, 12 two-seat 2000-5Dis, plus 120 Block 20 F-16As and 30 F-16Bs, started earlier in 1997. They have resulted in the Republic of China air force retiring by late 1997 its last F-104 Starfighters from the two remaining fighter/reconnaissance wings flying this type. Its last eight RF-104Gs operated for tactical reconnaissance by 12 Squadron of the 5th Tactical Fighter Wing were the first to go, in August, being replaced by eight Northrop Tigereyes converted to RF-5E standards with new camera-equipped nose fairings by Singapore Technologies Aerospace at Paya Lebar.

At Hsinchu, a dozen or so F-104Gs of the 2nd Tactical Fighter Wing's 42 Squadron were due for retirement in November, as the first multi-role Mirage 2000-5s entered RoCAF service. RoCAF F-104Gs have also been replaced in the 427th Fighter Wing at Ching Chuan Kang Air Base, Taichung, by deliveries from 1992 of the first of 130 indigenous Ching-Kuo air defence fighters. At least 220 Starfighters have been acquired by the

Two African rarities: above is a Falcon 900 of the Algerian air force during a visit to Brussels, while below is an MB-339C seen at the Aermacchi factory just prior to its delivery flight to the Eritrean air force.

RoCAF since the first ex-USAF F-104As were delivered in 1960. First RoCAF F-16 unit is the 455th TFW, operating three Northrop F-5E squadrons at Chiayi AB.

More US equipment sought

New US military equipment supplies requested by Taiwan through Pentagon letters of offer and acceptance were listed as including 21 AH-1Ws, plus AGM-114A Hellfires and other munitions, as well as AGM-84A Harpoon air-launched anti-ship missiles. The RoC army has already received 17 AH-1Ws from the US since 1993, towards requirements totalling 50 or more.

Once again, however, Taiwanese requests for AIM-120 AMRAAMs and more AGM-65G Maverick ASMs were vetoed by the State Department. Taiwan is already taking delivery of 960 MATRA MICA BVR active radar-homing AAMs for its Mirage 2000-5s. Taiwan has developed its own TC-II Sky Sword II medium-range AAM, and is initially producing 300, but the US refuses to release the software necessary to launch it from the F-16.

THAILAND:

More L-39s

Four more Aero L-39ZAs were delivered to the RTAF in 1996, supplementing earlier orders for 36 received in 1993-94. Further Thai L-39 requirements are also being discussed.

More Congolese AF aircraft at Maya-Maya included a Noratlas (left), An-24 (top left), Mi-8s (above) and MiG-17 (below), all of which were in open storage. Most of the aircraft wear the socialist-style national insignia, although a few carried the red/yellow/green roundel adopted after the 1991 introduction of democratic rule. The recent fighting in the republic centred on the airport, and many of the aircraft may have subsequently been damaged.

Africa

ALGERIA:

L-39 follow-up order

The Algerian air force recently took delivery of seven Aero L-39C trainers from the Czech Republic, to supplement 32 L-39ZAs equipped for light ground-attack and received between 1987-90.

KENYA:

Light transports from China

Six Y-12 transports shipped to Kenya by China's Harbin Aircraft Manufacturing Company on 2 April are believed to be scheduled for Kenyan government or air force operation.

Powered by two 620-shp (462-kW) Pratt & Whitney Canada PT6A-27 turboprops, the Y-12 has a maximum cargo load of 3,744 lb (1698 kg), or 17 passengers. HAMC has now delivered over 95 examples worth $160 million to 18 mainly Third World countries.

SOUTH AFRICA:

Rooivalk avionics order

Confirmation of the SAAF's promised order for 12 Rooivalk attack helicopters accompanied a South African government contract via ATE and Denel. France's Sextant Avionique is to supply advanced avionics for this requirement. New Sextant equipment will include LCD cockpit displays, laser-gyro INS and Topowl helmet-mounted sights, also selected for the Tiger and NH-90 helicopters, with day/night mission capabilities.

By late 1998, the IAF will receive 12 Su-30MKs with definitive avionics, including French systems, although India is evaluating rival radars from Phazotron and NIIP to replace the NO01 units from the same companies in the first examples delivered. Flight development of Phazotron's new NO011 development of the Zhuk with a bigger (3.11-ft/0.95-m) slot-array antenna has already started in an Su-27 at the Komsomolsk factory.

When the 12 Su-30MKs, which will still lack canards, arrive in India, the first eight Su-27PUs will be returned to Russia for rebuilding to full MKI standard, matching the last 20 IAF aircraft due for delivery between 1999 and 2004. All Su-30MKIs will have uprated (to 31,967 lb/142.2 kN thrust) Lyul'ka/Saturn AL-37FUs with pitch and roll thrust-vectoring nozzles, as well as canards, and India is negotiating a production licence for HAL to build 80-100 more at Ozhar. The first of two prototype canard-equipped Sukhoi OKB-built Su-30MKs with AL-37FU engines was due to start its flight development at Zhukhovskii in June. Three or four aerial tankers (probably Il-78s) are also being sought by the IAF.

PAKISTAN:

Mirage transfer details

Details of surplus Dassault Mirage III series fighters obtained from France in October 1997 by the PAF indicate that they involve six or more two-seat IIIBEs, plus eight Mirage 5Fs. They supplement the 50 Mirage IIIOs purchased earlier from Australia, and others from Lebanon in 1996.

CN.235 requirement

Negotiations have been reported with Turkey's TUSAS Aerospace Industries to buy up to 20 licence-built CASA/IPTN CN.235Ms for the PAF. They would follow the 50 CN.235Ms being completed by TAI in February 1998 for the Turkish forces.

Southern Asia

INDIA:

Su-30 delivery plans

Delivery by the Irkutsk Aviation Production Association of the 40 two-seat Sukhoi Su-30 multi-role fighters bought by the IAF for $1.9 billion started on 19 March 1997, when the first eight began arriving at Lohegaon air base, Pune, in An-124 freighters. Although described as Su-30KIs, they are reportedly Su-27PU trainers built to Russian air force standards, including avionics, and used mainly for pilot and ground crew training to replace the MiG-21Ms of No. 24 Squadron from Ambala.

Australasia

AUSTRALIA:

Hawk order finalised

The RAAF's BAe Hawk 100 lead-in fighter trainer requirement to replace its Aermacchi MB.326s was quantified for the first time as 33 aircraft on 22 June when Australian Prime Minister John Howard visited British Aerospace Military Aircraft Division's Warton factory. The aircraft were quoted by BAe as costing £425 million ($US700 million) overall, although Howard said that Australia would spend some $A850 million ($US638 million) on the Hawks in the first seven years of the programme.

Canada's 433 'Porcupine' Squadron has an anniversary aircraft to commemorate 130 years since Canadian Confederation. In 1867 the British Parliament passed the British North America Act, which formed the colonies of British North America into the Dominion of Canada.

Bell UH-1 upgrade contract

A contract is also being finalised with the Colombian government by Bell Helicopter Textron to upgrade up to 14 UH-1 utility helicopters from over 32 used by the armed forces and police mainly for drug interdiction roles. They will be fitted with uprated AlliedSignal T53-L-703 turboshaft engines, combined with Bell 212 main and tail rotors, plus transmission systems, for about $1 million each, to UH-1HP Huey II standards. From 25 April they were also supplemented by 10 Mil Mi-17 transport helicopters bought from Russia for $43 million.

PERU:

Russian combat aircraft delivered

Despite earlier difficulties in ensuring technical support from Russia, the Peruvian air force (FAP) was reportedly successful in taking delivery of 18 surplus MiG-29/UBS and 14 Sukhoi Su-25 ground-attack fighters from Belarus by mid-1997. These aircraft were accompanied by about 80 CIS technicians, some of whom may also be involved in planned upgrades of the FAP's 52 remaining Sukhoi Su-20/22M-2 strike/interceptors delivered from 1976.

The Hawk 100 contract was due for signature in Canberra in early July 1997, but with a current production two-year lead time, the first of 12 aircraft from BAe's Brough and Warton factories was not expected before 2000. The remaining 21 aircraft will be assembled under licence by the Australian Hunter Aerospace consortium, with components from Hawker de Havilland and other Australian companies, at a new factory at Newcastle, NSW, alongside the RAAF's main Williamtown fighter base. Offset contracts are expected to reach or exceed the initial programme value. A further $A400 million will be generated locally from maintenance and support expenditure between about 2007 and 2025, within the expected 25-year service life of the RAAF Hawks.

Seasprite numbers increased

Some 29 Kaman SH-2F Super Seasprites will now be involved in the Royal Australian Navy contract, although its original Project 1411 requirement was for only 14. Eleven will be upgraded jointly by Kaman and its Australian partners to SH-2G(A) standard for frigate-based anti-submarine and ASV operations, for delivery in 2001/02. The RAN requirement

included options for another 18 to operate from its nine proposed offshore patrol combatant (OPC) ships, which Australia's remaining Seasprites will fulfil, leaving some available as reserves.

NEW ZEALAND:

SH-2G contract

A $US185 million contract was signed by the New Zealand government with Kaman in June for the four SH-2G Super Seasprites, plus associated spares and support equipment, selected to replace the frigate-based Westland Wasp ASW helicopters of the Royal New Zealand Navy. Delivery is scheduled to start in 2000.

On 11 April 1997 MV-22A Osprey BuNo. 164939 was at MCAS Cherry Point for the first public showing of the dedicated Marine Corps variant. The 2nd MAW will equip first, the lead squadron being HMT-204 'White Knights', which will be redesignated as VHMT-204. IOC is slated for 2001.

more CASA C.212-300 light turboprop transports. They were ferried across the north Atlantic in the spring of 1997 to Santiago, supplementing earlier deliveries of six Chilean army Aviocars (the basic C.212-200 model).

COLOMBIA:

CN.235s ordered

An order for three CN.235M tactical transports has been placed with CASA by the Colombian air force. They have a reported programme cost of $48 million, or $16 million each, including spares and technical support, and delivery is scheduled for early 1998.

VENEZUELA:

Polish transport aircraft procurement

Deliveries started in late 1996 of the first of 24 PZL M-28 Skytruck twin-turboprop light transports for the Venezuelan army from an $80 million order, due for completion in 1998. Powered by 1,100-shp (820-kW) Pratt & Whitney Canada PT6A-65B turbo-props driving five-bladed Hartzell propellers, the 18-passenger (or freight) M-28 is also fitted with Bendix-King avionics and other Western equipment, and will operate mainly on drug interdiction roles.

South America

BRAZIL:

French Mirage transfers

Recent acquisitions have included two Dassault Mirage IIIEs from French air force surplus. They supplement a dozen upgraded F-103E and four two-seat F-103D Mirage IIIEBR/DBRs that remain in FAB service with a single squadron (1°/1° GDA 'Jaguares') of Dassault Mirage IIIEs, based at Anapolis in Goias province, for defence of Brasilia. The additional Mirages will probably undergo similar upgrades to the existing FAB aircraft, which include canards and lateral strakes at the pitot/radome junction, to increase combat manoeuvrability; single-point pressure refuelling; fitting two 30-mm DEFA cannon; provision for MATRA

R-530 AAMs; and HOTAS controls, with only limited avionics changes.

CHILE:

First export JPATS?

Plans for Chilean air force modernisation reportedly include the Beech Mk II (T-6A) to supersede 22 T-37Cs for basic training. The trainer requirement is now becoming urgent, and could result in the first export order for this upgraded Pilatus PC-9.

More army Aviocars

The Chilean army aviation inventory was augmented earlier this year by three

Central America

MEXICO:

US aircraft transfers for anti-drug roles

Earlier in 1997, Mexico was due to receive the remainder of 73 surplus US Army Bell UH-1H utility helicopters for anti-drug operations, following the first 20 from the US in 1996. Other current US military aircraft transfers for

similar duties include four Fairchild C-26 Metro III twin-turboprop light transports. Equipped with TCAS II, GPS, microwave landing systems and other digital avionics, plus multiple day/night sensors in a large underfuselage pod, they are among 30 C-26Bs operated by the USAF Air National Guard since January 1992, in support of US law enforcement agencies on drug interdiction roles.

North America

CANADA:

Hawks selected for NATO flying training

A requirement for 17-25 Hawk 100 lead-in fighter trainers, for which contracts with British Aerospace are now being negotiated, was confirmed in April, with inauguration of Canada's NATO Flying Training Centre (NFTC) programme. The Canadian government, in partnership with the Canadair Defence Systems Division of Bombardier Inc. and several international aerospace companies, is establishing the NFTC for its military jet pilot training requirements while offsetting much of their costs by making its facilities available to NATO and other air forces on a commercial basis. Interest in the NFTC facilities has already been expressed by Denmark, Germany, Norway and the UK.

Apart from British Aerospace, the NFTC group includes EMBRAER in Brazil plus CAE Electronics, CAE Aviation and Frontec of Canada. EMBRAER is expected to supply 23 EMB-314 Super Tucanos for the basic and some advanced stages of the NFTC's proposed flying training programme. The NFTC will initially train 20-25 foreign student pilots from Phase I primary flying national selection to advanced standards, from which they would transfer directly to national Operational Conversion Units (OCUs) on current combat aircraft.

The 18-month three-phase NFTC syllabus costs up to $1.25 million. It will cover 95-123 hours (the latter for fast-jet students) for basic flying in the Tucano (Phase II), 80 hours of advanced (Phase III) and 47 hours of tactical/lead-in fighter training (Phase IV), the latter two in the Hawk. NFTC operations, beginning in 2000 with students from Canada and Europe, will be centred at CFB Moose Jaw, Saskatchewan. Phase IV training will utilise over 700,000 sq miles (1.813 million km²) of tactical ranges at CFB Cold Lake, Alberta.

UNITED STATES:

'No-Fly Zone' participants changes

Six F-16Cs of the 149th FW from Kelly AFB, TX deployed to Al Jaber AB, Kuwait during mid-March 1997 for a 45-day stay as part of Operation Southern Watch. The aircraft joined a detachment of OA/A-10As of the 74th FS, 23rd Wing (now 23rd Fighter Group) from Pope AFB, NC which was already in-theatre. The squadron was deployed to Kuwait just a few days after it was declared combat ready following conversion to the Thunderbolt II from the F-16C/D. The A-10 rotation consists of 18 aircraft not 24, since the number was reduced in mid-March 1997. Al Jaber also hosts a small contingent of F-117As.

Above right: One of three Phantoms built as F-4Bs but converted to YF-4J standard, BuNo. 151473 is active again with the NWTSPM 'Bloodhounds' at Point Mugu. It is assigned to ejection seat trials for a new F/A-18 seat.

Right: USS Rainier (AOE-7) visited Port Phillip Bay, Australia in March 1997. On board was this immaculate HH-46D from HC-11 Det 1.

Below: Following the B-1B and the B-2, the Boeing B-52H is being cleared for carriage of JDAM. The trolley in the foreground carries several 2,000-lb Mk 84 bombs which (apart from the pair in the middle) have been modified with the JDAM kit to become GBU-31s. The work is being performed by the 419th Flight Test Squadron, which performs test work on the B-1B and B-52H. On 1 January 1998 the unit will add the work of the B-2 test unit (420th FLTS), and fully occupy the Edwards South Base complex.

The 366th Wing from Mountain Home AFB, ID was deployed almost in its entirety to Al Kharj AB, Saudi Arabia during March and April 1997 for Operation Southern Watch. During early March, 18 F-15Es arrived to replace a similar number of F-16C/Ds of the 347th Wing, and 12 F-16C/Ds of the 366th Wing replaced a dozen 20th FW F-16C/Ds. The interceptors were swapped during April, with 18 F-15C/Ds replacing 18 33rd FW F-15C/Ds. In addition, the 366th Wing deployed four KC-135Rs to the Gulf in support of its forces. The F-15Es and F-16Cs were replaced during June by similar quantities of aircraft from the 4th FW at Seymour Johnson AFB, NC and the 20th FW from Shaw AFB, SC. The F-15Cs were expected to be replaced in-theatre by aircraft from the 1st FW at Langley AFB, VA during June.

Further north at Incirlik AB, Turkey, the F-15Es of the 48th FW returned to RAF Lakenheath on 6 April 1997 when their participation in Operation Northern Watch was completed. The Eagles had been replaced by a dozen Reserve F-16C/Ds drawn from the 115th FW at Madison, WI, 178th FW from Springfield, OH and the 419th FW stationed at Hill AFB, UT. The F-16s remained in Turkey

until early July, when they were replaced by 12 F-16C/Ds of the 482nd FW from Homestead AFB, FL. The latter were due to be assigned for one month before being replaced by another Reserve unit.

The 493rd FS also returned to RAF Lakenheath during April when six F-15As of the 131st FW from St Louis, MO arrived to perform air defence duties. The electronic warfare rotation by the EF-111A Ravens of the 27th FW came to an end during June 1997 when the three aircraft at Incirlik AB were flown home to Cannon AFB, NM. The aircraft are believed to have been replaced by the EA-6B. The four EF-111As at Al Kharj remain, although they too are due to be replaced later in 1997 by the EA-6B crewed by both Navy and Air Force personnel.

Theatre airlift reorganisation

On 1 April 1997 the theatre airlift C-130s of Air Combat Command (ACC) and the C-21A Operational Support Aircraft (OSA) were transferred to Air Mobility Command (AMC). At Pope AFB, NC the 43rd Airlift Wing was activated to take charge of the 2nd AS and 41st AS, both operating the C-130E. Pope AFB

was also transferred from ACC to AMC, with the 23rd Wing becoming the 23rd Fighter Group as a tenant unit. Little Rock AFB, AR and the resident 314th AW became part of Air Education and Training Command (AETC), along with the 53rd AS (tasked with basic aircraft qualification for personnel transitioning to the Hercules), and the 62nd AS (performing mission qualification). The two squadrons have 38 C-130Es assigned. The 463rd Airlift Group was also activated at Little Rock AFB under AMC as a tenant unit, with the 50th AS and 60th AS operating 30 combat support C-130E/H models. AETC has also become the gaining command for the C-130Es of the 189th AW/Arkansas ANG as the unit performs training of Reserve C-130 crews. The 317th AG was formed as a tenant at Dyess AFB, TX, with the 39th AS and 40th AS both operating the C-130Hs which were previously assigned to the 7th Wing.

AMC has gained the Stateside active-duty fleet of C-21A Learjets which were formerly operated by ACC, AETC, Air Force Space Command (AFSPC), and Air Force Materiel Command (AFMC). The centralisation involved the transfer of 41 aircraft which join 18 already oper-

installed by Boeing, along with modifications to the cockpit and boom operators' instrumentation to enable the three fuel dispensers to be monitored simultaneously. The French air force has begun to fit these kits to its C-135FRs, and the US Air Force is planning to have one aircraft modified for tests by Boeing in mid-1997, with the remainder converted by 2001. The aircraft involved in the tests is believed to be 62-3499 of the 22nd ARW, which was with Boeing at its Wichita, KA facility during March 1997. The fitting of the two additional pods will enable the USAF to air refuel aircraft compatible with the flying boom system as well as those which utilise the hose-and-drogue method (including Navy, Marine Corps and many NATO types) simultaneously during a single mission. At present, missions involving the latter are accomplished by attaching a hose and drogue to the rear of the flying boom. The new pods can transfer fuel to receivers at a rate of 400 US gal (1514 litres) per minute. Forty-five KC-135Rs are due to be modified by Boeing at a cost of $204 million.

Weapons separation tests continue apace at NAWC-AD, Patuxent River for the F/A-18E/F Super Hornet. F/A-18F2 undertook the first live launch of an AIM-120 AMRAAM on 5 May 1997 (left), while (above) F/A-18E5 is seen above dropping Mk 20 CBUs. By early May 1997 the test fleet had amassed more than 960 hours in 624 flights.

Quadrennial Defense Review

The results of the Quadrennial Defense Review were released in mid-May 1997, providing the three armed services with details of the changes to manpower levels and the quantity of new equipment to be ordered during the coming fiscal years. The US Army will cut back its personnel by 15,000 but will maintain its present level of 10 active-duty divisions. Surprisingly, the two attack helicopters for the next decade – AH-64D Longbow Apache and RAH-66 Comanche – have both survived the review unscathed. The Navy will shrink by 18,000 personnel but will keep its current structure of 12 carrier battle groups and 11 air wings. However, 15 surface combat ships and two submarines will be axed. Procurement of the F/A-18E/F Super Hornet will be significantly reduced from 1,000 to 548, although the number may be increased if the Joint Strike Fighter is not available for service entry in 2008. The order for the Bell-Boeing MV-22 Osprey for the Marine Corps will be reduced from 425 to 360, but production will be accelerated. The planned acquisition for 48 RV-22As for the US Navy and 50 CV-22As for the Air Force remains unchanged.

The Air Force appears to be the loser as it will need to shed 25,000 personnel, and the equivalent of one wing of F-15Cs. As a consequence, the acquisition of the Lockheed Martin F-22A Raptor will be reduced from 438 to 339. The Air Force is to have its allocation of E-8C J-STARS cut

ated by AMC. The 375th AW with headquarters at Scott AFB, IL is the parent organisation for the OSA, with the 457th AS at Andrews AFB, MD responsible for the 12th, 47th and 54th Airlift Flights stationed at Langley AFB, VA, Wright-Patterson AFB, OH and Maxwell AFB, AL, respectively. At Scott AFB the 458th AS has the 84th, 311th and 332nd Airlift Flights located at Peterson AFB, CO, Offutt AFB, NE and Randolph AFB, TX. The C-21s stationed in Europe and the Pacific are unaffected by the change.

Airlift recommendations

The Air Force has completed a major mobility requirements study to determine a new lower total number of C-130 Hercules needed to support two near-simultaneous major regional conflicts. The changes will be implemented during the coming year and include the inactivation of the 52nd AS at Moody AFB, GA. At Little Rock AFB the 61st (AMC) will lose two C-130Es, while the 62nd AS (AETC) will redesignate 14 C-130Es from combat support to the training role exclusively. Three Air Force Reserve Command units will each lose two aircraft, consisting of the 302nd AW at Peterson AFB, CO, 440th AW at Milwaukee, WI and the 913th AW at Willow Grove JRB, PA. The latter operates the C-130E and the other two fly the C-130H, which will be redistributed. Five Air National Guard units will each lose four aircraft, consisting of the 123rd AW at Louisville, KY, 145th AW at Charlotte, NC, 146th AW at NAS Point Mugu, CA, 147th AW at Nashville, TN and the 167th AW at Martinsburg, WV. All except the 146th AW operate the C-130H, which again will be reassigned. The 193rd SOW at Harrisburg, PA will place one of its four EC-130Es in back-up status, although it could be returned to service in an emergency. Within PACAF, the 36th AS at Yokota AB, Japan will transfer six C-130Hs to the 517th AS at Elmendorf AFB, AK during FY 1998.

Other imminent changes to the transport fleet include the inactivation of the 20th AS at Travis AFB, CA following the retirement of its nine C-141B StarLifters later in 1997. The 62nd AW at McChord AFB, WA will also commence the retirement process for its C-141Bs as crews are sent to Altus AFB, OK to receive training to operate the C-17A. The two CT-43As operated by the 200th AS at Buckley ANGB, CO will also be retired.

Stratotanker to receive wingtip refuelling pods

The Air Force has funded a programme involving the supply by Flight Refuelling Ltd of Mk 32B wing-mounted hose-and-drogue refuelling pods kits for the KC-135R. The pods will be

Seen at Fort Worth, this Lockheed Martin-owned Sabreliner has a missile seeker head fitted in the nose for trials. The 'PAC-3' badge on the fin suggests it is connected with Patriot missile testing.

from 19 to 13, but the Department of Defense hopes that NATO will acquire the other six to help maintain the cost per aircraft within budget. There will be no additional Northrop B-2A Spirit bombers past the planned 20 plus one prototype. Sixty active-duty fighters will be transferred to the Reserves to form the equivalent of one additional Reservist fighter wing. Six Air National Guard squadrons currently fulfilling the role of defence of the continental United States will switch to general-purpose fighter operations or to other missions altogether.

The reduced F/A-18E/F and F-22 totals do not preclude the acquisition of further derivatives of these two types at a later date. It is possible the former will eventually provide the platform for an EA-6B Prowler replacement, and the latter is being considered as a replacement for both the F-15E and F-117A. The planned overall Joint Strike Fighter purchase has been reduced from 2,978 to 2,852, consisting of 1,763 for the Air Force, 480 for the Navy and 609 for the Marine Corps. The Air Force total is slightly reduced, while that for the Navy shows a slight increase, although this is dependent upon programme costs and no slippage in timescales.

T-6A 'Texan II' makes its debut

The Raytheon T-6A 'Texan II' primary trainer received its nickname in a ceremony at Randolph AFB, on 2 June 1997. The T-6A (JPATS) will replace the Cessna T-37B 'Tweet' in the US Air Force and the Beech T-34C Turbo Mentor in the US Navy. Most new Air Force and Navy pilots will be trained on the T-6A by 2010.

The first aircraft will go to the 559th Flying Training Squadron (which trains instructors) at Randolph in March 1999. The first T-6A training of student pilots will begin with the 85th Flying Training Squadron at Laughlin AFB, TX in June 2001. The first naval aviators will train in the T-6A at NAS Whiting Field, FL from 2003.

The T-6A designation reflects improper use of the Department of Defense aircraft designation system, administered by the Air Force. If the system were followed correctly, the aircraft would be the T-4A. The designation, and the 'Texan II' nickname, are a rip-off from – or a tribute to – the immortal North American AT-6 Texan advanced trainer of World War II (which was redesignated T-6 in 1948). The new aircraft will be assembled not in Texas but in Wichita, KS.

The T-6A 'Texan II' is being sold at a flyaway cost of $1.9 million (as measured in 1992 dollars). The T-6A uses GPS navigation and digital instruments, and is 'anthropometric' – which is the Pentagon's term for the interior being redesigned to accommodate women as well as men. The T-6A's Powerplant is a 1,150-shp (858-kW) Pratt & Whitney Canada PT6A-62 turboprop.

Above: Back in the air again after nearly 19 years in open storage at Tucson, Arizona, is the McDonnell Douglas YC-15. The aircraft was taken from the Pima Air & Space Museum and refurbished at neighbouring Davis-Monthan AFB for a 'first' flight on 11 April 1997. The aircraft was then flown to Long Beach to act as an advanced transport technology demonstrator.

Right: One of two assigned to the US Army's 207th AvnCo at Heidelberg, this is a Cessna UC-35A. It is a military model of the Cessna 560 Citation V.

Right: This F-16D Block 25 of the 416th FLTS, 412th Test Wing was seen in April 1997, configured for trials linking GPS to the LANTIRN system for precise targeting. Note the GPS receiver on the spine.

OH-58Ds with digital messaging

Bell OH-58D Kiowa Warriors participating in March 1997 in the US Army's Task Force I experiment at the National Training Center, Fort Irwin, CA, were equipped with a new digital messaging system to improve connectivity with ground units. Eight OH-58Ds were equipped with the Embedded Tactical Information Control System (ETICS) manufactured by Honeywell Defense Avionics Systems. Operational testing will determine whether the US Army proceeds with further development of the system.

X-36

The McDonnell Douglas X-36 made its first flight on 16 May 1997 at NASA's Dryden Flight Research Center, Edwards AFB, CA. Two X-36s have been built as 28 per cent scale models of a planned future fighter. The X-36 is powered by a 700-lb (3.11-kN) Williams Research F112 turbofan.

Gulfstream V is C-37A

The US Air Force has ordered two Gulfstream Vs, to be designated C-37A, to meet its VC- requirement for a long-ranged, medium-sized VIP transport. The deal includes an option to purchase four more aircraft before 2003. Both aircraft will join the 89th Airlift Wing at Andrews AFB near Washington, DC.

V-22

Production of the Bell Boeing V-22 Osprey tilt-rotor aircraft may increase to between 30 and 36 aircraft per year, cutting unit costs slightly and easing the Osprey's introduction into operational service. The current requirement is for 360 MV-22Bs for the US Marine Corps, 50 CV-22Bs for US Special Operations Command, and 48 HV-22Bs for the US Navy.

Gulf War re-examined

A reassessment by the General Accounting Office (GAO), the auditing agency of the US Congress, of the Gulf War of 1991 suggests that precision-guided munitions (PGMs) did not perform as well as originally thought. For example, it says that Lockheed F-117 Nighthawk, which had exclusive purview to bomb targets in the Iraqi capital of Baghdad, hit 41 to 60 per cent of their targets, not 80 per cent as previously stated, and that 22,000 lb (9980 kg) of guided ordnance had to be expended on each target destroyed.

The GAO acknowledges that figures such as this can bolster claims of the weapons' effectiveness if contrasted with past wars. The findings are important because US strategy relies heavily on employing advanced technology to compensate for reduced numbers. So, although PGMs produced "perhaps the most successful war fought by the US in the 20th century,"the results were not always what they seemed. The GAO and other sources have said that, contrary to reports at the time, no coalition aircraft ever detected or destroyed a mobile 'Scud' missile site.

The GAO said that the effectiveness of Tomahawk cruise missiles was reduced by vague aimpoints, poor intelligence, and employment against targets that were too hard or too mobile. In the air-to-ground realm, of 2,665 main battle tanks in 12 Iraqi divisions, the 43 per cent that were destroyed by aircraft before the ground war began, along with the 32 per cent of 2,624 armoured personnel carriers that were wiped out, constitute less than half of the quantity that had been claimed. A total of 313 of Iraq's 724 fixed-wing aircraft survived the fighting intact and 121 escaped to Iran, leaving 290 destroyed by coalition forces, most by air-to-ground strikes. The report also noted that Iraqi air defences were not degraded to the extent claimed at the time, and that Iraq shot down 11 aircraft in the final three days of the war.

BRIEFING

Mil Mi-28N 'Havoc-B'

Mil joins battle on attack helicopters

In mid-March 1997, the Mil Design Bureau informed journalists that the Mi-28N (*Nochnoy*) 'Havoc-B' night-capable version would be demonstrated in flight at the end of the month. The helicopter is equipped with a mast-mounted sight (MMS) combining a millimetre-waveband radar and an IR seeker. Inputs from these are processed by a computer and displayed by the pilot's EFIS, enabling the helicopter to operate day and night in any weather, even in total darkness, including NoE flying at 5 m (16 ft). The Mi-28N has already earned such nicknames as 'Night Hunter' and 'Night Pirate'.

The first prototype, coded 'White 014', was rolled out following completion at the company's experimental plant near Moscow on 16 August 1996. (During the static display at the 1995 Moscow air show, the prototype lacked much of its avionics and equipment.) The engines were ground-run for the first time on 14 October that year, and on 14 November the Mi-28N made its first flight, hovering briefly at 5 m (16 ft). Additional test flights were delayed due to a small malfunction of the main rotor, as a Mil representative put it. The Mi-28N features new main rotor blades with swept tips and a new main gearbox. The latter's malfunction during test

The Mi-28N is powered by a pair of uprated (2,500-hp/1863-kW) Klimov TV3-117VK turboshafts. The original TV3-117VMs of the Mi-28 are rated at 2,200 hp (1639 kW).

flights meant that the defective part had to be taken to the manufacturer in Perm. This caused the delay, because Mil does not have the several hundred million roubles to pay for a replacement.

Mil is now putting great emphasis on the Mi-28N, despite the fact that the type has lost out to the Kamov Ka-50 'Hokum'. On 5 October 1994, the Russian Ministry of Defence signed a protocol to the effect that the Ka-50 be adopted by Russian army aviation and the Mi-28 be discontinued. This should have ended the fierce competition for the new assault chopper between Mil and Kamov.

The Ka-50 has entered production in Arsenyev in the Far East, yet no more than 20 have been built to date. Most were delivered to the Army Aviation Training Centre at Torzhok, about 300 km (186 miles) from Moscow. The slow production rate is primarily accounted for by lack of funding. Still, the Ka-50, dubbed 'Black Shark', and its two-seat version, the Ka-52 'Alligator', are being actively promoted both by the Russian and foreign media, while the Mi-28 has almost faded into oblivion.

Of course, Mil is unhappy about this. The company's situation is critical, among other things because of the death of general designer Mark Weinberg. So, Mil has embarked on a counteroffensive. The Mi-28N is its only weapon against its adversaries (notably Kamov, the Ministry of Defence

and the Russian government). As the first strike, the first and so far only prototype was prepared for demonstration to Prime Minister Viktor Chernomyrdin, military leaders and the media.

The demonstration took place on 30 April 1997; the prototype hovered and made a few pedal turns at 10-15 m (32-49 ft) with test pilot Colonel Vladimir Yudin and weapons operator Sergei Nikulin. After that, Colonel General Vitaly Pavlov, army aviation C-in-C and Hero of the Soviet Union, climbed into the cockpit and tried a hover at 5 m (16 ft). Permission to demonstrate the Mi-28N in flight to the public was not given.

The greatest philosophical difference between the two competitors is Mil's adherence to conventional layout. The main shortcoming of this layout, says Yevgeni Yablonskiy, a high-ranking Mil specialist, is the long tailboom and transmission shaft; the coaxial

Russian army funding for the Mi-28N was announced in 1994 and the basic airframe was unveiled at the 1995 Moscow Aero Show.

layout is more compact and simple. On the other hand, the coaxial layout has a very serious shortcoming – the blades of the two rotors get dangerously close and may collide during manoeuvres. This can only be avoided by separating the rotors, but this separation has a limit and is insufficient for a combat helicopter which has to manoeuvre sharply to avoid enemy fire. The helicopter must be able to perform all sorts of manoeuvres, including those not allowed by the flight manual. This ability saved many Russian lives in Afghanistan when Mi-8 'Hip' and Mi-24 'Hind' pilots took the machines to their limits. That is why the coaxial layout may increase attrition considerably.

Mil believes that the Ministry of Defence has made a gross blunder by choosing the Ka-50 over the

Mi-28. Yablonskiy is perfectly right, according to Colonel V. Bukharin, who was a helicopter pilot in the Afghan war. "On one occasion we were flying top cover for a convoy of trucks going along a canyon near Kabul. Suddenly a hail of fire came at us from the mountain side. I had no choice but to make a sharp U-turn at full power; my wingmen followed suit. We exceeded every possible speed, bank, pitch and *g* limit, but stayed in one piece and no-one was hit. Another incident happened over the Salang pass when we encountered severe turbulence or possibly wind shear, but got through. A coaxial-layout helicopter would have surely crashed because of a blade collision."

According to test pilot Colonel Vladimir Yudin, who had a chance to fly both the Ka-50 and Mi-28, there are few coaxial-layout helicopters. They only make up about ⅕₀th of all helicopters built worldwide; none has been built outside the USSR since 1952. About 1,500 such helicopters have been built in Russia in the last 30 years or so, and none has been used in combat. Conversely, the Mi-24 with its conventional single-rotor layout has been in action in more than 30 wars. "Coaxial-layout helicopters are great flying cranes, but I wouldn't dream of going to war in such a helicopter, even the most modern one," said Yudin.

One reason is that certain horizontal/vertical speed combinations are unfavourable for this layout, e.g., descent speeds from 3-4 to 9-10 m/sec (10-13 to 29-32 ft/sec) and airspeeds around 30 km/h (18.6 mph) lie within the ring of turbulence zone. Investigation of the crash of the first prototype Ka-50 ('White 010' which encountered severe turbulence and crashed out of control, killing the pilot) showed that the critical speed increases as *g* loads grow. At 2*g*, critical speed is about 70-80 km/h (43-49 mph), i.e., a helicopter's speed over the battle area. In other words, some suggest that coaxial helicopters are dangerous to fly in combat at 0-80 km/h (0-49 mph). They also have directional control

problems at descent speeds of 5 m/sec (16 ft/sec) and higher and airspeeds up to 60 km/h (37 mph), which are also in the speed range of a combat helicopter in action.

Why are these speeds typical for a combat helicopter? When flying over hilly terrain (to say nothing of mountainous areas), the helicopter cannot climb higher than 15-20 m (49-65 ft) AGL in order to avoid detection. Thus, it has to veer around obstacles rather than fly over them, making turns of up to 60°. Forward speed cannot exceed 30-60 km/h (18-37 mph) because of the danger of hitting high terrain. Thus, the helicopter is constantly within the ring of turbulence zone and in constant danger of blade collision or hitting high ground because of poor directional control during descent or turns.

Finally, coaxial helicopters have never been used in combat and defects may be encountered in operational conditions which cannot be eliminated. Conventional helicopters are more reliable. On one occasion, an Mi-24 and an Mi-26 'Halo' collided in mid-air when training for an air show, the main rotors striking each other. Despite violent vibration, both helicopters landed safely.

Colonel General Pavlov, who flew the giant Mi-26 transport helicopter during the Zhukhovskii air show, confirmed this. Both

helicopters involved in the accident have been repaired and are still operational, and the crews alive and well. Conversely, on a different occasion a coaxial-layout helicopter struck the tail rotor of a parked Mi-26 and both main rotors disintegrated instantly on impact, tearing the gearbox loose.

General Gherman Samoylov, a professor of the Russian Air Force Academy named after Yuri Gagarin (in Monino near Moscow) and a long-time teacher of combat helicopter manoeuvring techniques, agrees with the above-mentioned views on the inherent dangers of the coaxial layout. He also points out that during the Afghan war many SovAF helicopters returned from sorties with parts of main rotor blades shot away by Mujahideen ground fire. The helicopter stayed airborne but experienced violent vibration, and the damaged blade would go outside the main rotor cone. On a coaxial helicopter this would greatly increase the danger of blade collision, not only at low speed but at any speed.

Considering all this, why did the USSR still use Kamov coaxial helicopters for a long time (and why does Russia, and others, still do so)? First, since the late 1950s Soviet naval doctrine has included the use of large ASW ships armed with helicopters. Compactness – a

characteristic of coaxial helicopters – is a must for an ASW helicopter because more can fit into a ship's hangar. Secondly, wind speed is much stronger over water than it is over land. Tests have shown that coaxial helicopters are much less sensitive to crosswinds than conventional ones and are thus better suited to deck landings. Kamov's coaxial helicopters have proved this by doing sterling service with the Soviet navy for four decades.

Assault helicopters, however, are a different story. Most navies of the world still use conventional helicopters for ASW and SAR tasks, the advantages of the coaxial layout notwithstanding; only India, Yugoslavia and Vietnam use a few Soviet-supplied Kamov Ka-25 'Hormone' and Ka-28 'Helix' helicopters. Coaxial helicopters have been under development in the USSR for the same 50-year period as conventional ones; why are there so few, then? And why have they never been used in real combat? The reason is that while a conventional helicopter can land successfully after sustaining battle damage to the main rotor, this is completely impossible for a coaxial helicopter because a damaged blade can flap 1.5 m (5 ft) up and down, and blade collision is imminent.

General P. Bazanov, who often chaired state commissions during state acceptance trials of new military aircraft, is convinced that the AH-64 would emerge as the winner in a dogfight with the Ka-50 because the Apache can perform complex manoeuvres in the vertical plane which the 'Black Shark' cannot. Mil engineers believe that even the Mi-24 has a chance against the Ka-50 because of the latter's poor manoeuvrability. Iraqi Mi-24Ds shot down 53 Iranian helicopters of US origin (including 10 Bell AH-1 Huey-

The Mi-28N was on show at the 1997 Paris air show, with its systems and sensors installed. Note the twin Igla (SA-16 'Gimlet') air-to-air missile tubes in front of the aircraft.

the world lets combat pilots fly coaxial helicopters. It is not that Kamov knows how to make such helicopters and everybody else does not; there are coaxial designs elsewhere in the world, but all of them are non-combat types or pilotless.

Yablonskiy names other serious disadvantages of the coaxial layout. Speaking specifically of the Ka-50/52, they include poor directional control in the autorotation mode and high rotor loading because of the rotor's relatively small diameter, which causes the high-energy rotor downwash to raise clouds of dust on dirty or snow-covered areas, rendering landing impossible due to zero visibility and increasing engine wear by abrasive dust. In addition, power and telegraph cables become a major problem when flying at low altitude; no effective cable cutters can be devised because the rotor mast contributes half of the helicopter's overall height. For the same reason, the Ka-50/52 cannot be airlifted by an Ilyushin Il-76 freighter without difficult disassembly and reassembly.

The Ka-50/52 has other shortcomings not related to the coaxial layout. The side-by-side seating (of the Ka-52) is unacceptable because both crew members have a seriously restricted field of view. (By comparison, the tandem layout provides an approximately 120° field of view.) The equipment is placed in bays closed by outward-hinging panels, which is inconvenient on dusty or snow-covered airfields, especially in bad weather (wind and rain), and may lead to multiple failures. The high-pressure tyres may create problems on soft surfaces. The crew rescue system is dangerous during concerted action, as the blades, which are jettisoned before ejection, may strike other helicopters in the formation; at 50 m (164 ft), hit probability is 35 per cent. Besides, there is no provision (i.e., no free space) for picking up a crew which has been shot down. The Mi-28 can evacuate three people.

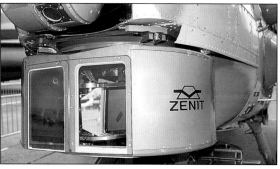

The box turret beneath the Mi-28N's nose houses the (daylight) Zenit TV/FLIR system behind doubled-glazed glass. The turret can move through an arc of ±110°. Above the Zenit system is a ball turret with the Mi-28N's laser spot tracker/designator.

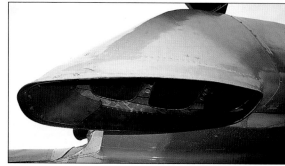

Both TV3-117VK engines are fitted with a (composite) downwards-facing shroud that would appear to direct the Mi-28N's exhaust plume directly at ground-based IR SAMs. An upwards-facing shroud has reportedly been tested on an earlier prototype.

Details of the Mi-28N's millimetre-wave radar are scant, as are those relating to its US rival on the Longbow Apache. The Russian system is claimed to provide 360° coverage but its associated weapons are unknown.

The prototype Mi-28N has been seen carrying this pod, which is reported to carry 'test instrumentation'. The wingtip pods contain some form of RWR or laser warning system, plus chaff/flare dispensers.

An assault helicopter should have a movable gun, and the gun of the Ka-50/52 is, in effect, fixed. Using the movable gun, a second crew member (weapons operator) can engage targets lying outside the helicopter's path while the pilot is firing at another target. The pilot may fly at higher speed and

Cobra assault helicopters) and an F-4 Phantom II during the Iran-Iraq war, losing six of their own.

The Ka-50's aerobatics displays at air shows certainly look impressive to the public. However, General Bazanov points out that the Ka-50 makes sharp turns only in a sharp climb, and then only left turns because a right turn in these conditions would very probably lead to blade collision. Conversely, Russian specialists judge the manoeuvres demonstrated by the Apache as usable in combat. Many Russian

officers (and, of course, Mil) believe the only combat helicopter capable of matching the Apache's performance is the Mi-28, which can perform a series of loops, pulling 3g repeatedly. Incidentally, Mil claims that the Mi-28 is the world's only helicopter capable of doing so and that such unusual manoeuvres can assure victory over the Apache.

There have been media reports that a new ambush tactic has been developed for the two-seat Ka-52 to protect it from enemy fire. This

tactic actually is not new at all, being developed by NATO some 20 years ago. It is well known that this tactic was seldom successful during regional conflicts; to quote a Mil representative, one would be a perfect idiot to fall for this trick. There are several ways of countering this tactic, including counter-ambushes.

Mil believes that the coaxial layout has just too many disadvantages and is therefore unacceptable for a combat helicopter because it jeopardises crew safety. Nobody else in

To date, a total of four Mi-28s (012, 022, 032 and 042) has been built, along with a single Mi-28N (014). The Mi-28 first flew in 1982 and the Mi-28N followed in 1996.

manoeuvre more sharply, staying within the target's field of view for a shorter time. A fixed gun imposes limitations on the pilot's actions, forcing him to aim the helicopter at the target and wasting time on targeting manoeuvres.

The second crew member gives the Ka-52 an advantage over the Ka-50. It is an established fact that a combat helicopter should have at least a crew of two; US companies gave up on single-seat assault helicopters after much research. However, the addition of a weapons' operator increases the Ka-52's gross weight (as compared to the Ka-50) by 10 per cent, with a corresponding deterioration in performance and combat efficiency.

Mil has analysed media reports on the Ka-50/52 and come to the following conclusions. The Ka-50 can meet the stated performance figures only at its normal TOW (9800 kg/21,604 lb), i.e., with practically no armament. With a full weapons load the TOW exceeds the normal value, which means the ceiling, speed, range, rate of climb and other performance figures will not be met. This also means the helicopter will always be operated above normal TOW and in some cases (ferrying etc.) above MTOW, which will lead to an abrupt shortening of its service life (1.5 to 2 times).

An attempt to keep maximum commonality between the Ka-50 and Ka-52, with the latter grossing at 600-1000 kg (1,322-2,204 lb) more, means that the latter's performance and service life will not be good. Even if performance can be improved by uprating the engines, the gearbox and other units of the Ka-50 cannot be used for the Ka-52 because they were not designed for bigger loads. Thus, Mil states that there cannot possibly be 80 per cent commonality between the two and the Ka-52, so to say, is not an alligator at all but a mutant shark.

Its hard to say why the Ministry of Defence chose the single-seat coaxial Ka-50 over the two-seat conventional Mi-28. Contributing factors included a large-scale propaganda campaign by Kamov, and the Communist Party's desire to have a breakthrough in helicopter engineering (because the US had by then designed great assault helicopters and left the USSR behind). The Ka-50's unusual layout for a combat helicopter seemed to

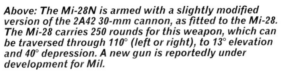

Above: The Mi-28N is armed with a slightly modified version of the 2A42 30-mm cannon, as fitted to the Mi-28. The Mi-28 carries 250 rounds for this weapon, which can be traversed through 110° (left or right), to 13° elevation and 40° depression. A new gun is reportedly under development for Mil.

Above right: The Mi-28N displayed at Paris in 1997 carried a loadout of ground attack weapons including 9M114 Shturm (AT-6 'Spiral') anti-tank missiles and 20-round UB-20 rocket pods (for 80-mm C-8 rockets), as seen here. Up to 16 Shturms can be carried, in groups of eight on either pylon. Large-calibre 130-mm C-13 rockets can also be carried. As in the AH-64 Apache, guns and rockets can be fired by either crew member but any guided weapons can be fired from the front seat only.

Right: Millimetre-wave radar provides precision guidance for missiles and is unaffected by atmospheric conditions, unlike laser guidance. The radar should also provide a degree of target identification.

be the required breakthrough. Incidentally, concurrent with the Ka-50, the coaxial Sikorsky S-69 and the conventional RAH-66 Comanche were under development in the USA. Unlike Kamov helicopters, the S-69 had rigid rotors without flapping and drag hinges, which effectively precluded blade collision; however, that would be an American breakthrough, not a Soviet one. When the Comanche was revived it was changed from a single-seat to a tandem two-seat configuration.

In 1993 a Ministry of Defence commission reviewed the Mi-28N project and was very positive in its assessment; still, no funds to

produce it could be found. Mil has tried to source funds elsewhere and succeeded, to a certain extent.

The day version (the basic Mi-28) participated in a fly-off for a new army helicopter held by the Swedish air force in the autumn of 1995, competing against the MDH AH-64 Apache (see *World Air Power Journal*, Volume 29). The Russian helicopter managed to penetrate 20 km (12 miles) into Swedish defences, flying at 20 m (65 ft) to avoid detection by radar. "The Mi-28 can carry a sizeable payload," said Thomas Edholm, Director of the Swedish Army Aviation Centre. "The optical targeting system works well and

our pilots had no trouble learning to use it. The Mi-28's survivability is also impressive; besides armour protection, there are systems ensuring survival, including RHAWS and ECM equipment. Night capability will be of prime importance for the Swedish army's new assault helicopter. We are well aware that the Mi-28 is a day helicopter, but the Mi-28N will meet our demands."

There is a Mil in-house joke that sharks and crocs cannot be tamed and sooner or later they will eat their masters. Or, as the late general designer Mark Weinberg put it, you can't trick nature.

Yefim Gordon

BRIEFING

188th Fighter Squadron/150th Fighter Wing 'Tacos'
The 'Killer Scouts'

Based at Kirtland AFB, near Albuquerque, New Mexico, the 150th FW is the pre-eminent ANG unit in the state. The 'Tacos' returned to their home base at the beginning of April 1997, after another successful deployment to Aviano AB, Italy, for two months in support of Operation Deliberate Guard. The aircraft arrived in Italy on 29 January 1997. The New Mexico ANG deployed more than 600 members and eight F-16Cs, and flew 280 sorties, including 250 in support of Deliberate Guard. In the last 18 months, aside from their deployment to Aviano, the 150th FW has deployed to exercises at Nellis AFB plus Singapore and Australia.

The history of the 188th FS dates to January 1943 when the 61st Bomber Squadron was constituted. On 24 May 1946, the unit was assigned to the New Mexico Air National Guard, operating from Kirtland AFB. The 'Tacos' were successively equipped with the P-51, B-26, F-86, F-80, F-100A and A-7D (LANA). With the Super Sabre, the 188th FS flew over 6,000 combat sorties in the Vietnam War. During this duty, unit pilots chose the callsign TACOS as a replacement for the Air Force callsign SQUID. In January 1971 the unit established Det 1, a detachment of F-100s stationed at Holloman AFB, with the mission of supporting US Army R&D programmes. This detachment returned to Kirtland in the spring of 1974, and continued operations as the Defense Systems Evaluation (DSE) contingent of the New Mexico ANG.

Today, the 188th FS has 18 Block 40 F-16Cs on strength. It is the only ANG unit flying with this version of the 'Viper' to also employ the AN/AAQ-13/14 LANTIRN system. In addition, the wing has eight Block 30 F-16Cs to support the DSE test mission – DSE being one of the few Air Force units to get funding from the Army. DSE aircraft are marked with a black band on the tail fin, as opposed to the 188th FS's yellow tail band. The DSE-assigned F-16Cs are used for many tasks, particularly to support the US Army missile works on White Sands Weapons range. The aircraft also fly simulated target missions in support of surface-to-air missile testing. Only eight 188th FS pilots are qualified for and assigned to the DSE mission, and they can also undertake all the missions flown by other 'Tacos' pilots.

Foremost among these is the mission known as Killer Scout, in which the F-16C Block 40 is used as a 'precision weapons multiplier' and high-tech Fast FAC. The Killer Scout mission was first undertaken by F-100Fs and F-4s in Vietnam and was revived by 4th TFS F-16s during Operation Desert Storm. The 188th FS has pioneered the modern Killer Scout mission, solely for PGMs. Using LANTIRN, the 'Tacos' unique (in the ANG) Block 40 F-16Cs can cycle other PGM-carrying aircraft, from A-10s to F-16s to B-1s, through a target area while designating for them, to bring massive precision firepower to bear. The 188th's Killer Scout F-16s are also equipped with GPS. The ANG plans to equip three other squadrons with the LANTIRN targeting pod, allowing them to undertake similar missions. However, the 188th FS will remain the only ANG squadron with the full LANTIRN fit for the foreseeable future.

Luigino Caliaro

The 188th flies General Electric F110-powered F-16Cs. The extra thrust of these engines (29,000 lb/ 129 kN compared to the 23,770-lb/ 106-kN F100-PW-220 engine of other F-16s) allows them to operate fully loaded, for long-endurance Killer Scout missions. Such a full load could comprise two AIM-9s, two AIM-120s, two LANTIRN pods, two 370-US gal fuel tanks, one ALQ-184 ECM pod plus four 500-lb GBU-12 LGBs or two 2,000-lb GBU-10s.

Naval Air Warfare Center-Aircraft Division

The 'Patuxent Pioneers'

Nestling in the heart of Maryland, NAS Patuxent River is the home of US naval flight testing. The natural boundary of the Patuxent River provides a ready identity for the US Naval Air Warfare Center-Aircraft Division (NAWC-AD), the 'Patuxent Pioneers'. Commissioned in 1943 to centralise air testing facilities, NAS Patuxent River (invariably abbreviated to 'Pax' River) has become the fastest growing base in the United States. It serves as a headquarters for the NAWC-AD, along with 50 other directorates reporting directly to the US Navy.

The Naval Air Test Center (NATC) was established at 'Pax' River on 16 June 1945 and by 1948 a dedicated Test Pilot Training Division had been formed. Progress through the Korean and Vietnam War eras led to a sweeping reorganisation and restructuring in

1975, preparing the NATC for its role as the Naval Air Systems Command's principal site for development testing. The plan included the disestablishment of the three major divisions of the NATC – Flight Test, Service Test, Weapons Systems Test – and the forming of more streamlined directorates able to evaluate aircraft by type and mission. The new face of the NATC comprised Strike Aircraft, Rotary Wing, Systems Engineering Test and Anti-Submarine Aircraft directorates (the latter became Force Warfare Aircraft Test). The US Naval Test Pilots School remained unscathed.

In 1991 the Department of the Navy began a further consolidation programme to improve its products and services, which resulted in the formation of the Naval Air Warfare Center (NAWC), again streamlining resources into just three divisions –

Aircraft Division (HQ at Patuxent River), Weapons Division (HQ at China Lake) and Training Systems Division (HQ at Orlando).

The Naval Air Warfare Center-Aircraft Division was formed through the decommissioning of the NATC and the amalgamation of the Naval Air Development Center formerly at Warminster, PA, the Naval Air Engineering Center, Lakehurst, NJ, the Naval Air Propulsion Center, Trenton, NJ and the Naval Avionics Center, Indianapolis, IA. So began the base's role as a facility that incorporated the full spectrum of test and evaluation, fleet support and engineering. The consolidation is about to take another turn with the imminent closure of the naval facilities at Warminster. The main element of the Aircraft Division at 'Pax' branches into four efficient sub-divisions. These comprise Force Aircraft Test, Strike Aircraft Test, Rotary Wing Aircraft Test and the US Navy Test Pilots School – all supported by the Test

And Evaluation Group which was born from the original Systems Test Directorate.

Today, 'Pax' River and its unique facilities are known as Test Wing Atlantic, and serve to bridge the gap between manufacturers' production lines and the carrier deck. All directorates report to the Naval Air Systems Command (NAVAIR), which combines all its subsidiaries' expertise to provide world leadership in the design, development, procurement and support of aviation systems and related equipment to be used by the Navy and Marine Corps.

Force Aircraft Test

The Naval Force Aircraft Test Squadron performs technical test and evaluation programmes on fixed-wing jet and turboprop aircraft (excluding fighter and

Development Super Hornets from NAWC-AD wait alongside a Force Test Squadron KC-130, as one of the Strike Test Squadron's F/A-18Cs takes on fuel during a trials sortie.

Left: The Strike Test Squadron maintains Patuxent River's 'front-line fighter fleet', and flies a mix of F/A-18C/Ds, F-14s and now the new F/A-18E/Fs. This is one of its F/A-18Cs.

Below left: The S-3 Vikings based at 'Pax' are currently involved in a major systems and avionics upgrade programme.

Below: The Naval Research Laboratory was formerly known as VXN-8 'World Travellers'. This is the unit's sole EP-3A.

attack types). The unit is composed of military and civil contractor partnerships operating and maintaining various aircraft types. The unit's backbone is a fleet of 13 Lockheed P-3 Orions.

Each airframe has a dedicated mission to evaluate at any given time, reflected in its external and internal retrofitted appendages. Current programmes include a constant ASW assessment under the Air Sea Warfare Improvement Program (AIP) resulting in continuing refinements to the Orion's sensor and communication fit. It is not unusual for the Force squadron to work in tandem with its neighbouring unit, VX-1 'Pioneers', on joint ASW tests. For example, on 12 September 1996 a combined test team launched the first Stand-off Land Attack Missile (SLAM) from a P-3.

The latest generation of this weapon is being integrated with the NAWC-Weapons Division at China Lake, CA. In a new guise, the Sea SLAM is launched from a ship and controlled from the air by day or night, in adverse weather, with over-the-horizon precision. The first Sea SLAM launched in precision strike tests in April 1996 hit a small land target guided by an SH-60 helicopter. The following day a second missile, controlled by a USMC F/A-18 Hornet, flew through the hole made by the previous day's launch.

The jewel in the crown of Force testing is a P-3 Orion that has been

The Naval Test Pilots School operates a raft of unusual types, including this DHC NU-1B Otter. Fourteen Otters were originally acquired by the Navy for Antarctic service with VXE-6, in 1962.

fitted with a laser for underwater mapping and detection. The entire ASW fit has been replaced by the blue/green laser mounted in the belly of the fuselage. The airframe has also been littered with sensors and air cooling inlets to assist the mission.

The squadron's three KC-130s are currently providing valuable support for the F/A-18E/F trials. Their missions include tanker compatibility trials and support for long-endurance missions such as supersonic evaluations. The aircraft are also called upon to support team detachments from 'Pax' River. They carry out their own evaluation duties, and have aided the development of HUDs and chemical and biological warfare suits for the Marines.

Another de Havilland Canada type unique to the NTPS is the U-6A Beaver. The Navy acquired its initial small handful of U-6s from the US Army, but later purchased two more on the open market.

Findings from these trials are reported directly to the C-130 Program Manager at Lockheed and also to NAVAIR, which receives all data collated by the Naval Air Warfare Centers in the US. All major projects are instigated with a tasking statement (AIRTASK), issued from NAVAIR. The process of reporting conclusions from evaluations can vary. A report will be compiled with input from the project managers, pilots, navigators and engineers within the 'Pax' River infrastructure, which affords Force Aircraft Test 24 buildings from where they can collate the research data in order to incorporate it into naval policy. All research project write-ups from the NAWC are typically commenced with a written or e-mailed report, which can vary in size depending on the trial in hand. If the trial is particularly large, a series of small reports will be sent as results come in, followed by a summary upon completion of the trial.

The three S-3 Vikings on strength are involved with various computer, radar and avionics upgrades, which also includes the installation of a global positioning system. It is planned to extend the expected service life of the S-3 within the US Navy, so one of the aircraft is involved with structural analysis and recording, in order to monitor fatigue. In the past, Force Aircraft Test initially qualified the S-3 as an air-to-air tanking platform, and continually stretched the aircraft and its systems to understand its full potential in all environments such as submarine hunting against real or simulated targets in the Atlantic Underwater Test Evaluation Center (AUTEC) ranges near Free Point, Bahamas.

Three E-2 Hawkeyes operated by the unit are facilitating vibration tests as well as avionics and computer upgrades that are planned for the type. Other turboprops employed by Force consist of a single C-2 Greyhound on avionics upgrade and stress evaluation duties, while a T-34C Mentor is regularly used for NVG, 'night spotter' trials and chase duties. The latest innovation being studied utilising the T-34 is a gyro-equipped flight suit that employs gyro sensors incorporated in the suit itself. This is intended to eradicate pilot disorientation with the help of fail-safe attitude indications.

The directorate also augments its fleet with squadron-assigned aircraft when necessary, one example being the T-45s acquired as evaluation dictates. Future plans for the unit's schedule include an avionics upgrade for the C-9 in 1997.

Strike Aircraft Test

The Naval Air Warfare Center's Strike Test Squadron works directly with carrier battle groups. Strike relays the conclusions drawn from all experimental fixed-wing attack and fighter evaluations for implementation on the front line. Testing is carried out on a similar structure to that at Force, with the main difference being the aircraft assigned. The roles of these aircraft also include the evaluation and integration of weapons systems into front-line strike aircraft. The unit has a predominantly F/A-18-equipped fleet, with other types currently on strength such as the F-14 and EA-6B. When the need arises, other types are recruited from operational squadrons, such as AV-8Bs.

Strike's complement of F/A-18s is currently involved with JDAM and SLAM integration trials. It is envisaged that the unit will soon be

Above: This F/A-18E is seen overhead the NAWC-AD's large airfield complex at Patuxent River, which juts out into Chesapeake Bay.

Right: The Tomcat has been transformed into the 'Bombcat' through the addition of LANTIRN pods and LGBs. The NAWC-AD was at the forefront of this development. Here one of the unit's F-14s, carrying a pair of GBU-16s, fires a Sparrow AAM – underlining the Tomcat's new-dual role capabilities.

involved with the integration of the new Joint Air-to-Surface Stand-off Missile (JASSM) – if the Navy elects to continue its involvement with this joint project. Of particular note is a new aircraft skin applied to one F/A-18, intended as a more durable, low-maintenance, stealthier replacement for paint. The unit's F-14s are continuously paving the way for avionics and flight systems upgrades, including in-depth work to further exploit the aircraft as an air-to-ground platform. A handful of NAS Oceana-based F-14s supplement the fleet for precision strike trials.

The most notable programme underway at Strike is the eagerly awaited F/A-18E/F. This is a joint effort between the US Navy and civilian contractors to produce a multi-mission evolution of the already proven F/A-18C/D. The Super Hornet offers greater range, endurance and enhanced survivability with the potential to incorporate even more new advanced systems. However, its most important feature is its ability to return to the carrier deck without expending its payload unnecessarily. The

Navy is keen to promote the new aircraft's increased 'bring-back' capability as a distinct advantage over the C/D model. Maximum landing weights for the older Hornet models mean that in some cases an unexpended war fit may need to be jettisoned so that a carrier deck recovery can be completed without exceeding weight limitations. As potential weapons fits increase due to mission flexibility, the current C/D models must compensate with reduced onboard fuel loads, thus rendering the aircraft less effective. The Super Hornet has a distinct advantage in this area as its overall structural configuration, combined with a new GE F414 engine, overcomes these deficiencies.

Patuxent River is the principal site for the Super Hornet evaluation, which is expected to last for at least the next two years under the command of Captain Kevin Thomas at the Strike Test Directorate. Since the first flight of the Super Hornet on 29 September 1995, the rigorous flight test programme, set for around 2,000 flights, has escalated to utilise all seven of its assigned test airframes (five single-seat E models and two twin-seat Fs). The jets assigned have all been fitted out for individual taskings with instrumentation specifically designed for each test requirement. The programme can therefore take advantage of the advanced telemetry systems at 'Pax', enabling ground-based staff

BRIEFING

Above: The USMC has been adding FLIR systems to its UH-1s for some time, chiefly to give them all-weather casevac capability. However, this aircraft is involved with weapons trials at 'Pax'.

Below: The NTPS flies OH-58As, on loan from the US Army, which have been modified with instrumentation booms. Naval TH-57 SeaRangers are also operated by the NAWC-AD.

An SH-60B Seahawk is seen here in the foreground as an SH-60F Ocean Hawk departs from the Rotary Wing Test Squadron's ramp, in the background. The Test Squadron is heavily involved in developing the new hybrid SH-60R, which will combine the functions of the two earlier SH-60s in a single airframe.

to evaluate each mission on a real-time basis. Missions can be extremely complex, sometimes including up to 70 tasks on a single flight. This can result in some missions lasting up to five hours with support from KC-130s.

Flight testing to date has revealed a wholly satisfactory product, with the only negative flight characteristic being a wing drop tendency at high angles of attack. This was subsequently cured by wing leading edge modifications. Other milestones reached so far include land-based catapult launches and arrested landings, as well as steam ingestion tests and jet blast deflector trials. Super Hornet F1 embarked

on the USS *John C. Stennis* on 17 January 1997 for carrier trials.

A trial flight in late November 1996 resulted in the first major hitch for the development programme. One of the aircraft's GE F414 powerplants suffered a compressor stall, leading to engine shut-down at supersonic speeds, but the aircraft made a successful single-engined recovery to Patuxent River. This led to the precautionary suspension of all Super Hornet flying while compressor blade cracks were investigated by General Electric.

Some of the aircraft will venture away from 'Pax' River for cross-wind tests at Edwards AFB, CA,

and shipborne arrester suitability trials at Lakehurst, NJ. The second two-seat test aircraft (F2) has been configured as the weapons trials aircraft. Munitions separation is seen as a major challenge for the team, and the project will involve the delivery of over 50 different types of ordnance. This weapons phase is being conducted at Patuxent River as part of the test programme and fully utilises the services provided by the 'Pax' ranges. NAS China Lake will utilise F2 for software development and verification.

Rotary Wing Test

The Naval Rotary Wing Aircraft Test Squadron is primarily responsible for development, test and evaluation of all new rotary projects for the Navy and Marine Corps. The unit also provides access for the US Army and Air Force to their unique facilities, avoiding the duplication of trials with similar aircraft types.

As with the other directorates, the number of aircraft assigned to

the unit fluctuates, depending on the programmes underway. The variety of types on the flight line overlooking Chesapeake Bay is an indication of the diverse array of projects undertaken. The workhorse of the Navy and Marine Corps helicopter units, the H-46 Sea Knight, is currently undergoing a lengthy upgrade programme to extend its service life. The Sea Knights (from the USN and USMC) at 'Pax' are involved with reliability testing and improvement, to refine the rotor heads.

Marine Corps AH-1 Cobras are currently undergoing NVG and FLIR cockpit compatibility, including exterior NVG lighting tests. An example of the programme's flexibility to meet requirements manifests itself in work carried out on H-53 Stallion rotor heads. This has resulted from problems in US and foreign fleets with failures that, in some cases, caused loss of aircraft.

Sikorsky is working in conjunction with Rotary Wing to investigate airframe loading and its long-term effects on major components. These tests, along with powerplant developments, are being carried out with the H-3 Sea King complement. An example of a Marine Corps H-3, from Presidential transport squadron HMX-1 at Quantico, is being used to test countermeasures, navigation and communication systems to be introduced fleet-wide. Another of these H-3s is configured with a VH-3 cockpit on the port co-pilot's position and VH-60 instrumentation and systems on the right-hand captain's seat.

The SH-60B Seahawk and SH-60F Ocean Hawk will become the subject of an extensive remanufacturing programme to provide the Navy with a multi-mission platform, capable of conducting

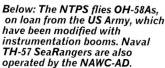

The OH-6A is another US Army type on loan to the NTPS. Note the instrumentation boom clamped onto the undercarriage skids.

In November 1996 the new Digital Flight Control System (DFCS) for the F-14 Tomcat – which will improve high-g manoeuvrability and low-speed handling – had its first sea trials in conjunction with the USS John C. Stennis (CVN 74). After qualification at the NAWC-AD, the DFCS will be installed in fleet aircraft in 1998.

undersea and surface warfare for the next quarter of a century: the SH-60R. This is expected to become operational by 2002 and the 273 projected examples will be derived from upgraded testbeds currently on the line with Rotary Wing at Patuxent River. Improved radar, sonar, FLIR, additional Hellfire missile capability, SATCOMS, laser detectors and advanced ECM suites all serve to make the SH-60R a multi-mission helicopter for the future. Supporting all operations, the unit's TH-57 Sea Rangers offer chase and pilot proficiency services.

In keeping with the commonplace joint service evaluations conducted across US services' test fleets, an integrated test team was formed in November 1993 for the development and procurement of the V-22 Osprey. This team combines Bell, Boeing and US military personnel from all forces and comes under the jurisdiction of Rotary Wing Test. The team's dedicated tasking is to take the V-22 programme from the drawing board to the operational theatre

Major update work now being conducted for the US Navy's and Marine Corps' CH-46 Sea Knight is largely due to delays in the V-22 Osprey project.

of the 21st century.

The project aircraft arrived at 'Pax' River in December 1993, and flight trials commenced in February 1994. Many pitfalls have been experienced, including the disastrous loss of two airframes in accidents.

NTPS

Undoubtedly the most famous unit at Patuxent River is the US Naval Test Pilots School. For over 50 years the School has trained Navy aviators to perform duties as flight test pilots for the purpose of trials on naval aircraft. Two courses run in parallel over an 11-month period and the graduates are instructed to meet the requirements of Naval Development Test and Evaluation (DT&E), and Operational Test and Evaluation (OT&E). Students not only include Navy, Marine, Air Force and Army officers, but also include foreign nationals and civil service engineers.

The unit maintains and operates 42 aircraft of 12 types to provide varied air vehicles and airborne system capabilities necessary to train efficient test pilots and engineers. In addition to providing fixed-wing aircrew, the School also provides helicopter test pilots, and is the only source of such pilots for the US government or industry. As well as the training of new pilots and engineers in the testing environment, the School investigates and develops new flight testing techniques.

Typically, 36 candidates will be selected to embark on a course which represents a formidable cross-section of aviation knowledge. Fixed wing, rotary wing and systems students all work together to promote greater understanding for future 'live' testing. Fixed wing students can expect to enter into initial handling evaluations on the T-2 Buckeye and T-38 Talon to promote greater awareness of aircraft handling in order to effectively glean flight test data. The OH-6 and the OH-58 provide similar tasks for the rotary wing students. The systems students are exposed to cutting-edge technology which includes the ability to evaluate live data in a classroom environment aboard the School's P-3, on loan from Force/NRL. This NP-3D, *El Coyote*, is equipped with an F-16 APG-68 radar, representing a readily available advanced-technology piece of equipment that the systems students would expect to encounter in the operational trials field. The aircraft is also fitted with

BRIEFING

Above: This P-3C is one of those operated by VX-1 'Pioneers', the US Navy's dedicated ASW test and trials unit.

Left: The only Navy T-38As are those flown by the NTPS, which were acquired through the USAF and NASA. They are used for high-speed training tasks.

Below: This F/A-18D is the NTPS commander's personal aircraft. Interestingly, for a Test Pilot School's aircraft it is carrying the AAS-38 NITE Hawk FLIR pod.

a dummy cockpit to prepare systems students for future live-fly missions, teamed with their fixed wing colleagues and working together in the School's F/A-18s. Final evaluation of a systems student will take place in an airborne classroom – an F/A-18 – with an instructor taking the front seat to evaluate his student in the back as the mission develops. Fixed wing students will eventually be competent with rotary-wing aircraft (and *vice versa* for the helicopter students), which is typical of how the course confronts students with unfamiliar territory.

The School has access to every aircraft necessary to complement the courses. Of particular note are the two X-26A Schweizer gliders. They are used to demonstrate energy management in unpowered flight and to investigate high-lift and drag situations. These gliders serve similar tasks to the School's U-1 Otter and U-6A Beaver, providing the vital variety of aircraft types to make graduates masters of their trade.

Atlantic Ranges

The Atlantic Ranges and Facilities Department provides management for the extensive airspace resources covering Chesapeake Bay and over the Atlantic Ocean as far as Delaware and Virginia. The 'Pax'

River complex is known as the Mid Atlantic Test and Training Range. It is a demanding sea-level theatre, augmented by the Air Combat Environment Test and Evaluation Facility, and is the most advanced facility in the world. Its many virtual and simulated qualities are supported by state-of-the-art laboratories, including flight simulators, EW simulations and an anechoic chamber. The unique operations focus largely on carrier aviation, supplemented by steam catapult and arrester gear at 'Pax' and a landing systems test facility.

Each unit at Patuxent River has the benefit of unlimited access to these facilities which continually complement their aeronautical evaluations, with datalink systems feeding back real-time data to ground-based systems analysts. These home-grown specialists are

in many cases graduates of the Test Pilots School systems course, and, via the datalink system, can work with manufacturing teams at their plants across the country to evaluate test flights as they happen.

Major tenant units

VX-1 'Pioneers' was established on 1 April 1943, and currently evaluates and develops the US Navy's fleet of ASW and special mission VQ aircraft weapons and systems. The unit serves to complement Force Aircraft Test and Rotary Wing Aircraft Test. The command is directly responsible for the constant updating of ASW tactics, producing doctrines and modifying training procedures. The fleet operates P-3s, S-3s and SH-60s, reporting to the Commander of Operations Test and Evaluation force. The unit has been

based at 'Pax' River since 1973.

The Naval Research Laboratory Flight was formed in July 1965 as the Oceanographic Air Survey Unit (OASU), redesignated VXN-8 'World Travellers' in 1969 and is now known as the Naval Research Laboratory Flight (NRL). This unit is dedicated to airborne geophysical survey work, operating a fleet of RP-3Ds and a single EP-3A. The unit moved into Patuxent River in 1965, bringing its complement of aircraft involved in geographic survey work that is known to the Navy as Project Birdseye.

Fleet Composite Squadron Six (VC-6 'Skeet of the Fleet') maintains a UAV detachment at 'Pax' River. In addition to land- and shipborne deployments, the unit is responsible for factory acceptance trials and evaluating fleet readiness training. The unit's Pioneer UAVs are used for surveillance, over-the-horizon targeting, gunfire spotting and the relay of real-time battle damage assessment. The UAV detachment at 'Pax' River has flown from the decks of operational battle ships during Operation Desert Storm on reconnaissance and battle damage assessment missions.

VQ-4 'Shadows' replaced its EC-130Q Hercules in 1991 with the Boeing E-6A Mercury. The TACAMO (Take Charge And Move Out), as it is known, fulfils a role as a strategic communications aircraft in support of fleet ballistic missile submarines. This long-endurance communications relay aircraft carries a state-of-the-art airborne very low frequency system. At patrol altitude, the aircraft deploys a Long Trailing Wire Aerial, which reels out from the underside of the rear cabin; once in a tight orbit, the wire stalls and the now-vertical cable becomes an antenna for sub-sea communications.

Richard Cooper and Jamie Hunter

General Atomics RQ-1A Predator

Tier II UAVs in service

In late 1995 the US Air Force established the 11th Reconnaissance Squadron (parented by the 57th Wing) at Indian Springs AFAF to prepare for operations with unmanned air vehicles for reconnaissance purposes. The current drone programme first saw action over Bosnia in February 1994, when the CIA briefly operated General Atomics Gnat-750 (Tier I) drones from Albania. Later in the year Gnat-750s began flying from Croatian bases.

Early experience with the Gnat-750 led to General Atomics being awarded an urgent contract to develop an enlarged version, known as the Predator, to fulfil the DARO (Defense Airborne Reconnaissance Office) Tier II requirement for a medium-altitude UAV. The first aircraft flew in mid-1994, and at the end of the year a joint-service team deployed to Fort Huachuca, AZ for evaluation. In May 1995 the team flew Predators in the Roving Sands exercise in New Mexico, in preparation for deploying to Gjader in Albania in July for operations over Bosnia.

Three Predators were deployed, of which two were lost (one was probably shot down and one was command-destroyed after an engine failure): both were replaced. The deployment lasted until November and around 80 sorties were flown. After a recall to the US to have TESAR equipment fitted, the Predators returned to the warzone in March 1996, flying from Taszar in Hungary. On 3 September 1996 control of the Predators was officially handed over from the Army-led joint-service team to Air Combat Command's 11th RS.

Designated RQ-1A, the Predator has a maximum endurance of 40 hours, and can maintain a 24-hour patrol at a radius of 500 miles (805 km), which is its normal maximum radius. It is powered by an 85-hp (63-kW) Rotax 912 four-cylinder engine and has a fuel capacity of 650 US gal (2460 litres). Overall length is 26 ft 8 in (8.13 m) and wing span is 48 ft 8½ in (14.85 m). The aircraft incorporates RCS-reducing design, most notably around the chined nose, and has the provision for stores hardpoints under the wings.

Initially the RQ-1A carried only EO/IR sensors mounted in a steerable Versatron Skyball turret under the nose, but later the TESAR (Tactical Endurance Synthetic Aperture Radar) was added. Sigint sensors and a laser designator are also being incorporated.

Data can be transmitted by three links. Out to 150 nm (278 km; 173 miles) a standard G/H-band line-of-sight datalink is used, this being able to transmit EO/IR video. The antenna is mounted underneath the aircraft. At greater distances a UHF SATCOM link can be used for the same imagery. Both of these links are located in the mobile UAV ground control station. For SAR frames (and EO/IR video) a Ku-band SATCOM link is needed, which requires an external ground antenna. Airborne antennas for the two SATCOM links are located in the top of the Predator's airframe.

The RQ-1A is fully integrated with the Trojan Spirit data dissemination system, which uplinks imagery and receives tasking information from higher command through the Comsat system. A Trojan Spirit ground unit is attached to the ground control station to link the Predator system to the wider net. Predator can also be controlled from other platforms, notably J-STARS, and even submarines (demonstrated in 1996).

All three datalinks can be used for command and control of the vehicle, allowing direct control inputs to the flight control and sensor system from offboard users. The air vehicle also has GPS/INS navigation, and will automatically fly a preset route pattern. Take-off and landing is controlled using the direct line-of-sight datalink, and is operated by a rated pilot in the command vehicle. A forward-looking TV camera in the extreme nose provides the necessary visual clues to the operator. Seated alongside the 'pilot' is the sensor operator. Both consoles have two large screens for displaying sensor imagery, moving-map displays or TV imagery. A stick control allows direct control inputs. **David Donald**

The 'stealthy' nose mounts an air data probe, and incorporates a forward-facing TV camera. The latter provides a real-time image on a screen in the ground station for take-off and landing.

The Skyball turret mounts the EO/IR sensors. Video imagery is received at the ground station in real-time and can then be relayed to the customer via various links, including the Trojan Spirit net.

Above: An unmarked Predator takes off from Taszar in Hungary for an operational mission over Bosnia in 1996, by which time the deployed UAVs had been fitted with TESAR imaging radar equipment. The long stalky undercarriage is required to provide enough ground clearance for the downturned low-RCS tails, and retracts backwards into the fuselage. Noteworthy is the additional fin area between the primary surfaces.

Right: The 11th RS RQ-1As at Indian Springs wear full markings, including the 57th Wing 'WA' tailcode and fin-band. The badges are those of Air Combat Command (fins), 57th Wing (starboard side of fuselage) and 11th Reconnaissance Squadron (port side).

Marham
Reconnaissance Wing

RAF Marham's station motto is 'Deter'. A vitally important role in the act of deterrence is to gather as much intelligence as possible concerning the military capabilities and intentions of a potential enemy. With the concentration of recce-roled Tornados and PR Canberras at one base, Marham is now at the forefront of the RAF's ability to gather intelligence, and is recognised the world over as a centre of excellence for the art of aerial reconnaissance.

Above left: Marham has been Tornado country since 29 June 1982, when the first aircraft for No. 27 Sqn arrived (long before the squadron officially reformed). Today No. 27 and its Marham partner, No. 617, have moved on, allowing the Norfolk base to become the centre for GR.Mk 1A tac recce operations.

In an era of ever-shrinking defence budgets, there are few areas of any air force that are on the increase. One area in the Royal Air Force that is of rising importance, with continuing funding for new equipment, is that of reconnaissance. Given the reordering of world politics in the post-Cold War era, and the greater uncertainty of where the next threat may come from, reconnaissance has assumed an ever-greater importance. With its high-profile international role in peacekeeping and policing operations, the United Kingdom requires a highly capable reconnaissance force which can respond rapidly to new situations, providing the ammunition for commanders and politicians to enable them to make quick intelligence assessments and deploy their forces accordingly.

Marham has been developed over recent years to provide just such a force. Reconnaissance assets had previously been spotted throughout the RAF organisation, but a concerted effort has been made to concentrate the reconnaissance force at one base to provide a reduction in overlapping missions, streamline the chain of command and ease rapid deployment. The airfield itself was previously home to two Tornado GR.Mk 1 squadrons, with an overland strike/attack commitment, and the Victor tanker fleet.

In the aftermath of the Gulf War the Victors were retired and the two GR.Mk 1 squadrons were moved to Scotland to take over maritime attack duties from the retiring Buccaneer force,

leaving Marham free. The first unit to move in was No. II(AC) Squadron, the first Tornado reconnaissance unit, which transferred to the Norfolk base from Germany when Laarbruch Tornado operations ended. Next followed No. 13 Squadron, which had only recently been re-established as the second UK Tornado recce unit. It relocated the short distance from Honington, the two Tornado squadrons inheriting the two HAS complexes from the departing Nos 27 and 617 Sqns.

Finally, the Canberras of No. 39 Squadron moved in when Wyton was closed to flying operations, a move further consolidated in 1996 when parentage for the Canberra unit was switched from No. 18 Group to No. 1 Group, bringing it under the same aegis as the Tornados. No. 1 Group does maintain other reconnaissance assets, notably the single recce-tasked Jaguar squadron (No. 41) at Coltishall. In addition, the Harrier force has a tac recce pod capability, which it has used on Operation Warden over northern Iraq, but it is not classified officially as a reconnaissance asset.

Tornado GR.Mk 1A

Spearheading the RAF's tactical reconnaissance force is the Tornado GR.Mk 1A, which serves with two squadrons at Marham: No. II (AC) and No. 13. In addition to the primary reconnaissance role, both units have a secondary attack role, the split being 80 per cent recce and 20 per cent bombing. As will be seen, the

preparations and execution of both missions are similar. In the bombing role the free-fall weapon is the main ordnance employed, there being no speciality attack task (such as LGB or ALARM) assigned to either unit.

In addition to normal reconnaissance tasks, both squadrons regularly support Out of Area operational commitments in Turkey (Operation Warden) and Saudi Arabia (Operation Jural). Consequently, the majority of each squadron is away for three months each year, quite apart from other overseas deployments such as the annual Western Vortex training period at Goose Bay, armament practice camps and participation in a variety of exercises.

As a reconnaissance system, the GR.Mk 1A remains a world-leader. When it entered service in 1989 it was the world's first filmless reconnaissance aircraft, thanks to its revolutionary infra-red (IR)/video system. Fourteen were initially converted from standard Batch 4 GR.Mk 1s by British Aerospace, the modification entailing removing the two cannon, installation of the sensors and recording equipment, additional cockpit controls and integration of the reconnaissance system into the nav/attack system. Another 16 were built as GR.Mk 1As as new (two from Batch 5 and 14 from Batch 7), although the recce system integration for them was performed by the RAF itself.

Infra-red reconnaissance

In the late 1990s air arms queued up to procure IR-based reconnaissance systems, many as a result of seeing first-hand the capabilities of the Tornado system. The advantages of using IR for tactical reconnaissance are many, the

for film processing greatly outweighs the drop in quality over traditional systems for tactical reconnaissance requirements.

Although less impaired by weather conditions than light cameras, IR systems do suffer loss of quality, especially in heavy moisture conditions and at certain times of day. Another problem is IR cross-over, when the heat energy of the target object matches that of the background, rendering it invisible to the sensor. In such cases the wind shadow effect is often useful in discriminating the object from the background.

Processing speed

Despite these drawbacks, the overwhelming advantage of the Tornado's IR/video system is the speed with which gathered imagery can be processed into usable intelligence. In the tactical reconnaissance arena it is that speed which is the vital factor. Intelligence from a conventional system may tell a commander that there is a mobile 'Scud' launcher at this location, and it has so many track segments and a number '12' on the side; intelligence from the Tornado's system arrives an hour earlier, telling the commander that there is a 'Scud' launcher at this location and the engine has just been turned off, indicating it may be preparing to launch.

Giving the Tornado GR.Mk 1A this outstanding low-level reconnaissance capability

most obvious being the complete disregard the system has for ambient light. IR systems are as equally effective at night as they are in daylight, and are much less affected by meteorological conditions.

Furthermore, the heat picture can reveal far more intelligence than a light picture can, providing the interpreter is fully versed in the relatively new skill of IR imagery exploitation. For instance, fuel in an aircraft's tanks will show up as colder than the airframe, indicating whether an aircraft is fuelled or not. Engines glow hot many hours after they have been shut down, giving experienced interpreters a good approximation as to how recently they have been moved. Even a departed aircraft will leave a shadow on an apron some time after it has taken off. In addition to sun shadows, IR shows

up wind shadows, which can sometimes reveal the location of objects which would be otherwise be obscured. Camouflage of objects on the ground becomes far more difficult.

A classic example of what an IR system can discover was provided by an archaeological find close to Marham. An infra-red image taken from a Tornado shows clearly a large circle in a field, which upon excavation was found to be a historically significant earthworks. A pin-sharp conventional photograph taken by a Canberra of the same location reveals nothing at all.

There are, of course, disadvantages to the system. It is primarily of use at low level, putting the carrier at a tactical disadvantage in some scenarios, while the resolution is nowhere near as sharp as a wet-film process. However, the ability to view imagery without the need

is the TIRRS (Tornado Infra-Red Reconnaissance System), which consists of three sensors, recording equipment and cockpit controls. The primary sensor is the Vinten Type 4000 IRLS (Infra-Red LineScan), mounted in a blister on the underside of the fuselage. This is a panoramic sensor with horizon-to-horizon coverage, operating in the 8- to 14-micron waveband. It peers through a slit aperture, which is covered by a protective door when not in use.

Augmenting the IRLS are two SLIR (Side-Looking Infra-Red) sensors which peer sideways from either side of the forward fuselage. Each sensor is provided with a gold-coloured window, which is actually a glass sandwich with thorium fluoride inside for enhancing the image. The SLIR has a field of view from the horizon down to 10° depression, and is used to fill in the image close to the horizon in better detail than possible with IRLS. A recent modification to SLIR allows the sensor to be depressed further to give a coverage of +4° to -14° from the horizon, making the imagery more useful. However, this extra depression can only be selected on the ground prior to take-off.

The SLIRs can be roll-stabilised, so that they remain looking at the horizon when the aircraft banks, within the limits of the look angle governed by the size of the windows and the mechanism of the sensor mounting, or they can

be locked to the aircraft. The latter allows the side-facing sensors to be used at any angle by rolling the aircraft, in much the same way traditional oblique wet-film cameras are used to gain vertical or shallow oblique photography. In this mode a simple chinagraph line drawn on the canopy serves as a rudimentary yet effective sighting system.

Imagery is produced by an EO (electro-optical) back which is made up of thousands of CCDs (Charge-Coupled Devices). Each CCD can be likened to a rod or cone in the human retina, or indeed the bromide grains on conventional film. Lenses focus the heat energy onto the EO back, and each CCD is energised to a greater or lesser degree according to the amount of energy striking it. This creates a digital electric signal. The signals from all of the CCDs are combined to form a complete image.

Video tapes

This imagery is handled by a Computing Devices Ltd recording system and transferred to analog video tape in real time. These tapes are essentially the same as standard E-180 household VHS tapes, but run at three times the speed for better definition. Each holds 60 minutes of imagery. Imagery can also be viewed on one of the navigator's 625-line TV Tab screens in the cockpit, although only one sensor at a time can be displayed.

The tapes/recorders are numbered from 1 to 6, and each has a specific function. No. 1 is the primary recording tape for the IRLS, No. 2 is the primary for the left-hand SLIR and No. 3 the primary for the right-hand SLIR. No. 4 is the reversionary, or back-up, tape for the IRLS, but the first 10 minutes can also be used for inflight editing, as described below. No. 5 is a back-up for the left SLIR, and No. 6 performs a similar job for the starboard SLIR. The latter tape also has 10 minutes of editing time available.

In addition to the TIRRS, the GR.Mk 1A can carry a podded sensor system, although this is not unique to the reconnaissance-dedicated Tornado, and is routinely carried by other variants during the continuing UN-monitoring missions over Iraq. Political sensitivities preclude low-level operations, rendering the TIRRS virtually useless. Manufactured by W. Vinten Ltd, the GP.1 pod is a member of the Vicon 18 Series 601 family, and is essentially a medium-altitude, wet-film, daytime-only system. It contains as its primary sensor a Type 690 LOROP camera, shooting on to 126-mm film. The main 450-mm lens and focal plate are mounted longitudinally within the pod with a 45° mirror at the front reflecting the image through 90° into the camera. The mirror and sensor window are mounted in a rotating nosecone, which allows the camera to peer out at any angle, including vertically downwards. In the rear of the nacelle is a smaller Type 900B panoramic camera which provides limited coverage and can be used as a tracker for accurate orientation of the LOROP imagery. It has a 3-in lens and employs 70-mm film.

Both reconnaissance Tornado squadrons operate twin-stick GR.Mk 1 aircraft for continuation training duties. No. II's are coded 'II' and 'IV' (illustrated), while No. 13's is coded 'XIII'.

Reconnaissance missions fall into three basic categories. The first is known as point-of-interest (POI), where a mission is planned to gain imagery and intelligence on discrete targets (there can be several such targets planned for each sortie). The second is a line search, which is traditionally aimed at reconnoitring a specified length of coast, road or railway, while the third is an area or strip search, in which the Tornado(s) covers a specified area of interest in a series of passes.

Much of the success in a mission lies in careful planning. The two-man crew works closely together, but generally it is the pilot who plans the target approaches while the navigator plans the routing. In peacetime, the navigator checks the NOTAMs and plans the flightpath to avoid any potential danger areas. In wartime, or in simulated combat exercises, special attention is paid to threats which have to be avoided during the ingress. An Army officer (the GLO – Ground Liaison Officer) is permanently attached to the squadron, and one of his tasks is to brief the crews on the latest intelligence reports. In peacetime exercises the GLO carefully constructs realistic threat scenarios and briefs the crews accordingly. In wartime, the squadron's Recce Leader (one of the flight commanders) would assign targets to the crews as required by the ATM (air tasking message), which is received from higher command.

ATTG

Depending on the nature of the target and available intelligence, the crew may have the luxury of an ATTG (automated tactical target graphic). This consists of a description of the target and known local threats, and may include previous reconnaissance photos or diagrams. In many cases it would be the job of the GR.Mk 1A to go out and produce such an aid for subsequent attack. For the bombers, targets are broken down into categories to optimise attack profiles and weapon loads.

Once a target has been assigned, the crew sets to work planning the mission. Planning a POI (point-of-interest) target run is very similar to planning a bombing attack. The pilot's first task is to plot the POI (or for a bomb run the DMPI – desired mean point of impact) on a 1:50,000 map. For UK training targets standard Ordnance Survey maps are used. The target is marked as 'X'. The second task is to decide on the best direction of approach, based on several factors. Terrain, local threat array, the nature of the target and sufficient features on the ingress for offset points are all considered. For a bombing run the need to minimise the potential for collateral damage may also be a factor.

TIRRS

The Tornado Infra-Red Reconnaissance System takes the place of the two 27-mm Mauser cannon in the strike variant. It comprises three sensors (two SLIRs and an IRLS) and a recording unit. The system is easily accessible for removing tapes and for maintenance.

The SLIRs peer sideways through these gold-tinted windows. The panel mounting the window is hinged for rapid access to the sensor.

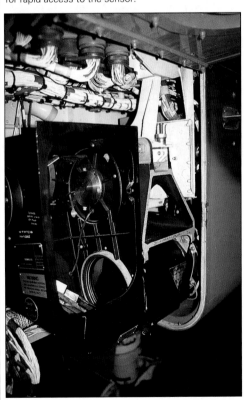

This is one of the SLIRs mounted in the side of the forward fuselage. The infra-red image is reflected through 90° into the sensor itself which is mounted longitudinally.

This view is looking directly up into the recorder bay, which holds the six tape machines. Drop-down doors on the aircraft's underside provide ready access.

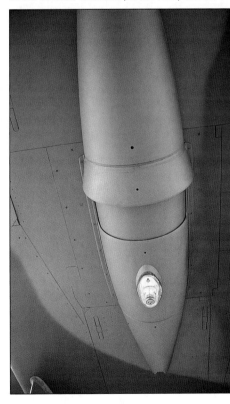

On the underside of the aircraft is the bulge for the IRLS sensor. It has a slit window which is covered when not in use, and is protected by an airflow baffle. The sensor gives panoramic coverage.

With the target and ingress direction plotted, an IP (initial point) is chosen. This is an easily recognisable feature for both visual and radar confirmation, and is generally about 20 miles (12 km) from the POI. The IP is labelled 'X1' and a line drawn between it and the POI, along which the pilot marks off the miles from the target on one side, and then marks the time from target on the other, having decided on the optimum attack speed. In order to facilitate cal-

culations both in this phase and, more importantly, in the air, crews usually use speeds which are multiples of 60 kt (420 kt, 540 kt, etc.).

Having drawn the IP-to-target run, the pilot then plots offset points, which are used to refine the aircraft's position and direction during the attack run. Normally three points are used, although up to five can be plotted. The offset points are features which lie off to the side of the IP-to-target run, and are chosen, using the

TIRRS controls

Control of the TIRRS is handled by the navigator, who is provided with a control panel (right) in the port side console in the rear cockpit. This is a menu-driven unit which enables the tapes to be replayed and edited. For 'tagging' events of opportunity the navigator has a small toggle switch forward of the radar control stick (below). It can be used to mark individual sensor tapes. A simple all-sensor marking device is situated on the pilot's stick-top.

large-scale map, as points which will provide an obvious radar return. Visual cues are also important. Buildings and masts are obvious choices, but if they are not present a corner of a wooded area or similar feature can be equally effective. These offsets are drawn on the map, and labelled 'X2', 'X3' and so on. If the points are only radar points, requiring no visual confirmation, the suffix 'R' is added (e.g., 'X2R') to signify their radar-only status. The map is then cut into a suitably small section, and is ready for use. For a bombing attack, weapon release information is also added, depending on the nature of the attack. A normal loft bomb requires a 3g pull-up 3 miles out (23 seconds), while a mini-loft is initiated closer to the target (15 seconds out). Other standard profiles available include a classic level laydown with the Tornado flying directly over the target, or a dive attack from any angle between 5° and 45°.

In order to load the IP and POI positional data into the master route plan, the exact National Grid reference is calculated, which is then mensurated into latitude/longitude co-ordinates by a hand-held Casio computer. Offset points are expressed in terms of distance in feet from the target, based on northings and eastings, etc. A typical offset description may be

For operations over Iraq the GR.Mk 1A adopted the Vinten GP1 pod, which has a steerable high-resolution camera in the forward portion and a panoramic camera in the rear. It provides the Tornado with a high/medium-level capability not catered for by the internal TIRRS.

'X3R – 15,500 ft North, 2,750 ft West'. This allows the weapon system to accurately generate the theoretical position of the offset.

For the navigator the first task is to draw on his route map the threat and NOTAMed areas to be avoided, followed by three lines corresponding to the real or simulated battle scenario. They comprise, from the rear of the battle area to the front, the 'IFF On' line (beyond which the aircraft must have its IFF equipment working to avoid the dangers of fratricide), the FLOT (forward line of own troops) and the FSCL (fire support co-ordination line, or furthest extent of direct friendly action against opposing troops). To them are added safety altitudes and range radius rings from base. Each of the range rings is annotated with a 'chicken fuel' figure, which is the amount of fuel required to get back to base efficiently from that particular radius.

Plotting the ingress

Taking into account the opposing threat array and terrain, the navigator then plots the best route into and out of hostile territory. The crew confers over the best route to the target, allowing the navigator to complete the routing, which is drawn on the map. The mission is flown as a series of straight lines with standard-rate turns at predetermined points, making speed/time calculations much easier. A plastic template is used to draw turn radii based on standard bank angles (usually 60° for visual flight, less for terrain-following) and at various

speeds (naturally multiples of 60 kt). All the various points are then fed into the mission planning computer.

Available to the navigator are a few fixed points, notably the runway threshold. In the NATO training area there are pre-surveyed points whose lat/long co-ordinates are already stored, and for regularly visited targets offsets are also pre-surveyed. The turn points are entered sequentially, labelled alphabetically from A to a 'maximum' of W (X being the target label). The fixed points are also entered, followed by the desired speeds and altitudes of each leg between points.

Armed with this information, the mission planning computer can produce a complete plan of the sortie, generating a figure for the amount of fuel theoretically required to complete the flight. Once the crew has entered the actual figure of fuel to be taken aloft, the computer then produces a detailed flight plan showing vital fuel and time data. For each waypoint there are theoretical fuel used and fuel remaining figures, cumulative flight time and elapsed flight time readouts. Times for each leg are computed and displayed along with the desired track to reach the next waypoint. This data provides the crew with invaluable checks all along their route to monitor the navigational progress, fuel flow rates and timings of the mission as it unfolds, allowing them to take remedial action if the theoretical does not match the actual.

Computer-predicted timing

A highly useful function of the planning computer is to provide timing information. If the aircraft is required to be at a certain location at a certain time, then that time and waypoint can be entered and the equipment then plots back to a theoretical take-off time to meet the schedule. This usually concerns TOT (time over target), but could also be useful as a deconfliction tool when other friendly aircraft are operating in the same area.

The above mission planning is common to both attack and POI reconnaissance missions, but the GR.Mk 1A can also use two other functions of the computer not required by the bombers. In many cases it may be required for the GR.Mk 1A to produce oblique imagery of the target rather than from directly overhead. In this case an offset track factor can be lodged into the system, the computer automatically modifying its predicted offset point positions during the ingress accordingly. Secondly, the computer flight plan can be annotated with various target locations so that the aircraft's systems automatically label the reconnaissance video tapes at the appropriate point, in turn allowing these 'events' to be found rapidly for analysis.

As mentioned previously, the mission can include several POI targets, all of which are plotted in a similar fashion. Mission planning for line searches is similar, although there are start and end points to be plotted. Features such as roads and coastlines rarely follow straight lines, so turnpoints are often plotted along the track to keep the area of interest within the field of view of the GR.Mk 1A's sensors. In some cases, the line of interest may change direction so dramatically that the aircraft cannot turn sharply enough to follow it. In these instances the crew's experience is brought into play in plotting the optimum turns to gain as

much coverage as possible without having to make a potentially dangerous second pass.

Area searches are also complicated to plan, as they may require several parallel passes across the area with the sensor 'footprint' overlapping to provide complete coverage. GR.Mk 1A reconnaissance missions are usually flown single-ship, although large-area missions are often flown with two aircraft to achieve the desired results in half the time.

Once all the flight plan has been entered, the computer provides a printout for checking, and then the plan is downloaded onto a tape for entering into the aircraft's own central computer. Such information can be entered into the system from the rear seat, using map slewing on the display, but is a task performed far more comfortably in the planning room. It should be noted that, even with the sophistication of the Tornado's planning system, the navigators are still fully conversant in the skills of map and stopwatch.

Booking the slots

For peacetime training missions the crew must book in to the low-level flying system using a standard form. The UK is sub-divided into set regions for this task, and the crew enters the expected times they will be operating within certain areas. Inside those areas they have relative freedom to operate, although key locations with heavy traffic, notably long valleys, have one-way flow patterns imposed to minimise the risk of mid-air collisions. Range slots and time at Spadeadam EW range are usually pre-booked on a squadron-by-squadron basis, although it is possible to get 'bootlegs' into these areas if there is no other booked traffic.

The navigator loads the precious mission tape into the aircraft, and checks that the data has been transferred correctly. In the near future the TAMPA (Tornado Advanced Mission Planning Aid) equipment will be introduced. This new kit employs off-the-shelf PC technology, which is much faster and has greater processing power than the computers presently in use. A useful by-product will be the ability to download the plan for detailed briefing.

In wartime, crews allocate about 20 minutes of planning time per target, and with the mission fully planned then receive a final briefing. A senior squadron member authorises the flight, and the crew takes a final check of the MIST computer which gives the latest weather update. In winter, or when immersion suits have to be worn, the crew 'walks' about 45 minutes before take-off; in summer this is cut to 30 minutes, as it takes less time to get comfortably strapped in. The tapes are collected for loading into the aircraft, the aircraft signed for and the mission begins for real.

GR.Mk 1A mission execution

Generally operating alone, the GR.Mk 1A sets out on its mission, the central computer drawing on the pre-loaded mission tape to provide control inputs to the autopilot or to provide navigation cues to the crew. The navigator checks times and bearings, as well as using basic map-reading, to confirm that the aircraft is established on its pre-planned routing and schedule. Unmistakable features or constructions whose precise locations are already known are used to continually update the accuracy of the INS (Inertial Navigation System) upon which the route information depends; this is done using the radar. Similarly, features with known elevations (lakes are the best example) are used to refine the system's altitude settings.

Nearing the front line, the crew switches on the IFF system, and as they cross into denied territory the video tapes are turned on. The tapes run continuously until turned off when the Tornado returns to friendly airspace, or when their 60 minutes' endurance is reached. The Tornado and its system are optimised for

A rare view from the front seat shows the GR.Mk 1A's HUD. The aircraft is flying due south over the desert, at 340 kt and at a height of 381 ft.

Left: A trio of GR.Mk 1As from No. 13 Sqn flies over Turkey during an Operation Warden deployment.

The Tornado GR.Mk 1A's reconnaissance suite works as well at night as it does in daytime. The TIRRS is restricted to low-level use, but the new RAPTOR pod will add medium-level IR night reconnaissance to the GR.Mk 1A's repertoire.

low level and the entire flight through enemy airspace will normally be made at very low altitudes to avoid radar detection, using the TFR. In a textbook mission the aircraft should follow its pre-planned route exactly, but in realistic exercises or actual combat many factors, not least of which is the attention of enemy fighters, can cause the crew to deviate from the intended path. Rapid risk assessment and a recalculation of routing and times can easily rescue the mission in such cases.

IP approach

As the IP is approached, the crew prepares for the most task-saturated portion of the mission. The radar is used to provide accurate positional data of the IP in relation to the aircraft, and any deviation between actual and theoretical is removed at this point. As the aircraft crosses the IP, the navigator starts the stopwatch and begins looking on the radar for the first offset point. The aircraft's nav/attack system generates a cross on the screen where it believes the offset point to be. The navigator looks at the radar imagery to find the returns from the actual offset point, and any discrepancy is removed by slewing the theoretical cross onto the actual offset point return. The aircraft's central computer compensates accordingly and subtly alters the flight path. If an offset point also requires a visual check, the central computer generates a cross in the pilot's HUD (Head-Up Display) corresponding to the point where it thinks the offset is.

With the revised offset point position entered into the system, it is cancelled and the navigator begins looking for the next offset further down track. By using up to five offsets, the aircraft's track is continually refined to a point of extreme accuracy, allowing a computer-

controlled weapon release in the bombing role or a pinpoint pass for reconnaissance purposes. As the aircraft crosses the target the central computer labels the reconnaissance event with an electronic tag on the running tapes in much the same way as most home VCRs can be tagged with the start of a programme.

Despite the technical merits of modern reconnaissance systems, the Mark One Eyeball remains one of the most sophisticated sensors ever carried aloft. Throughout their route through enemy territory the crew keeps a constant vigil for targets of opportunity which may fall within the scope of the TIRRS sensors, or even areas which may not be instantly recognisable as targets but which may show some promise of bearing fruit under closer examination of the tapes. Each crew member is provided with a switch – the pilot's is on the control column and the nav's is a small toggle in front of the radar controller – which, when activated, enters a label on the tape to tag the event.

Once through the target area, and away from the pressures of dealing with defences, the navigator then has the task of roughly analysing the 'take'. If the event has been seen, and is of an extremely time-critical nature, an immediate VisRep (Visual Report) can be transmitted back by HF radio. Normally, however, the navigator will review the tape by rewinding to the electronic tags and playing back the event. A panel is provided on the left-hand console for controlling the tape and display system. From this the navigator can rewind or fast-forward the tape, command a slow-motion replay and zoom the TV Tab image up to 8x magnification. After reviewing the tape, he or she can transmit an inflight report back to base.

This immediate review facility has great applications to the concept of recce/attack interface. In this, the GR.Mk 1A directly supports attacking aircraft by providing intimate target information immediately prior to the attack. A good illustration would be a mission dispatched to destroy enemy aircraft on an

airfield. Although the situation and layout of the airfield is known, the precise locations of the aircraft on it would not be known.

Prior to the launching of the mission the airfield would be divided into a matrix of numbered boxes. The GR.Mk 1A would make its pass across the airfield, and immediately afterwards the navigator would review the tapes, perhaps creating a freeze-frame image on the TV display, locate the positions of the parked aircraft and radio the positions according to matrix box number back to the attacking force, which could then refine its target positions accordingly. In another example of the recce/attack interface, the GR.Mk 1A can slip in across a target between attacking waves, providing immediate post-strike assessment of the damage inflicted by the first wave, and then radio back details of the targets which were untouched or required further attention from the second wave.

For deeper analysis of the gathered imagery, the navigator uses the system to produce an edited highlights tape. This task is usually undertaken once the aircraft is away from hostile airspace and the tapes have stopped running. Again, the electronic tags are used to find the events on the tape, which are then recorded across to one of the reversionary tapes. It is this tape which is initially seized upon by the interpreters once the Tornado has landed.

Imagery exploitation

Inflight review can provide much useful intelligence in a timely manner, but detailed analysis can only be performed on the ground with more sophisticated equipment by specialised PIs (Photographic Interpreters). Each of Marham's squadrons has an RIC (Reconnaissance Interpretation Centre) which houses the PIs and their equipment.

When the GR.Mk 1A was conceived, the aircraft was intended for a Cold War-style operation, flying from fixed bases. The initial ground interpretation equipment was installed at the two main bases (Laarbruch for No. II Squadron and Honington for No. 13), and consisted of several IAWs (Imagery Analysis Work-stations), each contained in its own hardened shelter called the GEE (Ground Exploitation Equipment). With the end of the Cold War the needs for deployed forces increased, leading to the introduction of the EIAW (Enhanced Imagery Analysis Work-station), which was of more modular form. The EIAW is air-deployable, and takes approximately two hours to strike down and two-and-a-half to three hours to reassemble. In 1997 the fully mobile TREF entered service.

The EIAW is a means of displaying the gathered imagery and enabling it to be enhanced for full interpretation and exploitation. As soon as the Tornado is back in its shelter, the tapes are downloaded and rushed to the RIC, where they are loaded into an EIAW. The workstation digitises the imagery to allow its enhancement. At the centre of the EIAW is an 875-line screen upon which the imagery is

*The GR.Mk 1A first saw action during **Operation Granby**, being employed on low-level sorties deep into Iraq to find mobile 'Scud' launchers. Several aircraft are still deployed in the region to provide reconnaissance (and bombing) cover to UN operations monitoring Iraq.*

Panavia Tornado
GR.Mk 1A
No. II(AC) Squadron
RAF Marham

Markings
Marham's GR.Mk 1As have been in the forefront of receiving the medium sea grey scheme which is slowly being applied across the Tornado fleet. No. II(AC) Sqn's markings consist of white triangles (carried since World War I) and one Wake knot. The latter commemorates the unit's traditional role of army co-operation, Hereward the Wake being the guardian of the army. This aircraft also carries a commander's pennant below the cockpit.

Self-defence
In the fin fairing are antennas for the GEC-Marconi Hermes RHWR. Carried underwing are either two BOZ-107 chaff/flare pods, or alternatively one BOZ and one Sky Shadow ECM pod (as illustrated here). Tornado GR.Mk 1As may also carry the GEC-Marconi Ariel towed radar decoy in a converted BOZ pod.

Weapon options
Although primarily tasked with recce missions, the GR.Mk 1A retains full attack options (apart from the cannon). Nos II and 13 Sqns practise with 1,000-lb (454-kg) free-fall bombs, and also with the BL755 cluster weapon. The GR.Mk 1A is believed to have been WE177B nuclear capable, although this weapon has been withdrawn from the inventory.

GR.Mk 4A
The recce Tornados will be among the first to go through GR.Mk 4 MLU, adding FLIR, new HUD, new HDD, Mil Std 1760 weapons interface, better defences and other improvements. The updated aircraft will also be able to carry the RAPTOR LOROP dual-band pod.

Intakes
The Tornado's wedge-shaped intakes were designed with variable geometry for Mach 2 performance. Such speeds are not required by the low-level strike/recce mission, so the ramps of RAF aircraft are locked in the fully open position.

Tactical reconnaissance had been one of the original MRCA requirements, and it was obvious from the early days of the programme that the Tornado would be an excellent tac recce vehicle, thanks to its low-level flying qualities and accurate navigation suite. Whereas the Luftwaffe, Marineflieger and AMI initially opted for external camera pods for their recce-tasked Tornados, the RAF went one stage further and introduced an internal system. It was the first filmless recce system to enter service anywhere, and greatly decreased the time between initially acquiring imagery and delivering usable intelligence to the end customer. RAF experience with the system, backed up by demonstrations by the GR.Mk 1A fleet during overseas deployments, has encouraged other nations to embrace video-backed infra-red systems. Saudi Arabia has procured TIRRS-equipped Tornados as part of its Al Yamamah II purchase, for initial service with 66 Squadron.

Internal fuel
Fuel is held in Uniroyal self-sealing tanks in the wing box structure (210 Imp gal/955 litres) and fuselage (1,075 Imp gal/4887 litres). The RAF-only 121-Imp gal (551-litre) fin tank is no longer used due to fatigue problems.

No. II(AC) Squadron
No. II (Army Co-operation) Squadron previously flew recce-configured Jaguars as the main tac recce squadron in RAF Germany. It began receiving Tornado GR.Mk 1As in the late summer of 1988 but they were initially operated without reconnaissance equipment. With the deactivation of the Laarbruch wing, No. II returned to the UK in 1993.

Braking
In addition to the multidisc brakes (with Goodyear anti-skid units), the Tornado employs bucket-type thrust reversers. An airfield arrester hook can be used in an emergency.

IRLS imagery

This is a typical example of a linescan hard-copy as printed out by the ground console. Shown at right is the full horizon-to-horizon image produced by the IRLS. Noteworthy is the digital 'flattening' of the main swathe of terrain beneath the aircraft to produce a rectilinear image. IRLS image quality falls off rapidly near to the horizons, the SLIRs being employed for

better imaging of this region. Below is a magnified image from the full-size IRLS image, showing detail of a viaduct. Clearly, any traffic would be easily visible. TIRRS imagery is optimised for exploitation on screen, and the image is far better when viewed on the TREF/EIAW screen than on a hard-copy. The capability to pause the video and print out a copy (similar to a fax machine) has obvious benefits for briefing and for explaining the results of the tape interpretation to a non-specialist audience.

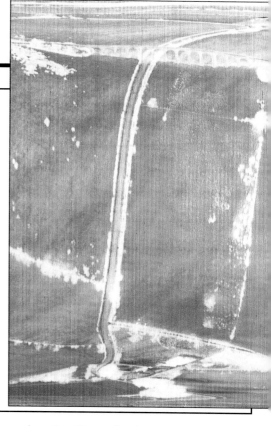

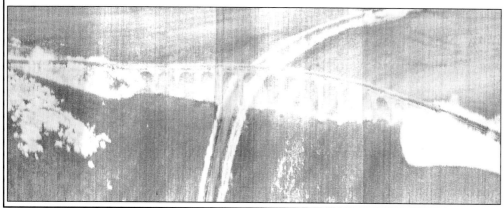

displayed, surrounded by controls for play speed and direction, magnification, contrast and other functions. Depending on conditions, the imagery can be displayed as either white-hot or black-hot, whichever provides the greatest contrast.

For immediate reports the crew will fill in a VisRep form while the PI views the edited tape of the primary mission objective events. The IRLS imagery is primarily used (SLIR imagery covers less area and is generally more difficult to enhance), and the EIAW can produce a rectilinear version of this, although it does lose some quality. This is a digital flattening-out of the basic imagery (thereby 'unfolding' the earth) to produce a near map-like image, at least over the main swathe of the sensor beneath the aircraft. The imagery width in real terms is approximately 4-5 km (2.5-3.1 miles) at normal altitude and in normal terrain. Imagery is seamless, and can be played forwards, backwards or frozen without any flicker on the screen. The basic screen image is usually played at 1x magnification, but areas of special interest can

be pulled out onto a second display at great magnification.

Measurements can be made rapidly by using a trackball and screen cursor, the EIAW computing distances based on the known altitude of the aircraft and screen magnification. PIs are extremely skilled at rapid interpretation of the imagery and within minutes can file a detailed report for dispatch by secure comms to the tasking command or end-user of the intelligence. The EIAW does have the facility for printing a hard copy of a frozen image, but the vast majority of the product is written report.

Once the immediate report has been dispatched, the PIs will take a more leisurely look through the whole mission imagery to spot any events of opportunity that may have escaped the crew. The EIAW has an event marker function itself to tag the tapes. In wartime the tapes would be stored for future use. It is possible that an object or area which just happened to be along the Tornado's flight path has no significance on that day, but the situation may change later, and the tape will provide ready-made imagery without having to

send an aircraft to gather it.

Each squadron operates approximately 10-12 GR.Mk 1As as its primary mission aircraft. No. II Sqn flies the Batch 4/5 aircraft while No. 13 uses the new-build Batch 7 machines. Both squadrons have standard GR.Mk 1s assigned (No. II has two and No. 13 one), albeit in twin-stick form. They are used mainly as training aircraft to relieve the hard-pressed GR.Mk 1A fleet. The squadrons operate out of two hardened shelter complexes at either end of Marham's runway, each with its own RIC.

In personnel terms, each squadron has a wing commander as OC, aided by his second-in-command, the Executive Officer. There are four flights, the commanders of which (usually squadron leader rank) have specific functions in addition to their flight-lead duties. OC 'A' Flight is concerned with the day-to-day operations of the squadron, OC 'B' is in charge of the training syllabus, and OC 'C' handles exercises. OC 'D' Flight is also known as the Recce Leader, and it is his task to aid reconnaissance training and to liaise with other agencies regarding modifications and procurement, and with Recce 1 (a Ministry of Defence officer responsible for policy and management of reconnaissance forces). Other key personnel in the squadron are the Senior Engineering Officer ('Sengo') and the OC RIC.

GR.Mk 1A training

Initial training for the GR.Mk 1A reconnaissance mission is the same as that for standard bombing, as the basic POI mission is itself very similar. That training is still highly valid to the crews of Nos II and 13 Sqns, given their secondary strike/attack role. However, for the overall reconnaissance mission more specialisation is required, and a recce work-up typically takes from six to nine months.

In addition to flying, much of this time is spent in intelligence lectures, learning how to recognise potentially hostile equipment and installations. The importance of the visually-recognised event of opportunity cannot be overstated, and it is vital that the recce crew is fully versed in what to look for while over enemy territory. Special attention is paid to the

Left: For exercises in Norway, No. II(AC) Sqn's jets received this temporary snow-cam scheme. The white areas were sprayed on in soluble distemper over the permanent grey paint.

Below: High over the Saudi desert, a gaggle of No. 13 Sqn jets is seen being trailed by a No. 10 Sqn VC10 C.Mk 1K. Both Marham Tornado squadrons are used for deployments to both Jural (Al Kharj) and Warden (Incirlik) detachments.

Above: This No. II(AC) Sqn GR.Mk 1A carries a GP1 camera pod for UN monitoring operations over Iraq. For operational sorties GR.Mk 1As routinely carry the 495-Imp gal (2250-litre) tanks, politely nicknamed 'Hindenburgers' but more colloquially referred to as 'Big Jugs'.

Right: Both Marham squadrons retain and regularly practise the overland strike role, which in many ways is identical to the tac recce mission. Here a No. II(AC) Sqn jet flies with a standard 'strike' GR.Mk 1 from No. 14 Sqn, both armed with four live 1,000-lb (454-kg) bombs.

idiosyncrasies of an IR-based system as opposed to light-sensitive systems; many of the identification clues are different in heat than they are in light.

A key part of teaching and maintaining these skills is the TRST (Tornado Reconnaissance Systems Trainer) which, despite its rudimentary appearance, is an ideal vehicle for training. TRST consists simply of a wooden mock-up cockpit complete with a single TV Tab and the reconnaissance systems control panel. Real mission tapes are played through the system and displayed on the TV Tab, providing the navigator with all he or she requires to perform the tasks of identifying events of opportunity, and reviewing and editing tapes.

To extract maximum training benefit from a peacetime sortie, up to six targets are planned. The Tornado crews try to get on to a weapons range to practise bombing (with small practice bombs which mimic the ballistics of the full-size weapon), and also aim to fly through the Spadeadam range in Cumbria which has extensive EW threats. Occasionally, air-to-air refuelling is worked into the plan using areas over the North Sea. Aircraft from the two squadrons regularly visit the Army's Salisbury Plain training area to work with ground-based forward air controllers. The GR.Mk 1A is also used in support of Special Forces, and occasionally trains with them in setpiece exercises.

Many of the training sorties involve fighter affiliation work, and the GR.Mk 1As regularly become potential prey for patrolling Tornado F.Mk 3s and other NATO fighters. Both fighters and recce aircraft work with the Sentry AWACS platform, often using a 'Bullseye' reference point. This is standard wartime procedure: a fixed yet arbitrary point is nominated as the 'Bullseye' for the day, and players use a

bearing and distance from that point for positional data rather than standard grid references. In wartime this point would be changed at regular intervals, as would an arbitrary base altitude which is used in a similar fashion.

Canberra

If the Tornado squadrons represent the cutting edge of new systems and concepts in the tactical reconnaissance world, the Canberra operation across Marham's runway is, at least for the time being, the high temple of traditional reconnaissance skills and processes. Until new sensors are introduced, the world of video backs, digital enhancement and electronic event tagging – and there is considerable experience in the use of such systems in the squadron – does not yet intrude on the daily working lives of the Canberra force. Yet, with the versatility of its camera platforms, highly-developed skills of its aircrew and PIs, and the diversity of its missions, No. 39 Squadron offers the RAF a unique capability unmatched by any other single unit in the world.

With its high-altitude capability, the Canberra was an obvious choice for a reconnaissance platform from the outset of its design. The first dedicated version, the Avon Mk 101-powered PR.Mk 3, was introduced in 1952, and was followed by the PR.Mk 7, based on the Avon Mk 109-powered B.Mk 6 but with a lengthened fuselage for greater sensor carriage and fitted with a belly tank for greater range. In 1959, the Canberra PR.Mk 9 entered service, sporting a fighter-style cockpit for the pilot, navigator position in the nose with hinging

nosecone for access, considerably uprated Avon Mk 206 engines, extended square-cropped wingtips and extra wing sections between the engine nacelles and fuselage. This was a very different bird, with exceptional altitude performance and a good range, which could be further extended by rarely-used underwing tanks. It has remained the RAF's standard medium-level photo-reconnaissance platform to this day.

For much of its career the PR.Mk 9 operated in the tactical role, equipped with a flare-bay for the carriage of photoflash bombs to allow night photography. The bay was a shortened bomb-bay with an extra fuel tank added in the front. The arrival of the Jaguar in service in the mid-1970s allowed the Phantom fleet to be reroled, in turn allowing the passage of the recce Phantoms' infra-red linescan equipment to the Canberras. The photoflash capability was deleted. At that time the PR.Mk 9 operated in the low-level role, albeit in less dangerous areas such as NATO's northern flank.

Navigation equipment has received constant update over the years, with the addition of Sperry TANS in the mid-1970s which incorporated a Doppler-sensed sea drift function and Omega in the 1980s. Most recently, GPS was added in 1993, although this is not a primary navaid. New radios have been fitted, and new sensors have been added to the repertoire. The most notable of them is the Zeiss RMK mapping camera, which required airframe modifications in order to enable its use with the flare-bay options.

The current Canberra operation is entirely based on wet film with a variety of sensor

Canberra cockpit

The Canberra cockpit belies the aircraft's age, featuring a mass of dials and switches. To complicate the work of No. 39 Sqn's crews further, the three variants in use have vastly differing cockpit layouts.

The PR.Mk 9 navigator sits behind the nosecone, which hinges to starboard to allow access. The instrument panel is dominated by the hooded circular screen for the periscope. A fold-down map table is provided.

The PR.Mk 9 navigator's seat ejects upwards through a frangible panel. The seat is surrounded by instrumentation, with most of the camera controls being on the port side.

With its fighter-style cockpit the PR.Mk 9 offers its pilots much better visibility than the other variants. The cockpit is narrow, with the result that some instruments (notably the fuel gauges) are located in the side consoles. The yoke control column provides better control at high altitude and on long sorties than a fighter-style stick.

The pilot of the PR.Mk 7 sits alone up front, offset to port. To starboard is a crawlway through to the glazed nose position. The T.Mk 4 trainer seats two pilots side-by-side with only one seat in the back.

The periscope is located underneath the nosecone, with direct optics to the navigator's sight. The prism can be swivelled through 180° along the line of flight to give full fore and aft coverage.

options. Remaining from the old tactical reconnaissance fit are three F95 cameras, one in the 'forward fire' position in the extreme nose and one each facing obliquely out from either side of the forward fuselage. They use 70-mm film and are essentially low-level sensors. Another 'relic' from the tac recce days is the IR pack, which fits into the flare-bay. Although this senses heat energy, it records the image on constant running film. Both of these sensors are of limited military application today, but are still routinely carried as they receive a 'free ride' during operations of more important sensors, and do have some uses. The F95s are certainly used widely for low-level training missions.

Oblique camera

For general-purpose photography the F96 camera remains in use; it has a variety of focal-length lenses available (24-in being the most common) and shoots onto 9-in x 9-in film. Occasionally, two are fitted in the forward camera bay (just in front of the flare-bay) in a near-vertical arrangement. However, the normal fit is a single PFO (Port-Facing Oblique) installation with a 24-in lens. A sensor rarely seen is the System 3 long-range oblique camera, which provides far better stand-off capability than an oblique F96.

The workhorse of the Canberra's camera battery is the Zeiss RMK, available with either 6- or 12-in lenses, and shooting on to 9x9 film. It is mounted in the rear camera bay aft of the flare-bay, and peers vertically downwards. The Zeiss has proved extremely effective in a number of applications, and has replaced the F49 Mk IV survey camera which was previously accommodated in the flare-bay. As a hang-over from the use of photoflash bombs 20 years

Marham is one of the last places left where one can witness a cartridge start. The Canberra T.Mk 4 has a single cartridge system, while the PR.Mk 7 (illustrated) employs three. The PR.Mk 9 uses AVPIN starting.

ago, the task of changing sensors in the flare-bay is still designated as an armourer's role rather than that of a reconnaissance specialist.

Canberra missions

No. 39 Sqn does not have a NATO-declared commitment but is now considered to be part of the Joint Rapid Deployment Force, and is available for a wide variety of tasking from UK agencies. Requests are made to a centrally-managed MoD office which prioritises them. Each task is presented on a standard form, stipulating the type of imagery required (oblique or vertical, colour or black and white, transparency or print, etc.), at what scale, whether there are any time limitations/deadlines, and other special requests such as orientation of the imagery. The squadron has the task of drawing up a tasking schedule based on this information.

High-priority tasks obviously take precedence, but, as several tasks can usually be performed in one sortie, it is usually possible to undertake some of the lesser-priority tasks in the general vicinity of the high-priority target, or if the primary flight-path takes the aircraft near to the lower-priority locations. A large map on the wall of the ops room, annotated with all the taskings, makes this an easier undertaking. Similarly, the squadron has its own ongoing training syllabus, elements of which are worked into tasked sorties.

Planning the sortie follows the standard pattern, with special attention paid to the NOTAMs affecting the flight-path, especially those concerning weather balloons and low-level activity. Naturally, mission planning concentrates on the camera run, based on the information provided in the tasking form. Many mapping tasks may stipulate a north-orientated product. The height at which the run is made is a function of the camera in use and the required scale of the end-product. End-users unfamiliar with the finer points of aerial reconnaissance draw heavily on the squadron's experience to help them formulate their individual tasking.

Tasking is many and varied. The majority are flown over government or military installations for accurate mapping and security purposes, allowing security procedures to be reviewed or installed. Heat-loss missions are occasionally flown, using the IRLS to pinpoint areas where energy-saving measures can be made. Major constructions and industrial complexes are also regularly photographed at various times to provide a ready-made database for security purposes; these images also prove very useful for training intelligence officers.

Precise navigation and flying is crucial to the success of the mission: the crew's job is to put the aircraft at exactly the right location, on the right heading and at the right height for the camera run. Sensors are operated from the nose compartment by the navigator, aided by the use of a calibrated periscope which provides fore and aft visibility through 180° below the aircraft. On the Zeiss imagery the camera prints level, height and time data in small bubbles in the rebate between each frame.

No. 39 (1 PRU) Squadron maintains the traditions of two famous RAF units. The badge is that of No. 39 Sqn, depicting a winged bomb. Note the 'Avtur' marked refuelling points.

Aperture and shutter speed are set by the navigator. Image movement compensation (IMC) must be applied to the film as it passes over the camera plattern to reduce the effect of relative target movement while the camera shutter is open. This can either be set manually by the navigator, or automatically via a Nav Automat. This equipment is fitted behind the Zeiss in the rear fuselage and uses three light sensors to determine the relative speed of ground movement. This in turn is translated into electrical signals applied to the camera to control the film movement.

Film processing

After return to base, the film is unloaded and processed in the RIC. Large Kodak Versamat processors handle the film at between 10 and 15 ft (3 and 4.5 m) per second. The processed film (usually in negative form) is then taken to the PIs for exploitation. The aircraft crew is present and, together with the PIs, reel through the film to find the best images for the tasking. If, for example, cloud cover has precluded satisfactory target acquisition, it remains on the squadron's list of assignments for future missions. Once the required negative frames have been marked (having been numbered on the F96 film), they are printed and dispatched to the end-user. Much of the squadron's

No. 39 Sqn maintains a pair of Canberra PR.Mk 7s for training, these providing a useful stepping stone between the T.Mk 4 and PR.Mk 9. Until recently, the PR.Mk 7s also had a chaff-laying and target facilities role.

All three Canberra variants in use with No. 39 Sqn are represented here. The T.Mk 4 has a solid nose, while the PR.Mk 7 has a glazed navigator position. The PR.Mk 9 has a completely redesigned forward fuselage.

The most likely replacement for the Canberra PR.Mk 9 will be a converted executive jet. However, none can match the aircraft's high-altitude performance.

product is processed through the JARIC (Joint Air Reconnaissance and Intelligence Centre) for distribution.

PIs are highly expert in rapidly spotting objects of interest that would be lost to most onlookers. There are several 'tricks' which can be used to enhance the usefulness of imagery, notably the use of three-dimensional effects. The classic example is the stereo pair, which is usually provided courtesy of the sideways-looking F95 oblique framing cameras. By viewing two adjacent frames through a stereoscope (two lenses mounted on a frame side-by-side),

the brain forms a combined image much as that seen through binoculars. As each frame has been taken from a slightly different position along the aircraft's path, the combined image has added depth perception. In another process, an overhead image can be split into a base image and two coloured overlays. By partially offsetting these overlays, and then viewing the three together through 3-D glasses, the combined image has three-dimensional qualities.

One task at which the Canberra excels is mapping. Cartographic surveys are long-lead tasks because they may require an aircraft to be away from Marham for weeks at a time. In addition to UK mapping tasks, requests are also received from other nations, such tasks being channelled through the Foreign Office.

Funding for these jobs varies, often being split between the UK and the other nation, the UK receiving detailed maps back in return for its own investment.

Mapping requires a highly systematic approach, much of which is organised by the 1 Air Survey Liaison Section of the Royal Engineers, a unit permanently attached to No. 39 Sqn at Marham. 1 ASLS prepares the flight plans for the crews to provide precise coverage of the area to be mapped. They consist of a series of parallel tracks, flown at a specific height to produce the required map scale, and offset by a set distance so that the imagery from one track overlaps that from the adjacent track by about 25 per cent. Predetermined aircraft speed and film frame drive rate are set to provide a 60 per cent fore/aft overlap along the flightpath. With a 6-in lens, coverage from 10,000 ft (3048 m) altitude is 5,000 yd (4572 m), this moving forward by 2,000 yd (1829 m) for each successive frame. The Zeiss RMK is used for these tasks, and from the results a highly detailed map can be produced. In 1996/97 the squadron is involved in the mapping of Zimbabwe, and may also carry out survey work in Kenya in 1998.

No. 39 Squadron has five Canberra PR.Mk 9s on charge, of which three are operational and two designated as in-use reserves. At any one time one aircraft is usually away on a major overhaul, which can take from between six and nine months to complete. In addition, the squadron has two PR.Mk 7s and two T.Mk 4s assigned, one of which is in use, with the other in storage. Until 1996, 50 per cent of the

PR.Mk 9 sensors

F96 camera
For general oblique work the F96 is carried in the forward camera bay, peering through this large window. The camera usually has a 24-in lens.

Nav Automat
Situated behind the rear camera bay (note open door and RMK window), this equipment automatically detects angular velocities to enable the cameras to be set correctly.

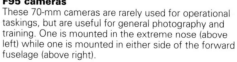

F95 cameras
These 70-mm cameras are rarely used for operational taskings, but are useful for general photography and training. One is mounted in the extreme nose (above left) while one is mounted in either side of the forward fuselage (above right).

Infra-red linescan
The IRLS pack is mounted in the flare-bay (left). Unlike the modern IR equipment in the Tornado GR.Mk 1A, the imagery is recorded on film.

Zeiss RMK
The principal survey camera, the RMK is mounted on a sliding pallet in the rear camera bay (right), shooting through a circular window in the lower fuselage. A drop-down door provides access to the camera.

PR.Mk 7's tasking was for target facilities, the aircraft being used as a radar target or for chaff-laying in support of air defence training. This role was subsequently contracted out to FRA and its Falcon 20 fleet, leaving the PR.Mk 7 with a training-only commitment.

Six crews staff the flying element of the squadron, and new pilots and navigators still periodically arrive on the unit. As the last UK military operator of the Canberra, all training is conducted in-house using live aircraft (there is no simulator). The Canberra is described as "easy to operate, difficult to fly," and there are key areas which require much experience to handle comfortably. The most obvious is the appalling (by modern standards) asymmetric handling with an engine out, caused by the wide spacing and high drag of the engine nacelles. Another is the 'graveyard gap' – the uncomfortable difference between the unstick speed and the single-engine safety speed, which in the low power-to-weight ratio T.Mk 4 can be about 45 kt (52 mph; 83 km/h) and take 20 seconds to achieve.

New recruits to the squadron are usually experienced aircrew. The first trips are made in the T.Mk 4, which has side-by-side seating for two pilots (other Canberras have only one pilot station) and one seat in the rear. Once the basic Canberra handling has been mastered, the more powerful single-pilot PR.Mk 7 is used, before progressing to the PR.Mk 9. Following the loss of the target facilities mission, the future of the PR.Mk 7s is under review in 1997, pending the outcome of an engineering assessment. The aircraft is a useful training tool, providing a handy bridge in performance terms between the T.Mk 4 and the PR.Mk 9. It also helps conserve fatigue life among the elderly T.Mk 4 population.

Recent operations

Canberra PR.Mk 9s have recently received considerable publicity due to two overseas assignments. The aircraft have been active over Bosnia for some time, undertaking regular deployments to Gioia del Colle in Italy to monitor the area of operations covered by Operation Lodestar, the UK contribution to SFOR. The outstanding quality of the photographs from the PR.Mk 9 has given the IFOR/SFOR commanders a new dimension in their ability to monitor the military position in the country. The grisly discovery of the locations of potential mass graves was widely attributed to Canberra imagery.

For operations over Bosnia the PR.Mk 9s were fitted with self-protection systems on underwing pylons. A BOZ pod is carried on either side, each of which can carry chaff or flares. The vertical Zeiss RMK has been the main sensor employed, although it is believed that the stand-off System 3 was used in the early stages of the operation.

More recently, a single Canberra PR.Mk 9 made a high-profile deployment to Entebbe in Uganda, the operation being codenamed Purposeful. The aim of the deployment was to track down thousands of 'missing' Rwandan refugees believed to be in the jungles of eastern Zaïre. In the course of 21 missions between 20 November and 19 December 1996, the Canberra surveyed a huge area of jungle to reveal the whereabouts of about 300,000

A Canberra PR.Mk 9 taxis in at Entebbe after an Operation Purposeful mission over Rwanda. The aircraft carried the BOZ-107 pods originally to provide extra protection over Bosnia.

refugees, all of whom appeared to be returning to their homeland. This information saved the UN from mounting a large-scale military peacekeeping effort. Finding what groups of refugees actually were in the surveyed area provided a considerable challenge owing to the thick tree cover, but the small groups were found, thanks to the eagle eyes of the photographic interpreters. The sorties were launched in the early morning to allow photography before storm clouds built up later in the day. An unusual obstacle encountered during these flights were the clouds of bats flying around Entebbe airport each morning and evening.

New systems

Reconnaissance systems figure prominently in the procurement budget, and both Tornado and Canberra forces are to receive new equipment in the near future as part of the ongoing strengthening of RAF recce assets. For the Tornado squadrons the first major event has been the arrival of the TREF (Transportable Reconnaissance Exploitation Facility) to replace the EIAWS previously in use. The first TREF package arrived at Marham in the spring of 1997 for service evaluation.

TREF is a 'swept-up' version of EIAWS utilising Sun Ultra Space computers, with greater imagery processing capability made possible by the recent advances in computer technology. It is of a modular nature and is fully mobile. The configuration also incorporates ergonomic advances to make it more user-friendly to the PIs working the system, and it incorporates a high degree of NATO standardi-

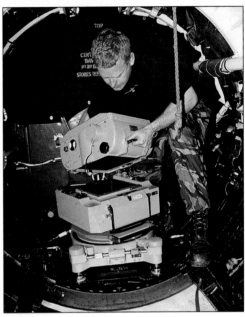

Working in the close confines of the PR.Mk 9's rear camera bay, a No. 39 Sqn technician removes the film back of the Zeiss RMK camera. The camera is mounted on rails so that it can be slid away from the hatch for easy access.

sation. Inbuilt growth potential allows TREF to handle imagery from the new sensors currently in the procurement process.

One TREF is allocated to each of the two

Until recently the Canberras were assigned to No. 18 Group, which is primarily concerned with maritime operations. Although it does not have a specific maritime tasking, the PR.Mk 9 is versatile enough to take on photographic missions at sea with ease. No. 39 Sqn is now part of the tactical No. 1 Group.

PR.Mk 9 imagery

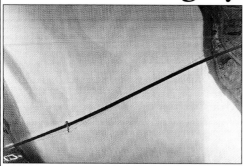

The image above is from the IRLS, which records the heat 'picture' on to continuous film. The twisting effect noticeable on the bridge is due to the aircraft flying across the centre of the target at an angle.

No printing process can adequately provide the required rendition to illustrate the clarity and quality of this Zeiss RMK overhead photograph of Cambridge city centre. The RMK uses 9x9-in film and is the main survey sensor. For mapping work the camera is set so that each frame overlaps the next by 60 per cent.

This view of Cambridge was taken using the F96 oblique camera. For long-range oblique work the Canberra also uses the System 3 camera. Both this and the F96 are to be supplanted from 1997 by a new LOROP sensor.

This is a good example of a stereo pair, produced by one of the oblique F95 cameras. By viewing consecutive frames such as these simultaneously through a stereoscope, a false three-dimensional image can be seen.

Processed RMK 9-in negative film is checked for quality as it emerges from the processor. Note the aircraft information presented in the rebate between each frame. The interpretation process uses large lightboxes, with the film held on these large reels.

stemmed from both tactical and political developments. Originally optimised for the Cold War Central European mission, the GR.Mk 1A was only ever intended to fly at low level over or very close to its target, and the TIRRS was designed accordingly. However, the broadening of potential combat scenarios since the end of the Cold War now means that the aircraft may fly in regions where it is safer to pop-up to high altitude and fly at some distance from the target to acquire the desired imagery. Furthermore, the heavy commitments to peacekeeping surveillance tasks place further emphasis on the high-altitude, stand-off mission, for it is politically unacceptable to have Tornados streaking across military installations at 200 ft (60 m)!

As an interim step the Vicon GP1 pod is in use, but the RAF is currently procuring a far more capable system for the Tornado known as RAPTOR (Reconnaissance Airborne Pod for TORnado). Although it will not displace the TIRRS as the primary sensor, RAPTOR will add a full stand-off capability for both day and night operations. The sensor is a dedicated EO-LOROP system, operating fully digitally, and will be pod-mounted for carriage on a shoulder station. Included in the package is digital datalink capability, and two deployable DLGS (DataLink Ground Station) systems. Each DLGS has two work-stations, and the

squadrons, and the complete package comprises eight 20-ft (6.1-m) cabins, each of which can be air-transported by Hercules. The eight cabins consist of two for imagery exploitation, two for management, two for engineering and two link cabins, the latter being equipped with a wide range of communications systems. It is SATCOM-capable although the SATCOM terminals are provided by other units; in most scenarios the reconnaissance force would deploy as part of larger packages which would have a SATCOMs unit attached.

A half-squadron of GR.Mk 1As can function with one of each type of cabin, enabling a maximum of four operating locations to be manned simultaneously by the two squadrons. Cabins will be maintained on specially-built hardstandings to allow rapid loading onto transport aircraft, although some of the equipment may be offloaded for peacetime operations into existing RIC facilities. However, the modular nature of the TREF system allows it to be repackaged into the cabins very rapidly.

Operations in the Gulf, both during the war and after, revealed a need for a stand-off sensor for the Tornado GR.Mk 1A. The requirement

Above: Initially fitted for Operation Hamden/ Resolute missions over former Yugoslavia, BOZ-107 chaff/flare pods provide the PR.Mk 9 with missile protection.

Right: This PR.Mk 9 is fitted with the circular Zeiss window in the rear bay. Note the bullet radomes for the radar warning receiver on the fin and tailcone.

processed data can be linked into the TREF system.

Tenders have been received from Hughes Danbury, Lockheed Martin and FRA (the latter using US-made sensors), and a contract award was expected in June 1997. IOC is planned for late 1999. RAPTOR is intended only for carriage by the GR.Mk 1A (and GR.Mk 4A after these aircraft emerge from their mid-life update), although it will be theoretically possible to fit the pod to other Tornado variants. RAPTOR is also being mooted as an option for EF2000.

EO/IR developments

Other reconnaissance improvements under study include the fitment of EO backs to the cameras contained in the Vicon pods, although this option is considered to be more applicable to the Jaguars of No. 41(F) Squadron. A key area for the Tornado is the continued development of the existing TIRRS, notably the move to an all-digital system. At present the imagery is converted between digital and analog format several times in the gathering process, before being eventually recorded onto an analog tape (and subsequently digitised for exploitation!). Using an all-digital system is now easily within the realms of technology, and would allow the recording of imagery on a solid-state tape. The lack of conversions between the two formats would also reduce the loss in picture quality between sensor head and analysis work-station. Also being investigated is the use of a new horn seeker in place of the current bifurcated unit, the horn being able to focus the gathered energy for higher resolution imagery. No contracts have been awarded yet for these developments, but studies continue.

Some thought has been given to datalinking the TIRRS imagery to a ground station, but the problems associated with this are huge. TIRRS is a low-level system, rendering useless a standard line-of-sight datalink. An uplink would therefore be required to a satellite or aircraft. With present technology such an uplink requires a large, high-gain antenna for large bandwidth transmission, and this would pose severe problems in accommodation in the already crammed Tornado airframe. Furthermore, the antenna tracking system needed to keep the antenna facing toward the data relay platform while the Tornado is banking and weaving along valley floors would have to be very sophisticated. However, in the future it may be possible to use the RAPTOR's equipment to downlink TIRRS imagery during the cruise back to base.

Not to be upstaged, the PR.Mk 9s of No. 39 Squadron are in the process of receiving a major new equipment modification, known as the CSSU (Canberra Sensor System Update). Two new sensors have been purchased to replace the F96 cameras and System 3 equipment currently in use. The first is officially known as the Panoramic Camera, a KA-93 wet-film unit manufactured by Recon Optical. This versatile sensor can scan from horizon to horizon, or can be restricted to narrower sweeps at any desired offset angle. Although it can be set to a wide variety of 'obliqueness' and sweep angles on the ground, the camera can also operate in four positions selectable in flight by the navigator. The Panoramic Camera occupies the forward camera bay currently usually used for the oblique F96.

For further back in the aircraft, a highly impressive EO-LOROP camera has been procured as a replacement for System 3. This all-digital sensor is packaged into a special crate which fits into the flare-bay, the bottom of which forms a bulge on the aircraft underside and incorporates camera windows.

At the time of writing the first aircraft was undergoing integration of the new systems with FRA at Hurn, and first flight in the new configuration was expected in the spring of 1997. Some airframe modifications are needed to accept the new equipment, and the aircraft receives a Mil Std 1553 databus during the rework.

All five operational PR.Mk 9s will receive the KA-93, but an unspecified number of EO-LOROP systems have been funded. IOC for the latter is expected in the autumn of 1997,

HDOS-Itek is one of the contenders for the RAPTOR contract with its DB-110 dual-band LOROP camera (full-scale model, right). The sensor was tested under DERA's Tornado ZA326, mounted in a converted fuel tank (below).

Relatively new additions to the PR.Mk 9 are the underwing hardpoints for BOZ-107 chaff/flare pods. The Canberra is undergoing a major update which includes adding a Mil Std 1553 databus. Some of the aircraft will gain the capability to carry a new LOROP sensor in a bulged bay.

although the system does not yet include a datalink. A single air-deployable GIEF (Ground Imagery Exploitation Facility) cabin is part of the acquisition, as the Canberra RIC has no current capacity to process anything other than wet film.

Eventual retirement for the Canberra PR.Mk 9 is slated for some time in the next decade, around the same time as the ASTOR stand-off radar platform is expected to enter service. It is possible that the EO-LOROP will be transferred from the Canberra to ASTOR, allowing the 'Queen of the Skies' to retire gracefully at the end of a long career at the forefront of reconnaissance and survey work.

ASTOR is the RAF's next major reconnaissance programme, and together with the steady move to electro-optical systems, with increasing digitisation and air mobility, will keep the service at the forefront of reconnaissance and surveillance technology. Marham's three squadrons have played a large and indispensable part in developing and introducing new concepts and technologies, while honing the skills of flying the reconnaissance mission to the point of excellence. **David Donald**

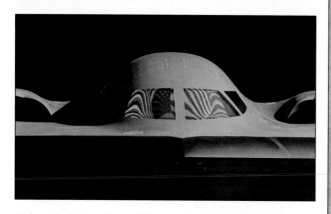

The B-2 is the ultimate symbol of the United States' supremacy as a military and technological superpower. An aircraft like no other, it was conceived with a single mission in mind: to range unseen into the Soviet Union's Arctic hinterland and destroy the ballistic missiles of the Strategic Rocket Forces before they could be launched at the USA. That mission was reason enough to pour immense sums of money into building the 'Stealth Bomber' – the ultimate monument to the Cold War. Now the USAF has to find new missions for its tiny B-2 force which has been cut back in numbers from 132 to just 21, but is still expected to meet a whole new range of tactical and strategic roles. This task may prove almost as complex as developing and building the B-2 in the first place.

It would have been cold in southern Missouri on 17 December 1993 if you were not standing in the middle of a windswept airfield, under a ragged and spattering sky. Kansas City, with its blues, barbecue and heating, seemed a long way off.

That was when the B-2 arrived, dropping through a rent in the clouds. Those who had never seen a B-2 in the air before forgot how cold they were, because a B-2 in flight is a strange and mystifying sight that changes from second to second. Head-on, it is barely visible at the other end of the airfield, a charcoal-pencil stroke across your vision. From the side, a flying saucer from a 1950s movie, its wings invisible. Overhead, a manta ray executed in black by Picasso.

The bomber landed, the first of its type to join the 509th Bomb Wing at Whiteman AFB, close to the bustling metropolis of Knob Noster, and was handed over in a brief ceremony. Defense Secretary Les Aspin, who had just tendered his resignation, was not present. Air Force Secretary Sheila Widnall was there, but answered few questions. The date at which the B-2 would become operational was still classified. Somehow, a grey cloud seemed to surround the B-2, even when the sun was shining.

Now, as the bomber finally nears a full operational capability with the 509th, more of its extraordinary story can be put together. It is a tale of determination and innovation that defies most comparisons.

The technology that would make the B-2 possible originated in the mid-1970s, from two unrelated developments. After the successful use of remotely piloted vehicles (RPVs) in Vietnam, USAF and industry researchers were looking at smaller, less complex mini-RPVs. In the process, a Teledyne Ryan mini-RPV had been flown against both US and foreign radars at Eglin AFB, and proved very difficult to detect.

Lockheed and Northrop were the two greatest American rivals in the quest for stealth. A wise official decision to keep both company's R&D efforts alive meant that Lockheed built the Have Blue/F-117 for the USAF, but Northrop 'won' the B-2.

UNITED STATES AIR FORCE ★ NORTHROP
★ ★
B-2 TEAM

B-2 Spirit
The 'Stealth Bomber'

B-2 Spirit: The 'Stealth Bomber'

The Pentagon's scientific consulting group, the Defense Science Board, had meanwhile completed its annual Summer Study for 1974. With fresh experience of Vietnam and the 1973 air battles over the Middle East, the DSB concluded that conventional aircraft would face severe challenges surviving against the type of robust, networked air defence system which the Soviet Union was developing.

In the early autumn, the Pentagon's deputy director for research and engineering, Malcolm Currie, brought a request to a group at Wright-Patterson AFB which supported the Defense Advanced Research Projects Agency (DARPA), and which had links to the USAF scientists who had been researching the subject of radar cross-section (RCS) for decades: could they build a manned aircraft with a signature as low as the tiny mini-RPV?

Despite a great deal of work on RCS reduction in the 1950s and 1960s – including the testing and operational use of stealthy drones and reconnaissance aircraft, and the use of RCS-reduction technology on the Hound Dog missile – the smallest RCS achieved for a real aircraft was still too large for the aircraft to survive by stealth alone. On the Hound Dog, stealth bought time as the missile bored in on the SAM sites it was intended to destroy. On the Teledyne Ryan AQM-91 Firefly drone, it was combined with high altitude, and on the SR-71 it was combined with altitude and speed.

Project Harvey

Late in 1974, DARPA contacted the main US manufacturers of fighters and other military aircraft, to determine which of them might be interested in bidding on the study. It was codenamed Harvey, in an ironic reference to the 6-ft (1.8-m) invisible rabbit which haunted James Stewart in the film of the same name. It was a low-profile project, but not particularly secret, because nobody knew whether or not it would even be important. In January 1975, DARPA awarded small contracts to McDonnell Douglas and Northrop, calling for designs for a low-RCS manned aircraft. Neither weapons nor sensors need be carried and at that stage there was no guarantee that there would be money to take the project further.

At Northrop's Aircraft Division, the DARPA proposal arrived two months after John Cashen joined the Division. Cashen had been a phenomenologist at Hughes, tasked with defining what targets looked like to the company's radar and infra-red sensors, and had come to Northrop in 1973 to work on lasers.

Cashen had gathered a solid background in signatures through his work at Hughes, including the work that had been done on SRAM and other missiles. A forceful personality, not reticent about putting his views forward, Cashen became the leader and spokesman for the more junior electromagnetics experts on the team. "I was well aware that RCS was not dependent on size, area or volume," he says. RCS "is local. If you deal with each local phenomenon, you can make a very large object very small on radar."

Headed by Cashen, and using the RCS-prediction equations that had been developed at universities in the 1950s and 1960s, the Northrop group started to work on the DARPA requirement.

They were joined by Irv Waaland, a veteran hands-on designer who had come to Northrop from Grumman barely a year earlier. The work started with "a lot of systems analysis," Waaland recalls. "While the RCS people were estimating how low they could get, we did systems analysis to determine what kind of reductions would be required to impact the air defences."

Northrop's goal was to develop a low-altitude attack aircraft, and the analysts concluded that it was most important to reduce its RCS from the nose and tail. Detecting a low-flying aircraft from the side is difficult (because look-down radars rely on the Doppler effect caused by the target's movement relative to the radar and to the ground beneath it); and, because it is less easy to shoot down an aircraft in a tail-chase, the tail-on signature was less important than the nose.

The 'Northrop approach' and XST

It has often been stated that Northrop's approach to stealth relied on advancing computer technology, but Cashen tells a different story. "If we'd had a computer (that could predict RCS) we'd have used it," he says. "We were not able to synthesise RCS, we couldn't get a complete answer. It was better to use experience and the tools that we had, and do it experimentally. We ended up using a shaping solution that, in general, ended up working when we tested it."

Lockheed's Skunk Works had not been asked to compete in the Harvey project, but found out about the project and entered the fray using its own funds. The Lockheed and Northrop companies both outperformed their competition, and in September 1975 they were awarded contracts to design a stealth demonstrator – known as the Experimental Survivable Testbed, or XST. Each company would build a full-scale RCS model for a 'pole-off' at the USAF's RCS range at Holloman AFB in New Mexico.

Northrop had two problems. First, the Northrop XST had been designed on the assumption that the nose-on RCS was more important than the rear aspect. Its planview shape was a diamond with more sweep on the leading edges than the trailing edges. From the rear, it sustained its low RCS as long as the radar was no more than 35° off the tail, but beyond that, the radar would be at right angles to the trailing edge.

Unfortunately, the DARPA requirement treated RCS by quadrants: the rear quadrant extended to 45° either side of the tail, taking in the Northrop design's RCS 'spikes'. Waaland could not solve the problem by stretching the tail and increasing the sweep angle, because the diamond-shaped aircraft would become uncontrollable. Lockheed, however, had made the jump to a swept wing with a deeply notched trailing edge, and could handle the problem.

Northrop's other shortcoming was radar absorbent material (RAM). Northrop was unaware of Lockheed's long background of work on RAM, including the sophisticated high-temperature plastic used in the SR-71's leading edges. In June 1975, the USAF convened a secret Radar Camouflage Symposium at Wright-Patterson, where the Skunk Works' Kelly Johnson revealed the decade-old secret of the SR-71's stealth technology, but it was too late to catch up in time to compete in XST.

Lockheed also proved bolder in designing its XST. Northrop's design had curved wing surfaces; Lockheed built its entire shape from flat plates. Northrop used a top-mounted inlet with a serpentine duct and a mesh screen; Lockheed adopted inlet grilles. There was disappointment but little surprise when Lockheed was selected to build XST in March 1976, under the codename Have Blue, which ultimately evolved into the F-117 (see *World Air Power Journal* Volume 19).

DARPA and the USAF wanted a second source of stealth technology, but did not want to focus attention on the secret magic of stealth by holding another open competition. In December 1976, DARPA approached Northrop about an agency project called Assault Breaker. Its goal was to stop a Soviet tank attack in Central Europe with preci-

B-2 Spirit: The 'Stealth Bomber'

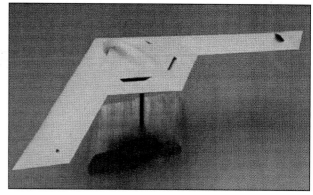

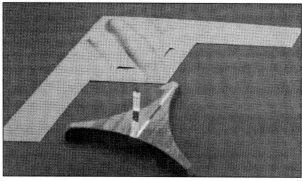

These early ATB models from Northrop give some idea as to the configuration changes that the 'Stealth Bomber' went through on the drawing board. Although the concept of a 'notched' flying wing seems to have been determined from an early stage, refining that design was far less straightforward. Three stages in the evolution of its directional controls are seen here. The first design (top left) featured inward-canted vertical tails at the extreme rear of the centrebody, which was longer than that of the ultimate configuration. In the next version (top right), the outer wings were longer and the aircraft used small outboard vertical tails and jet-reaction controls at the wingtips. The third version represents the design submitted in late 1980, with split rudder/brakes and differential engine thrust.

This is the only known public photograph of Northrop's 1975 XST design, seen here as a full-scale RCS model on a pylon at Holloman AFB. The XST (Experimental Survivable Testbed) competition was originally aimed at McDonnell Douglas and Northrop. Lockheed 'discovered' the project and, together with Northrop, so out-performed the competition that both companies were then selected to build an XST demonstrator. On that occasion Lockheed won through, building the Have Blue flying prototypes that led to the F-117. The XST programme was the last 'open' competition that the US DoD hosted for stealth research and development – the subject had become too sensitive. Instead, DARPA selected Northrop to build the BSAX (Battle Surveillance Aircraft – Experimental) that flew as Tacit Blue. In 1979, aware that Lockheed was working on a similar project, Northrop presented plans for a large stealthy nuclear bomber. In 1980 the USAF issued its own RFP for an Advanced Technology Bomber. By then Northrop's 'know-how' had advanced far beyond the days of the XST and by 1981 the die was cast.

sion-guided weapons. It depended on an airborne radar to track the tanks and the incoming missiles – but how would a radar-carrying craft survive within line-of-sight of its targets? The answer was what DARPA called Battlefield Surveillance Aircraft – Experimental (BSAX). DARPA planned to award this programme to Northrop, both to keep Northrop's stealth technology moving and to avoid the risk of distracting Lockheed from Have Blue.

BSAX was considerably more difficult than Have Blue. A stealth aircraft has been described as a very inefficient antenna that flies; but a radar antenna has to be an efficient reflector. The radar-range equation was also at work: a radar signal that is strong enough to detect a target can itself be intercepted at a much greater distance.

Although Have Blue was an attack aircraft, intended to make a straight run for its target and to spend as little time in a defended area as possible, BSAX would have to loiter over the battlefield for hours, during which it would be illuminated by many radars from different directions. Unlike Have Blue, which was more detectable from the side than from the front and rear, BSAX would have to be the first 'all-aspect stealth' design.

Part of the solution was in hand at Hughes, which was already working on low probability of intercept (LPI) technology, the radar world's equivalent of stealth, and designing low-RCS antennas.

The pace quickens

As Northrop started to design BSAX, the Ford administration packed its bags in Washington. The incoming Carter team, including Defense Secretary Harold Brown and Under-Secretary William Perry (who would become Secretary from 1993 until 1996), was heavy with engineers and academics. Perry himself had built up his own company to manufacture electronics for the Pentagon and intelligence agencies. One of Perry's first actions on stealth was to appoint Air Force scientist Paul Kaminski "to serve as his technical conscience," as Kaminski puts it. "Was it real or not?" Kaminski's report was positive. The next step was more difficult. Assuming that Have Blue worked, how should stealth be used?

Some high-level discussions followed in the spring of 1977, involving Perry, General Al Slay – the chief of USAF research and development, and General Robert Bond, a rising Air Force star who later died while flying a MiG from the Nellis ranges. The support group included two majors, Ken Staton and Joe Ralston: today, the latter is vice-chairman of the Joint Staff.

At a conference in 1990, Ralston remarked that one option studied by the group was whether stealth research should be shut down, the programmes stopped and the data locked away, because the potential of stealth was so explosive. Stealth did not discriminate between US and Soviet radars, and the Soviet Union was showing a disconcerting tendency to develop new generations of weapons on a shorter cycle than the US, and to field them more quickly once developed. But Perry, as Kaminski recalls, "thought it was better to run fast than to behave like an ostrich."

The study group looked at how stealth could be applied to any type of conflict, ranging from counter-insurgency operations through regional and European conventional conflict to nuclear deterrence. Large-scale conventional warfare and nuclear attack were seen as the missions where stealth provided the greatest military advantage.

Stealthy bomber studies

Next, the Pentagon group examined what kind of operational stealth aircraft could and should be developed first. The debate closed in on two concepts. The 'A airplane' was a scaled-up Have Blue, with the fewest possible changes to its shape, and off-the-shelf systems. It was designed to be fielded quickly with minimum risk and to be built as a 'silver bullet' system for attacks on a few crucial targets. The 'B airplane' was much larger, around the size of the 45-ton FB-111 bomber, with a two-member crew, and would be more expensive but more flexible.

There was some enthusiasm for a larger aircraft within the USAF, particularly after the new administration cancelled the B-1 in June 1977. "We had much less confidence that we could pull that design off," says Ralston. "There were some tough decisions that had to be made by a small group of people." One critical issue was whether or not a single pilot could perform the mission envisaged for the smaller aircraft. "We flew a simulator and found one person could do it."

During 1977, the USAF decided to focus on the A design first, but continued to fund Lockheed's studies of the larger 'B airplane'. After the cancellation of the B-1, the design started to grow in size and performance, until it was capable of both conventional and nuclear missions.

These decisions had little impact on Northrop, which was preoccupied with BSAX. The design matured as an awkward-looking aircraft designed rather like a 'Huey' helicopter, around a huge box with open sides. The concept was to concentrate all the radar reflectivity into one 'spike' at right angles to the body, and to manoeuvre the aircraft so that the 'spikes' never dwelt on a hostile radar.

Northrop put the first BSAX models on the pole in the summer of 1977. "It was a disaster," says Waaland, who

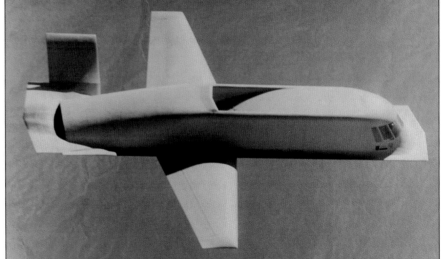

was quickly summoned to rescue the programme. DARPA's Ken Perko, worried that Northrop might not now be able to make BSAX work, quietly invited their rivals at Lockheed to study the concept also.

Above and top: Northrop's BSAX design, Tacit Blue (above), was not successful but did make a contribution to the ATB design, which was proceeding in parallel. The B-2 seen here is AV-4, pictured during flight no. 80 on 2 May 1995.

Left: The jet-powered Northrop YB-49 was developed from the piston-engined XB-35 that first flew in June 1946. The YB-49 took to the air in October 1947. The two YB-49s had very unpredictable handling characteristics and one crashed in June 1949 after back-flipping into a high-speed spin.

B-2 Spirit: The 'Stealth Bomber'

Above and right: The first images of B-2s on the production line at Northrop's Plant 42, in Palmdale, were released only in 1989. Subsequently, it was reported in the US media that Northrop still stood to make a profit even if the final production run was cut to as little as 15 aircraft.

It was Fred Oshira, one of Cashen's electromagneticists, who saved Northrop's face. With the BSAX problems constantly in his mind, Oshira had taken to carrying a piece of modelling clay at all times – even when he took his family to Disneyland. Sitting on a bench, watching his children on the teacup ride, Oshira moulded the clay into a new shape, with a rounded top and flat sloped sides that flared down and outward into a knife-edge.

It worked like a charm, flowing the radar energy around the body rather than scattering it like a mirror. Northrop had not only found a way to remain stealthy from any direction, but had significantly expanded the range of radar frequencies that stealth technology could defeat. Northrop's philosophy was also inherently compatible with curvature, promising greater aerodynamic efficiency. Again, better computers helped, "but we didn't design the aircraft on the computer," says Waaland. "Computers allowed us to look at parts of the aircraft in two dimensions. We could blend them together but we didn't have an integrated model."

Northrop's BSAX emerges

With the major RCS problem solved, the BSAX design came together in the second half of 1977. It had a bluff-nosed, bulky body to accommodate the radar. The engines were buried at the rear behind a flush dorsal inlet, with no screens or grilles. It had an unswept wing, which used a Clark Y airfoil section that had not been seen since the 1930s – the advantage was that the lower surface was flat. Pitch and yaw were controlled by a fly-by-wire system driving two all-moving V-tails. Worried about how the ends of the angled tail would appear on radar, the designers curved the tips of the V-tails towards the horizon. It was a final, organic touch to the design, which acquired the nickname 'Whale'. DARPA awarded the company a contract for a single prototype in April 1978, under the codename Tacit Blue.

By the end of that year, there were several stealth programmes under development. Have Blue was flying. Its operational derivative, the F-117, was the subject of a development contract late in 1978. Lockheed was working on the still-classified Senior Prom air-launched cruise missile – and a stealthy nuclear bomber.

Above and right: The roll-out of the B-2 on 22 November 1988 was intended to be a carefully managed affair, as most details of the new aircraft, even its exact shape, were still classified. Few people were invited (fewer than 500 guests and 50 from the media) and all were kept at a distance, screened from the aircraft. Experience with the F-117 dictated that a night-time flight test programme for the B-2 would not be possible, which was the driving reason behind its public unveiling. However, not enough planning had been devoted to the security of the Plant 42 area and so a single light aircraft with a photographer from Aviation Week and Space Technology *cruised overhead to take photos that, for a while, were the scoop of the decade.*

Even though the Carter administration had cancelled the B-1 only months before, it was increasingly committed to developing a new bomber. US nuclear deterrence relied on a 'triad' of systems – bombers, ICBMs and submarine-launched missiles – which supported one another, because it was almost impossible for an adversary to attack them all at the same time.

In the late 1970s, however, CIA analysis identified an emerging 'window of vulnerability'. More accurate Soviet ICBMs would destroy more US ICBMs on the ground. This would mean that the bombers would be attacking an almost intact and fully operational Soviet air-defence system, and this system itself was being strengthened. Cities and other targets were being ringed with high-power radars and new missiles. The new long-range MiG-31 interceptor was designed to push the air battle hundreds of miles further from the targets, over the Arctic, so that the vulnerable B-52s could be engaged before they were within cruise-missile range of their objectives.

Stealth bomber go-ahead

By 1979, the Carter administration had secretly authorised the start a stealth bomber programme. The requirement had become more demanding, and the Lockheed design had evolved to meet it. It acquired curvature on the wings, and rounded edges rather than sharply defined facets – although its surfaces were curved in one dimension rather than two, and the shape still retained flat surfaces. But because the USAF was looking at a stealth bomber which could penetrate for hundreds of miles into an undamaged Soviet air defence system, Northrop's all-aspect, wide-bandwidth stealth technology began to look promising.

Northrop was not known as a builder of large aircraft, and its last bomber programme (the B-35/B-49) had almost destroyed it, so it took some high-level persuasion from the Air Force before the company would even begin a small-scale bomber study.

Northrop's analysis of the threat showed a weakness: the Soviet air defences were being bolstered against low-level penetrators and cruise missiles, but remained thinner at high altitudes. The designers concluded that they needed a bomber capable of U-2-like altitudes, with a planform shape that generated the smallest possible number of RCS 'spikes'. High altitude meant a large wing area and span.

It was natural for Northrop to look at a flying wing design: not only did it recall Northrop's most famous product, the XB-35/YB-49 of the late 1940s, but the wing had been the subject of numerous studies in the 1970s.

In the summer of 1979, designer Hal Markarian produced a sketch that is recognisably an ancestor of the B-2 in the arrangement of its basic components and the philosophy that drove them. Each feature was determined by a different sub-set of the mission requirements. It was a flying wing, because there is nothing quite as stealthy as a flat plate viewed edge-on, and the wing is the closest

approach to such a shape. Payload and range set a lower limit to the wing span. The leading-edge sweep angle was determined by the desired high subsonic cruising speed and by the need to locate the aerodynamic centre close to the centre of gravity: given that the wing extends to the front of the vehicle, it must be swept back to place the centre of lift where it needs to be.

The length of the centrebody section was determined by depth: it had to be deep enough to accommodate a normal cockpit and the weapon bays, and this meant that it had to be a minimum length to avoid excessive drag at high subsonic speeds. Outboard of the centrebody section, the chord was set by the need to integrate the engines and their low-observable inlet and exhaust systems into the wing. The inlets and exhaust were set well aft and well forward of the wing edges, the better to shield them from radar.

Although the chord close to the centreline had to be long, the planform area of a flying wing sets its weight and drag. As a result, the design had a long, deep centre-section, married to slender outer wings. With just eight ruler-straight edges, it presented only four main-lobe reflections.

In August 1979, Northrop presented Perry with two designs: Markarian's flying-wing design with parallel edges, using the shaping techniques developed on Tacit Blue, and a diamond-shaped aircraft similar to its Have Blue. Perry asked for a further study to flesh out the flying wing design. The maximum cost was $2 million, because a $2 million project did not have to be reported to Congress.

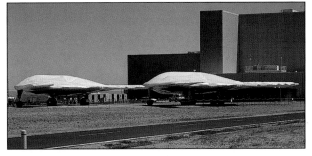

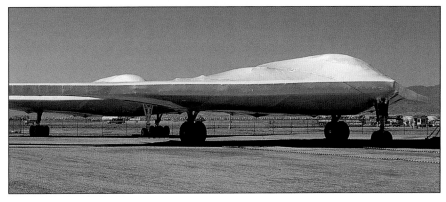

The B-2 made a successful first flight on 17 July 1989, departing from Palmdale's runway 04 at 06.36 PDT. The 112-minute maiden voyage of AV-1 had been preceded by initial taxi tests on 10 July and high-speed taxi tests on 13 July, at Palmdale. During the high-speed runs the B-2 reached a speed of 115 kt (213 km/h; 132 mph) and the nosewheel lifted off the runway. To protect the B-2 from FOD (Foreign Object Damage) the area around Plant 42 began to receive regular FOD sweeps as early as June; a major 'FOD walk' was organised on the morning of 10 July and the airfield was closed to other traffic. This heightened concern followed an incident in May when AV-1 suffered minor ingestion damage during engine runs – but also provided a good clue to the 'stealth watchers' around the fence at Palmdale that the B-2 was about to re-emerge.

Left and below: These strange shapes are the two little-known static ground test airframes, built for the B-2 programme. Note the completely non-standard undercarriage on one of the airframes. Both 'iron birds' are seen in storage at Plant 42, in March 1994.

Above and opposite page: The B-2's first flight took it from Palmdale to Edwards AFB. It had originally been planned to make the journey on 15 July but a fault in the aircraft's heat exchanger (which uses fuel to cool accessory drive oil) forced the flight's postponement.

Landing the B-2 requires virtually no back pressure on the stick. When its 172-ft (52.4-m) wing enters ground effect (at approximately half a span's distance from the ground) sink rate decreases almost automatically. In the words of one pilot, "think about flaring – and you're down."

The team was joined by Dick Scherrer, who had joined Northrop from Lockheed. Scherrer, Waaland and aerodynamicist Hans Grellman started to work out the design details. They developed a $14 million, 11-month proposal (with a $2 million contract price), including wind-tunnel and RCS tests, and Northrop received a contract for the Advanced Strategic Penetration Aircraft (ASPA) in January 1980. "There was one condition," Waaland recalls. "We were advised at the highest levels that we were an insurance policy. We were told not to start lobbying."

The ATB emerges

A steady stream of visitors from Wright-Patterson, Strategic Air Command and the Pentagon passed through Northrop's offices. Northrop learned from them that the USAF and SAC were pushing for more weapons capacity and more flexibility, and responded by making the bomber's centre-section deeper, increasing its weight and reducing its U-2-like cruising altitude.

When the USAF issued a request for proposals for development and production of the Advanced Technology

Bomber (ATB) in September 1980, there was little doubt that Northrop had advanced from an insurance policy to at least equal standing. Lockheed had already teamed with Rockwell for the bomber competition, and Northrop's leaders realised that they would have to find a partner as well. Jones asked for a meeting with Boeing's chairman, Thornton 'T.' Wilson. With one company chief on either side of a long table, flanked by their subordinates, Jones told Wilson about the ATB competition and invited Boeing to join Northrop. It was one of the most valuable contests in history, but Wilson had heard next to nothing about it. Waaland recalls that Wilson accepted Jones's offer, turned to the Boeing executive next to him and said, "Don't ever let me be in this position again."

Senior Ice and Senior Peg

The Northrop proposal, codenamed Senior Ice, was submitted in December. "It was one of the best proposal efforts I'd been on," says Waaland, "and we ended up feeling pretty buoyant. It was part exhaustion, part fatigue and part euphoria." By the early spring "we had indications that we had buried the competition."

Lockheed's Senior Peg design is still classified, making a comparison impossible. In his autobiography, Skunk Works leader Ben Rich claimed that the Lockheed design was more stealthy and that Northrop prevailed because of a small edge in aerodynamic performance and because it was a larger aircraft. Cashen disputes that claim. "We had a hell of an aircraft, it's as simple as that. We beat them on the pole, we beat them in the air, we beat them on everything."

As the engineers prepared their final proposals, President Jimmy Carter and the Congressional Democrats were defeated by Ronald Reagan in the November 1980 election. Under Carter, several options for renewing the bomber force had been studied. One option was to bring the ATB into service as soon as possible; another was to delay the ATB and concentrate on a more stealthy development of the B-1; and at one point, Strategic Air Command favoured a plan that would have produced an interim bomber by radically modifying its existing FB-111As.

Reagan's defence secretary, Caspar Weinberger, decided on the most expensive option: a full-speed-ahead programme to build 100 B-1s in the mid-1980s, followed by 132 stealth bombers.

Northrop was awarded the ATB contract in October 1981, covering full-scale development, preparations for production and the manufacture of six flying aircraft and two static-test airframes. Including options for the production of 127 more bombers (one of the prototypes would not be operational), the contract was worth $36.6 billion in 1981 dollars. The Pentagon wanted to keep the award secret –

announcing, for legal reasons, nothing more than the award of a 'study' to Northrop – but Northrop chairman Tom Jones pointed out that securities law required disclosure of contracts that would materially affect the company's business. A 12-line statement was issued – the last that would be heard of the programme, officially, until 1988. The programme was codenamed Senior CJ in tribute to Connie Jo Kelly, the indispensable and hard-working secretary to the stealth programme office in the Pentagon.

Although Northrop had a contract to build the new bomber, its design was not frozen, and, in fact, it would change dramatically in the first year of the programme.

Planning for operations

In 1980, in the Pentagon, Paul Kaminski had decided to invest one per cent of the stealth budget in counter-stealth studies. The Red Team was divided in two. One group worked with full knowledge of stealth; the other worked from public sources. The effort led to major changes in the bomber design.

The most important lesson was that a stealth aircraft was not invisible. It could and would be detected if its operators did not use tactics that exploited its stealth. The Red Team underscored the importance of planning routes so that the stealth aircraft would show its least visible side to known radars. This led to the development of the first automated mission planning system for the F-117A. Constantly updated with the location of hostile radars, the system devised the stealthiest routes to any chosen target. (Pilots nicknamed it 'Elvira', after late-night TV's Mistress of the Dark.) A similar system would be developed to support the ATB.

More significantly, the Red Team suggested that, within the new bomber's service life, the Soviet Union might build large ground-based radars that could overpower stealth technology at a useful range. The USAF decided to design the bomber so that it could bypass those radars on the deck, using terrain to protect itself.

The design that Northrop had submitted for the ATB competition in 1980 was very similar to Hal Markarian's first sketches, with the exception that it was noticeably deeper at the centre-section: in response to Strategic Air Command's indications that they wanted a multi-mission bomber, the aircraft had grown heavier, with larger weapons bays. This had been accomplished within the original planform at the expense of some altitude performance.

ATB changes

When the Red Team's low-altitude requirement was added to the specification, Northrop initially offered a revised ATB that would fly at Mach 0.55 at low altitude (about the same as the B-52). However, as the competition entered its final stages, it became clear that the bomber would have enough power (because of its low drag) to reach Mach 0.8. Northrop adjusted its final offer to reflect this, while cautioning the USAF that it had not had time to fully model the aeroelastic effects of the higher loads and more rigid structure. Designers expected that some local stiffening would be required, along with changes to the environmental control system (ECS) to deal with friction heating encountered at high speed and low level.

The issue turned out to be more complex. The designers developed a new computer model that took account of external air loads, the internal structure and the control laws. This showed that the control surfaces – all of which were on the relatively flexible outer wings, apart from a gust-alleviation flap on the extreme tail – were located ahead of the primary longitudinal bending mode line, which curved across the centrebody. In low-altitude turbulence, these controls would tend to excite bending in the structure as they attempted to counter gust-induced pitch movements. Stiffening the structure would add at least 10,000 lb (4500 kg) to the empty weight.

Instead, the bomber was redesigned. The outer wings became shorter and thinner, and carried only two control segments instead of three. The outboard centrebody sections were extended backwards, creating the characteristic 'double-W' trailing edge, and the exhausts were changed to a V-shape. Two elevon sections were added to each side of the centrebody, placing them on a stiffer part of the structure, and further aft for greater effectiveness.

At the same time, the RCS group at Northrop produced a different type of radar absorbent structure for the leading edge of the wing, which could provide the required absorption with less depth. This meant that the wing spar and cockpit could be moved forward. The inlets had originally been designed so that part of the duct passed through the spar, with a stream-wise vane to help conceal the compressor face from the engine. With the spar moved forward, it was possible to move the entire duct behind the spar and simplify the structural design.

The revised aircraft would not only be lighter but would have a better ride at low altitude, so it was possible to eliminate an isolated, palletised cockpit which had been incorporated in the original design.

Low-altitude performance was only one area in which the USAF and Northrop raised their sights as the design evolved. The customer was well aware that the B-2 would be the last new bomber for a long time. With strong support from those members of Congress who were permitted to know about stealth, and encouragement from a hawkish administration, the USAF wrote the toughest set of requirements ever seen. "In the requirements stage, money was no object," one engineer recalls.

Demands of the strategic mission

The ATB design assumed that the bombers would have to penetrate Soviet territory after a successful first strike by Soviet missiles had destroyed the US ICBM force. This meant that they would have fully operational threat radars all around them: hence, the requirement for a very low RCS in all bandwidths and from all directions. Moreover, the bomber's crew would have to be able to detect and avoid threats that had not been predicted.

The bomber was intended to be fully autonomous and able to attack almost any target, ranging from deeply buried bunkers – using high-yield thermonuclear weapons such as the multi-megaton B53 bomb – to mobile, protected missile launchers. Its radar would have to combine LPI with long range and high resolution.

Since the bombers and submarines might be the only surviving element of the US nuclear strike force, the ATB was designed to be recovered and reconstituted. After their first nuclear mission, the bombers would return to the US and land at dispersal airfields (the ATB can operate from any airfield that can handle a Boeing 727), where they could be rearmed and launched on a second strike.

No previous bomber, including the B-1, had been designed to meet such a requirement. It meant not only that the bomber needed a high level of reliability and redundancy, but that every part of the aircraft had to be radiation-hardened to an unprecedented degree, to survive the blasts of radiation from its own nuclear bombs and from Soviet nuclear air-defence warheads. Even mundane components like the TACAN receiver had to be specially designed. "About the only thing that was not rad-hardened was the anti-skid system," Waaland recalled.

When it came to deciding how to meet these requirements, the Air Force and civilian engineers worked closely together – but in a management system which, programme participants recall, did not allow them to see the cost impacts of their decisions. "There was a lack of cost information to the engineers," Waaland remarks. "If engineers are left unchecked, they will always go for the best solution." One example was as simple as the radio: from the early stages of the programme, it was decided that the ATB should have an advanced anti-jam radio. "After we put it in," says Waaland, "we had nobody to talk to, because apart from the B-2 the programme had been cancelled."

Moreover, there are features of the aircraft that apparently have not been discussed at all. "From the beginning, it was the Advanced Technology Bomber," one insider notes, "not just the stealth bomber. That's where the money is, not in the stealth. There are certain special technologies that cost a fortune."

The bomber described

In 1984, with its redesign complete, the bomber passed an unusual second preliminary design review. The challenge was to build it. This was to prove more difficult than expected, and as always the devil was in the details.

Bombers present a unique design challenge because of their combination of transport-like size and fighter-like intricacy, and the B-2 is an elegant, densely packed aircraft.

The centrebody is little longer than the fuselage of an F-15 but is as deep as a B-52 fuselage, accommodating two large weapon bays, one each side of the centreline. Each bay contains either a Boeing-developed Advanced Rotary Launcher (ARL) capable of carrying eight 1000-kg (2,204-lb) class weapons, or, alternatively, two Bomb Rack Assembly (BRA) units for carrying smaller conventional weapons.

The centrebody accommodates the crew compartment, reached through a ventral hatch. The B-2's cockpit windows are so large that they make the aircraft look smaller than it is. They are large for the same reason that the cockpit windows of a DC-10 are large: a cockpit window has to provide the pilot with a given angular field of view, and the further the window is from the pilot's seat, the bigger it has to be. Comparing the location of the ejection-seat hatches with the width of the dorsal hump shows how wide and high the latter is. Even so, fighter pilots transitioning to the B-2 sometimes feel "that they are trapped in a dumpster" because of the restricted field of view. The nose-down view is limited.

Stealthy features

The engines, outboard of the weapon bays, are buried completely within the wing. The S-shaped inlet ducts curve down to the engines, which are accessible from below the aircraft. Curvature conceals the compressor faces from direct line-of-sight illumination by radar, and RAM on the duct walls suppresses any radar energy which could bounce off the duct walls to reach the engines. Ahead of each inlet is a jagged slit-like auxiliary inlet which removes the turbulent boundary layer, and provides cool air which is mixed into the exhaust to reduce the bomber's infra-red signature. The bizarre, modern-sculpture shape of the inlets results from the combination of the straight-edge planform alignments with the curvature of the surfaces.

The exhaust ducts are curved in profile. They flatten out to wide slits and open into overwing trenches. As in the case of the F-117, the exhaust system exploits the Coanda effect (the phenomenon that causes spilt water to follow the curved side of a glass rather than falling straight down) to direct the thrust aft while concealing the nozzle openings from a direct rear view.

The B-2's aerodynamic characteristics are unique. Compared with a wing-body design of the same weight, the B-2 has much more span and wing area, so the lift coefficient (a measure of how much lift must be produced

Above: AV-2 joined the flight test programme when it departed Palmdale for the first time on 19 October 1989. It was flown by Northrop pilot Leroy Schroeder and Lt Col John Small of the (then) 6520th Test Squadron. The first flight of the second B-2 was nearly aborted by high winds which were gusting outside the aircraft's limits. As a result the crew elected to depart on runway 25, to avoid an excessive tailwind component, but had to make a snappy right turn on departure to avoid downtown Palmdale. Rising crosswinds at Edwards AFB forced the crew to land ahead of their scheduled time, after 67 minutes in the air. AV-2 was instrumented for load testing and was originally the only one of the six-strong test fleet that was not scheduled to be returned to active service at Whiteman AFB.

The B-2 was rolled out during the transition from the Reagan to the Bush administration, and began flying when the first deep cuts in the US military budget were being initiated, in the early 1990s. F-117 procurement had been cut almost in half, rail-basing plans for the MX missile (MGM-118) force were slashed, the small ICBM programme was cancelled (as ultimately was the rail-based MX) and the B-2 had to compete for funds with other high-spenders such as the ATF and SDI.

by each square foot of wing) does not have to be as high. While conventional aircraft have complex flaps to raise the lift coefficient for take-off and landing, the B-2 needs none, and lifts off at a conservative speed of just 140 kt (160 mph; 258 km/h).

Another effect of the big wing is that the B-2 operates over a smaller angle of attack range than a conventional aircraft and flies in a fairly flat, constant attitude regardless of speed and weight. A sophisticated fuel-management system is used for zero-drag trim. The net result is that the B-2 is very efficient, even though the lift distribution was not what it would be in an ideal flying wing.

The B-2 is lighter than the B-1, but has a far better warload and range performance. It can carry about as much and as far as the B-52, which is 59 tons heavier.

The B-2's weight is a curious subject. Early fact sheets gave the maximum take-off weight as 375,000 lb (170500 kg). Later, this number was reduced to 336,500 lb (152600 kg), and other documents place the aircraft "in the 350,000-lb (158730-kg) class." The most probable explanation for this discrepancy is that the bomber's structural life is based on the lowest figure, reflecting a take-off with full fuel but no weapons. Since a full load has relatively little effect on the bomber's flying qualities, a B-2 will probably never fly with a full load except in combat, which represents a tiny percentage of its lifetime sorties.

Its aerodynamic efficiency is close to that of the Lockheed U-2, a very specialised aircraft with a much smaller design envelope. The B-2's altitude performance is another interesting question: with its great span and wing area, the B-2 is

certainly capable of exceeding the nominal 50,000-ft (15000-m) ceiling cited in official statements. The only real question is by how much.

In most respects, the B-2 is close to neutrally stable. If it had conventional controls, any disturbance would tend to push the aircraft on to a new flightpath. It would not diverge further from its original path unless it was disturbed again, but it would require an action by the pilot to resume its former attitude and speed. However, it is rendered stable by a quadruplex fly-by-wire (FBW) system. The flight control computer (FCC) units were developed by General Electric, which provided the hardware for the F/A-18 and Tacit Blue. (This GE unit is now part of Lockheed Martin.)

Control system and surfaces

The FBW system drives nine very large control surfaces which occupy the entire trailing edge, apart from the area behind the engines. The outermost pair of surfaces is split horizontally and operates symmetrically as speedbrakes, and asymmetrically as rudders. The flattened, pointed tail of the centrebody – known as the gust load alleviation system (GLAS) or simply the 'beavertail' – is primarily used to counter pitch movements caused by vertical gusts at low level. The remaining six surfaces are elevons for pitch and roll control, although the outermost pair functions purely as ailerons at low speed.

The absence of a vertical fin is one of the B-2's unique features. B-2 designer Irv Waaland describes a conventional aircraft without a vertical fin as "like an arrow without feathers." The flying wing is different, because it is short from front to rear and has no features to generate destabilising side forces. "The all-wing design is neutrally stable directionally," Waaland says: "all you need is adequate control." Northrop's first designs had small, inward-canted vertical control surfaces on the centrebody, immediately outboard of the exhausts. Alternative approaches were evaluated, including a combination of small outboard verticals and reaction controls, before Northrop settled on the brake-rudder surfaces.

The brake-rudders are the primary means of yaw control, but because of the boundary layer over the wing, the surfaces are ineffective until they have moved about 5° from their trail position. The B-2 normally flies with the rudders at 'five and five' – that is, slightly displaced so that any movement takes it immediately into a responsive zone. This is not compatible with stealth, so the rudders are closed when the cockpit master mode switch is in its 'go to war' position. Instead (according to a 1991 technical paper, although this area is now classified), the B-2 uses differential engine thrust for stealthy directional control.

The flight control system presented its own challenges. Because the B-2 is short, the elevons have a short moment arm in pitch, and must be large to provide adequate power. Being on the wing trailing edge, they are not mass-balanced, so the loads at the hinge line are high. On the other hand, the designers had also elected to use the controls to counter gust loads in low-level flight, so the controls had to be able to move very quickly.

To meet these conflicting requirements, Moog and Lear Astronics developed a unique actuation system. The B-2 is fitted with eight actuator remote terminals (ARTs) spread out along the wing span, which receive their instructions from the GE flight control computers over a quadruplex digital bus. The ARTs issue analog commands to the actuators and control all the necessary feedback loops, saving complexity and weight in the wiring between the FCCs and the actuators. The entire system runs at 4,000 psi (27580 kPa) to reduce the size and weight of the actuators.

The Rosemount air data system is also new, but proved less troublesome than the air data system on the F-117. (For one agonising period in the F-117's development, the team was working with several air-data systems, none of which had yet been made to work.) The B-2's system is based on a circular heated port which can measure both normal (static pressure) and pitot pressure. There are five groups of four ports, each arranged on a common pressure line. The system compares pressures at upper and lower ports to determine Alpha, and left and right to determine sideslip.

Aerodynamic design

The B-2 aerodynamic design was primarily based on computational fluid dynamics (CFD), according to aerodynamicist Hans Grellmann, although CFD for whole-airframe design was in its infancy when the programme started. "We had to make do with tools that were never designed to do the job," he says. A transonic wing analysis code was adapted to define the entire wing. CFD could not directly account for engine flows, so the aerodynamics team subtracted the engine flow from their calculations, leaving only the spilling airflow. CFD was also used to investigate important handling areas such as inflight refuelling and behaviour in ground effect. "We relied on CFD, and used the wind tunnel to tell us that our codes were valid," says Grellmann. Several models – all produced by numerically controlled machines, driven from the same computer database which was used in the production of the full-size aircraft – were used for more than 24,000 hours of total tunnel time. The 'workhorse' was a sting-mounted force and moment model with working primary and BLC inlets.

Detail design challenges included the need to push the thickness of the centre-section to the limit of flow separation,

to accommodate a body depth equal to that of the B-52 in the bomber's 69-ft (21-m) overall length. The aircraft was also to have conventional pitch and stalling characteristics, even though Cashen's stealth group wanted the leading edge to be as sharp as possible. The wing section itself is a modified NASA laminar-flow profile, chosen because it can combine the camber demanded by cruise aerodynamics with a sharp leading edge. The high degree of twist and drastic leading-edge camber variation which are visible on the B-2 evolved as a complex compromise between aerodynamics and stealth.

All-new engine

Northrop selected a new engine from General Electric in the early stages of the ASPA contest. It was based on the F101-X, a fighter engine derived from the B-1's powerplant that later became the F110. Compared with the F101, the F101-X had a smaller low-pressure spool, scaled up from that of the F404, which reduced the bypass ratio from 2:1 to 0.87:1. The F101-X was attractive for two reasons. Although a higher-bypass-ratio engine would be more

Above and top: In these two views the 5,000 sq ft (464.4 m²) wing area of the B-2 can be compared to that of a KC-135E and a KC-10A. The B-2 has a wing span of exactly 172 ft (52.43 m) which, co-incidentally, is the same as that of the XB-35/YB-49. The B-2 was originally designed with a pair of split flaps located under the aft centre fuselage. Tunnel tests indicated that they would probably not be needed, so the actuators were removed and the flaps were bolted shut on AV-1. Vestiges of the flaps remain on later aircraft.

Ahead of each B-2 engine inlet is a small auxiliary inlet which removes the turbulent boundary layer that might otherwise impede engine performance. It also provides cool air to mix with the exhaust efflux to reduce the bomber's infra-red signature. The exhaust ducts themselves are curved in profile. They flatten out to wide slits and open into overwing trenches, blocking them from ground-based IR sensors. Note the frangible panel markings for the ejection seat of the third crewman, which is particularly clear in these two views from a KC-135 tanker.

efficient, it would need a bigger exhaust and inlet system that would add to the bomber's weight, and it would lose thrust more rapidly with altitude.

The definitive B-2 engine was originally referred to as F101-F29, but was officially designated F118-GE-100. Compared with the F110, it has a redesigned, higher-airflow fan that provides more non-afterburning power. Its high-altitude potential is indicated by the fact that it has been retrofitted to the Lockheed U-2S.

Inlet design was difficult. The completely flush inlet used on Tacit Blue had worked adequately, but had experienced starting problems (at one point, the flight test crew borrowed a C-130 to generate airspeed over the inlet of the 'Whale') and Northrop was looking for better pressure recovery and efficiency on the bomber. However, the last place to put an efficient inlet is on top of the wing.

Supercritical wing

Although the B-2 is subsonic, its thick supercritical wing sections accelerate the air to supersonic speeds over the wing. The inlet region resembles two supercritical wing sections in series. The first is the area behind the leading edge, where the airflow accelerates to supersonic speed and is then recompressed to subsonic speed before being swallowed by the main inlet and the auxiliary boundary-layer/IR suppression scoop. The second supercritical section comprises the region from the inlet lip to the exhaust exit, where the flow is accelerated and recompressed once again. In cruising flight, the inlet is spilling air (as most inlets do) and the interaction with the flow over the wing translates all the way to the wingtip. Because of this, it was impossible to predict or test the B-2's aerodynamic performance without taking the propulsion system into account.

In the early days of the programme, Northrop built a full-scale replica of the inlet, complete with two engines,

and tested it on the ground. Only one serious problem turned up: a certain amount of flow separation in the tightly curved duct, leading to a loss of power at low speeds. The solution was to add retractable auxiliary inlet scoops above the wing.

Structural elements

Structurally, the B-2 consists of six major assemblies. The centre wing assembly, built by Boeing, contains the weapon bays and the avionics bays above and behind them. In front of this is the crew station assembly, produced by Northrop in California. On either side are the two very complex intermediate wing assemblies, which house the inlets, exhausts, engine bays and main landing gear bays. (The company responsible for them at the start of the programme – Vought – has since been acquired by Northrop Grumman.) The outer wings are produced by Boeing, which is also responsible for the weapon launchers and landing gear.

The components of the B-2 actually built by Northrop are only a small proportion of the total weight – the cockpit and the entire perimeter of the aircraft, comprising the leading edges, wingtips, control surfaces and fixed trailing-edge structure. For Northrop, this makes good business sense. Much of the value of a contract resides in the design, the integration (which includes the cockpit) and the use of company-proprietary technology, such as the radar-absorbent edges of a stealth aircraft.

Inside the centre and intermediate wing sections are two very large titanium carry-through box (CTB) structures, one behind the cockpit and the other one aft of the engine bay. Otherwise, the primary structural material is carbon-fibre/epoxy composite, which is used for most of the skin and the spars of the outer wing. The B-2 includes many of the largest carbon-fibre parts ever made, including centre-section skins that are more than 1 in (2.5 cm) thick, and spars and skins more than 70 ft (21 m) long, and is still by far the largest aircraft ever built primarily from composites.

One of the most important reasons for choosing the new material had to do with stealth. Carbon-fibre is less dense than metal, so carbon-fibre skins are thicker than metal skins of the same strength, and composite parts can be assembled by 'co-curing' them: autoclaving them together, so that the parts bond together with a strength equal to that of the original material. Most of the stiffeners are co-cured to the skins. The thick, fastener-free skins produced by this method are smoother than riveted metal skins, and will stay that way in service – a characteristic that was critical to Northrop's 'seamless' stealth design technique. Large skin panels reduced the number of joints, which were possible sources of unwanted radar reflections. The result was a durable and relatively simple structural design: the question was whether anyone could draw it, let alone build it.

Building the B-2

Northrop's stealth design philosophy, with its continuous flowing curves, had worked on the hand-built Tacit Blue prototype, but a large mass-produced bomber was a different matter. Most aircraft are built from the inside out, starting with spars, ribs and frames. They are all parts which are defined in two dimensions, and are assembled into the complete structure. Any deviances from the design accumulate into small errors in fit and surface finish, which are fixed during final assembly; and errors are usually larger on large aircraft.

The B-2 could not be built this way. The major skin components had to fit almost perfectly, so that there would be no gaps or steps even when the aircraft was pummelled and bent by turbulence. The classic methods of ensuring that parts conformed to the design shape were inadequate, being basically designed for single-curvature surfaces.

Since stealth was a critical aspect of the design, and would have to be demonstrated by the first B-2s, the first aircraft off the line would have to be exactly the same in every external detail as all the others; that is to say, it would be built on hard tooling. This tooling would have to be

As the combat assets of SAC and TAC were merged into Air Combat Command, plans for the B-2 entered a state of flux. From a proposed total of 132, by late 1991/early 1992 a force of 75 B-2s was looking unlikely and as few as 15 aircraft seemed more like the truth. It was the then-Chairman of the House Armed Services Committee, Les Aspin, who coined the phrase 'silver bullet' force for such a tiny number of B-2s. Deep splits arose between factions in the USAF and the DoD as to whether some aircraft were better than none at all, and quite what the value of a single B-2 might be when compared to existing assets. Major General Stephen Croker, the architect of ACC (and a Vietnam MiG-killer), said, "[there will be a] serious practical problem day-to-day to use 15 aircraft for a long period. You could get a job done with 15 airplanes, 10 of which you have access to, five of which you used on any given day, but it would take an awful lot of days." Croker oversaw SAC's SR-71 operations, and said, "those eight aircraft cost me more in operations and support for a year than 3½ B-52 wings."

installed and aligned to unprecedented standards of accuracy before the first bomber was built.

The answer was twofold. First, the B-2 would be defined and built from the outside in. Instead of being made of flexible sheets fastened to substructure, the skin panels would be laid up in precise female moulds. Second, to make sure that everything would fit, the entire aircraft would be designed on computers.

As the company renovated the massive Ford automobile plant at Pico Rivera, where much of the B-2 was to be built, it did so according to a new concept: computer integrated manufacturing (CIM). At Pico Rivera, the image of

computer-aided design became the reality. The external shape of the new bomber was defined on a computer database, not in terms of sections and stations, but in its totality; the database could define the precise three-dimensional co-ordinates of any point on the skin. The database was housed on banks of tape drives and managed by a Cray supercomputer. Connected to the database were more than 400 computer work-stations at Pico Rivera; the database was shared with major sub-contractors Boeing and Vought, and their own engineers. As detail design proceeded, the engineers could work from the outside in; as the design of each part was completed, it was added to the database. The computer system grew to define the shape and location of every component of the B-2, down to the smallest fastener.

New approaches, new materials

Quite early in the programme, the database took over from the first 'engineering fixture' produced to support the B-2 design, so that the aircraft became the first to be created without a true mock-up. Computer-aided design is standard practice now, but it was far from being so in 1983, and the Northrop team found itself breaking new ground. Even with CIM, the internal plumbing and wiring of AV-1, the first aircraft, proved to be a voracious consumer of manhours.

Materials were another problem area. The skin had to be made thicker and heavier than predicted, because its stealth characteristics might be compromised if it buckled under loads. Other requirements compounded the problem, Waaland said later: "We entered the programme with what we thought was a full range of validated materials, both low-observable and non-low-observable. We were required to validate our materials for nuclear flash and dust, long-life ultra-violet exposure, rain, supportability, producibility and a lot of other concerns. The bottom line is that nothing that we started with survived."

Before the first B-2 was completed, Northrop and its team-mates tested more than 900 materials. Where the chosen approach seemed risky, the customer demanded extensive demonstrations: for example, three complete 15-m (49-ft) composite wing skin panels were built in 1982-83 before the USAF was satisfied that the material would be durable, that there would be no problems with

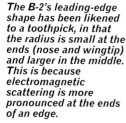

AV-1008 (88-0329) is seen here, outside the B-2 engine run dock at Edwards AFB, with the name of General Mike Loh inscribed on the nose-wheel door as mission commander. General Loh was the commander of Air Combat Command until 22 June 1995 (and a former commander of TAC for four days until ACC was established on 1 June 1992).

The B-2's leading-edge shape has been likened to a toothpick, in that the radius is small at the ends (nose and wingtip) and larger in the middle. This is because electromagnetic scattering is more pronounced at the ends of an edge.

lightning and that the promised 3.2-ton weight saving would be achieved. Only then could Northrop and Boeing cease working on a back-up aluminium-alloy design.

In many cases, new materials not only cost money to develop, but were more expensive in production as well. Like other manufacturers, Northrop had to switch from early epoxy resins to new formulations which offered better through-the-skin toughness and resisted delamination better. Around the engines, epoxies gave way to new heat-tolerant bismaleimide and polyimide resins. Many of these materials and processes have or will become standard on later programmes.

The third principal driver behind the design, along with aerodynamics and structures, was stealth technology. The concept of 'balanced observables' is essential to understanding the design of the B-2. In the ideal 'balanced' aircraft, its detection range in any spectrum – radar, IR, visual or acoustic – will be much the same.

The demands of 'stealth'

On a stealth aircraft, routine things can become difficult. Because access panels have to be treated so carefully, it is best to eliminate as many of them as possible. This involves careful design. On the B-2, one panel usually gives access to several systems; other sub-systems, such as the avionics, are installed so that they can be reached through existing apertures such as the crew boarding hatch, weapons bay and landing gear bay. The B-2 is also unusual in that it has no drain holes. Instead, drain paths lead to collectors that can be emptied on the ground.

RCS reduction is the most critical element of stealth, because radar provides the defender with the most information at the longest range. Denys Overholser, one of the key

players in the Lockheed Have Blue design, lists the four most important factors in RCS reduction as "shape, shape, shape and materials." Shape is by far the biggest factor in reducing RCS, but special radar-absorbent material (RAM) is necessary to mop up residual scattering from the shaped surfaces and to suppress reflections from features such as inlets, which cannot be totally stealthy in their basic design. RAM is applied to an existing structure and adds to its weight without increasing its strength; radar-absorbing structure (RAS) involves building these materials into load-bearing structure. Most of the B-2 is covered by multi-layer sprayed-on elastomeric coatings that maintain a uniform conductivity at the surface. RAM is used selectively in areas such as control-surface gaps, doors and other apertures, and inside the inlet ducts.

The principles of RAM

RAM consists of an active element – a material such as carbonyl iron particles, which transform radar energy into heat – embedded in a dielectric plastic matrix. It is usually formulated and applied so that the small reflection from the front face of the absorber is cancelled by a residual reflection from the structure beneath it. The basic technique is to make the total pathway of energy within the RAM equal to half a wavelength, so that the residual reflection is exactly out of phase with the front-face reflection. The RAM can be much thinner than the nominal wavelength of the radar and still achieve cancellation, because the wavelength inside the material is much shorter than it is in free space.

Solid RAM coatings cover a frequency range of about 20:1. This is enough to address air-to-air and surface-to-air missile radars (from the L-band up to the Ku-band) but

more elaborate schemes are used to cover the full radar spectrum, which includes VHF radars with wavelengths of almost 2 m (6.5 ft).

Although the leading edges of the B-2 cannot be described in detail, a wide-band radar-absorbent structure (RAS), used on the edges of a stealth aircraft, has been compared to a stereo system, with a 'tweeter' and a 'woofer'. The 'tweeter' is a high-frequency ferromagnetic absorber, applied over a resistive layer that reflects higher frequencies but allows low-frequency signals to pass through. Beneath this resistive layer is the low-frequency 'woofer': a glass-fibre honeycomb core, treated from front to back with a steadily increasing amount of resistant material. Behind this is a sharp-edged, wedge-section reflective surface. What little energy reaches this surface will be attenuated once again before it escapes from the absorber.

Suppressing the IR signature

After radar, infra-red systems have the greatest potential range of any sensor. There are many types of infra-red sensor in service, and their different capabilities are sometimes confused. At a range of a few miles, a small IR sensor can receive enough energy to produce a TV-type image of the target, but this capability diminishes quickly with range.

Longer-range IR sensors, such as the infra-red search and track systems (IRSTS) fitted to fighters and the homing heads of IR-guided missiles, do not usually detect the IR emissions from the aircraft itself, but instead detect the radiation from the hot gas and water vapour emitted by its engines. The stealth designer's first task is therefore to deal with the exhausts.

The B-2's exhausts are built into the top of the wing. The primary nozzles are well ahead of the trailing edge, and lead into a pair of soft-lipped trenches, which flare outward. The engines are fitted with flow mixers to blend the cold bypass air with the hot core stream, and cold boundary layer which is swallowed by the secondary inlets is injected into the exhaust stream to cool it further. The exhausts are wide and flat, so the perimeter of the plume is longer than the perimeter of a round exhaust stream, and mixing takes place more quickly. Finally, the interaction between the exhaust stream and the airflow over the aircraft, at each angled side of the exhaust 'trench', creates a vortex which further promotes mixing.

At shorter ranges, IR systems detect radiation from the aircraft's skin. This is produced in two ways: from reflected sunlight and skin friction. IR-absorbent paints are widely used; containing compounds such as zinc sulfide, they work exactly like paints with visual colours, absorbing energy in a certain waveband. In this case, they absorb IR radiation from sunlight.

Heat generated by skin friction cannot be affected by an absorbing paint, but coatings have been developed which change the 'emissivity' of the surface – that is, the efficiency

with which it converts heat into IR radiation. Only certain bands of IR radiation travel efficiently through the atmosphere, so if the aircraft is coated with a substance that can shift energy into a different band, an IR detector may not be able to see it. IR emissions can also be reduced by slowing down or climbing into thinner air – both of which a B-2, with its modest wing loading, can do.

The most conspicuous element of the visual signature is not part of the aircraft, but its contrail, which can be suppressed by changing altitude. In 1995, NASA released

On 14 July 1994, during flight no. 36, AV-6 staged this unique formation with a pair of Lockheed F-117s. The orange diamond on the B-2's spine is a temporary test antenna (for TACAN or GPS, etc.). Another temporary test fit, the trailing wire rig, is seen here on AV-1 (above).

B-2 Spirit: The 'Stealth Bomber'

In October 1996 General Richard Hawley, Commander of Air Combat Command, stated that, "the B-2 is almost as revolutionary as the concept of flight itself. And true to its revolutionary capabilities, the B-2 is opening up new frontiers in the planning and execution of our national military strategy...it's an aircraft for all seasons – a true renaissance in aerial achievement." USAF air power theory proposes that the B-2 combines four characteristics never before combined in one aircraft: intercontinental range, large payload, precision weaponry and stealth technology. As the denial of foreign bases to US forces becomes increasingly likely, the B-2 is intended to stage from its home at Whiteman AFB, or from secure forward locations such as Guam in the Pacific Ocean or Diego Garcia in the Indian Ocean, from where it can strike virtually any target on the globe. The key to this capability will be the new range of precision-guided weapons now being fielded for the B-2. However, not one of the weapons currently earmarked for the B-2 yet has sufficient stand-off range to ensure that the B-2 will not come within lethal range of enemy air defences – so its stealthy credentials must be unassailable.

details of a LIDAR (light detection and ranging) system, being tested on an F/A-18, which would allow pilots to see their own contrails and change altitude to reduce them. The agency was later asked to stop talking about it in public, suggesting that a similar system may be used on stealth aircraft.

Suppressing the visible

Contrails can be made less visible by injecting chemicals into the exhaust that break the water into droplets which are smaller than the wavelength of visible light. In the 1960s, the USAF tested a system that injected chloro-flouro-sulfonic acid (CSA) into the exhaust stream on B-47 and B-52 bombers. CSA is toxic and corrosive and was abandoned in favour of a new, classified system that is in use on the B-2 and F-117. (One alternative in the open literature is an alcohol/surfactant mixture.)

Because the B-2's underside is a dark grey, people tend to think that it is intended to fight only at night. This is unlikely, because the B-2 was designed to bomb the Soviet Union, and the direct route from the central US to Central Russia lies smack across the Arctic Circle, where it is daylight 24 hours a day for a large part of the year.

Altitude is critical to visual signature. An airliner at its cruising height always appears brightly lit against the sky, regardless of whether it is finished in American's bare metal or United's formal grey. This is because both the aircraft and the sky above it are illuminated by light that is scattered by dust and moisture in the air. There is not much of either in the thin air above the aircraft, and lots of both below it.

The higher the aircraft flies, the more light is scattered onto its underside and the darker the sky behind it. The B-2's undersides are dark because it cruises at altitudes as high as 50,000 ft (15240 m), where a dark grey blends into the sky. It would not be surprising if the B-2 had an upward-facing light sensor that would instruct the pilot to increase or reduce altitude slightly to match the changing luminance of the sky.

Again, the goal is not to be invisible, but to be so hard to detect that no reliable and affordable detection scheme can be found. The sharpest fighter pilot has a hard time seeing another aircraft more than 5 nm (5.75 miles; 9.2 km) away, in the absence of a contrail or a 'cue'. The B-2 is likely to be at least 2 miles (3.2 km) away from any loitering fighter in the vertical plane alone – which also reduces the chance that it will be back-lit against the horizon.

The Red Team studied, built and tested acoustic detection devices, and determined that they did not present a threat to high-altitude aircraft. Even the quietest places on earth have too much background noise to permit high-flying aircraft to be detected. Finally, there is one signature that exceeds the range of radar, and provides even better identi-

One of the great benefits of Edwards AFB as a base for testing is the wide diversity of terrain and aerial climatic conditions that are just a short flight away. Though situated in the Mojave desert, Edwards is within 30 minutes flying time of the Pacific Ocean. The Sierra Nevada mountains and more rugged terrain are also close at hand to the flat dry lake bed at Muroc – which is not always dry and does receive some rainfall. Nearby Mt Whitney is the highest point in the 'lower 48'. This is an early view of AV-3 seen during B-2 test flight no. 8 on 22 November 1991.

fication: emissions from the aircraft's own systems. Stealth has been a major influence on the design, manufacture and cost of the B-2's mission avionics, which are designed to detect, identify and locate virtually any large surface target with no outside help, under any weather conditions – something which no other aircraft can do.

The mission crew and mission systems

The system is managed by the B-2's two-member crew. Both are rated pilots: the pilot occupies the left seat, and the mission commander sits on the right and has primary responsibility for navigation and weapon delivery. Behind the crew station is an area which is shared by avionics racks and space for a third crew station.

The cockpit is designed so that either crew member can perform the complete mission. Each pilot has four 6-in (15-cm) square, full-colour cathode ray tube (CRT) cockpit displays arranged in a T shape: they can display flight information, sensor inputs or systems data on command. Each pilot also has a data entry panel to his right, and a set of throttles to his left. (The throttles, like the flight controls, are linked electronically to the engines.) There is also a set of 'master mode switches' which configure the displays and computers for pre-flight, take-off, cruise and landing.

The space for a third seat, well behind the pilots' seats, was retained in case the workload proved too great. As it was, more than 6,000 hours of manned simulation had been carried out before the B-2 was unveiled, convincing SAC that two pilots would be enough.

The primary functions of the mission avionics are navigation, target detection and self-defence. The navigation sub-system (NSS) initially combined two units, either of which is capable of navigating the aircraft on its own but which are most accurate and reliable when they work together. One of them is an inertial measurement unit (IMU) from Kearfott, and the other is a Northrop NAS-26 astro-inertial unit (AIU). Northrop pioneered this technology in the early 1950s, when it developed the Snark long-range cruise missile.

The astro-inertial system developed for the Snark was based on a stabilised electro-optical telescope, capable of locking on to a pre-selected star even in cloudy daylight. A version of this system was used on the A-12 and SR-71, and an improved descendant is fitted to the B-2, with an observation port to the left of the windshield.

The Block 20 upgrade to the B-2 includes a global positioning system (GPS) receiver, with a specially developed low-observable antenna. GPS equals or surpasses the accuracy of the AIU, and will replace it in routine operations, although the AIU will remain in use as an unjammable backup.

LPI radar for the B-2

The B-2's APQ-181 radar (known as the radar sub-system or RSS) is developed by the Radar Systems Group of GM-Hughes Electronics. In the early days of the programme, B-2 critics often complained that the bomber would have no way of finding its targets at long stand-off ranges without betraying its presence by radar emissions. This argument was a measure of the effectiveness of the security which protected the development of low-probability-of-intercept (LPI) radar technology over many years. By the time the B-2 development programme started, in 1981, Hughes and Northrop had been actively developing LPI airborne radar for more than three years, under the Tacit Blue programme.

Weapons of the B-2: Past, present and future

B83

The B-2 was originally designed for nuclear strike, and its principal weapon in this role would be the B83 nuclear bomb. The B83 is the newest type of strategic nuclear bomb developed for the USAF, and was designed by the Department of Energy's Lawrence Livermore Nuclear Laboratory in California. It has a selectable yield of 1-2 MT (megatons), and is the first production bomb to be designed for 'laydown' delivery against hard, irregular targets. In such a delivery, the bomb is delay-fused so that the bomber can escape to a safe distance before the explosion. In contrast to airburst or contact fusing, however, this means that the bomb must survive the initial impact with the ground, and land without bouncing or rolling.

B61-11

The B-2 can also carry the B61-11 penetrating nuclear weapon, a newly developed bomb which has been produced by Sandia National Laboratory by modifying older B61s. The weapon has a needle-nosed casing packed with depleted uranium and no parachute, and is designed to bury itself up to 50 ft (15 m) into the ground before exploding. Sandia has also studied a gliding B61, but this has not yet been tested.

AGM-131A SRAM II (Short-Range Attack Missile)

The B-2 was also designed to use the Boeing AGM-131A SRAM II missile. SRAM II was a direct replacement for the original Boeing AGM-69 SRAM, which was designed in the 1960s. It consisted of a 200-kT warhead, a rocket motor and a Litton laser-gyro inertial navigation system. The SRAM II was due to enter service in 1993, but its development was terminated as part of the nuclear weapons cutbacks ordered by President Bush in September 1991.

AGM-137A TSSAM (Tri-Service Stand-off Attack Missile)

Another weapon intended for the B-2 was the Northrop AGM-137A TSSAM, a stealthy missile with a 250-nm (287-mile; 462-km) range, an 800-lb (360-kg) hard-target penetrator warhead and an autonomous precision guidance system. After a series of problems and cost overruns, however, TSSAM was cancelled in 1994.

GATS/GAM (GPS-Aided Targeting System/GPS-Aided Munition)

The demise of TSSAM left the B-2 in a paradoxical situation: the world's most sophisticated military aircraft, with an extremely accurate targeting system, was without any kind of precision weapon. This gap has been filled by a new class of weapon, which approaches the precision of a laser-guided bomb but is much less expensive and fully autonomous. The concept was simple: fit an inertial measurement unit in a bomb tail with moving fins, and, just before release, programme the weapon with the flightpath that the aircraft's weapon control system predicts that it will follow to the target. The guidance system will then take out random errors (such as those caused as the bomb wobbles through the aircraft's flow field) and unpredictable factors, such as changes in wind speed and direction. A number of companies, including Northrop, worked under USAF contracts in the later 1980s to develop this class of weapon.

After the Gulf War, in which coalition aircraft were forced to bomb from unexpectedly high altitudes, this concept was refined, with the addition of a global positioning system (GPS) receiver, and became the basis of a high-priority, large-scale programme: the Joint Direct Attack Munition (JDAM). Because this weapon would not be available until late in the decade, however, Northrop Grumman proposed a quick-reaction programme to build a small number of similar weapons for the B-2 force and to integrate a GPS receiver on the aircraft. This system is known as GPS Aided Targeting System/GPS Aided Munition. GATS is designed to reduce the target location error (TLE) of the B-2's bombing systems. Although the B-2's radar is capable of very high resolution, it includes inherent errors – such as INS error, uncertainty in the relative altitude of the target and the bomber, and Doppler error – which prevent the system from computing the exact distance from the aircraft to the target. This remaining zone of uncertainty is the TLE.

GATS uses GPS to correct for inertial error. In a GATS attack, the bomber makes a dog-leg approach to the target, taking several radar shots at the target and another fixed point from positions at least 30° apart. This changes the relationship among the components of TLE, allowing system software to estimate Doppler and altitude errors. The result is that GATS/GAM meets a circular error probability (CEP) requirement of 20 ft (6 m) (at least half the weapons will fall within 6 m of the target), compared with a 40 ft (13 m) CEP requirement for the standard JDAM. All 16 weapons can be released against different targets in a single pass. Alternatively, multiple weapons can be aimed at one target: the weapon is manoeuvrable enough to allow several weapons launched in sequence to strike the same target from their different release points.

The gliding bomb, a 2,000-lb Mk 84 bomb with a readily installed tail-kit, has a significant stand-off range. From a 40,000-ft (12195-m), Mach 0.8 release, the weapon can glide more than 13 nm (15 miles; 24 km) downrange, or 8 nm (8 miles; 15 km) downrange and crossrange, and hit its target at a 60° impact angle with undiminished accuracy. An all-up demonstration of GATS/GAM took place in October 1996. Three B-2s launched from Whiteman and dropped 16 live GAMs on 16 semi-trailers located on the Nellis AFB range. The leading aircraft dropped eight weapons, the rest being shared with the other two. All the targets were hit, and the third bomber used its radar to perform bomb damage assessment, imaging wreckage and the bomb craters.

JDAM (Joint Direct Attack Munition)/GBU-31

GATS will work with JDAM (Joint Direct Attack Munition) in exactly the same way as with GAM. McDonnell Douglas was selected to develop and produce JDAM in October 1995, and the weapon should achieve early operational capability on the B-2 Block 30 in July 1997. Its significance for the B-2 is that it can be used with the BLU-109 hard-target munition, allowing the B-2 to attack deeply buried or fortified targets. The Pentagon plans to acquire 87,000 JDAM guidance kits. The overall aim is to provide enough JDAMs to meet the needs of any future conflict without resorting to heavy unguided weapons. JDAM comprises a new tail with movable fins, containing a Honeywell ring-laser-gyro inertial measurement unit, a Lockheed Martin (Loral) computer, a Rockwell Collins GPS receiver and an HR Textron actuator

system. The weapon is powered by a thermal battery. Mated to a 2,000-lb warhead, either a Mk 84 blast/fragmentation type or a BLU-109, the weapon is designated GBU-31. From the outset, JDAM has been designed to be mated with a nose-mounted seeker for greater accuracy. Under current plans, a demonstration/validation programme for the seeker will start in 2002, which implies serious study of cost and performance issues from 2000 onwards. Another possibility is an extended-range JDAM with folding wings. Also under study is a 500-lb inertially guided weapon, of which the B-2 could carry and launch 76.

BLU-113/GAM-113

As JDAM enters service, it appears likely that the now-redundant GAM tail-kits will be mated with the BLU-113 hard-target penetrator. The 4,695-lb (2130-kg) BLU-113 warhead was originally developed in a quick-reaction programme during Desert Storm, in a thinly veiled attempt to 'decapitate' the Iraqi command by killing Saddam Hussein and his principal commanders. The first bombs were modified from Navy-surplus 203-mm gun barrels, fitted with nose and tail caps and mated to Texas Instruments Paveway III laser-guidance kits. In this form, the bomb was designated GBU-28. Since the retirement of the F-111F, it has been carried on the F-15E, and the USAF has acquired at least 100 new munitions from National Forge. A GAM-equipped version of the weapon, designated GAM-113, was test-dropped from a B-2 in early 1997: the bomber can carry eight GAM-113s, four on each rotary launcher.

The USAF is looking at other improvements to the BLU-113, including a hard target smart fuse (HTSF) which can count the layers in an underground structure (as the bomb passes through a void, its deceleration rate changes) and can be programmed to detonate at a certain level. A variant of the weapon with a tungsten-loaded explosive charge, weighing around 3200 kg (7,055 lb), could be used to increase the weapon's mass-to-diameter ratio and hence its penetration depth.

'Big BLU'

Before leaving the subject of deep-penetration weapons, it might be appropriate to mention the ultimate hard-target weapon, proposed by Lockheed Martin and known as 'Big BLU'. This would be a 10000-kg (22,045-lb) class bomb with a high-density nose section (filled with depleted uranium or a similarly dense material) and a GPS/inertial guidance system. In early 1997, 'Big BLU' was a candidate for Advanced Concept Technology Demonstrator funds, which would support the building of a small number of weapons for test and contingency operational use.

JASSM (Joint Air-to-Surface Stand-off Missile)

The USAF firmly plans to equip the B-2 with the JASSM, which is being developed as a less costly substitute for TSSAM. Lockheed Martin and McDonnell Douglas are competing to develop JASSM, and the USAF expects to announce a winner in the summer of 1998. The weapon is due to enter service in 2001, on the B-52. JASSM will be a 1000-kg (2,204-lb) class weapon with a 350-400-kg (771-881-lb) hard-target warhead, an autonomous precision guidance system (most likely, a GPS/INS mid-course system with an imaging infra-red terminal seeker) and a Teledyne J402 engine. The range is classified, but will be more than 250 km (155 miles). The B-2 will carry up to 16 JASSMs on its rotary launchers.

JASSM is the subject of some controversy, because the US Navy is campaigning to have the weapon cancelled in favour of its own SLAM-ER Plus. However, the USAF counters that the SLAM derivative will not fit on its bombers – a fundamental requirement for JASSM – and will probably cost more than JASSM, which is being developed under new procurement practices and is expected to cost at most $700,000 per round.

AGM-154 JSOW (Joint Stand-Off Weapon)

In early 1997, a contract was being negotiated to integrate the B-2 with the Texas Instruments AGM-154 JSOW. In its basic AGM-154A version (the only model to which the USAF is committed), JSOW is a GPS/inertial-guided gliding dispenser with a range of 75 km (46 miles) from the B-2's operating altitude, carrying a payload of Combined Effects Bomblets. It was originally developed for the US Navy as a defence-suppression weapon, because the CEBs are effective against targets such as missile sites. The B-2 can carry 16 JSOWs.

Other weapons

The Bomb Rack Assembly units can carry smaller weapons, including up to 80 225-kg (496-lb) Mk 82 bombs or 36 450-kg (992-lb) class Tactical Munitions Dispenser (TMD) weapons. The TMD is a USAF-standard weapon which can be loaded with CEBs or mines, and also forms the basis of the Textron Defense Systems Sensor Fuzed Weapon, which dispenses 40 IR-fused anti-armour weapons over the battlefield. Lockheed Martin is developing a Wind Corrected TMD with a simple inertial guidance system, which will allow weapons such as the SFW to be released at high altitude. So far, the WC-TMD is not slated for integration with the B-2, but it would pose no serious technical problems.

Above and left: The B-2 carries the majority of its weapons on a rotary launcher (above). Smaller bombs are dropped from the bomb rack assembly.

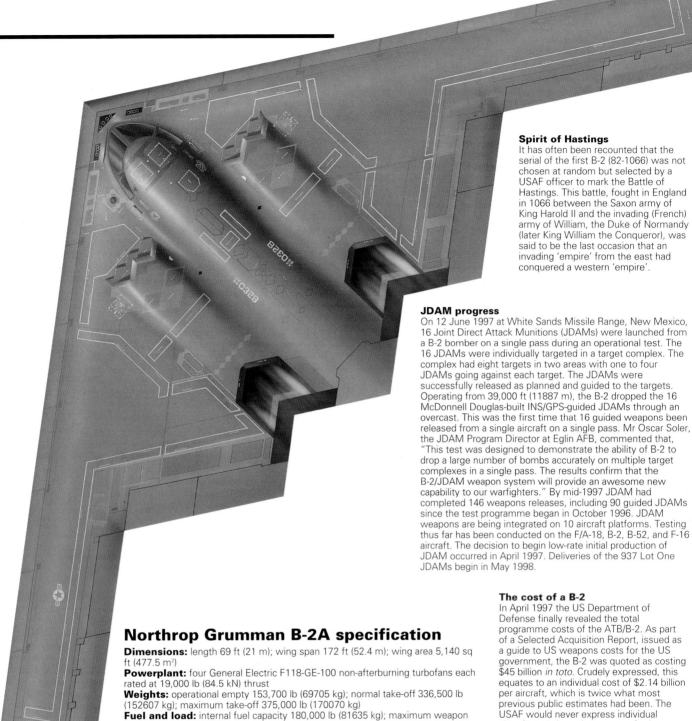

It has often been recounted that the serial of the first B-2 (82-1066) was not chosen at random but selected by a USAF officer to mark the Battle of Hastings. This battle, fought in England in 1066 between the Saxon army of King Harold II and the invading (French) army of William, the Duke of Normandy (later King William the Conqueror), was said to be the last occasion that an invading 'empire' from the east had conquered a western 'empire'.

JDAM progress
On 12 June 1997 at White Sands Missile Range, New Mexico, 16 Joint Direct Attack Munitions (JDAMs) were launched from a B-2 bomber on a single pass during an operational test. The 16 JDAMs were individually targeted in a target complex. The complex had eight targets in two areas with one to four JDAMs going against each target. The JDAMs were successfully released as planned and guided to the targets. Operating from 39,000 ft (11887 m), the B-2 dropped the 16 McDonnell Douglas-built INS/GPS-guided JDAMs through an overcast. This was the first time that 16 guided weapons been released from a single aircraft on a single pass. Mr Oscar Soler, the JDAM Program Director at Eglin AFB, commented that, "This test was designed to demonstrate the ability of B-2 to drop a large number of bombs accurately on multiple target complexes in a single pass. The results confirm that the B-2/JDAM weapon system will provide an awesome new capability to our warfighters." By mid-1997 JDAM had completed 146 weapons releases, including 90 guided JDAMs since the test programme began in October 1996. JDAM weapons are being integrated on 10 aircraft platforms. Testing thus far has been conducted on the F/A-18, B-2, B-52, and F-16 aircraft. The decision to begin low-rate initial production of JDAM occurred in April 1997. Deliveries of the 937 Lot One JDAMs begin in May 1998.

The cost of a B-2
In April 1997 the US Department of Defense finally revealed the total programme costs of the ATB/B-2. As part of a Selected Acquisition Report, issued as a guide to US weapons costs for the US government, the B-2 was quoted as costing $45 billion *in toto*. Crudely expressed, this equates to an individual cost of $2.14 billion per aircraft, which is twice what most previous public estimates had been. The USAF would never express individual aircraft costs in such terms, preferring instead more nebulous calculations such as 'flyaway cost' or 'then-year dollar price'.

Northrop Grumman B-2A specification

Dimensions: length 69 ft (21 m); wing span 172 ft (52.4 m); wing area 5,140 sq ft (477.5 m²)

Powerplant: four General Electric F118-GE-100 non-afterburning turbofans each rated at 19,000 lb (84.5 kN) thrust

Weights: operational empty 153,700 lb (69705 kg); normal take-off 336,500 lb (152607 kg); maximum take-off 375,000 lb (170070 kg)

Fuel and load: internal fuel capacity 180,000 lb (81635 kg); maximum weapon load 50,000 lb (22700 kg)

Performance: cruising speed Mach 0.85/485 kt/900 km/h at 36,000 ft (10972 m); speed at sea level Mach 0.8/530 kt/980 km/h; service ceiling above 50,000 ft (15240 m); range, unrefuelled with 8 SRAM and 8 B83 (37,300-lb/16919-kg) warload, 4,410 nm (8167 km; 5,075 miles) with a 1,000-nm (1852-km; 1,151-mile) low-altitude segment, or 6,300 nm (11667 km; 7,250 miles) at high level

Penetrating weapons
Lessons learned during the war against Iraq provided fresh impetus for research into weapons designed to destroy hardened or underground targets. Such research had been underway in the USA and UK since the 1980s, but at a leisurely pace. The realisation that many potential 'threat nations' such as Iran, Libya and North Korea were investing huge sums in developing large underground weapons manufacturing and operational facilities (in some cases for so-called Weapons of Mass Destruction/WMD), changed all that. By 1995, as part of its Advanced Concept Demonstration (ACTD) programme, the US had begun tests of 2,000-lb GBU-24 LGBs with BLU-109 penetrating warheads and new 'smart' fuses against earthmounded bunkers at the White Sands Missile range. Phase II of this testing (planned for 1998) calls for a weapon that can penetrate up to 6 m (19.6 ft) of hardened concrete. Such weapons are primarily intended for targets believed to be storing chemical or biological weapons. As such, they must be capable of destroying CW/BW agents without releasing them into the atmosphere. An air-droppable environmental sensor to detect agents in the air (before and after the attack) is also part of the potential package.

Controlling the RCS

The second element of the bomber's configuration was common to the F-117. While most of the surfaces could be concealed from radar by making them sloped or curved, the upper and lower surfaces of the aircraft would have to meet at some point. Wing and tail surfaces would also have distinct edges. How should this 'waterline' around the aircraft be handled? The edges and body sides could be treated with RAM, but not well enough to match the surfaces. Instead, the designers on both Have Blue teams realised that while the residual reflection from the edges could not be eliminated, it could be controlled, exploiting the fact that the strongest reflection was at right angles to the edge. The design was laid out so that all the edges were grouped along a small number of alignments. The RCS would peak when the radar was normal to one of these edges – but this would happen only transiently, as the aircraft moved relative to the radar and its bearing changed. Since there is scattering both from the edge of the aircraft that faces the radar and from the edge that faces away from it, the smallest practical number of 'spikes' is four. This can be produced from a pure diamond shape or – since a diamond will not fly very well – from a shape in which all edges conform to two alignments, as on the B-2. In a later refinement, both Lockheed and Northrop designers realised that the problem of combining stealth with doors and other apertures could be eased if they conformed to the same alignments as the wing and body edges. If necessary, door edges could be serrated so that the edges were angled while the aperture itself was rectangular. The breakthrough that got Northrop out of trouble on Tacit Blue in 1977 was the shaping technique that combined the sharp edges with the curved surfaces: a gradual flare to the knife-edge, still very visible on the lower surfaces of the B-2, combined with continuous curvature to make the energy flow around the aircraft. It is this combination of smoothly curved, seamless surfaces with jagged edges that makes the bomber's appearance so distinctive. Other aspects of low-RCS design had been clear from the first Harvey studies in 1975. Conventional engine installations and external weapons were dominant RCS contributors and would have to be eliminated. Tail surfaces were not impossible to deal with, but required careful design and had to be minimised in size and number.

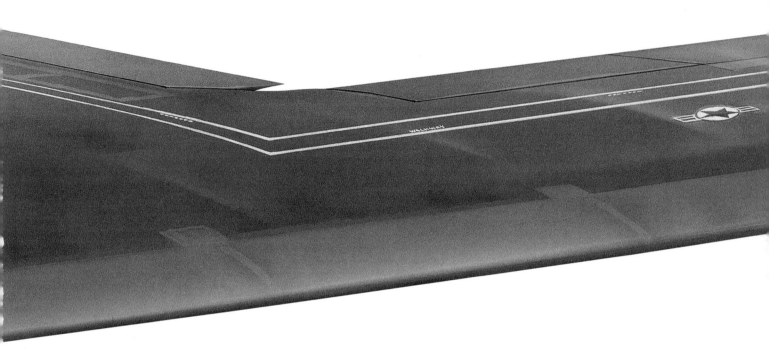

Northrop flying wing heritage

Jack Northrop's interest in tailless aircraft began when he was still an employee of Loughhead (before it became the Lockheed Aircraft Company), between 1919 and 1927. Northrop began working on his own design in the late 1920s and his Experimental No. 1 model flew in 1929. This aircraft did have a tail, but was a stepping stone to bigger and better things. The first true 'flying wing' was the unsuccessful N-1M which flew in July 1940. The N-1M's performance was very poor and the aircraft was reluctant to climb on take-off, let alone fly. With some changes to the aerofoil design its performance improved, and the N-1M itself survived and can be found today in the US National Air and Space Museum's Garber facility. The roots of the subsequent great Northrop flying wing bombers lay in the dark days of World War II when it looked as if Hitler's armies might overrun Britain, leaving the United States with a transatlantic war to fight. Preliminary requirements for a 'super bomber' that could make the round trip from the USA to Germany, carrying a 10,000-lb (4536-kg) bombload, resulted in several competing designs including Northrop's piston-powered B-35. The B-35 had the same 172-ft (52.42-m) wingspan as today's B-2 and weighed 100 tons. To build such an unprecedented aircraft was considered to be too great a technological leap, so Northrop first built the scaled-down N-9M (one-third the size of the B-35) to prove the concept. Though unpredictable in handling and at times downright uncontrollable, the N-9M proved that a flying wing could be built and flown. However, so great were the delays in the test and development programme that by the time the B-35 was ready to fly, the war was virtually over. As a result, all contracts were cancelled, leaving only two XB-35 experimental prototypes and 13 YB-35 service development aircraft to be built. Powered by four 3,000-hp (2238-kW) Pratt & Whitney Wasp Major R-4360-17 engines, the XB-35 first flew on 25 June 1946. Flying was such a mechanical nightmare that the two XB-35 aircraft spent a grand total of 36 hours in the air. The B-35 was already obsolete with the coming of the jet age, however, and USAF attention instead turned to building a jet-powered, eight-engined flying wing, the B-49. The B-49 simply swapped the new engines into the airframes of nine YB-35s and production proceeded smoothly and quickly. Fitted with eight General Electric TG-180/Allison J35 axial turbojets, the first YB-49 flew from Northrop's Hawthorne factory on 21 October 1947. The YB-49 encountered some minor problems such as its lack of fuel baffles, which left fuel sloshing back and forth through the large span-wise tanks, More serious was the loss of the stabilising effect of the piston-engines, prop-shafts and props, which lead to wing fences being incorporated on the jet flying wings. Most importantly, the YB-49 soon proved to be deficient in range, load-carrying ability and overall performance, and was essentially unable to carry out its intended mission as a long-range nuclear bomber. The seal was set on the story when aircraft No. 2 crashed on 5 June 1948, wildly out of control after having entered a tail slide during stall testing, killing test pilot Glen Edwards. The place of the B-49 was soon taken by Boeing's B-47, and all flying wing contracts were cancelled.

B83 nuclear bomb

In the strategic role the primary weapon of the B-2 is the B83, a megaton-class weapon with variable yields. It is cleared for carriage by a variety of aircraft, including tactical aircraft such as the F-16, F/A-18 and F-15E, but its high yield make it more applicable for carriage by the B-1B and B-2. It was developed as a cheaper alternative to the B77, development of which was cancelled in 1978. The B83 emerged with similar characteristics, and was the first strategic yield weapon designed for low-level laydown deliveries, replacing the B28, B43 and B53 weapons. Safety and versatility were the keywords in the bomb's development. It can be used from as low as 150 ft (46 m) and has a fully-variable fusing and yield, this being programmed by the crew in flight. The bomb uses very safe explosive initiators, which will not ignite even under extremes of temperature (such as may be caused in an aircraft fire) or if inadvertently dropped. The security code number system is highly complex, and if after a certain number of attempts the correct sequence has not been entered, a self-destruct mechanism is triggered, disabling key components without damaging the integrity of the radioactive material. The B83 was primarily targeted against hardened military targets such as ICBM silos, underground facilities and nuclear weapons storage facilities.

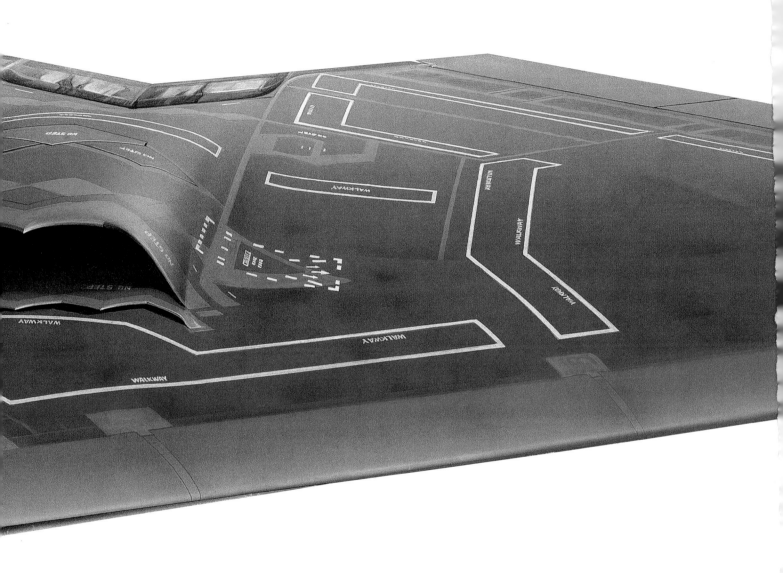

Defining the B-2 shape

The B-2's shape is the result of adding a new factor – observability – to the considerations which normally determine the general configuration of an aircraft, such as aerodynamics and the integration of the aircraft's major components. Northrop's low-RCS design philosophy, developed and tested on Tacit Blue, was quite straightforward but resulted in very unusual-looking aircraft, because it rested on two fundamental principles that drove different parts of the aircraft in opposite directions. The RCS of a conventional aircraft, which is a random irregular shape from an electromagnetic viewpoint, varies sharply with the aspect angle – that is, the radar's bearing from the aircraft. Whenever a radar illuminates the aircraft, most of its energy bounces off the surface like light from a mirror. The energy may well be reflected again from another part of the aircraft (bouncing off the body to the wing, for example). Some of the energy, too, will creep along the skin like St Elmo's fire, and will be scattered whenever it reaches a gap or a change in conductivity. A basic principle behind low-RCS design is that a flat plate has both the largest and smallest RCS of any simple shape. If the plate is normal to the radar beam, its RCS is enormous; but if it is rotated away from the beam in one dimension, its RCS is far smaller, and if it is rotated in two dimensions (rotated and canted) its RCS is minute. In the F-117, Lockheed's designers produced a shape composed entirely of flat plates, aligned so that they were, at almost all times, angled away from the radar beam in two dimensions. Most radar sources that matter are now located in a narrow band of elevations around the aircraft. However, this led to a secondary problem: creeping waves over the surface tended to be scattered from the sharp edges of the shape. Unable to model these effects fully, Lockheed beat them into insignificance by 'candy-coating' the entire aircraft with RAM. Cashen's electromagneticists saw that the same results – ensuring that every part of the surface was angled away from the radar in two dimensions – could also be achieved if the surface was curved. Indeed, if the entire skin of the aircraft comprised one surface, with curving contours of constantly changing radius and direction, there might be no edges or creases at all, avoiding any 'hot spots' in the RCS. This was the first basic principle of the B-2's shape.

Northrop Grumman B-2A

The only aircraft which have ever looked remotely like the B-2 were flown in the 1940s, when designers in the United States, Britain and Germany were pursuing the idea of an all-wing aircraft, or flying wing. As its name suggests, the all-wing aircraft has neither fuselage nor tail, but carries all its payload, fuel and components inside the wing. Even those distant ancestors did not share the single dominating, most bizarre feature of the B-2's shape. Viewed from directly above or below, the B-2's boomerang-like shape comprises 12 ruler-straight lines. The leading edges, the long sides of the boomerang, run straight from the extreme nose to the extreme tips of the wing. The wingtips are not parallel with the airflow, like those on most normal aircraft, but are cut off at a near-right angle to the leading edges. Apart from the tips, the outer wings have no taper: again, this is completely unlike any normal aircraft. The inner trailing edges form a jagged shape, jutting rearward toward the centreline. A closer inspection shows that the edges form two groups of six exactly parallel lines. Look at the B-2 from any point in the horizontal plane, however, and the shape changes. In front, rear or side view, the bomber has virtually no straight lines and no hard edges. The top and bottom surfaces are both continuous, three-dimensional curved surfaces. Even the overwing air inlets, which look jagged from a distance, can be seen at close range to be made up of many curved segments. There are even very few curves of constant radius; rather, the surfaces change radius continuously, as though they were produced from segments of a spiral. The shape has no abrupt distinctions between body and wing; a dorsal hump with the cockpit in front rises smoothly from the top surface, but the underside swells gradually from the outermost trailing-edge kink to the centreline.
Combined with the things that the eye expects to see, but which are not there – engine pods, a fuselage, a vertical fin and a stabiliser – the effect is to make the B-2 look like something organic rather than a machine.

Spirit of Texas
As it is handed over to the 509th Bomb Wing, each B-2 is named – all but one for a US state. Cynics might point out that the choice of names parallels the voting record of particular Congressional delegations when it came to making crucial B-2 funding decisions in Washington, DC. The first production aircraft (88-0328) was named *Spirit of Texas* when it was delivered to Whiteman AFB in September 1994. It is seen here armed with GAM-113 GPS-aided penetrating bombs, which are carried on a rotary launcher in the B-2's bomb bay. The B-2 can carry up to 16 of the 4,700-lb (2132-kg) weapons.

Future B-2s
As Congress continued its work on the FY 1998 Pentagon budget in the summer of 1997, the House of Representatives voted to spend $331 million on keeping the B-2 line open, with a view to ordering another nine aircraft for delivery in the first decade of the 2000s. These funds would have to be approved by the Senate or by a House-Senate conference,which is believed by all concerned to be a very remote possibility. The USAF itself has not requested any B-2 funding since the early 1990s – a tacit acknowledgement that the sparse available funds might be better spent elsewhere. However Congressional supporters of the B-2 consistently attempt to have more aircraft built.

B-2 Production and Deliveries

Development

Construction number	Air Vehicle	Serial	First flight	Delivered as Block 30
1001	AV-1	82-1066	17/7/1989	6/2000
1002	AV-2	82-1067	19/10/1990	8/1997
1003	AV-3	82-1068	18/6/1991	10/1999
1004	AV-4	82-1069	17/4/1992	2/2000
1005	AV-5	82-1070	5/10/1992	7/1999
1006	AV-6	82-1071	2/2/1993	1/1998

Production

Construction number	Air Vehicle	Serial	Name	Delivered	Block	Upgraded/delivered Block 20	Upgraded/delivered Block 30
1007	AV-7	88-0328	*Spirit of Texas*	9/1994	10		9/1998
1008	AV-8	88-0329	*Spirit of Missouri*	12/1993	10		11/1997
1009	AV-9	88-0330	*Spirit of California*	8/1994	10		6/1998
1010	AV-10	88-0331	*Spirit of South Carolina*	12/1994	10		4/1998
1011	AV-11	88-0332	*Spirit of Washington*	10/1994	10		1/1999
1012	AV-12	89-0127	*Spirit of Kansas*	2/1995	10	9/96	12/1998
1013	AV-13	89-0128	*Spirit of Nebraska*	6/1995	10	7/96	3/1999
1014	AV-14	89-0129	*Spirit of Georgia*	11/1995	10	5/97	4/1999
1015	AV-15	90-0040	*Spirit of Hawaii*	1/1996	10	3/97	7/1999
1016	AV-16	90-0041	*Spirit of Alaska*	12/1995	10	11/96	8/1999
1017	AV-17	92-0700	*Spirit of Oklahoma*	7/1996	20		11/1999
1018	AV-18	93-1085	*Spirit of Florida*	6/1996	20		1/2000
1019	AV-19	93-1086	*Spirit of Kitty Hawk*	8/1996	20		4/2000
1020	AV-20	93-1087	*Spirit of*	10/1997	30		
1021	AV-21	93-1088	*Spirit of*	12/1997	30		

The first production B-2 to be delivered: AV-8 (88-0329)

The second production B-2 to be delivered: AV-9 (88-0330)

The third production B-2 to be delivered: AV-7 (88-0328)

The fourth production B-2 to be delivered: AV-11 (88-0332)

The fifth production B-2 to be delivered: AV-10 (88-0331)

The sixth production B-2 to be delivered: AV-12 (89-0127)

The seventh production B-2 to be delivered: AV-13 (89-0128)

The eighth production B-2 to be delivered: AV-14 (89-0129)

The ninth production B-2 to be delivered: AV-16 (90-0041)

The 10th production B-2 to be delivered: AV-15 (90-0040)

The 13th production B-2 to be delivered: AV-19 (93-1086)

 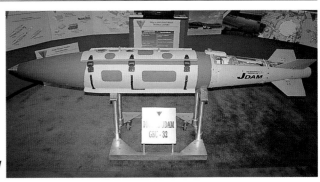

Left: On 15 June 1995 the first GAM bomb drop (a GAM-84) was made by a B-2 over the China Lake ranges. The test was a 'long-range' drop, made 45,000 ft (13716 m) 'uprange' of the target.

Right: The GBU-31 JDAM (which, like GAM-84, is based on a 2,000-lb Mk 84 bomb) will be the second PGM to be B-2 qualified.

Top: AV-4 is seen here in November 1993, in formation with one of the test force's F-16B chase planes, before all the F-16s adopted a red and white 'high-vis' scheme. The F-16s accompanied the B-2 as a 'visual augmentor' because, in many circumstances, they were easier for other traffic to see than the B-2 itself.

Right: AV-3 seen hooked up to a KC-135E at dusk during its flight no. 57, on 10 June 1993.

The APQ-181 has two 265-kg (584-lb) electronically scanned antennas built into the lower leading edge of the wing, one on each side. Each radar antenna has its own power supply, transmitter/receiver and signal processing unit, and the two chains are cross-connected so that the radar can continue to perform even if part of one chain fails. The radar operates in the Ku-band (12-18 GHz), which is a higher frequency and shorter wavelength than the X-band (around 10 GHz) where most airborne radars operate. Ku-band radars suffer from more atmospheric absorption than X-band, and are less suitable for large-area searches because, all other things being equal, they require more power and more time to scan a given volume. However, they have inherently higher resolution than X-band radars, and, for a given antenna size, a Ku-band radar will have smaller and weaker sidelobes that will dissipate more quickly.

APQ-181 modes

Among the most important of the radar's 20 modes are a synthetic aperture radar (SAR) mode, and terrain following and terrain avoidance (TF/TA). The latter modes provide data to dual TF/TA processors which interface with the flight control system. The radar has a ground moving target indication (GMTI) mode to detect vehicles on the ground,

The basic principle of LPI is to emit the least amount of energy required to detect and track the target, while manipulating the signal to make it difficult for an adversary to detect it among all the electronic burps, honks and squeals that pollute the high-tech battlefield. LPI techniques include the adaptive management of power (the radar gradually increases its power until it can see a target, and then holds its power level or reduces it as the range declines), the use of very-low-sidelobe antennas, and constant variations in frequency and waveform.

and an LPI air-to-air mode which may be used during inflight refuelling, as well as more conventional long-range mapping and weather modes.

Radar development proved difficult and expensive. The first experimental radar antenna in the programme flatly refused to transmit a coherent beam. The problem caused near-panic in the programme office, but it was soon realised that it was due to leakage among the ports in the electronically scanned antenna: the antenna had not been built to sufficiently tight tolerances. Each antenna included more than 400 precision-machined parts with a total of 600,000 high-tolerance features. Among those parts were 85 'phasor plates', machined from a solid slab of magnesium in a cutting process during which the machine head moves 6.4 km (3.7 miles). Using conventional machining, each plate would take 25 hours of cutting work – which meant that one machine working regular hours would take two years to build this single part for one aircraft. Hughes addressed the problem by introducing the emerging technology of high-speed machining, with cutter heads rotating at 25,000-75,000 rpm. This reduced the machining time to 4.5 hours for each of the plates, making the manufacture of the antenna practicable – if still not exactly cheap.

ZSR-62 and -63: the mystery DMS

The third main element of the B-2 mission avionics is the defensive management sub-system (DMS). Details of the DMS, which includes components from Lockheed Martin, Raytheon and Honeywell, are largely classified. However, its most important element appears to be the Lockheed Martin (formerly Loral, and before that, IBM) APR-50, which has also been identified by the internal designation ZSR-63.

The ZSR-63 replaced an earlier Northrop-developed system called ZSR-62, which was abandoned after encountering development problems. As far as is known, this was the only major sub-system to be scrapped during development, a measure of the difficulty of the DMS task. All details of the problems with the ZSR-62 remain secret.

The APR-50 is designed to detect, classify, identify and locate hostile systems that emit radio-frequency energy. Although the B-2's mission can be pre-planned to present

the aircraft's least detectable aspects to known threats, there is always the risk that some radars have been moved or have not been detected before the mission. The APR-50 – which has been compared to the electronic surveillance measures capability of a dedicated electronic warfare aircraft such as the EA-6B – provides the B-2 crew with real-time updates. It consists of an automated signal-processing and analysis system, linked to receiver antennas distributed across the airframe.

In combat, the B-2's information management system and cockpit displays should be able to 'fuse' data from many sources. Radar imagery, for example, will be superimposed on maps of the target area, acquired by satellite and stored onboard the B-2. The physical and electronic characteristics of known threats can also be stored and fused. If an SA-5 radar is detected, the system can display its location, its predicted area of coverage and the bomber's projected track on the CRT; the crew can determine instantly whether a course change is necessary.

Above: AV-4 seen during flight no. 194 on 28 February 1997 in the pattern for Vandenburg AFB. The white marks on the leading edges are for icing tests – the tests were long since finished but the markings were never removed. Note the drag rudders open to 45° for approach and the drooped gust alleviation surface on the tail.

Top: AV-6 is seen here on a rare humid day over Edwards in March 1994 with a strong laminal condensation flow building up as the aircraft approaches its critical Mach number.

Much of the avionics system is based on 13 common avionics control unit (ACU) processors (built by a former Unisys unit which is now part of Lockheed Martin), which carry out several functions which, in earlier systems, were performed by special-purpose computers: TF/TA, navigation, defensive systems and stores management are all carried out by ACUs. Designed to stringent requirements for radiation-hardening and vibration tolerance (some of them are installed in the aft centrebody, between the engine exhausts), the ACUs can be expanded to handle more complex processing tasks through new software.

The navigation and radar systems have been tested on a Boeing C-135, known as the flight-test avionics laboratory (FTAL), which made its first flight in January 1987. The FTAL was needed because many radar modes cannot be adequately tested on a static test rig and some (such as SAR) cannot be demonstrated at all except in the air.

Programme history

In 1997, more than 15 years after the B-2 was designed, it is interesting to ask how many other combat aircraft in service have multi-mode LPI radars; how many incorporate what can almost be classed as a signals intelligence system; how many use differential thrust for control; how many are primarily built from composite materials. The answer to these and many other questions is a Big Fat Zero. Little wonder, then, that the B-2 development was not easy.

In mid-1997, the initial B-2 flight-test programme is drawing to a close, eight years after the bomber's first flight, and the first fully operational aircraft is ready for delivery to the USAF. Quite clearly, there have been some delays in the programme, along with the cost overruns that inevitably accompany such delays. Pervasive secrecy has made it extremely difficult to put together the entire story of the programme. Even what follows is a preliminary account of a story that remains very sensitive, for reasons of politics and national security.

When the B-2 programme started, in October 1981, the first aircraft was planned to fly around the end of 1987. By that time, a concurrent production programme would be

under way, with the rate increasing as the 'learning curve' took effect. The bomber would attain an initial operating capability (IOC) in 1991 or 1992; around then, the production rate would attain a peak of 30 aircraft per year.

A common factor in almost any project that runs late is excessive optimism at the outset, and the B-2 was no exception. In a 1996 interview, Dr Paul Kaminski noted that hopes for stealth were high when the B-2 started. "The success of the F-117 had set up expectations. It was a given that we could achieve everything that we could do on the F-117, while eliminating all its deficiencies and limitations. But it wasn't just like falling off a log."

B-2 versus B-1

From the start, the B-2 was affected by the progress of the B-1B programme. In fact, work on the B-2 was quite slow for the first year, because the B-1B was 'ramping up' so quickly and absorbing most of the available money. Most of that time was taken up with the wing redesign; by extensive penetration studies, to validate the basic principles of the design; and by a lengthy study of the two-versus-three-crew issue.

However, the target first-flight and IOC dates did not change during 1983, despite the fact that the wing redesign had put the programme about a year behind where it was expected to be. The reason was in large measure political. Rockwell, teamed with Lockheed, was still actively promoting a follow-on B-1, and there was some concern that delays in the B-2 programme, acknowledged so early in its life, would make an improved B-1 more attractive.

The USAF was concerned about technical risks, and set up a 'risk closure' programme in which large-scale tests (such as the full-scale inlet rig) were used in an attempt to identify and solve problems before they could manifest themselves on the full-size aircraft. Designer Irv Waaland calls it "the world's most complete R&D programme." There was a belief that nothing should go untested. This philosophy has been sustained throughout the programme. To this day, it ensures that what is delivered to the user actually works, but it does not foster rapid progress.

Security was a larger-than-expected factor in the cost of the programme. Have Blue and Tacit Blue had been developed in strict secrecy, but they were smaller programmes. They were developed by small, hand-picked teams, and as few people as possible were told that they existed. The companies did not need to hire new people to build the aircraft, and many components were bought from third-party suppliers who did not need to know to purpose to which their products were put.

On those programmes, "we protected the perimeters," says Waaland. "We researched people, investigated and did background checks, but information within the programme was free-flowing. On the B-2, we introduced total accountability for everything." At any time, the USAF expected to be able to ask the location of any document in the programme. "It really added costs and reduced productivity."

Secrecy, on the B-2, "had many non-beneficial aspects," Kaminski says now. The classification level meant that the most stringent regulations had to be put into effect over thousands of sub-contractors. Tens of thousands of newly hired people had to be security vetted and tested for drug use (this in Los Angeles, in the early 1980s). The vetting system was swamped, and many employees spent weeks in limbo, on the payroll but unable to work. Overall, secrecy added 10-15 per cent to the cost of the programme.

Together with the technical challenges in every area – manufacturing, controls, avionics – these measures drove up costs and caused delay. However, since no schedule had been published, and since the project was shrouded in secrecy, public criticism was muted – at least for a time.

Out of the black and into the flak

The B-2 emerged from the black on 22 November 1988, when AV-1 (82-1066) was unveiled at Palmdale. Invited guests were allowed to view only the front of the bomber, and no pictures of the planview were released – a security measure that failed to deter *Aviation Week*'s Mike Dornheim, who flew a photographer over the roll-out site, above the minimum altitude set by the FAA, and secured clear shots of the planview shape and exhaust nozzles.

By this time, the programme was drawing more criticism from the media and from politicians. The fact that the production and service-entry schedule was still secret tended to heighten speculation that there were serious problems with the B-2. In fact, the programme was running 18-24 months behind the original schedule, and AV-1 was far from ready to fly: many internal parts had not been installed when it rolled out.

There were understandable reasons behind the delays: the B-2 had undergone a major redesign, it was breaking ground in many areas, and the programme philosophy favoured completeness over schedule. These were all secret, so the public and the media were left to draw their own conclusions as the winter of 1988 turned into the summer of 1989 and AV-1 remained firmly on the ground. Scepticism about the management of Air Force programmes in general, and bombers in particular, had been fostered by intractable problems with the B-1B's defensive avionics system. Ironically, the root of these problems was that crucial tests had not been performed before the design was committed to production, in direct contrast to the cause of the B-2 delays. Nevertheless, Congress became reluctant to commit the B-2 to production until flight tests were well advanced. Representative Les Aspin, the Wisconsin Democrat who chaired the House Armed Services Committee, used his committee to block full-rate production.

Under the original plan, B-2 production should have picked up pace in the FY88-89 budgets. B-2s could be delivered 60 months after being ordered, putting large-scale deliveries and full operational capability in 1994-95. But

The 509th BW at Whiteman AFB, MO gained Initial Operational Capability (IOC) on 1 April 1997. The granting of IOC enables the B-2 to be included in any contingency plans for combat operations on a limited basis. On 19 and 20 March the type performed one of its longest non-stop Global Power missions to date when 92-0700 flew from Whiteman AFB across the Atlantic Ocean before heading for the Vieques Range off Puerto Rico to deliver live conventional weapons. The 30-hour mission involved four inflight refuellings, including one by a KC-135R of the 100th ARW from RAF Mildenhall which rendezvoused near the Azores.

On 11 June 1995 B-2 88-0329/Spirit of Missouri (AV-1008) made the type's first appearance outside the USA, with a 1-hour 20-minute visit to the Paris air show. The aircraft was flown by Brigadier General Ronald Marcotte, commander of the 509th BW, and Major Jim Smith, who acted as mission commander.

The B-2 dropped out of the grey skies over Le Bourget right on schedule, at 10:00 a.m., and made several figure of eight circuits around the airfield, including steeply banked turns, before landing to steal the show at the 41st Paris Salon. The Paris appearance was part of an 11-hour 30-minute Global Power training mission from Whiteman AFB to the Vliehors bombing range in the Netherlands, where the B-2 simulated the dropping of 16 Mk 84 bombs before arriving at the show. The B-2 remained on the ground under heavy guard, with its engines running.

The GBU-31 JDAM (Joint Direct Attack Munition) is a 2,000-lb Mk 84 bomb body (with an optional BLU-109 hardened target penetrating warhead) fitted with a laser-ring gyro, GPS receivers and actuated fins along the body. JDAM was built to a requirement that demanded a CEP of 13 m (42.6 ft), but has demonstrated a CEP of 9 m (29.5 ft). The first JDAM was dropped from a B-2 on 28 February 1997. From a release point of 40,000 ft (12192 m) – at Mach 0.8, with an impact angle of 60° – JDAM can travel up to 13 miles (21 km) to the target.

Congress refused to appropriate the money. The start of production was, first, delayed to take account of the late start of flight-testing; then, it was further postponed so that more flight tests, including the first stage of observables testing, could be completed before production could begin. Preparations for production were well under way, and more than 40,000 people were working on the B-2 programme. Suspending production would have had a catastrophic impact; workers would have been lost, together with their hard-earned knowledge, and many sub-contractors would have had to find other business. Instead, the programme was stretched out, so that the USAF would buy only two or three B-2s per year until the start of full-rate production was authorised.

The maiden flight, and storm clouds

On 17 July 1989 AV-1 made its 2-hour 20-minute first flight from Palmdale to Edwards AFB. Pilots were Bruce Hinds, chief test pilot for the Northrop B-2 Division, and Colonel Richard Couch, commander of the B-2 Combined Test Force at Edwards AFB.

The mass media, which had largely ignored the B-2 during its years of secret development, were overwhelmingly negative in their coverage of the bomber in 1989 and 1990. Influential outlets such as *Newsweek* and the high-

rated TV magazine *60 Minutes* ran damning anti-B-2 diatribes, long on hyperbole, short on evidence and entirely free of balance. Flying-wing critics from the 1940s emerged from holes in the woodwork and were reverently quoted in major newspapers. Northrop employees alleged that there were safety-of-flight problems with the bomber. They were also widely quoted, and the media seldom explained clearly that they were allied with attorneys bringing actions under the Civil War-era False Claims Act, under which the whistle-blowers and their lawyers stood to make fortunes if claims were upheld or settled.

In June 1990, the Air Force held a B-2 media briefing at Palmdale, and described the B-2 and its planned missions in unprecedented detail. The *Wall Street Journal*'s reporter summed up the USAF's entire case in one word: "tendentious". In the same report, he quoted Congressman John Kasich, an opponent of the B-2, as saying that the B-2 would "bankrupt America". Considering that the programme's peak annual cost at the time was one per cent of the defence budget, that statement could (and should) have been called something more than tendentious.

The case for the B-2 was not helped by the fact that the apparent progress with the programme was slow. By June 1990, AV-1 had flown only 16 times, for some 67 hours. There had been one mechanical problem – cracking in the aircraft mounted accessory drive (AMAD) casings – but it had been anticipated as a result of earlier tests and was solved fairly quickly. AV-2 (82-1067) was still in final assembly, and would not fly until 19 October 1990. On its maiden flight AV-2 followed AV-1's original route, flying from Palmdale to Edwards also.

Although the programme was behind the original schedule, it was not out of control; the USAF was doing what it could to mitigate the impact of Congress's changes to the programme. By mid-1989, it was clear that the B-2 could not be declared fully operational for many years, because there would not be enough aircraft available to form a squadron. Congress had authorised procurement of only 11 flying B-2s – six development aircraft and five production aircraft, the last of which would not be delivered until late 1994. Long-lead items for five more B-2s had been authorised, but these aircraft would not be ready until 1995.

Congress had blocked full-rate production until the B-2 passed its critical RCS tests, but AV-1 would not be ready to perform them until late 1990 and they would not be complete until the summer of 1991. Since it took five years from go-ahead to build a B-2, full-rate deliveries could not start until 1996, even if everything went perfectly.

Accordingly, the B-2 programme office, in 1989, defined a test programme that would finish in June 1997. The last items to be completed would be the final radar modes, because some of them (such as TF/TA) could not start their testing until other parts of the system, such as the navigation and flight control systems, had been fully validated.

The long gap between AV-1 and AV-2 reflected Northrop's concentration of its efforts on getting AV-1 in the air, to validate the bomber's flight performance and to prepare for the RCS tests, because until that could be done there would be no go-ahead for production. The company was reluctant to increase its workforce to build the development aircraft, and then end up with more people than were needed for low-rate production, so work on AV-2 and subsequent aircraft slowed down.

But the USAF, still under heavy fire from the media and Congress, was justifiably concerned about what might happen if it were revealed that the new bomber was still seven to eight years away from a full operational capability – even though the bulk of the delay could be attributed directly to Les Aspin and the House Armed Services Committee. The IOC date for the bomber remained secret.

Affirming its LO credentials

AV-1 went into a lay-up period in the late summer of 1990, and resumed flying in November to carry out initial RCS measurements. Details of the process are still classified, but the tests were carried out incrementally, with components being adjusted and individual 'hot spots' being treated between flights until the desired RCS was attained.

Some of the tests involved flights against ground-based radars, while other tests were performed on the ground, with radars that moved on tracks to image parts of the aircraft. For air-to-air measurements – the only opportunity to examine the aircraft with its wheels up, its engines running and with no interference from the ground – Northrop used a NTA-3B Skywarrior bomber modified by Metratek to carry its Model 100 AIRSAR radar, in a bizarre frying-pan-shaped radome on the rear fuselage.

There were two significant differences between the B-2 and the F-117, the only stealth aircraft to have passed through full-scale development before it. First, it was much bigger, and it was too large to test on an RCS range at anything like full scale. The largest B-2 model that could be

To many, the prospect of the B-2 carrying loads of dumb bombs is alarming, but these weapons (including CBUs and mines) are still included in its notional warloads. AV-4 is seen here conducting conventional bomb drops with a full load of 500-lb Mk 82 bombs in August 1995 (above left) and then, in March 1997, with 750-lb M117 bombs. The B-2 can carry 80 Mk 82s or 36 M117s. The Vietnam-era M117 is an anachronism and quite why such a vintage weapon has been qualified for use with the B-2 is a mystery.

The first bomb to be tested by a B-2 was a 2,000-lb Mk 84, which was dropped from AV-4 on 12 September 1992. The Mk 84 forms the core of the GAM-84 (GPS-Aided Munition), part of the family of GAM bombs now in development for the B-2 and other aircraft. By January 1997 B-2s had reached limited operational capability with the GAM-84, which is essentially a Mk 84 bomb centrebody with a new tail section. The tail kit, which can be bolted on to any existing bomb, contains two GPS antennas and steerable fins with a MIL-STD 1760 interface for the B-2. A grooved 'tie-on' sleeve is also fitted to the nose of the bomb, which keeps it aerodynamically stable while guiding.

B-2 Spirit: The 'Stealth Bomber'

tested was about one-third of full size, whereas Lockheed had tested the F-117 at 70 per cent scale. The B-2 was also designed for stealth across a wider range of aspects and frequencies than the F-117; in particular, its leading edges were required to attenuate VHF frequencies – used by the Soviet 'Tall King' early warning radar – more efficiently than those of the F-117. These differences were at the root of the problems encountered in RCS testing. Higher-than-predicted reflections were found very early on, and by the summer it was clear that simple adjustments were not enough. The media and Congress panicked, and Air Force Secretary Donald Rice issued elaborate statements to quell the crowd without betraying any significant information.

Behind the scenes, the Pentagon's Defense Science Board reviewed the problems. Although details are classified, most observers believe that the problems were encountered in the VHF realm, where stealth is hardest to achieve, and that they were attributable to problems such as gaps, surface discontinuities and creeping waves, which are very difficult to model or predict and which cannot be adequately tested on a scale model.

An early conclusion was that the problems could be solved by changing coatings and edge materials; there was no need to alter the basic structure of the aircraft, so that any solution to the problem could be retrofittable, and B-2 production could be continued. The DSB also noted that, with the break-up of the Soviet Union, it might make sense to relax the RCS specification in some respects, to reflect threats that the bomber was likely to face, rather than to spend far more money to meet the original requirement.

It was announced in early 1993 that Northrop, Boeing and Lockheed had developed a set of RCS improvements that would be applied to the last B-2s off the line and retrofitted to earlier aircraft. This fix was described as the least costly and risky of three options which had been studied.

More B-2s in the air

Meanwhile, the remaining test aircraft had joined the programme. AV-3 (82-1068), first flown on 18 June 1991, was the first radar and navigation test aircraft. AV-4 (82-1069) and AV-5 (82-1070), designated for avionics and weapons testing, followed on 17 April and 5 October 1992, respectively. The last development aircraft, AV-6 (82-1071), flew on 2 February 1993. The NKC-135A avionics testbed resumed flying in 1992 to support tests of the TF/TA radar modes. In early 1993, AV-1 was placed in storage – with its incomplete avionics suite and non-standard instrumentation, it could no longer contribute to the programme.

The first production B-2, AV-1007 (88-0328), was delivered to Whiteman AFB, Missouri, in December 1993.

By then, however, it was clear that – barring a miracle – Whiteman would be the only operational B-2 base, because the programme had been scaled back to near extinction.

By 1990, with the Soviet Union on the verge of breaking up, the Democratic Congress was pressing the Bush administration for cuts in defence expenditures – the so-called peace dividend. The B-2 was a prime target, but the larger concern was that several large aircraft programmes – the B-2, the Navy's A-12 attack aircraft, the Advanced Tactical Fighter and the C-17 transport – were expected to be in full-rate production by the mid-1990s, and they could not all be supported by lower budgets.

A temporary compromise was announced in April 1990, when Defense Secretary Richard Cheney unveiled the results of the Pentagon's Major Aircraft Review (MAR).

The MAR kept all the Pentagon's aircraft projects alive, but sharply reduced production numbers in the mid-1990s. Under the MAR, the total planned B-2 buy was cut from 132 to 75, and the production rate was cut drastically; instead of a steady increase to a maximum of 33 aircraft in the final year, the rate would reach a plateau of 12 aircraft a year in the mid-1990s. Then-year programme cost would decline from $75.4 billion (having increased since late 1988 due to the delay in production) to $61.1 billion.

A 19 per cent cost saving as a result of a 43 per cent cut in output may seem asymmetric, but it has to be remembered that the non-recurring costs of the programme were unaffected by the cutback (most of them had been spent) and savings were further offset by the lower and less efficient production rate.

Ironically, one of the programmes preserved by the MAR, largely at the B-2's expense, was the Navy's A-12.

Cheney and Congress were equally unaware that the A-12 was in grave trouble, because the Navy was concealing the problems that had resulted from the arrogance and ineptitude of the service's top commanders and civilian leaders. Nine months later, the programme was dead.

Production freeze

Neither did the MAR satisfy Congressional foes of the B-2. In October 1991, Congress froze production at 16 aircraft, in the aftermath of the summer's failed military coup in the Soviet Union, the irreversible rupture of the Warsaw Pact, and the bad news from the RCS tests. In an attempt to turn the apparently inevitable halting of the programme into a political asset in an election year, President Bush announced in January 1992 that the administration would seek funds for only five more B-2s, bringing production to 21 including the six test aircraft. The cutback

Left: The B61-11 bomb is now the other arrow in the B-2's nuclear quiver. The B61-11 is a modification of the existing B61-7 bomb, specially altered for a specific task – destroying underground targets. The USAF already had a nuclear weapon tasked with this job, the 9-MT B53. However, the B53 is an old weapon, one which weighs 8,800 lb (3992 kg) and is 4 ft 2 in (1.28 m) in diameter. The B53 is so large it can only be carried by the B-52, but it has been retained in the inventory as it was the only US weapon capable of destroying a buried target. In 1987, Sandia National Laboratories proposed a penetrator modification of the B61, but approval for the actual B61-11 version was not given until August 1995. Drop tests were first made by the F-16, B-1B and the B-2, followed, in July 1997, by the B-52. The B61-11 is a rugged weapon, designed for high-speed 'laydown' deliveries, though most tests (to date) have been made at altitude. Exact release parameters are classified, but Donald McCoy , the programme manager, was quoted in Aviation Week as saying, "this one will skip. If you get it too shallow, it'll go in and come back out."

was one of a group of post-Cold War changes to the US strategic forces, which included a fundamental restructuring of the US Air Force. In June 1992, Strategic Air Command ceased to exist, and the USAF's heavy bombers were reassigned to the newly formed Air Combat Command (ACC).

The last significant event of 1992, for the B-2 programme, was the Presidential election. The incoming Democratic administration, accompanied by a new and largely liberal influx of Representatives and Senators, was hardly likely to authorise an increase in the number of B-2s; this was confirmed by the appointment of Les Aspin as Secretary of Defense. As the former chair of the House Armed Services Committee, Aspin had been instrumental in delaying and cutting back the B-2 programme.

Hopes rise and fall

Hopes that more B-2s might be produced rose in November 1994, when the Republican party unexpectedly seized control of the House and Senate. In May 1995, the House added $500 million to the FY96 defence budget to start producing two more B-2s, and Northrop Grumman (Northrop had acquired Grumman in 1994) offered to build 20 more B-2s at a flyaway cost of $566 million each.

The logic behind the proposal was solid. The 1993 Bottom-Up Review of the US military posture had confirmed the need for long-range bombers, because of their ability to bring heavy firepower to bear anywhere in the world at short notice, and supported the retention of the B-52H, B-1 and B-2. Building more B-2s, at a slow rate, would keep the force effective, despite attrition, and in the longer term provide a replacement for the B-52.

The action was supported by the Senate, but opposed by the administration and the Air Force, and the money was earmarked instead to bring AV-1 to operational status and to fund other improvements.

The administration's opposition to the B-2 is political. The cutbacks in production have driven the 'then-year unit programme cost' of the B-2 above $2 billion. This number is based on dividing the total cost of the programme by the

number of aircraft built, and is a fiscal fiction – for example, you could never have saved $2 billion by cancelling one B-2, nor does an additional B-2 cost $2 billion. However, braying politicians and know–nothing columnists have now lodged the number in the public mind, to the point where few people will advocate building more B-2s.

Generally, too, the Clinton administration has been content to defer major military modernisation costs until after 2000, keeping the current budgets balanced and leaving later administrations to pay the bills, a pattern which is also visible in fighter modernisation.

The B-2 and the USAF

The USAF's opposition to more B-2s is pragmatic: the service considers that the money would be better spent elsewhere. The B-2 is a valuable aircraft, but it is not cheap to acquire or to operate, and the USAF's tactical forces have already been substantially cut back. The demise of SAC has not favoured the B-2; while ACC has not ignored bomber modernisation, the new command is inevitably dominated by fighter pilots, who are reluctant to see more fighter wings shut down in order to fund small numbers of bombers.

Another argument with some merit is that the B-52H, armed with JASSM, will be useful until 2015-2020, and that by that time a replacement long-range aircraft may be very different from the B-2. A future bomber might not need the same payload as the B-2, particularly with today's smaller, more accurate weapons. Unrefuelled range could be traded off against tanker support: there is no need for a 1,000-nm (1,148-mile; 1847-km) penetration of hostile territory if the Soviet Union is not the target. A new bomber would take advantage of the more modern stealth technology developed for the F-22 and Joint Strike Fighter, and it would certainly use less costly avionics. Despite the development bill, it might be cheaper in the long run than more B-2s. The USAF's Scientific Advisory Board, in its

1996 New World Vistas study, postulated an even more radical solution for long-range attack: a large global-range aircraft that would combine the roles of transport and strike, carrying uninhabited combat air vehicles (UCAVs) into the battle area.

Return to flight test

While this debate drew to a close, testing proceeded on a deliberate, complex schedule, with aircraft being grounded periodically so that they could be upgraded with new hardware and software for the next series of flights. Avionics hardware and software paced the schedule, but the programme office noted in late 1996 that development had broadly followed the schedule laid down in 1989. While not every radar and DMS mode was available for testing on time, many of the modes were not dependent on others, so

This photograph shows AV-2 engaged in 'splash' tests on a wet runway at Edwards. For these tests the runways were flooded by fire trucks – though in the desert heat the water would evaporate after only 30 to 45 minutes. Crews were concerned mainly with testing the brakes, steering and anti-skid mechanisms under these conditions. Water ingestion via the engine inlets is not a problem for the B-2.

Above and left: Initial terrain-following (TF) certification flights were undertaken by AV-4 in September 1996. Low-level penetration is still considered to be an important potential element of the B-2's mission profile and the aircraft will ultimately be cleared to TF down to a height of 500 ft (152 m) in Block 30 aircraft. Block 20 standard B-2s are cleared to fly manual terrain-avoidance profiles down to 600 ft (182 m).

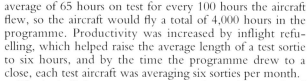

Above and top: B-2s have no obvious surfaces on which to carry their serials, tailcodes and assigned names. Instead, they have set a unique trend in carrying this information on their main gear doors.

Below: This view of an operational B-2 (88-0330/Spirit of California) shows the airflow baffles that drop down in front of the weapons bays to ensure clean separation of bombs.

average of 65 hours on test for every 100 hours the aircraft flew, so the aircraft would fly a total of 4,000 hours in the programme. Productivity was increased by inflight refuelling, which helped raise the average length of a test sortie to six hours, and by the time the programme drew to a close, each test aircraft was averaging six sorties per month.

The basic B-2 test programme was due to be completed by 1 July 1997. It has been a long, drawn-out effort, but, as we have seen, the bulk of the delays and many of the associated increases in the programme's cost are directly attributable to decisions taken on Capitol Hill.

The aircraft itself works much as it was initially designed to do. The major exception has been the RCS shortfall, but the modifications to correct this problem do not affect the basic structure or the systems. On the other hand, the B-2 has already acquired a unique multi-target near-precision conventional strike capability, using existing sensors and inexpensive weapons. Most of the charges levelled at the aircraft by its critics in the late 1980s have proved to be groundless.

It now seems unlikely, nonetheless, that any more B-2s will be built. The cost of doing so increases day by day, as suppliers wind up their production lines and as experienced workers move to other jobs. However, the Palmdale plant remains busy, because a good deal of work is still to be done on the 21-aircraft programme.

The B-2 blocks

Because of the production delays imposed by Congress, it was clear that more than three years would elapse between the delivery of the first production aircraft, AV-1007, and the completion of flight testing. The USAF and Northrop accordingly laid out a three-stage plan that synchronised deliveries, flight-testing and the working-up of the operational wing at Whiteman.

The plan defined three B-2 configurations or blocks. To ease entry into service, two principles were adopted: the operational unit would always have at least eight aircraft in a common configuration and there would never be more than two versions in the field at the same time.

The first 10 production B-2s – AV-1007 through AV-1016 – were delivered as Block 10 aircraft between December 1993 and the end of 1995. The Block 10's primary role was as a trainer for pilots and maintenance crews. It did not operate at full flight loads (being limited to a maximum take-off weight of 305,000 lb/138300 kg), had no terrain-following or precision-weapons capability and had a limited capability in the DMS.

Three new Block 20 aircraft (1017-1019) were delivered in 1996, the last arriving in August. Starting in mid-1996, the five newest Block 10s (1012-1016) went through a 12-16-week modification programme to bring them up to Block 20 status.

With the arrival of the fifth modified aircraft in May 1997, the 509th had eight Block 20s on strength. The B-2 had been declared operational for conventional strike missions in January 1997, and – after passing standard

another part of the test programme could be brought forward to use the aircraft and other resources. As a result, some modes were delivered ahead of schedule and the entire programme remained on track.

Apart from the RCS problem and the anticipated detail headaches with radar performance, only two substantial problems emerged during flight testing: structural cracking in the aft decks, and problems with the radomes. A new aft deck material (unspecified, but possibly based on carbon-carbon composites) was developed for retrofit to the aircraft and incorporated from the 14th aircraft. The original plastic radomes were found to absorb water, degrading the performance of the radar, and have been replaced by a honeycomb material.

The flight-test programme was planned to comprise 2,359 'test point hours'; throughout the programme, the Combined Test Force at Edwards AFB accomplished an

nuclear certification tests – the 509th attained initial operating capability (IOC) in April 1997.

The Block 20 is described as "contributing to the integrated air campaign" because it is armed with GATS/GAM (see weapons section). It operates up to a peacetime take-off weight of 336,500 lb (152600 kg). It is cleared for manual terrain following down to 600 ft (182 m), and the DMS is operational in Bands 1-3. The Block 20 also introduces an improved environmental control system.

Block 30: the ultimate B-2

By the end of 1997, the Block 20s will be joined by the first four fully operational Block 30 aircraft, comprising AV-1020 and 1021, the only new-production Block 30s; AV-1002 (formerly AV-2, the structures test aircraft); and AV-1008, the second Block 10. The scale of the Block 30 modifications can be gauged from the fact that the first modifications take two years; even later, when Block 20s are upgraded, the bombers will be on the ground for a year.

The Block 30 modification includes the removal and replacement of all the aircraft's edges, including the leading edges and control surfaces, in order to meet RCS requirements. The leading edges, visibly segmented on the Block 20, will be joined into an electrically continuous structure. Aircraft prior to AV-1014 receive the new aft deck structure.

All the surface coatings on the B-2, including absorbent and conductive layers, are removed and replaced with improved materials. After having a great deal of difficulty in finding an environmentally safe stripping medium that would remove the coatings without damaging the composite skins, Northrop Grumman developed a technique to 'depaint' the B-2 using crystallised wheat starch and high-pressure air.

The modification includes some rewiring, particularly for the test aircraft. New weapons include JDAM, and the Bomb Rack Assembly units are being used for the first time, allowing the B-2 to carry CBU-87s, mines or other small stores.

Avionics software and hardware changes include automatic TF/TA down to 200 ft (60 m) and the installation of a Milstar satellite communications terminal. DMS reaches its full capability with the addition of Band 4, allowing crews to replan their missions in flight when an unexpected threat is detected.

Another change, introduced in two phases in Blocks 20 and 30, is the integration of the B-2 with the Air Force Mission Support System (AFMSS). This replaces the Strategic Mission Development and Planning System (SMDPS), which was originally developed for the B-2. The SMDPS was designed for nuclear warfighting, and was never intended to be installed outside the B-2's main operating bases. The switch to the transportable AFMSS will allow

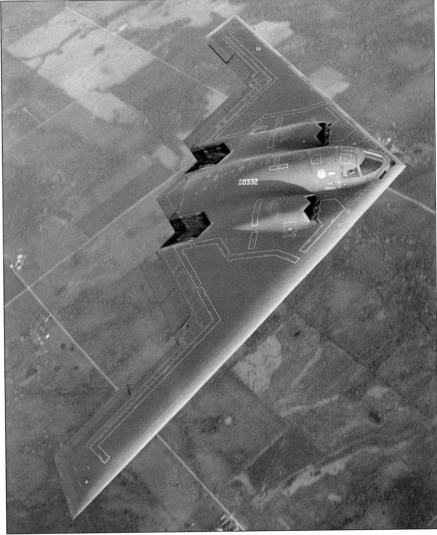

the B-2 to sustain operations from bases around the world, and makes it easier to integrate the B-2 with other USAF operations.

Stealth performance parameters are, naturally, classified. However, the Block 30 aircraft, with the final signature modifications, should have an RCS that is at least two to three orders of magnitude less than the kind of conventional target which radars are designed to detect. The effect is to reduce the radar's range by a factor of four to eight. The radars are less effective, and their areas of coverage no longer overlap; with mission planning and the DMS, the

Above: 90-0332/Spirit of Washington was the 11th B-2 and the fifth production aircraft.

Top: B-2 89-0129/Spirit of Georgia approaches a KC-135 over New Mexico. With a full warload, the B-2 has a maximum unrefuelled range of 6,300 nm (11660 km; 7,245 miles).

Flying wings and their advocates – including Hugo Junkers, Jack Northrop and the Horten brothers, Walter and Reimar – have existed as long as the aircraft itself. The flying wing, these advocates argue, will carry the same payload as far as a conventional aircraft while weighing less and using less fuel. The weight and drag of the tail surfaces are absent, as is the weight of the structure that supports them. The wing structure itself is more efficient because the weight of the aircraft is spread across the wing rather than concentrated in the centre. Northrop's XB-35 was designed to equal the warload and range of the Convair B-36, but with two-thirds the gross weight and two-thirds the power. What made the flying wing attractive for the B-2 was stealth, its basic mission and the intended mission profile. From the stealth viewpoint, the flat, low-profile shape of the flying wing and the absence of tail surfaces were clearly advantageous. As a long-range bomber, it would carry a dense, compact payload that would fit inside a wing. And, since Northrop had concluded that a high-altitude aircraft would fly above the detection range of many threats, the flying wing's large span and wing area were positive advantages. The new bomber, the designers believed, would cruise with the U-2, above 70,000 ft (21336 m).

bomber can weave between them. It is worth noting that the F-117, with a not-dissimilar RCS to the B-2 and much less real-time data on hostile radars, was able to raid Baghdad and survive even though the Iraqi defence forces had good reason to guess when and where the fighters would attack.

Still stealthy after all those years?

Claimed 'detections' of B-2s making air show appearances should be taken with more than a pinch of salt. The F-117 is equipped with means to increase its RCS at will, for two good reasons: to ensure that civilian ATC can see the aircraft in a 'skin paint' mode, and to prevent any unauthorised radar operator from acquiring real RCS data. The B-2 indubitably has the same capability, and uses it routinely. As for British Aerospace's much-touted imaging of a B-2 at a few kilometres' range at Farnborough: how often will a defender see the top of a B-2, and how useful is it to see an aircraft at 3 miles (5 km) when it flies 9 miles (15 km) high – or more – and can deliver a conventional bomb from 13 nm (15 miles; 24 km)?

Five more Block 30s, modified from Block 10s and flight-test aircraft, will be delivered during 1998: by the late summer, therefore, the bomber should be declared fully operational. Eight more Block 30s will arrive during 1999, and the last four in 2000. On present plans, the first phase of the B-2 programme will be completed in June 2001, when the first prototype, AV-1, joins the 509th as a fully operational Block 30.

In the hands of the 509th BW

The 509th is mainly dedicated to missions which are of high importance and which only the B-2 can perform. If, for example, the US decided to destroy a chemical weapons factory in Libya without the B-2, the US government would have to secure landing and overflight permission from one or more NATO allies, either for the attack force (if F-117s were used) or the support force (if B-52s delivered the attack). In either case, the preparations would send a strong signal that an operation was under way. The B-2 can perform the mission, non-stop and unsupported, from Missouri, with one refuelling outbound, and can either recover to a secure base such as Diego Garcia or return with another refuelling direct to Whiteman.

Training and tactics development are focused on such special, B-2-unique missions. "Gulf War-type operations, where we deploy into a situation and perform like everyone else, are not in the plan now, but we will become deployable," remarks Lieutenant Colonel Jim Whitney of the 394th Combat Training Squadron.

The 509th is highly selective. Out of 60-70 pilots with the necessary paper qualifications to fly the B-2, 20 were selected for interview. After an interview and a check ride in the Hughes Weapon System Trainer, seven were chosen.

The trainees are mid-level captains with 1,000 hours in bombers or 600 hours in fighters, and ample tanking experience. Roughly one-third come from B-1s, one-third from B-52s and one-third from fighters – mostly F-15s or F-117s. As well as experience and piloting skills, the 509th is looking for people with leadership potential – "people who can be trusted to fly an expensive asset" – and individuals with initiative.

Flying the B-2

Training starts with 178 hours of academics, followed by 60 hours in the cockpit procedures trainer – a fairly basic replica of the B-2 cockpit. The next step is 40 hours of 'real time' practice in the mission trainer, another fixed-base system that "teaches pilots to be navigators."

The student then moves on to the Hughes-Link Division Weapon System Trainer (WST), an extremely sophisticated full-motion simulator that doubles as a mission rehearsal system, with access to a global database of targets and threats. Block 20 training required 15 WST flights; the Block 30 takes 19 rides, most of the increase being due to the later version's TF/TA capability. (From the pilot's viewpoint, the Block 10 to Block 20 change has been much more significant than Block 20 to 30.) After seven WST rides, the pilot takes his first flight in the B-2, and is ready for a check ride by the ninth sortie.

This process, known as initial qualification training (IQT), takes six months. After passing IQT, the pilot typically flies two sorties per month on the B-2, interspersed with four to six flights on the unit's charcoal-grey T-38 companion trainers. Like other specialised USAF units, the 509th uses the T-38s to maintain hands-on flying skills and to keep the pilots accustomed to making quick decisions.

The pilot will typically fly for about a year before upgrading to mission commander. The B-2 has a crew of two: the pilot, and the mission commander who combines the roles of pilot and weapon system operator and is additionally responsible for targeting and weapon release. As was done on the FB-111, the 509th tries to match pilots and mission commanders according to personality and compatible working methods, and to keep crews together over the long term.

Pilots describe the B-2 as a pleasant, undemanding aircraft to fly, a factor which helps to keep the workload reasonable. As in any fly-by-wire aircraft, leaving the stick in the centre position means that the aircraft will hold its

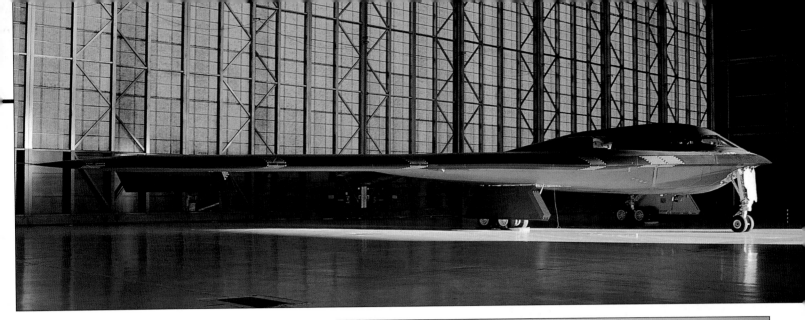

current attitude. The B-2 is not a fighter: its flying-wing design limits it to a relatively small Alpha range, its long wing span precludes a rapid roll rate, and it does not have the thrust for high-*g* manoeuvring or rapid acceleration. But it is more responsive than most large aircraft, because the control system is powerful and the airframe is stiff. Its low drag means it out-accelerates most aircraft of its size, and the fighter-type engines respond quickly to throttle inputs. The verdict, according to one operational pilot: B-52 pilots think the B-2 is manoeuvrable and B-1 pilots less so. As for fighter pilots: "It's still a Mack truck to them."

Good handling qualities

Before the B-2 flew, many critics expected the aircraft to be only marginally stable. Even on the first flight, however, observers noted the B-2's almost unnatural steadiness on final approach, with absolutely no visible wing rock or 'hunting' in Alpha. The speedbrakes are left open 45° up and down on the approach, increasing drag and placing the engines in a more responsive thrust range.

One of the bomber's quirks is apparent on landing: the broad centrebody generates a powerful ground cushion, so landings are no-flare, carrier-style affairs. One pilot notes, "If you do try to flare, the airplane says, 'You want to fly, let's go fly.' It's obvious when you see someone do that on one of their first landings." Another pilot observes that "you don't need the flight engineer barking out the radar altitude so that you don't pancake the airplane." On the other hand, the 509th pilots have noticed a tendency towards 'firm' landings on the part of pilots making their first T-38 approaches after a series of B-2 flights.

The flight control system normally keeps the B-2 at zero Beta (that is to say, with no sideslip or crab) and a constant Alpha, selected by the pilot. At low level and high speeds, the constant-Alpha law tends to counteract wind gusts immediately: an upward gust increases the aircraft's Alpha, and so the FCS commands the aircraft to pitch down. At the same time, the abrupt Alpha increase is detected by the gust-alleviation laws in the FCS, which signals the elevons and beavertail to apply more nose-up trim on the outer wings and less on the centreline. This reduces the peak bending moment. The ride quality is not quite as good as that of the B-1 – there is no substitute for very high wing loading – but is much better than a B-52's.

Low-level training was temporarily suspended in early 1997 because of the risk of birdstrikes. Crews do not expect the B-2 to be susceptible to catastrophic damage (of the kind that caused the loss of one B-1). Most vital systems are buried deeply behind the leading edges and front spars, and even the largest bird will have been slowed down by a few authoritative ricochets before it can reach the engines. However, the B-2 force cannot afford to have an aircraft down for extensive repairs, because it would disrupt the training schedule.

The entire B-2 inflight refuelling envelope was cleared in a single flight, a first-time achievement for a brand-new aircraft. This is not to say that refuelling is always easy. The KC-10 is not much of a problem, with its size and a very

long boom, but the KC-135 represents a unique situation. The B-2's refuelling slipway is located well aft, and, unlike most conventional aircraft, is behind much of the wing. The entire aircraft must be driven through two 'down-bursts' – one of the engines, and one of the wing – to reach a contact position. Once the B-2 is in position, it is well inside the KC-135's 'bubble' and the two aircraft interact strongly: any movement of one aircraft tends to affect the other. "Once you're inside the tanker's envelope, the B-2 tends to slide forward on you because you're so clean."

Flying the B-2 is a great deal more than stick-and-rudder skills, because of the bomber's complex systems. "If an individual likes computer games, it suits them very well," says one pilot. "You can fly for a long time and never touch the stick or throttles. The automation frees up a lot of brainpower for other tasks." The challenge is teaching the pilot where to find the information he needs to accomplish the mission. Pilots who have grown up with computer games sometimes forget that the B-2 was designed in the early 1980s. One pilot calls this the "shock,

Above and top: AV-4 is seen here hiding in a hangar at Edwards AFB in 1993 (top). All five of the developmental aircraft will now be returned to active service, the last joining the 509th BW by June 2000. 89-0127/Spirit of Kansas (above) – the sixth production aircraft – was delivered to Whiteman AFB in February 1995.

As part of its ongoing B-2 upgrade programme, Northrop Grumman developed an environmentally friendly paint-stripping system for the aircraft that uses wheat starch.

From the very first sketches at Northrop, after the company had been dragged into the ATB competition, it was clear that conventional designs were not on the table. It was remarkable how quickly the designers gravitated toward the flying wing shape, given Northrop's history. The designers were looking for a simple planform shape – with few RCS 'spikes' – and a low wing loading for high altitude. The two alternatives that emerged from the original studies were a flying wing and a diamond-shaped aircraft. Modern technology promised to solve some of the problems that had afflicted earlier flying wings. In particular, fly-by-wire flight control could solve some of the stability and control problems that had never been alleviated on the XB-35 and YB-49.

For the US Air Force's 50th anniversary show, held at Nellis AFB in April 1997, the Air Force displayed two B-2s, including one static aircraft (89-0128) marked with the name of General Ronald Fogleman, Chief of Staff of the US Air Force.

denial and acceptance" syndrome. "When you start, you're always behind the system. Once you've trained, you can be waiting for the system and saying, 'Come on, I'm burning nanoseconds here'."

A GATS/GAM attack is one of the most difficult tasks on the B-2. The pilot has to fly an indirect path to the target, while the mission commander searches for the target and a secondary reference point on the SAR scope. F-15E and B-1 people find it easy, apparently, but others find radar signal interpretation (RSI) difficult. The APQ-181 is good, but performance does vary with obscurants and the size of the targets. "We start with big buildings in the

middle of nowhere, and move on to more difficult targets." GATS/GAM is "not a problem with the processors on the airplane, but with the grey matter in the pilot's head."

One unique aspect of the 509th's operations, directly related to its 'sniper squadron' role, is that some of its missions may be extremely long. The worst case is a non-stop mission halfway around the world and back, using an indirect route to avoid violating airspace. So far, the longest real mission flown by a B-2 has been 30 hours, but crews have flown mission rehearsals for up to 44.5 hours in the WST.

The simulations are as realistic as the WST can make them, including equipment failures and threats, and if the real mission would start at 02.00, the simulation does so as well. Pilots have experimented with different kinds of bedding and food; the B-2 cockpit is just large enough for a roll-up mattress and can accommodate a chemical toilet and a few personal items. Crews on the simulator rides are heavily instrumented, including an eye-blink-rate sensor attached to the oxygen mask, and their performance in air-to-air refuelling and weapon delivery is carefully monitored. So far, tests have shown that a combination of pre-flight rest and 'power napping' during the tedious parts of the flight should make it possible to fly missions of more than 50 hours without degrading the crew's performance over the target.

B-2 at Whiteman AFB

Whiteman was selected as the first home for the B-2 in 1986; it had not hosted large aircraft since the 1960s, when a B-47 wing gave way to Minuteman missiles. The base has been largely rebuilt to accommodate the new aircraft, including a row of individual docks for each bomber. Each dock opens at both ends (so that engines can be started under cover), has underfloor plumbing for fuel and fluids, and includes comprehensive test equipment and a fire-suppression system.

The B-2 maintenance crews typically compare them-selves to the 'Maytag repairman', referring to a long-running advertising campaign for Maytag dishwashers, featuring the repairman whose phone never rings. The B-2 does require a fair amount of scheduled maintenance, because of its complexity, but it seldom breaks – a result of the rigorous specifications, long development and meticulous testing.

The main area where maintenance lessons are still being learned is in RCS maintenance. The normal flexing of the airframe, gust loads and vibration all affect the surface of the aircraft, and physically small discontinuities may sharply increase the RCS. The USAF and the contractors are working on maintenance materials (such as tapes and caulking compounds) and on new diagnostic tools which will allow RCS to be measured on the flight-line.

B-2: past, present and future

What the B-2 does not have, as yet, is a name. In accordance with USAF tradition, the official name of 'Spirit' is never heard around the aircraft. The name 'Bat' has been suggested (it fits neatly with the one-syllable 'Buff' and 'Bone') but has not caught on. Neither has 'Voron' – Russian for raven, and the callsign for B-2 flight tests. Meanwhile, crews call it simply 'the jet' and there is no doubt at Whiteman as to what that means.

The B-2 is an extremely complex and technologically advanced aircraft that has emerged from a long, controversial development programme. It has suffered – and still suffers – from being at the mercy of decisions made by people who do not understand its capabilities.

Myths and misconceptions about the B-2 are everywhere, and will be destroyed only gradually; as Mark Twain remarked, "a lie can be half way around the world before the truth has got its boots on."

The B-2's builders and operators are confident that the fully operational aircraft will be stealthy enough to perform its mission: to deliver 16 near-precision, hard-target weapons per sortie, anywhere in the world, with no support except tankers. There is nothing else in the world that even comes close to this capability, nor will there be for decades – the B-2's capabilities will be unique when most of us have retired.

It still seems puzzling and incongruous that, while there is no money for more B-2s, the Pentagon is pushing hard for a Joint Strike Fighter which will not be much more survivable than a B-2, at best; carries one-eighth of its weapon load; has one-fifth of its unrefuelled range; relies on the availability of overseas bases; and will not be available for another decade. Are numbers everything?

More than half a century ago, the US Army Air Corps wanted to buy a new bomber. It was large, sophisticated and the most expensive combat aircraft in the world.

Critics in Congress and the other branches of the military argued that economic times were tight and that the United States was not about to become embroiled in any conflicts where the big bomber's unique assets – range and survivability – would be necessary. A cheaper warplane, based on an existing airframe to save money, would be adequate.

The Air Corps lost its fight and received only a small test squadron of the big bombers. Most of the money earmarked for bombers went to buy hundreds of the less expensive aircraft.

The cheaper bomber was the Douglas B-18A Bolo, a derivative of the DC-2 airliner. In the Air Force Museum, a plaque in front of an immaculate B-18 sums up its front-line combat career: "Several of these aircraft were destroyed by the Japanese on 7 December 1941."

The big, costly bomber that the nation could not afford was, of course, the Boeing B-17 Flying Fortress.

Bill Sweetman

Although this photograph is perhaps the result of a quiet afternoon at the Edwards photo section, it does have some small message to give about the B-2's effectiveness when compared to other, conventional, aircraft. According to USAF figures, the B-2's unique combination of abilities would allow just two aircraft to carry out the same mission as 32 'dumb bomb droppers' (F-16s) and obviate the need for their associated escorts (16 F-15s), SEAD support (EF-111s and EA-6Bs) and tanker support (15 KC-135s). To put a more precise figure on matters, other USAF figures state that a strike by two C-ALCM-armed B-52Hs, with 32 missiles, costs $92.8 million (in FY97 dollars, a C-ALCM costs $2.9 million). The same mission could be accomplished by a single B-2, armed with just 16 JDAMs (only FY97 $27,000 each), for a total weapons cost of $432,000. JDAM has a CEP of less than 20 ft (6.09 m) compared to 30-45 ft (9.1-13.7 m) for a cruise missile. JDAM's warhead is also twice as heavy as a conventionally armed cruise missile.

Continued production of B-2s remained a possibility in 1997, a further nine aircraft being suggested for delivery early next century. The follow-on batch would have a much cheaper unit price than the initial 21 aircraft.

B-2 Operators

B-2 Combined Test Force (CTF), Edwards AFB

The B-2 Combined Test Force (CTF) was a joint Northrop-USAF (later Northrop Grumman) effort that brought together employees of the manufacturer and Air Force personnel to test the B-2 bomber. This industry/military team was created in part to reduce duplication in the work performed by the manufacturer and the Air Force. Unlike other such efforts, the B-2 CTF began in the 'black' world during the Reagan years (1981-89) and was not publicly acknowledged in its early existence. Historians at Edwards say that the B-2 CTF began in July 1983 without a formal name. At that time, plans for the ATB/B-2 were still at an early stage and all relevant information was SAR (Special Access Required) classified. The B-2 CTF first appears on organisation charts in July 1988, two years before the first B-2 arrived at Edwards. The B-2 CTF adopted a badge which was in use before the CTF was formally established.

The CTF brought together four parties. They were the civilian contractors such Northrop Grumman plus other companies involved in B-2 operations, the Air Force Operational Test and Evaluation Center (AFOTEC), Air Combat Command, and Air Force Materiel Command. AFOTEC is an independent test agency responsible for testing new systems under realistic conditions to determine their operational effectiveness in the field.

The CTF was located at a purpose-built facility on 'South Base' (now renamed the Birk Flight Test Facility), site of the original Muroc Army Airfield and (subsequently) Edwards AFB, chosen because it is isolated, easy to keep secure, and has access to the main runway. The facility has its own communications, security, administration, and other support operations, styled to handle the SAR nature of all of the B-2 programme in the past, and some of it today. This is in contrast to the B-1B and B-52 test operation located on 'contractor's row' on 'Main Base' where most test aircraft have been located since the early 1960s. Each CTF at Edwards has evolved somewhat differently, including those on the C-17 and F-22. In the case of the B-2 CTF, the military commander was 'dual-hatted', serving also as commander of the 412th Test Group, parent unit of the 420th Flight Test Squadron.

First flight of the number one B-2A (82-1066 c/n 1001), known as AV-1 or Air Vehicle One, took place at Palmdale,

California on 17 July 1989, and was flown by Northrop's Bruce Hinds and Colonel Richard S. Couch. Both men became early, key figures in the B-2 CTF at Edwards. The second ship flew on 19 October 1990. Test flying to evaluate low observables (LO), or stealth, technology began on 30 October 1990.

B-2s are frequently identified by one- and two-digit 'air vehicle' numbers (AV-1 to AV-20), with the final ship presumably dubbed AV-21. Northrop c/ns, however, are four-digit numbers (1001 through 1020), with the final aircraft expected to be 1021; c/ns 998 through 1000 were assigned to three non-flying airframes, namely the static test vehicle, the durability test vehicle, and the 'iron bird' or static avionics vehicle, respectively.

Flight tests of the B-2 were expanded in late 1992 to include testing of the bomber's navigational accuracy and radar capability. The extended flights put the B-2 on a 3,100-mile (4990-km) 'box route' encompassing California, New Mexico, North Dakota, Washington, and return. By the time the no. 5 B-2, ship AV-5 (82-1070), was delivered on 5 October 1992, the B-2 CTF was growing and prospering. Weapons tests began. The B-2 logged its 1,000th flight hour in February 1993. By then, six aircraft had taken part in 217 developmental sorties (with the no. 1 B-2 going into temporary storage soon afterward).

At one time or another, the B-2 CTF operated seven B-2 airframes plus two Stratotankers (see 412th TW entry), with the eighth and subsequent B-2s going directly to the operational wing at Whiteman AFB, Missouri. At one point, the B-2 CTF numbered nearly 2,000 civilians and military people, and many of them used ingenuity to

create unofficial emblems to celebrate their work. Typically, employing used computer graphics, elements within the B-2 CTF transformed an official emblem into an unofficial one, with a personalised message for a particular office or branch. CTF data handlers, for instance, processed telemetry data and turned it into the findings that engineers used to analyse the tests – and came up with an emblem showing a computer reel on the CTF predator logo. Other such special projects logos were designed but never used, illustrating the old flight test truism that the first thing done in a programme is to design the logo.

A 'Frozen Spirit' motif was designed for AV-5's deployment to Eielson AFB, Alaska, in March 1997, where the B-2 CTF operated in snow, demonstrated snow removal and anti-icing. AV-5, nicknamed Fire and Ice, had been the climatic test aircraft and was 'stuffed' into the climatic test hangar at Eglin AFB, Florida for over two months in 1994.

Both the manufacturer and the service concluded that the joint effort had finished the EMD (Engineering and Manufacturing Development) phase of B-2 testing and evaluation, so the B-2 CTF lost most of its contractor personnel by 30 June 1997. Northrop Grumman, which once had hundreds of employees in the CTF and had 440 as recently as the start of 1997, had laid off all but 43 men and women by 30 June 1997.

At the peak days of B-2 testing, pilots and engineers of the CTF had up to 10 bombers at their disposal, including three deployed from the wing in Missouri and five assigned to Edwards. To mark the expiration of the EMD contract and the 'skeletonising' of Northrop Grumman's role in the CTF,

members were issued with a brass medallion commemorating the final flight in the EMD programme. On one side, the medallion is "dedicated to [the] B-2 test team, 1985-97." On the other is a notation commemorating the final EMD flight (no. 217) on 25 June 1997 by Colonel Mike Walker and Major Jay Schwindt in aircraft AV-3, a five-hour sortie. As of 1 July 1997, the much-reduced B-2 CTF was down to two aircraft: AV-3 (82-1068) and AV-5 (82-1070 c/n 1005), the latter being scheduled to be named Spirit of Ohio and moved to Whiteman AFB. The military component of the B-2 CTF was expected to be greatly reduced by 31 December 1997, when the 412th Test Group and 420th Flight Test Squadron were scheduled to go out of existence. On that date, the amount of SAR needed for the programme was to be reduced and the test force moved to 'Main Base'. In greatly reduced form and without an EMD contract, the CTF is expected to remain in existence throughout 1998 with one B-2 aircraft.

US Air Force Materiel Command

412th Test Wing

The 412th TW (tailcode 'ED', derived from Edwards) is the flying component of the Air Force Flight Test Center (AFFTC). The wing acquired its designation on 1 October 1992

through a renumbering of the former 6510th TW. (Four-digit numbers reflect 'provisional' status, and the '6' prefix was assigned to Air Force Systems Command (AFSC) and subsequently adopted by AFMC.) Under the 6510th designation, the wing dates to March 1978. The current designation was chosen to carry on the lineage and honours

of the 412th Fighter Group, which flew Bell P-59 Airacomets and Lockheed P-80 Shooting Stars at Muroc, California (the future Edwards AFB) during World War II.

The wing is responsible for virtually all aircraft tested at Edwards by the USAF. The wing is the parent for the 412th Test Group, which is concerned only with the B-2.

The 412th had a total of nine aircraft assigned during its B-2 test operations (seven B-2s and two C-135s) and has also,

on occasion, flown a B-2 borrowed from Whiteman. Some of the bombers had nicknames in test operations that are different from the names applied in operational service. The aircraft assigned to the wing were:

NC-135A 60-0377 c/n 18152, *Nasty Stuff* a.k.a. *Miss Piggy*, the 'hog-nosed' B-2 radar and avionics developmental flight testbed;
C-135C 61-2669 c/n 18245, apparently used for parts;
B-2A 82-1066 c/n 1001 AV-1, *Fatal Beauty*;
B-2A 82-1067 c/n 1002 AV-2 (no nickname), the aerodynamic test ship;
B-2A 82-1068 c/n 1003 AV-3, *Shady Lady/The Ghost*, the low observables and systems operations test ship, subsequently the Block 30 test ship;
B-2A 82-1069 c/n 1004 AV-4, *Deadly Attraction/Christine*, the performance and weapons development ship, equipped with external cameras for stores release tests;
B-2A 82-1070 c/n 1005 AV-5, *Fire and Ice*, the environmental capabilities test

CHRISTINE
21069

THE WORK HORSE

ship; evaluated at Eglin AFB, Florida and Eielson AFB, Alaska, the only test B-2 with nose art;
B-2A 82-1071 c/n 1006 AV-6, *Black Widow,* the 'easy maintenance'

demonstrator; the first ship to drop a bomb; **B-2A 88-0328 c/n 1007 AV-7,** the first production aircraft employed in the test programme for electromagnetic testing.

412th Test Group

The 412th TG at Edwards was formed in 1992 at the B-2 'South Base' facility to carry out B-2 tests as the military component of the B-2 Combined Test Force. The

commander of the group is also the military commander of the B-2 CTF. The group is scheduled to be deactivated on 31 December 1997, at which time bomber operations at Edwards will be merged into a single unit.

420th Flight Test Squadron

The 420th FLTS received its current designation on 2 October 1992, succeeding the 6520th Test Squadron. The squadron has the flying personnel (pilots and engineers) who carry out B-2 flight tests. The 420th FLTS is scheduled to be

deactivated on 31 December 1997, at which time B-2 flight personnel will shift to a different location on base to merge with, and assume the name of, the 419th FLTS, which currently handles B-1B and B-52H testing.

Air Combat Command

31st Test and Evaluation Squadron

The 31st TES is the Air Combat Command (ACC) test unit at Edwards AFB. It serves as ACC's 'window' to the B-2 world while the bomber is being tested at Edwards, which is an Air Force Materiel Command (AFMC) base. Most of the squadron's pilots are not Test Pilot School graduates, and their missions have more of an operational flavour than the earlier developmental missions intended to collect engineering quality data to evaluate the B-2 design.

The 31st TES was reactivated on 1 July 1986, taking over the functions of the 4200nd TES and bearing the lineage and honours of the 31st Bombardment Squadron, which dates to 1917. The squadron's emblem is a triangular skull emblem, which is linked to its origins as a bomb unit. From its reactivation, the squadron was a component of Strategic Air Command until ACC came into existence on 1 June 1992. The squadron provided flying personnel for B-2 test work beginning

in 1990. Squadron pilots have flown B-2s belonging to the 412th Test Group of the Air Force Flight Test Center (AFFTC) and, on occasion, B-2s on loan from Whiteman Air Force Base, Missouri.

509th Bomb Wing

The 509th Bomb Wing (tailcode 'WM') became operational on 1 April 1993 at Whiteman, preparing to operate the B-2. The USAF had announced in 1989 that the first B-2 operational unit would be stationed at Whiteman, then an inactive airfield 45 miles (72 km) from Kansas City, and that the unit would be the 351st Bomb Wing (by renaming an LGM-30F Minuteman II ICBM establishment). For reasons of tradition, however, there was strong sentiment to revive the 509th designation. The decision was reached in 1990 to pass the 509th flag to the first (and as it turned out, the only) B-2 wing at Whiteman. The wing's initial cadre came from Detachment 509, 351st Missile Wing, which had been the tenant at Whiteman AFB and was inactivated on that date.

To give an honoured name to its first operator of the 'Stealth Bomber', the US Air Force decided to carry on the identity of the 509th Composite Group, which was activated in secrecy on 17 December 1944 to organise, equip and train for atomic warfare. The 509th operated Martin-built 'Silver Plate' Boeing B-29s equipped to carry the first atomic bombs, and carried out the 1945 strikes on Hiroshima ('Little Boy', 6 August), and Nagasaki ('Fat Man', 9 August). In July 1946, the group was redesignated 509th Bombardment Group (Very Heavy), a change putting it in line with the terminology of the SAC, formed in March of that year. The 509th pioneered air-to-air refuelling in 1948 when it began flying Boeing KB-29M tankers in addition to its specially-modified B-29 bombers.

The group was redesignated 509th Bombardment Group (Medium) in July 1948, a step which reflected a changing view of the size of bombers as bigger aircraft began to join the inventory. The group converted from the B-29 to the B-50 shortly thereafter.

The USAF shifted from the combat group

to the combat wing as its principal establishment in 1952. Thus, although the 509th group was inactivated on 16 June 1952, the 509th Bombardment Wing (Medium) continued operations. The wing subsequently operated a variety of aircraft under 'medium' and 'heavy' designations before moving to Pease AFB, New Hampshire on 1 July 1958. As a B-52 operator, the wing deployed aircraft and crews to combat operations in Southeast Asia in 1968-69. In 1970, the 509th converted to the SRAM-equipped General Dynamics FB-111A, which it flew at Pease for almost two decades. When Pease was selected for closure and the FB-111A slated for retirement, the 509th Bombardment Wing (Medium) was inactivated in 1988.

The 509th, while inactive, moved to Whiteman on 30 September 1990 without personnel or equipment. By the time the 509th was resurrected at Whiteman to fly the B-2, the USAF had replaced the term 'Bombardment' with 'Bomb' in the designations of its units (squadrons and groups) and establishments (wings). The service had also (in mid-1992) restored the

combat group as part of its command structure while retaining the wing as its principal establishment. These changes having taken place while it was inactive, the wing began at Whiteman with the 509th Operations Group (OG) as part of its structure. The wing's flying units are the 393rd Bomb Squadron and the 394th Combat Training Squadron (CTS).

The 509th took over a base that had not handled large aircraft for three decades and all base facilities – buildings, hangars, taxiways, runways – had to be completely renovated and rebuilt. The first assigned aircraft, a Northrop T-38A Talon with a B-2-style paint scheme, joined the wing on 20 July 1993. Ten months after coming into existence, the 509th received its first B-2 bomber, AV-7 (88-0329) *Spirit of Missouri,* on 17 December 1993. A 509th B-2 participated in Exercise Red Flag at Nellis AFB, Nevada for the first time on 24 January 1995, dropping two Mk 84 bombs in a 7.5-hour mission. The 509th has since become a regular participant in Red Flag and other exercises throughout 1995. In May 1997, a B-2 crew from Whiteman flew the longest B-2 mission yet – a 30-hour round-trip to the Mildenhall Air Fete.

On 10 May 1996, the B-2 fleet was grounded for eight days while tailpipe clamps were inspected for cracks. The stand-down was ordered after mechanics at Whiteman discovered cracks in one aircraft's clamps; each bomber has eight of these titanium clamps. During the eight-day

period, 25 of 72 tailpipe clamps inspected were found to be faulty and were replaced. B-2 operations resumed on 18 May 1996.

In July 1996, the 509th announced that it had received the first 17 GAM-84 bombs for the B-2. Northrop Grumman and Hughes Aircraft Co. reportedly delivered 128 GAMs to Whiteman by the end of 1996. The bombs are considered an interim step for the B-2, providing precision-attack capability until the JDAM is fielded later in this decade.

On 1 January 1997, the USAF determined that B-2s at Whiteman had reached a 'limited' capability for delivering conventional weapons. On 1 April 1997, the USAF declared the 509th and its B-2s ready to take on nuclear and conventional combat missions. On that date, six B-2 Spirits (of 13 at the base at the time) became part of the SIOP (Single Integrated Operations Plan), the Pentagon's nuclear-warfighting plan. Two more B-2s were scheduled to be added to the SIOP on 1 January 1998.

Unfortunately, just days after the announcement of nuclear readiness, the Air Force had to ground its B-2 fleet. On 8 April 1997, the bombers were removed from flying status after an engine-shaft assembly broke during flight. An investigation revealed that the housing of the shaft assembly had nearly undetectable cracks that caused the shaft to turn in a slightly elliptical pattern rather than a circle. The bombers returned to flying status in mid-April.

393rd Bomb Squadron 'Tigers'

The 393rd Heavy Bombardment Squadron, under the command of Colonel Paul W. Tibbets, actually carried out the two atomic raids on Japan in 1945. The 393rd BS 'Tigers' ('WM' tailcode) was reactivated on 27 August 1993 as the first operational B-2 Spirit flying squadron of the 509th Bomb Wing. In addition to flying personnel, the squadron has support personnel, crew chiefs, maintainers, weaponeers, and other personnel. The 393rd is the USAF's principal B-2 combat formation and could be supplemented by personnel from the 394th CTS (below) in wartime.

394th Combat Training Squadron (CTS) 'Panthers'

The 394th CTS 'Panthers' (using the wing's 'WM' tailcode) was activated on 6 November 1996 as the second B-2 flying unit at Whiteman AFB, charged with both training and combat readiness. The 394th began as the 4th Aero Squadron in May 1917. At the time, the 4th was the fourth squadron to be activated in the group and chose the four-pointed star as its emblem. The new squadron patch has added the current squadron mascot, the panther, to its design. The 394th replaces a Formal Training Unit that had provided some aspects of B-2 type training. Its mission of training combat-ready pilots has three distinct phases, known as Initial Qualification (IQ), Mission Ready Status (MRS) and Continuation Training. The 394th, staffed with instructor pilots, is available to train and fight. CTS pilots can support the 393rd Bomb Squadron (to

which its trainees transfer when qualified in the B-2) with personnel as needed for contingency operations. The squadron's 51 people include T-38 and B-2 instructor pilots and students, weapons system trainer personnel, schedulers and other squadron staff members. The unique requirements of the squadron require support from other outside agencies to augment its academic and flight-line support requirements. USAF officials say the squadron operates 12 Northrop T-38A Talons, maintenance for which is handled by Lockheed. The USAF inventory lists 10 T-38As, however, namely 62-3690, 64-13206, 65-10324, 65-10418/10419, 66-8402, 67-14826, 67-14845, 67-14920 and 68-8179. An additional aircraft identified by other sources, 65-10361, may be a replacement for one of the 10, or may be the 11th.
Robert F. Dorr

Kaman SH-2G Super Seasprite

Kaman's single-engined HU2K-1 first flew in July 1959. Today's SH-2G is a very different aircraft to that which served with distinction during the Vietnam War and was once ubiquitous on the decks of US warships. The US Navy is retiring the last of its vessels which need a helicopter in the class of the Seasprite, but other nations are starting to eagerly snap them up. Meanwhile, the SH-2G/Magic Lantern MCM combination is unique to the USA.

The president of Kaman Aerospace International Corporation (KAIC), Admiral Huntington Hardisty, calls the Super Seasprite the "most advanced and robust small ship maritime helicopter designed." Having been prematurely dismissed as a relic (in operational terms) of the Cold War, the Kaman SH-2G Super Seasprite is now enjoying an unexpected, but welcome, revival. The United States Navy has cut back its once substantial

Seasprite fleet to just two Reserve squadrons of modernised SH-2Gs (a fleet that, albeit, is larger than the naval helicopter forces of many countries), and they are scheduled to remain in the US Navy until at least 2006. Since the sea service is retiring its few remaining 'smaller' warships from which the SH-2G routinely operates, the more distant future is uncertain for the squadrons HSL-84 'Titans' and HSL-94 'Thunderbolts'.

However, if the Seasprite itself is no longer in great demand in American colours, both the aircraft and the frigates from which it operates are coveted by other nations, some of which will almost certainly want to avail themselves of the remanufacturing talents offered by Kaman Aerospace Corp. in Bloomfield, Connecticut. Egypt has already done so. Australia and New Zealand have recently selected the SH-2G to augment their new frigates and smaller offshore patrol combatants. Several other nations have requirements for light helicopters (Kaman prefers to call the SH-2G an 'intermediate weight' naval helicopter) to fly from their new warships. As the US Navy divests itself of its smaller 'Oliver Hazard Perry'-class (FFG-7) frigates, other navies are scrambling to acquire these still-capable ships. The US has a long list of potential 'customers' for the FFG-7s, and for the ships to remain fully combat capable they must have a shipboard ASW helicopter. That helicopter should be the SH-2G.

The US Navy's 23 SH-2Gs (16 in operational service) are the last remaining helicopters which fly the LAMPS I mission. In the 1970s, chief of naval operations Admiral Elmo 'Bud' Zumwalt pushed hard for LAMPS (Light Airborne Multi-Purpose System) to provide picket ships at the outer edge of a carrier battle group with a helicopter able to act decisively against the Soviet submarine threat. Today, the principal anti-submarine warfare (ASW) weapon on board the fleet's surface warships is the Navy's Sikorsky SH-60B LAMPS III (while the SH-60F is deployed aboard aircraft-carriers). The US Navy has retired and sold abroad most of the frigates and light destroyers for which the SH-2G and its predecessor the SH-2F were designed. With the Navy on the verge of making the frigate a warship of the past – or at least of its overseas allies only – and the heavier SH-60B easily able to operate from the large destroyers and cruisers remaining in American service, the SH-60B is likely to emerge (with its planned successor SH-60R) as the only ASW helicopter on US naval decks.

The US Navy has standardised its active-duty fleet on LAMPS III and may elect to sell off its SH-2Gs along with the last of the smaller

Above: Integration of the AGM-65 Maverick ASM was an important element in the Seasprite's successful bid for the Royal New Zealand Navy order. The RNZN requirement, however, was less stringent than the Royal Australian Navy's which demanded a dedicated anti-ship missile.

Right: A crew from HSL-84 'Titans' banks their aircraft hard during another sortie from NAS North Island, California. In June 1997 the 'Titans' chalked up their 40,000th consecutive incident-free flying hour.

Above left: The SH-2G is equipped with the AN/ASQ-81(V)2 MAD – the standard US Navy system. The SH-2G can tow the ASQ-81 at speeds of 10-140 kt (19-259 km/h; 12-161 mph). Its cable is 180 ft (55 m) long.

Below left: Kaman has designed and built the unique Magic Lantern LIDAR mine detecting system for the SH-2G. The Magic Lantern is carried in a large pod, to port, replacing the MAD.

warships. But, for the near future, the Navy has decided instead to give the SH-2G new missions for a new world. The two Naval Reserve SH-2G squadrons now rehearse and carry out long-range surveillance, anti-surface warfare, anti-submarine warfare, search and rescue, and utility service. The Kaman-developed Magic Lantern device, a laser detector that finds mines from the water's surface to below the keel depth of most warships, gives the SH-2G Super Seasprite a much-publicised new mission in airborne mine countermeasures (AMCM).

History

Most of the men and women who fly and maintain the SH-2G were not yet born when the Seasprite helicopter first took to the air. Every aircraft in this series was manufactured at the Bloomfield facility of Kaman, a $1 billion-a-year company 'small' enough that founder, owner and aviation legend Charles Kaman, still has lunch in the employee cafeteria. The Seasprite has been improved so often, for so long, that several airframes have been upgraded more than once, producing a curious statistic: prior to the start of the Egyptian programme, Kaman had manufactured 250 Seasprites but had upgraded 268.

The Seasprite has a long history of naval service in single- and twin-engined versions, in a variety of duties, dating to before the US involvement in Vietnam. The prototype HU2K-1 (company K-20) made its first flight at Bloomfield on 2 July 1959. It became the only Kaman helicopter to go into production with a conventional main and tail rotor configuration, rather than the intermeshing twin rotors found on other Kaman products including the H-43 Huskie and K-MAX cargo hauler. The HU2K series was redesignated H-2 on 1 October 1962. Kaman manufactured 190 UH-2A and UH-2B single-engined Seasprites for liaison, utility, SAR and combat rescue (four YUH-2A, 84 UH-2A, 102 UH-2B).

On 19 June 1968, UH-2A Seasprite pilot Lieutenant Clyde E. Lassen of squadron HC-7 launched from USS *Preble* (DLG-25) on a daring night mission to attempt the rescue of two downed F-4 Phantom crewmen. Lassen and his crew shot it out with North Vietnamese troops close by, collided with trees, and rescued both crewmen. Together with an A-4 Skyhawk pilot, Lassen became one of only two naval aviators to be awarded the Medal of Honor in Vietnam. It was a swansong, of sorts: by the 1970s, single-engined Seasprites were beginning to vanish from Navy decks and were being replaced by twin-engined HH-2C and HH-2D rescue helicopters.

The twin-engined Seasprite helicopter was introduced in the ASW role in October 1970 when the Navy selected the SH-2D as an interim LAMPS platform. This version introduced an undernose radome housing a Litton LN 66 search radar and an ASQ-81 MAD on the starboard fuselage pylon, and a removable sonobuoy rack in the fuselage port side for 15 SSQ-47 active or SSQ-41 passive sonobuoys. Twenty were converted from HH-2D rescue craft and entered service in 1972.

Kaman began delivering the definitive SH-2F LAMPS I aircraft in May 1973. Its primary role was to extend the outer defensive screen of a carrier battle group. The SH-2F had upgraded General Electric T58-GE-8F engines offering 1,350 shp (1007 kW), Kaman's advanced '101' rotor which gave longer life (3,000 hours), improved performance, reliability and maintainability, and a strengthened landing gear. An identifying feature was the tail wheel, which was relocated forward (by 1.83 m/6 ft) for greater deck-edge clearance when operating from smaller warships. These modifications enabled the SH-2F to operate at higher all-up weights than the SH-2D.

Improved radar

The SH-2F featured an improved Canadian Marconi LN 66HP surface search radar, which is also on the subsequent SH-2G and on planned export aircraft, where it adds to the helicopter's versatility with its ability to spot small surface targets, including the periscopes of submarines and the helmets of airmen downed at sea. The SH-2F also had an AN/ASQ-81(V)2 towed MAD (Magnetic Anomaly Detector) 'bird' on a starboard pylon, and a tactical

Left: The Seasprite was the winner of a 1956 US Navy competition to find a light helicopter for plane-guard, transport, casevac and fire control/correction duties. The HU2K (which became the UH-2A) flew in 1959 and deliveries began in 1962. The first twin-engined Seasprite (powered by T58 turboshafts), the UH-2C, flew in March 1966, and it led almost directly to the SH-2F.

Below: Fitted with the APS-122 radar in a temporary fairing, this YSH-2E was one of two trials aircraft for Kaman's unsuccessful LAMPS II bid. LAMPS II gave way to the more demanding LAMPS III specification, won by the SH-60B.

nav/comms system, necessitating a sensor operator in addition to the two pilots. Offensive capability comprised two Mk 46 torpedoes to engage sub-surface threats. Eighty-eight aircraft were converted from earlier variants (using up virtually every surviving airframe) and 16 surviving SH-2Ds were also brought up to SH-2F standard in a programme completed in 1982.

In March 1972, Kaman completed two YSH-2Es as testbeds for the Navy's LAMPS II programme with a new Texas Instruments APS-115 radar in a reconfigured nose. The Navy cancelled the programme later the same year. Kaman proposed a derivative of the SH-2 known as the Sealamp as a contender for the LAMPS III requirement that was eventually fulfiled by the SH-60B. This aircraft remained unbuilt, although several SH-2s were used to test LAMPS III systems and equipment.

SH-2F LAMPS I aircraft remained on duty aboard US Navy 'Knox'- and 'Kidd'-class frigates, 'Truxton'-class cruisers, and the first two 'Ticonderoga'-class cruisers. All but the first 'Belknap'-class cruisers carried SH-2Fs, as did the first and third through the 25th 'Oliver Hazard Perry'-class ASW frigates. In 1981, the Navy ordered production of 60 new-build SH-2Fs in addition to those already converted from earlier airframes. The last six of them were delivered as SH-2Gs. In 1994, the SH-2F, once operated by 11 squadrons, was phased out, leaving the Navy with today's two SH-2G Reserve squadrons.

Many new-build SH-2Fs and some earlier ships received AN/ALQ-66A(V)1 RWRs and AN/ALE-39 chaff/flare dispensers. From 1987, 16 SH-2Fs received a package of modifications to allow them to operate in the Persian Gulf. The package included the provision of AN/AAQ-16 FLIR under the nose, AN/ALQ-144 IR jammer, AN/AAR-47 and AN/DLQ-3 missile warning and jamming equipment, and new radios. During the Gulf War of 1991, SH-2Fs tested the ML-30 Magic Lantern laser sub-surface mine detector, a predecessor of the

Magic Lantern system being placed into service aboard SH-2Gs in 1997.

SH-2G aircraft

The SH-2G programme began in 1985 when Secretary of the Navy John Lehman told a Senate panel that it would be more cost effective to upgrade an operational helicopter than to develop a new one to increase anti-submarine capabilities. The prototype YSH-2G which flew on 2 April 1985 was simply a conversion of an SH-2F to serve as a testbed for the powerplant for the new model, two General Electric T700-GE-401/401C turboshaft engines each rated at 1,723 shp (1285 kW). The new engines, offering 10 per cent greater power and 20 per cent lower fuel burn, were the principal change from the SH-2F to the SH-2G. Kaman says that these engines give the 13,000-lb (5896-kg) Super Seasprite far better power margins than the 22,000-lb (9978-kg) Seahawk. The G model is essentially rebuilt above the roof, the engines being heavier and more powerful: the

engine cowlings fold down to become work platforms and will support the weight of two maintenance people. The SH-2G has Kaman's signature servo flaps on its main rotors, in lieu of hydraulic assist.

The tilted rotor mast of the H-2 has always enabled the Seasprite to hover level, an important advantage in small-deck landings and search and rescue missions. A benefit of the T700 installation is the creation of an additional neutral centre of gravity (CG) as a result of moving the combining gearbox from behind the engines to the front. This change enabled the H-2 to accommodate a sonar in the aft cabin without adopting a nose-up attitude in the dipping hover.

KAIC president Hardisty claims that the SH-2G has "unequalled reserve engine power and reserve electrical power for future growth." The SH-2G has also flown with new composite main rotor blades. Composite blades were tested on the SH-2F but never put into production. Successful flight tests on an SH-2G in August

Left: This SH-2F of one-time North Island-based HSL-35 is seen here dropping a sonobuoy (probably an SSQ-41) from its side-mounted rack. Like the SH-2G, the SH-2F was fitted with the Canadian-developed AN/UYS-503 acoustic processing system, operated from the rear cabin.

Above: Late in their careers some SH-2Fs were converted to MEF (Middle East Expeditionary Force) standard with undernose FLIR, cabin-mounted M60 machine-guns, chaff/flare launchers and IR jammers (note the mountings for two ALQ-144 jammers on the spine).

Above and right: Magic Lantern received its final operational testing with HSL-94 at Panama City, Florida, in September 1996 (above) before the first system was formally delivered on 7 December 1996. Development of the electro-optical/LIDAR system began in the late 1980s, but in the light of the total shock and amazement caused each time a modern warship is disabled by an underwater mine, progress with Magic Lantern and similar systems has been leisurely.

1996 verified performance predictions for a second-generation Composite Main Rotor Blades (CMRB2) on the Super Seasprite. The new blades promise dramatic improvements in durability and reductions in lifecycle costs for the SH-2G. They have a 15,000-hour projected service life, depending on usage spectrum. The 'Dash 101' metal blades now on the SH-2G are cleared for 3,700 flight hours. The composite blades have been selected by Australia for its SH-2G(A).

The Kaman SH-2G Seasprite is a conventional helicopter light enough (design gross weight of 13,500 lb/6123 kg) to operate from small warships. The new aircraft still combines compact external dimensions, a rugged dependable airframe, and the good handling characteristics of earlier Seasprites, but has far more installed power and a capable new mission equipment suite. The crew is composed of a pilot, co-pilot/tactics, and an enlisted crewman operating the ASW or Magic Lantern equipment.

The SH-2G introduced an internal APU (auxiliary power unit) for autonomous engine start. Avionics improvements include MIL-STD 1553B digital databus, AN/ASN-150 tactical management system, and multi-function displays. The SH-2G radar is the same as in the SH-2F but its signal is digitally processed. The key system in the ASW role, of course, is the AN/UYS-503 onboard acoustic processor. The LAMPS I helicopter typically datalinks sonobuoy returns to the ship. The UYS-503 processes returns onboard and makes the SH-2G an autonomous sub-hunter with enormous capability. Replacing the 31-channel sonobuoy receiver on the SH-2F, the G model's kit has a 99-channel capability, a critical enhancement for operations with other aircraft.

An SH-2G crew of HSL-84 led its battle group to victory in the biannual WOLHUNT co-ordinated surface warfare (SUW) and undersea warfare (USW) competition off the coast of California in September 1996. The Super Seasprite pilot served as overall Scene of Action Commander for a battle group that

included helicopters and fixed-wing patrol aircraft. With its UYS-503 acoustic processor, ASN-150 tactical navigation system, and sonobuoys, the SH-2G was first in the battle group to acquire a contact on the opposing submarine.

Magic Lantern

Magic Lantern was developed by Kaman as a follow-on to an earlier system, dubbed ML30, which earned prominence in hunting mines during the Gulf War. Magic Lantern uses pulses of laser light to detect and provide images of sea mines located in the 'upper water column' (keel depth) using a process known as LIDAR (light detection and ranging). Although advanced naval mines are now found at greater depths, most damage caused by mines is attributed to those near the surface, which are vulnerable to this system.

Given the low priority assigned to mine warfare 'between wars', Magic Lantern (which has no military designation) has been slow to enter service. As of July 1997, only a single unit was operational. Magic Lantern has been tested on the MH-53E Super Stallion and will be tested on the SH-60B/R Seahawk, making it likely that a competitive evaluation between Magic Lantern and a rival system, the long-delayed ATD-111 from Lockheed Martin, will finally materialise, probably in early 1998.

Magic Lantern itself has a history almost as interesting as that of the Super Seasprite. Kaman, of course, has extensive experience

with the integration of weapons, navigation systems and sensors onto airborne platforms. The company has been developing LIDARs for detecting naval mines since 1987, following the effective use of moored sea mines to disrupt tanker traffic in the Persian Gulf during the 1980-88 Iran-Iraq war. This effort was intensified following the devastating damage caused to the USS *Samuel B. Roberts* (FFG-58) on 14 April 1988. In that incident, a primitive $1,500 Iranian M08 mine caused damage to the ship that cost $96 million to repair. Kaman devoted extensive IR&D resources between 1987 and 1992 to developing brassboard helicopterborne mine-detection LIDARs, performing early laboratory and field demonstrations, and developing essential hardware components, software algorithms and employment concepts which lead to a prototype mine-detection LIDAR built for the Navy in 1989. Following field testing and refinement during 1989 and 1990, in 1991 this system, now called ML30, was activated by the Navy for deployment to the Persian Gulf during Operation Desert Storm. Within 18 days, the ML30 system was reassembled, tested and deployed to the Gulf with a support crew of Kaman personnel. Operating from an SH-2F aboard the frigate USS *Vreeland* (FF-1058), the ML30 flew more than 80 sorties in the northern Persian Gulf between mid-February and mid-April 1991, detecting a large number of mines in areas otherwise thought to be clear. Despite the fact that the ML30 system was a brassboard never intended for deployment and was

Above: Kaman estimates that it has up to 60 extant airframes available for conversion to SH-2G Super Seasprite standard. This process involves 'cutting the top off' an SH-2F and adding a new titanium skeletal structure to accept the higher-powered T700-GE-401 engines.

Above and left: The existing SH-2G cockpit is quite conventional in layout. Onboard systems are structured around the AN/ASN-160 tactical management system, linked to the AN/UYS-503 acoustic processor, AN/ARR-84 sonobuoy receiver and AN/AKT-22(V)6 sonobuoy datalink. For the much improved Australian SH-2G(A) aircraft, Kaman has proposed a Litton Systems EFIS cockpit (left) as part of the Integrated Tactical Avionics System that combines '1760' databus architecture. Australian navy Seasprites will have only two crew, with the tactical operator in the left-hand seat.

subjected to dust, salt spray and heavy smoke from the Kuwaiti oil well fires, the system maintained a 90 per cent availability rating.

Based in part on the performance of the ML30 system in the Gulf, the Navy moved forward with the Magic Lantern Advanced Development Model (ML-ADM). The ML-ADM system represents a major increase in capabilities over the ML30 system used in the Persian Gulf, with a higher-power, all solid-state transmitter, an optical scanner and multiple receivers for much larger area coverage and better depth localisation, plus a powerful onboard computer for real-time automatic target detection, classification and localisation. The ML-ADM system underwent its first Contractor Test during October 1993 and its

second in June 1994. ML-ADM successfully completed its Contractor Testing during October 1993 and June 1994, and US Navy Developmental Testing and Operational Assessment during July and August of 1994 and June of 1995.

Reserve minehunters

Magic Lantern has been integrated into the SH-2G helicopters operated by the US Naval Air Reserve. This included integration of Magic Lantern and MAGR GPS into the ASN-150 TACNAV. Following a verification test in September 1996 flown at CSS by HSL-94, the first LIDAR-based AMCM capability in the world was stood up at HSL-94 with the formal roll-out of Magic Lantern on 7 December 1996.

It was subsequently announced that two Magic Lantern units had been delivered to the squadron. Both were withdrawn for fixes and one returned. As of mid-1997, the squadron had the US Navy's only operational Magic Lantern SH-2G (BuNo. 163214), while two SH-2F Seasprites were operating at the factory as Magic Lantern trials aircraft (BuNos 161641 and 161905).

Magic Lantern is an electro-optical sensor technology consisting of a short-pulse laser illuminating source (transmitter), electronically gated, intensified CCD cameras (receiver), control and image processing computers and an operator station. The transmitter and receiver are located in an externally mounted pod, while the computers and the operator's station are inside the aircraft. The control computer sets the delay time between the laser Q-switch (fire) pulse and the opening of the receiver gate, sets the receiver gains, and sets the scanner position for each laser shot. An inter-scene dynamic range of many orders of magnitude allows the intensified camera to image transmitter returns from targets over a wide range of depths and target reflectivities. In addition, the receiver gating switches the receiver sensitivity over six orders of magnitude from nearly zero to single-photon sensitive in a matter of nanoseconds. Because the delay time and the time duration of the receiver gate following the laser pulse can be set arbitrarily, electronic gating greatly enhances the flexibility and performance of the sensor by providing range selectivity and optical noise rejection.

Surface rejection

Gating is used to reject transmitter returns from the ocean surface and to reduce noise due to ocean-scattered sunlight. It also greatly enhances the sensor's ability to image targets which have a low reflectivity or low contrast with the background. For example, the sensor can image low-reflectance targets by gating the cameras so that they register light backscattered from the sea water below the target, rather than the light reflected from the target itself. In this mode the target appears as a shadow surrounded by a bright background and the return is independent of the optical reflectivity of the target, depending only on the target being opaque.

A unique feature of Magic Lantern is the ability to use and control multiple independent receivers. The receivers can be set to image the same area at different depths to increase volume search rate. Multiple receivers with different depth gates can be used to localise the target depth on a single laser shot, with the presence of a shadow or reflection image determining whether the target is above or below the camera gate depth.

Magic Lantern-Adaptation is a helicopter-based sensor system for the rapid detection and automatic classification of minefields in the shallow water and beach areas known as the craft-landing zone (CLZ). Magic Lantern-Adaptation is based on the Magic Lantern moored-mine sensor but includes additional functions to optimise sensor performance against small targets in the variable-depth, high-clutter environment typical of the CLZ. Magic Lantern-Adaptation was successfully tested during November of 1994 and August 1995. During 1996 and 1997 ATR refinements and a

Kaman SH-2G Seasprite HSL-94 'Titans', US Navy Reserve NAS Willow Grove

RAN and RNZN competitions

The battle to supply new ship-board helicopters to the Royal Australian and Royal New Zealand Navies was a hard-fought one. The two had very different aircraft and systems requirements. For example, the RAN set very specific requirements for its ESM fit (a 'tiny' angle-of-arrival for intercepted signals and wide bandwidth coverage), FLIR system (specifying a 3 to 5-μ system, with specific parameters for background humidity, delta-T, and target-to-background rejection at set ranges) and a missile that could manoeuvre within defined constraints and hit targets, at specified ranges, in confined littoral conditions. Australia has yet to choose a radar (from the APS-143(V)3 or Elta EL/M-2022) or ESM (Litton or Loral) for its aircraft, and New Zealand will most likely follow all of the RAN's mission fit choices.

Rotor system

The SH-2G has an auto-stability system that monitors main blade tracking in flight, and controls blade pitch using the servo flaps on the blade trailing edge. An accelerometer measures vibration and automatically trims the blades up and down. US Navy aircraft are fitted with CMRB 1 blades. SH-2G(A)s will be fitted with the CMRB 2 system, which has an even longer (15,000-hour) life.

The US Navy and abroad

The sudden decline in US Seasprite numbers has been attributed by many to the United States' 'carrier-happy Navy', which has decided to protect its 12 carrier battle groups from defence cuts by disposing of its 46 'Knox'-class ('1052') and 25 (SH-2-capable) Oliver Hazard Perry'-class (FFG-7) frigates, to foreign customers or the Reserve fleet. This is good news for Kaman as it has provided new customers such as Egypt, Australia and New Zealand, calls into question the long-term future of the two surviving Navy Reserve SH-2G units. Bahrain, Greece and Taiwan are among those who have taken delivery of Seasprite-capable ships recently – but all are existing SH-60/S-70 operators. Taiwan was to have taken delivery of 12 SH-2Fs in 1993 but lack of funding shelved the deal.

HSL-94 began SH-2 operations on 1 October 1985 when the unit stood up as a Navy Reserve squadron equipped with the SH-2F. HSL-94 received its first SH-2Gs in 1994 and survived the culling of the Navy's substantial SH-2F fleet in the early- to mid-1990s. In December 1995 the unit deployed in support of a six-month joint exercise (UNITAS) with Latin American navies. In June 1996 HSL-94 also took part in the major multi-national BALTOPS '96 exercise in the Baltic Sea and North Atlantic. HSL-94 is the only US Navy unit with the Magic Lantern system and so regularly deploys with active Navy vessels as part of that service's Defense Total Force concept.

Sonobuoys

In a vertical launcher mounted to port, the SH-2G can carry 15 sonobuoys. Buoys in use with US Navy units comprise either SSQ-41 DIFAR (Directional LOFAR) or SSQ-62 DICASS (Directional Command-activated Active Sonobuoy System) types. US Navy units also use the sonobuoy launcher cover as a convenient spot for 'nose art'.

Specification
Kaman SH-2G Super Seasprite

Powerplant: two General Electric T700-GE-401/C turboshafts, each rated at 1,723 shp (1285 kW)

Weights: empty 7,680 lb (3483 kg); maximum take-off gross weight (MTOGW) 13,900 lb (6305 kg); useful load 5,070 lb (2299 kg)

Performance: service ceiling, 21,000 ft (6401 m); hover ceiling OGE 15,600 ft (4755 m); hover ceiling IGE 18,600 ft (5669 m); rate of climb 2,360 ft/min (719 m/min); maximum range (no external tanks) 200 nm (230 miles; 370 km); maximum range (3 external tanks) 560 nm (644 miles; 1036 km); maximum endurance 5.7 hours

Dimensions: main rotor diameter 44 ft 4 in (13.50 m); length, rotors turning 52 ft 6 in (15.99 m); fuselage length excluding tail rotor 40 ft 0 in (12.19 m); fuselage with nose and blades folded 38 ft 4 in (11.68 m); height, rotors turning 15 ft 0.5 in (4.589 m); height, blades folded 13 ft 7 in (4.14 m); tailplane span 9 ft 9 in (2.97 m); wheel base 16 ft 10 in (5.13 m)

Above left and right: This is Kaman's own trials ship modified to test equipment for Egypt's 10 SH-2G(E)s. These aircraft will be uniquely fitted with the AQS-18(A) dipping sonar (and thus retain a three-man crew) and will be capable of carrying Mk 46 (above) or Mk 50 torpedoes – some sources indicate that Egypt will only receive early-model Mk 46s. Torpedo trials for Egypt also included final trials of a new digital autopilot hover coupler, integrated with ITAS.

Left: Australia's SH-2G(A) Seasprites will be armed with the Kongsberg Penguin anti-ship missile. Form and fit trials with the Penguin have been completed, but, at time of writing, a live missile had not been fired by the SH-2G.

Below: This scene on HSL-84's ramp at NAS North Island provides a clear view of the SH-2G's sonobuoy launcher and a 500-lb Mk 46 torpedo.

datalink for real-time display of mine and minefield locations on the ground will be added, and ML(A) will be featured in the Joint Countermine Advanced Concept Technology Demonstration (ACTD) during August of 1997.

Operations

In the post-Cold War US Navy, the SH-2G Super Seasprite is routinely deployed only on short-hull FFG-7 frigates which are not equipped with the Indal RAST (Recovery Assist Secure and Traverse) system and cannot accommodate the SH-60B. Kaman frequently makes the point, however, that the Super Seasprite can operate from any aviation-capable ship, including Coast Guard cutters. Although the US Navy has long ago disposed of the last of its '1052' or 'Knox'-class frigates (which have one hangar), it retains only eight of its short-hulled FFG-7s (which have two hangars but usually deploy with one helicopter). These vessels are operated by the Naval Reserve Force (NRF), which typically carries out operations in waters close to the US. Reserve forces are being used alongside active units in lengthy blue-water deployments around the world. A frigate typically functions as a picket ship, probing the outer fringe of a battle group for hostile submarines. SH-2Gs crews perform this role for

the NRF but the Reserve force does not routinely embark to distant locations as part of a carrier battle group. Under a May 1996 plan, these ships will be replaced in the Reserve by long-hull FFG-7s which can use the SH-60B/R, leaving the future of the Super Seasprite in doubt so far as US forces are concerned.

In American usage, the frigate – a much smaller vessel than the destroyer – is becoming a thing of the past. The May 1997 Quadrennial Defense Review (QDR) called for the accelerated retirement of all FFG-7s, although there

was no detail as how this would be achieved. With no change, all eight short-hull 'Fig Sevens' will be sold abroad by 2001. A frigate is a 'low end' blue water escort vessel lacking much of the offensive power found aboard destroyers and cruisers, and the US Navy purposely downsized the low end of its escort force to preserve the high end. The service is also going to retire seven early 'Spruance'-class (DD-963) destroyers which might otherwise have been candidates for SH-2G operation.

The Cold War was still a reality and '1052' and FFG-7 warships still part of the US fleet in

1987, when the US Navy began upgrading SH-2F helicopters to SH-2G standard with T700-GE-401 engines in place of T58s. The plan was to convert 61 SH-2Fs and buy 103 new-build SH-2Gs to provide LAMPS I capability from '1052s', for which the Sikorsky SH-60B LAMPS III is too heavy.

Unfortunately for Kaman, this programme began as the Cold War ended and the Pentagon decided to sell off all '1052s' to allies such as Egypt, Taiwan and Turkey. Thus, only 24 SH-2Gs were built (the final six 'new-build' aircraft in what had been the SH-2F production line, plus 18 conversions, one of which was a non-flying aircraft for parts). Eight aircraft each are operated by Reserve squadrons HSL-84 'Thunderbolts' at NAS North Island, California, and HSL-94 'Titans' at NAS Willow Grove, Pennsylvania. A single SH-2G performs developmental work at the Strike Test facility, NAS Patuxent River, Maryland.

North Island is also the headquarters of the Reserve helicopter wing and HSL-84 has an additional duty as the FRS (fleet replenishment squadron), or training unit, for the SH-2G type. Only HSL-94 is currently scheduled to acquire Magic Lantern capability. Both squadrons routinely operate from the NRF's short-hull, non-RAST FFG-7s in waters contiguous to the United States.

The H-2 series is credited with 1.1 million flight hours and more than 500 at-sea deployments of six months or more. Kaman's Hardisty claims that the Super Seasprite is the "smoothest helicopter in the world." It is single-pilot certified. Credited with superb gust response, it handles comfortably in turbulence at a ship's fantail.

US Navy crew

Its two pilots are naval aviators. The co-pilot is the tactics officer and is charged with planning and executing the attack on a submarine. The UYS-503 acoustic processor is operated by the third crew member, an aviation warfare systems operator (AWSO). AWSOs are also found on S-3B, P-3C, SH-60 and H-3 aircraft. The AWSO typically attends air crew school (five weeks), rescue swimmer school (five weeks), and basic ASW school (four weeks), all at NAS Pensacola, Florida.

Traditionally, ASW technicians have operated the sensors on both patrol aircraft and helicopters since World War II. Under the established division of responsibility, the enlisted member turns the knobs and gets the data while the officer interprets its tactical significance and prosecutes the attack (though each shares some of the other's roles in various degrees, based on experience and the individual platform).

The overall management of the anti-submarine warfare picture is managed through the

carrier battle group staff and with long-range support from the responsible submarine group commander's staff (far removed from the scene, but with a concentration of highly specialised skill) with support from various ocean surveillance platforms and networks. These staff jobs and ASWOCs (ASW Operations Centers) are manned by officers. They are supported by enlisted technicians and chief warrant officers who handle the computerised displays, consoles and datalink networks (though various officers have varying levels of expertise in these areas, often retained from prior enlisted service). The bulk of the data collection and initial compilation is handled by the enlisted ASW warfare specialists from the air, surface and submerged platforms. They often have cross training in maintenance and repair of the gear they operate, which is seldom the case for officers in similar jobs.

When a detachment goes to sea, it becomes a department of the ship, comparable to supply, operations, and engineering, with the detachment commander serving as the OIC (officer in charge) of the Aviation Department.

HSL-84 and -94 crews routinely train in alternate missions, including OTH (over the horizon) targeting of vessels for ASuW (anti-surface warfare) combat, search and rescue, utility work, medical evacuation, and the VertRep (vertical replenishment) mission – hauling supplies to ships to sea – for which the SH-2G has a limited capability. SH-2G crews say they could, if called upon, carry out conventional warfare in the MEF (Middle East Expeditionary Force) configuration that was employed by some SH-2Fs in Operation Desert Storm. The MEF package consists of two door-mounted M60 machine-guns, Hughes AN/AAQ-16 FLIR in a ball turret, ALQ-144 IR jammer, and two ALE-39 chaff units. The FLIR ball turret, when installed, is found on the forward port side on the SH-2G (but was forward to starboard on the SH-2F).

The Super Seasprite is now the ideal candidate for other navies operating '1052s', FFG-7s, or similar frigates. Thus, Kaman's ability to upgrade existing SH-2Fs – about 52 of which are in 'boneyard' storage – makes the company and its aircraft very competitive on the interna-

tional stage. To win purchase contracts from overseas navies, the Super Seasprite is pitted against competitors such as the Westland Super Lynx and, to a lesser extent, derivatives of the Eurocopter AS 565 Panther and Sikorsky S-70 Seahawk.

All future Super Seasprite upgrade work, beginning with those for Egypt, will follow the pattern established when SH-2Fs were brought up to SH-2G standard. The stored airframe is brought from the 'boneyard' (Davis-Monthan AFB, Arizona) first to Kaman's facility at Moosup, Connecticut, where it is stripped and blasted, creating an unpainted aircraft shell. The shell is then taken to the Bloomfield factory where an entirely new installation is made from the roof up, with titanium reinforcement to support the heavier, more powerful T700 engines. Final assembly and initial flight is performed at Bloomfield, where the aircraft receives the new rotor system, new drive train, cockpit and wiring, plus any mission equipment specified by the purchaser.

Egypt's SH-2G(E)

The Arab Republic of Egypt is the first non-US SH-2G operator, having ordered 10 of the aircraft for the two 'Knox'-class ('1052') frigates it obtained from the US Navy. To be initially delivered in late 1997, the Egyptian Super Seasprites will be fitted with the AlliedSignal AQS-18(A) digital dipping sonar, making them the only dipping-sonar Seasprites in the world. The AQS-18A processor can handle either buoy or dipping sonar inputs, but the SH-2G(E) package will use only the sonar. Active sonar is a more effective sensor in noisy environments (like in busy sealanes), and the Egyptians intend to work in the busy Mediterranean. Reports that a MAD detector will also be part of the package are in error.

The first Egyptian delivery was scheduled for October 1997. The first SH-2G configured for the Egypt programme (aircraft 162580, which will remain at the Kaman plant and is not slated for delivery to Egypt) tested the dipping sonar package at NAS Patuxent River, Maryland

earlier in 1997. The configuration includes the 572-lb (223-kg) AlliedSignal unit, 1,500 ft (457 m) of cable, and a digital hover-coupler enhanced stabilisation system that can fly an automated approach to a programmed altitude and hold a hover based on sonar cable angle or Doppler inputs.

The 10 SH-2G(E) Super Seasprites for Egypt, all former SH-2F airframes, were in various stages of construction at Kaman in mid-1997. Ships 1 through 10 for Egypt are former SH-2Fs with bureau numbers, respectively, 163212, 163213, 162577, 162581, 161652, 161906, 162587, 162582, 161909 and 161645.

Australia's SH-2G(A)

Australia is becoming a Super Seasprite operator to fill the needs of its requirement Project (Sea) 1411.1427, calling for a weapon system that is compatible with its new Meko 200-ANZ-class (more commonly called 'Anzac'-class) frigates. Australia will have eight Meko 200-ANZs by October 2004 (the first, now in

The Worldwide Kaman SH-2 Population

149030	SH-2F, to be SH-2G no. 2 for New Zealand	161906	Ship 6, Egypt	Ship no. 8	162582
150154	SH-2F, no. 3 for New Zealand	161907	HSL-94 NW-21	Ship no. 9	161909
150171	SH-2F, no. 4 (of 4) for New Zealand	161908	AMARC 05/06/97 (ex HSL-94 NW-20)	Ship no. 10	161645
152191	SH-2F, to be SH-2G no. 3 for New Zealand	161909	Ship 9, Egypt		
161641	SH-2F,	161912	HSL-94 NW-23	**HSL-94 NAS JRB Willow Grove, Pa.**	
	NASC (Naval Air Systems Command),	162576	HSL-94 NW-27	(tail code NW) as of 16 May, 1997	
	RD & TE at KAC flight test facility, Bloomfield.	162577	Ship 3, Egypt		
	04/06/97. Old paint scheme. Marked as SH-2F.	162578	HSL-94 NW-24	(20)	163214*
	Magic Lantern test aircraft. 'Magic Lantern'	162580	KAC Flight Test, 05/06/97,	21	161907
	in white paint beneath 'Navy' on fuselage.		marked as SH-2G(E) but is not one of	22	161644
	Scheduled to become the first of four interim		the ten aircraft to be delivered to Egypt;	23	161912
	SH-2Fs for New Zealand		tested the dipping Sonar to be used by Egypt	24	162578
161642	Strike Test, NAS Patuxent River 05/06/97	162581	Ship 4, Egypt	25	161658
161643	HSL-84, NW-06	162582	Ship 8, Egypt	26	161647
161644	HSL-94, NW-22	162585	SH-2F No. 2 for New Zealand	27	162576
161645	Ship 10, Egypt. Egypt ships 1	162587	Ship 7, Egypt	*163214, the only Magic Lantern aircraft in service,	
	through 6 were indoors at KAC	163212	Ship1, Egypt	is scheduled to be side no. 20 but does not have the	
	being upgraded from SH-2F to SH-2G(E)	163213	Ship 2, Egypt	number painted on yet.	
	on 03/06/97	163214	HSL-94; has been assigned NW-20		
161647	HSL-94, NW-26		but tail code and side number	**SH-2Fs for New Zealand:**	
161650	SARDIP 1, cocooned at KAC		were not yet painted on as of 16/05/97;		
161652	Ship 5, Egypt		only Magic Lantern aircraft in service; replaced	1	161641
161653	Struck at KAC for parts, *i.e.*		161908 as NW-20; apparently previously	2	162585
	officially made a non-flying aircraft.		at KAC for Magic Lantern program	3	150154
161657	SH-2F, to be SH-2G no. 1 for New Zealand	163541	HSL-84, NW-07	4	150171
161658	HSL-94, NW-25	163542	AMARC (ex HSL-84, NW-02)		
161899	SH-2F, to be SH-2G no. 4 for New Zealand	163543	HSL-84, NW-04	**SH-2Fs to become SH-2Gs for New Zealand:**	
161900	HSL-84, NW-05	163544	HSL-84, NW-00	1	161657
161904	SARDIP 2, cocooned at KAC	163545	HSL-84, NW-01	2	149030
161905	SH-2F at KAC. Old paint scheme.	163546	HSL-84, NW-03	3	152191
	Painted as HSL-32. Old paint scheme.			4	161899
	No designation painted on aircraft. Magic	**Notes to above list**			
	Lantern test aircraft. 'Magic Lantern' in white	***1.** All aircraft listed are SH-2G unless otherwise		*New Zealand's SH-2Fs will be serialled NZ3450/	
	paint beneath 'Navy' on fuselage.	indicated. Egyptian SH-2Fs being rebuilt as SH-2G(E).*		*3453 while the SH-2Gs will be NZ3440/3443.*	

2. *Identifications of current HSL-94 aircraft are valid as of 16/5/97, on which date 163214 was the only Magic Lantern aircraft in service. The squadron is due to send at least one more aircraft back to Kaman Aircraft Corporation for Magic Lantern conversion. After that, further Magic Lantern conversions will take place on site at Willow Grove, Pa. No plans exist for the other current squadron to acquire Magic Lantern capability.*

3. *Identifications of current HSL-84 aircraft are valid as of 05/06/96, but side numbers may have been recorded on earlier dates.*

4. *SARDIP (Selective Aircraft Reclamation and Disposal in Place) covers four SH-2Gs removed from flying status and used for parts at Kaman, namely 161650, 161904, 163209, and 163210. All four except for 163210, plus a 'SLAP' aircraft or proof of concept aircraft possibly assigned no buno. were cocooned at KAC 97-06-05.*

5. *Two US Navy SH-2Gs are stored at AMARC (161908, 163542).*

6. *Aircraft 163541 through 163546 were completed initially as SH-2Gs and never existed as SH-2Fs. All other SH-2Gs are former SH-2Fs.*

The Egyptian program

Ship no. 1	163212
Ship no. 2	163213
Ship no. 3	162577
Ship no. 4	162581
Ship no. 5	161652
Ship no. 6	161906
Ship no. 7	162587

Left: The last SH-2G was handed over to the US Navy in 1994/95, so the aircraft in service today are relatively 'young', having been rebuilt with a 10,000-hour airframe life.

Right: Egypt will be the first export customer for the Seasprite, in an FMS deal for 10 aircraft worth $170 million plus spares and training. Deliveries are expected to proceed at the rate of one per month from late 1997 and six additional SH-2G(E)s may be required in the future. By the end of 1997 Egypt will have three 'Oliver Hazard Perry'-class and two 'Knox'-class frigates in service.

Below: Throughout 1997 and 1998 Kaman will continue its export battles with Sikorsky, Westland and Eurocopter in one of the few military aviation growth markets left.

Zealand's two new Meko 200-ANZ-class and two modernised 'Leander'-class frigates.

New Zealand is very interested in the Super Seasprite's capability to fire the IR-imaging or TV-guided AGM-65 Maverick air-to-ground missile, demonstrated in missile qualification tests that consisted of three firings at the Yuma, Arizona proving grounds, 14-15 February 1996. The first firing was performed in a hover to test 'safe separation'. The second, with an unarmed missile, was conducted at 100 kt (114 mph; 185 km/h) forward speed. In the third firing, an armed Maverick was fired at 100 kt and made a direct hit on its target.

These firings were conducted by aircraft 163214, which was then assigned as a test ship at the factory. The live-fire demonstration was conducted with a TV-guided Maverick, although New Zealand will acquire the IR version. A final configuration for carriage of the Maverick has not yet evolved.

Other countries

Turkey – On 8 August 1994, the US Congress was notified of a planned FMS (Foreign Military Sales) deal involving 14 stored SH-2F Seasprites (12 intact aircraft plus two to be dismantled and used for parts) for use aboard '1052s'. Turkish-Greek tensions in early 1995 appear to have resulted on a US 'hold' on naval support for Turkey. Turkey has four '1052s' with four more currently tied up by the US 'hold', plus eight Meko 200 frigates, and operates three Agusta AB 204 utility and nine Agusta AB 212 ASW helicopters.

Malaysia – In 1996, Kaman made a bid to Malaysia, which is looking to introduce a new generation of helicopters for the Royal Malaysian navy to replace its Westland Wasps.

Apart from the obvious countries that operate frigates, the Super Seasprite is the ideal helicopter for the 80- to 100-m (263- to 328-ft) ocean patrol vessels being planned jointly by Australia, New Zealand and Malaysia, and known as Ocean Patrol Combatants (OPCs). The S-70/SH-60 is too heavy for these vessels. The future of the Super Seasprite will depend heavily on the ability of Kaman to 'sell' its ability to upgrade Seasprites now in storage at AMARC at Davis-Monthan and deliver them to new customers as Super Seasprites.

Robert F. Dorr

service, was commissioned in April 1996) and its order for 11 SH-2G(A) Super Seasprites is for these vessels. It should be noted, however, that Australia also has six FFG-7s (two of which were built in Australia) which normally carry one Sikorsky S-70B-2 Seahawk ASW helicopter plus one Aérospatiale AS 350BS Ecureuil utility helicopter in this class's two helicopter hangars. (Australia's three Bell 206B Kiowas and seven Sea King Mk 56s are land-based, non-ASW aircraft.)

The Royal Australian Navy's SH-2G(A) Super Seasprites will incorporate an Integrated Tactical Avionics System (ITAS) 'glass cockpit', new sensors, and AGM-119B Penguin Mk 2 Mod 7 missiles. All will be able to operate from any helicopter-capable ship in the RAN.

KAC president Hardisty says the SH-2G will "complement" the relatively new S-70B-2s, which use the same T700 engines, APUs and rescue hoist, and almost identical UYS-503 acoustic processor. However, Australia may be interested in expanding its SH-2G(A) purchase to 29, to add a second helicopter aboard its FFG-7s. The SH-2G(A) differs from the S-70B-2

in being point designed for the two-crewman ASuW mission with air-to-surface missiles.

For the Australia SH-2G(A) programme, Kaman has fielded a team which includes Litton, supplier of ITAS; CSC of Australia, to provide trainers and software; engine-maker General Electric; Safe Air Ltd (of New Zealand) for fabrication, assembly, and component overhaul; Transfield Defence Systems, for ship integration; and Scientific Management Associates for logistical support. The Australian aircraft are expected to have Telephonis APS-143 multi-mode radar with a potential for Inverse Synthetic Aperture Radar (ISAR) mode to classify as well as detect surface combatants.

New Zealand's SH-2G

After accepting tenders on 8 September 1995 and determining that the Super Lynx had less excess power and a lower fatigue life, New Zealand ordered four SH-2G Super Seasprites. The age of its four Westland Wasps, which date to 1966, mean that New Zealand also will acquire four SH-2F Seasprites on an interim basis. The helicopters will operate from New

HARPOONEX

Expanding roles for the US Navy Orion force

Though the size of the US Navy P-3 Orion fleet has been cut back, the range of roles and missions facing the aircraft and their crews has not. The Orion is no longer purely a long-range, blue-water 'sub hunter', but an important littoral warfare platform. The role of the US Navy Reserve is also expanding as it fills the gaps left in the active Navy 'Papa Three Charlie' inventory.

Between February and April 1997 live-fire exercises were held at NAS Barbers Point, Hawaii that involved both active and reserve US Navy P-3 squadrons from West and East Coast units. Harpoonex CPW-4 put P-3C Update III aircraft and crews to the test with ASW, mine, torpedo and Harpoon launching scenarios on the ranges of PMRF Barking Sands, Hawaii. The primary goal was to fire the Harpoon anti-ship missile, yet it was important to combine other tactical scenarios such as torpedo and mine delivery ('Torpex' and

'Minex', respectively). This involved the entire gamut of planning, loading and weapons execution followed by an 'Endex' review of the lessons learned.

Harpoonex was far from a routine exercise. The opportunity to fire a Harpoon does not come along often; per year, only one training missile is allocated to the four East Coast Reserve units, and one to the four West Coast Reservists. As a result, a squadron will only get to fire a Harpoon every four years, at best. Then, only one crew from each squadron gets

to make a shot. On this occasion two West Coast squadrons (VP-69 and VP-91) fired a missile together, but only because no firings had been made the previous year. For everyone involved, it was a first.

The location for the exercise was NAS Barbers Point, Hawaii, the permanent home for active-duty squadrons VP-4, VP-9 and VP-47. Three Reserve units – VP-62 of NAS Jacksonville, Florida, VP-69 of NAS Whidbey Island, Washington, and VP-91 of NAS Moffett Field, California – deployed to Barbers Point and flew their sorties in the PMRF (Pacific Missile Range Facility) Barking Sands ranges near the island of Kauai, which include underwater ranges.

The P-3's roots can be traced to the Lockheed L-188, which first flew in 1957. Since then, the Orion airframe has evolved into the United States' premier land-based sub-killing system. The aircraft operates as a comprehensive system, which involves detailed co-ordination of all 10 crew members. The basic mission crew complement of the P-3C is 10, though usually 12 crew members are onboard because typical P-3C flights are lengthy due to mission requirements (a backup pilot and flight engineer are required to reduce crew fatigue). The crew consists of two pilots (both rated for either left or right seat), a flight engineer, a TACCO (tactical co-ordinator), navigator, sensor 1/acoustic operator, sensor 2/acoustic operator, sensor 3/EW (radar) operator, IFT (inflight technician), and the ordnance man (on Reserve P-3s only).

Top: VP-65 'Tridents' is a US Navy Reserve Patrol Squadron, based at Pt Mugu, California. 'Patron 65' was established in 1970 and has always been a Reserve unit. It transitioned to the P-3C (from the P-3B) in 1991. VP-65 is typical of the Reserve units that routinely operate as the equals of their regular Navy counterparts. Note the AN/ALQ-78 ESM pod on the innermost pylon.

Left: VP-91 'Black Cats' was one of the participants in Harpoonex CPW-4. This view from the cockpit was taken during the ASW portion of the exercise when the crew were chasing a Mk 30 Mod 1 submarine target.

Above: At the peak of its Cold War strength, the
US Navy had 24 regular squadrons of P-3s, each
with nine aircraft. This total has now been
reduced to just 15, including two special
operations squadrons. This P-3C is assigned to
VP-62 'Broadarrows', based at NAS Jacksonville.

*Right: Seen in the evening light at NAS Barbers
Point, Hawaii, this Orion is a P-3C of VP-47
'Golden Swordsmen'. VP-47 took part in the
'Sinkex' portion of the Harpoonex exercise,
attacking the target ship (the former USS
Edwards) with Mk 82 bombs.*

The Orion is powered by four 4,910-ehp
(3662-kW) Allison T56-A-14 engines, similar
to those on the C-130, E-2C and C-2A. The
engines are always run at 100 per cent while the
fuel (JP-8) flow is regulated, which indirectly
alters the propeller pitch, thus changing air
speed. The incredible endurance of the P-3 on a
sortie can be in excess of 14 hours, which is
why the Orion never needed inflight refuelling
capability. Often during a mission, two of the
four engines are shut down and feathered while
the aircraft is loitering or patrolling to achieve
maximum range and efficiency. The maximum
take-off weight is 140,000 lb (63636 kg), and
speeds of up to 405 kt (465 mph; 748 km/h)
can be reached.

Orion weapons

The current and latest US Navy variant of the
ASW P-3 is the 'Charlie' Update III. The P-3C
has an internal weapons bay that has eight hardpoints. Weapons carried in the bay include
Mk 46 and Mk 50 Barracuda torpedoes,
Mk 82/83/84 GP bombs (although Mk 84s are
a rarity), Mk 36 Destructor/Mk 62 Quickstrike
mines (based on the Mk 82 500-lb bomb),
Mk 40 Destructor/Mk 63 Quickstrike mines
(based on the Mk 83 1,000-lb bomb) plus Mk 52,
Mk 55, Mk 56 mines, Mk 60 CAPTOR and
Mk 65 Quickstrike mines. There are 10 underwing weapon stations as well, and weapons that
can be carried on the racks include depth
bombs, mines and GP bombs, AGM-84
Harpoon, AGM-84E SLAM and AGM-65
Maverick. A wide range of rocket pods can be
carried by the P-3C, including LAU-10 (four 5-in
Zuni rockets), LAU-61 (19 2.75-in rockets) and
LAU-68 (seven 2.75-in rockets). The SUU-25
launcher (based on the LAU-10) is used to
dispense LUU-2 magnesium flares and has
replaced the older SUU-25/Mk 45 parachute
flare combination for this task. To simulate 500-lb
mine/bomb drops, BDU-45 inert practice
bombs are used. The P-3C can carry 48
sonobuoys in the sonobuoy launcher with
another 48 reloads carried inside the aircraft.
Sonobuoy tubes can also be used to launch Mk 58
or Mk 25 smoke markers, which are activated
upon contact with salt water. The Mk 58 burns
for one hour and the Mk 25 for 20 minutes.
AIM-9 Sidewinders have been trialled on the
wing pylons, but are not carried. The
P-3C no longer carries the Mk 54 depth bomb
or LAU-69 19-tube rocket launcher. The
nuclear role has also been removed from the
regular P-3 force.

All P-3Cs are equipped with the Texas
Instruments APS-36 IRDS (Infra-Red Detector
System). The IR sensor turret retracts behind a
protective door just aft of the nose radome and
just forward of the nosegear wheel well. The
turret is only extended when it is in use, so is
not noticeable when the Orion is on the ramp.
At the rear lower portion of the fuselage there is
an array of sonobuoy openings in the fuselage,
which is the easiest way to differentiate a P-3C
externally from the older P-3As and P-3Bs that
have since been retired.

Flying the P-3C

Senior VP-91 P-3C pilot Lieutenant
Commander Jeff Dodd, who has over 2,600
hours flying the P-3, stated, "(on an ASW
mission) we usually operate on our own in the
Orion and drop buoys at 300 ft (91 m) and 220
kt (252 mph; 406 km/h). Our bank angle is
typically 45° and when flying that low we
usually have our autopilot altitude hold on. The
P-3C has a maximum speed of 405 kt (465
mph; 748 km/h) at sea level and when we are
cruising, in transit, and flying for max range and
optimum fuel flow, the air speed is around
280-330 kt (320-378 mph; 518-609 km/h) true
air speed, dependent on weight, altitude,
temperature, etc. The engines are self-starting
and the Orion is APU-equipped. The P-3C is
rated as an all-weather aircraft since the engines
have anti-ice and de-ice capable leading-edge
surfaces that are heated via turbine bleed air.

"One thing that you need to be careful about
when flying the P-3C is that if you are unfortunate
enough to lose an engine or two engines, a
touchy asymmetrical thrust situation can
develop. The worst case scenario would be if
you lost two engines on the same wing, but
P-3s have safely recovered in that manner in the
past.

"When we start the P-3C, we start no. 2 first,
then no. 3 and begin taxiing. While taxiing, we
use a little steering wheel on the left side of the
cockpit. We then will start nos 1 and 4. For
take-off, the aircraft is usually heavy and the
thrust is sluggish. Rotation happens about 130
kt after a 6,000-ft (1829-m) take-off roll, and at
6 kt (6.8 mph; 11 km/h) later you are airborne.
Then we pull the nose up around 6° to 8°, and
once at about 40-50 ft (12-15 m) AGL, we raise
the gear (it has a 300-kt/344-mph/554-km/h
restriction). We start bringing the flaps up incrementally and begin our turn to our heading.
When landing, we use full flaps; our approach
speed is around 140 kt (160 mph; 258 km/h)

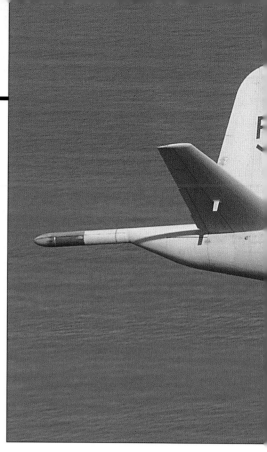

Sensor III manages the Orion's EW, ESM and radar suite. The radar can be either the AN/APS-115 or the improved AN/APS-137 ISAR set – both supplied by Texas Instruments.

Sensor I and II both monitor the Orion's sonobuoys. Underwater sounds from the buoys are displayed as waveforms on a screen, which demand substantial experience to interpret.

Above left: This VP-65 P-3C is seen taxiing out at NAS Pt Mugu. All current USN P-3Cs have been upgraded to Update III standard, which improves the onboard AN/UYS-1 Advanced Signal Processor set and AN/USQ-78 ASP displays.

and we touch down at 125 kt (143 mph; 230 km/h). The P-3 also has a great view, and when taxiing around the field you're sitting up 20 ft (6 m).

"Once you have finished the RAG and are assigned to your squadron, you are not plane commander qualified. After four to six months with the first P-3C assignment, you get a 3P rating. Four to six months after that, you get a 2P rating. Then six to 12 months later, and after 850 hours in the type, you finally become a plane commander and get the PPC rating.

"I had an opportunity to do an exchange tour with the Royal Netherlands Navy. I went to language school for six months and learned Dutch. The Dutch operate their P-3C Update IIIs under different rules and you need to have an open mind. They don't deploy, but do go on detachments. We participated in many NATO exercises and one of the benefits was sharing experiences and information."

Dodd closed with, "When I chose P-3s I also wanted that lifestyle as well. If I had to do it all over again, I probably would have still selected P-3s. It has certainly proved its worth and Lockheed is still building brand-new P-3s today. The P-3 is like the Energizer battery, it keeps going and going and going, a result of a very strong airframe. Some of the P-3s in the inventory are over 30 years old, and service life extension programmes are in place.

"VP-91 'Black Cats' won the Battle E in 1996. I like flying the P-3C and its a great airplane. It's not sexy and sleek like a fighter, but it is a good steady platform and a solid performer. It is aerodynamically stable, has good

power because the engines are constantly at 100 per cent power, and the design has been around since the 1950s. I like flying it from a crew concept, with 12 people coming together as a team. In the Tac Air community, the crews are one, two or four. A lot of chatter in the P-3 over the ICS in the form of a co-ordinated team effort is exciting."

Orion crew members

When asked about their jobs as flight engineers, AD1 Rich Belme and AD2 Chris Northern of VP-91 added the following. "We are responsible for pre-flight, fuelling, loading, aircraft weight balance before taking off, and working out aircraft performance via the charts. We also ensure that the Orion is mechanically safe, safe for flight, and we are the systems experts of the P-3. During flight, we monitor systems, do fuel management, monitor safety of flight, keep our eye on the altitude and air speed, monitor communications, and are an extra set of eyes looking for air traffic or obstacles while low. We will help the pilots tackle any emergency that arises and also we start and shut down the engines. During tactical missions we will often shut down both outboard engines (nos 1 and 4) for loitering, which results in fuel savings for mission economics. Typical loitering speeds are around 190-200 kt (218-230 mph; 315-370 km/h), and we also input data into the computer during the sortie."

The TACCO manages the entire tactical situation and often is the mission commander (although the aircraft commander can also be

the mission commander). Inputs from the Sensor 1, 2 and 3 operators/stations, navigator, pilots and ordnance man go to the TACCO. The TACCO makes the final attack decisions and almost always initiates the weapons release, and has the HACLS (Harpoon Aircraft Command Launch-control Set) computer at his station.

The navigator officer is responsible for keeping the aircraft at the proper locations throughout the flight and within the area the P-3C is working. The navigator sits next (on the starboard side) to the TACCO and both are just aft of the flight deck. Both the navigator and TACCO have large protruding observation windows and help visually identify targets and aid in search and rescue missions. They have a smaller polarised sliding window that limits the amount of light coming to their stations, making the electronic displays easier to see while working a target.

Sensor operators and systems

The Sensor 1 and 2 operators sit at a large side-by-side console, located on the port side of the fuselage aft of the TACCO station. They are the ASW acoustic experts, with Sensor 1 being the more experienced and senior of the two operators. The Sensor 3/EW (radar) operator is responsible for target IFF, the radar, the IRDS, the MAD, and the ESM suite.

The P-3C has one of two radar systems. The older radar is the less-capable AN/APS-115, although some aircraft now have been upgraded to the newer AN/APS-137 ISAR (Inverse Synthetic Aperture Radar), which is the same radar that the S-3B Viking has. Many squadrons have a mix of Orions, with two different types of radars assigned to their units. The ISAR has superior capabilities when compared to the older radar.

When asked about the AN/APS-115 versus the AN/APS-137 ISAR, Sensor 3/EW radar operator AW1 Don Jordan said, "The P-3 role in the past was sub-hunting only, then the

Above: Deliveries of Update III standard (production) aircraft began in 1984 and the upgrade was retrospectively applied across the fleet. The AN/APS-137 radar which is carried by some current aircraft was intended as part of a broader P-3C Update IV programme which was cancelled, after its initiation in 1987.

Right: This 1996 photo shows a VP-10 'Red Lancers' P-3C (Update III) Orion launching an ATM-84D Harpoon training round, near Viegues Island, Puerto Rico. The accompanying TA-4J is from VC-8, which flies Skyhawks and UH-3Hs from NS Roosevelt Roads.

Harpoon was introduced and we added the surface surveillance role to our operations. As a radar operator, you need to be fluent with both the AN/APS-115 and AN/APS-137 due to the mix in the squadrons. The more capable ISAR radar greatly enhances our stand-off capability." VP-62 AWC Don Henderson had the following to say about the ISAR. "When we did our Harpoon launch (during the exercise), there was a high sea state of 3. Our Orion had the older radar and the target would have been easier to maintain with an ISAR radar."

Next to the IFT on the rear starboard side is the ordnance man. The ordnance man is responsible for launching and organising sonobuoys, and observing weapons as they are released. During SAR sorties both the IFT and the ordnance man have a large observation window that they use. The ordnance man works closely with the TACCO and also can often be found manually loading the trio of internal sonobuoy chutes. There is an internal sonobuoy storage rack that holds an array of various sonobuoys.

The COMRESPATWINGPAC Operations Officer and now VP-62 XO, Commander John Flynn, commented, "Although we now perform a wide array of roles in addition to ASW (including surface surveillance, sea control, SAR and medevac), we need to keep ASW skills honed because the threat still exists."

The primary role for the P-3C is USW/ASW and, although the Cold War is over, training for this mission has not decreased. All P-3 crews feel strongly that the anti-submarine mission is still paramount, particularly with the proliferation of advanced submarine technology among potentially aggressive nations. However, with potent littoral (coastal) threats emerging from the same nations, the P-3C has now been tasked with additional duties. Crews have to be able to counter surface vessels in both shallow 'white water' and deeper 'blue water' environments. The Orion community has begun training with Mk 20 Rockeye cluster bombs, Mk 80 series GP bombs, AGM-65 Mavericks and, most importantly, AGM-84 Harpoons for surface vessel attacks.

Harpoon launch

Manufactured by McDonnell Douglas, there are several species of the turbojet-powered Harpoons. The live Harpoon is an AGM-84. There are Alpha, Bravo, Charlie, Delta, and land-attack Echo (known as SLAM) variants. Prior to executing one of its several terminal attack manoeuvres, the Delta model Harpoon has the ability to navigate to several turn points en route to the target. One of the more effective attacks is a sea-skimming entry to the area and a final pop-up manoeuvre to achieve a better kill. The missiles used during Harpoonex were a single live AGM-84D and a trio of ATM-84D training missiles. The missile weighs 1,200 lb (545 kg) and can be launched by ships, submarines and other aircraft.

The Sensor 3/EW (radar) operator plays an important part in a Harpoon launch. AW1 Don Jordan of VP-91 said, "First we identify the target that we are after, which is usually the biggest. Then I get a positive ID on the vessel and the data is relayed to the TACCO. The ball is now in the TACCO's court." VP-91 TACCO Lieutenant Commander Randy Britt then described, "The Harpoon is radar guided and we can work in conjunction with other Harpoon platforms such as F/A-18s, other P-3Cs, or ships. This scenario would result in a volley of shots from all different locations at our primary target. I then initiate the launch when ready and our number one goal is to put the target out of commission."

VP-62 TACCO Lieutenant Guy Jackson commented, "I assisted TACCO Lieutenant Tim Belluscak during the Harpoon launch. This was the first time a Reserve crew launched a Harpoon using online capabilities. We have a new programme that allows us to select and launch the Harpoons. The system had to go through several modifications and a lot of practice back at Jacksonville prior to us coming to Barbers Point. Seeing the actual launch happen successfully, exercising the software, and then with the missile going down range, was a great feeling."

On the way to Barbers Point for Harpoonex CPW-4, VP-62 and VP-91 stopped by NAS Point Mugu, California to load and ferry four Harpoons to Barbers Point. Point Mugu-based VP-65 'Tridents' were instrumental in helping both VP-62 and VP-91 with the Harpoon

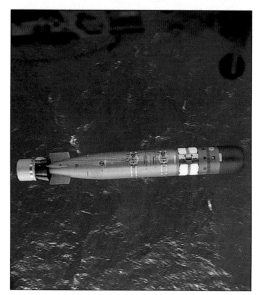

for years. The event is an excellent morale booster for the squadrons and all members involved. All the Reserve crews and squadron members are doing a great job, all the time they put in is greatly appreciated and they are individuals who are dedicated and love the Navy. All the crews are very well trained and are very professional at what they do. Seeing people who display such pride and satisfaction really makes the event exciting and fun as well. Most importantly, this is a combined effort with both the Reserves and active-duty working together to do the Harpoon shots. The result is good communications and also a significant cost savings at the same time."

Vital ASW training

For ASW training the US Navy uses a submarine simulator – the torpedo-shaped Mk 30 Mod 1 mobile underwater target – which can go as deep as 2,000 ft (609 m). The maximum endurance of the Mk 30 Mod 1 is seven hours and maximum speed is 22 kt (25 mph; 40 km/h). It is just over 20 ft (6 m) long and has a diameter of 21 in (53 cm). The Mk 30 Mod 1s can be launched or recovered by helos and range crafts. The target is used for training with the USN submarine, air and surface forces.

The Mk 30 has no limits on its manoeuvring capability and 'flies' underwater like a full-size submarine. Although the Navy is tight-lipped about the details, the Mk 30 can presumably replicate the acoustic signature and performance characteristics of a wide range of nuclear- and conventional-powered submarines. The US Navy expends substantial effort on collecting, cataloguing and maintaining a 'threat library' of submarine signatures and on ASW exercises Orion crews will presumably be faced with both 'hostile' and 'friendly' submarines. The 2,700-lb (1227-kg) Mk 30 target is pre-programmed to follow tactical and evasive patterns, which can create interesting twists and provide more realistic training for the P-3 crews. It can also be

loading in the red label weapons loading area.

The commander of the exercise training, Reserve Patrol Wing Pacific Commander Lieutenant Commander Bob Galloway, operated out of PMRF Barking Sands facility during the Harpoon shoots. Galloway is responsible for

co-ordinating and overseeing all aspects of air crew training for West Coast Reserve P-3 squadrons. He had the following to say regarding the event, "Every year the Reserve Wing Pacific is allocated one Harpoon to shoot. Last year we didn't have an opportunity to shoot the one allocated, so this year, as soon as we were allocated a Harpoon, we talked with the Reserve LANT Wing back east and asked if they would like to join us at PMRF Barking Sands. An active-duty unit, VP-4, was very helpful in setting up the range dates and co-ordinating, and wanted to join in the Harpoon shoot as well since they also had one to launch. The result was the range being reserved for only one day for the Harpoon launches, and three different units making use of the area within a couple of hours. This was a very well thought out and planned design, and is very cost-effective. It also allows us to share our experiences between all three organisations – the West Coast Reserve, the East Coast Reserve, and active duty. It was good for both the Reserve and active duty, and enabled us to teach each other different things.

"Having been active duty for years, the Reservists bring a lot of experience with them because most members have been flying P-3s

set for slow or fast speeds – battery life at slow speeds is seven hours and fast is four hours.

The 57-ft (17.4-m) long QST-35 Mod 1 SEPTAR (Seaborne Powered Target) was used for the Harpoon shots. It has a 34-ft (10.3-m) high tower that supports a large radar reflector and side-mounted radar enhancement screens. The radio-controlled QST-35 is a low-cost target, has a gasoline engine, and a maximum speed of 34 kt (39 mph; 63 km/h). Active radar threat simulators and rocket-boosted chaff can be provided on the target. The QST-35 Mod 1 is usually only used for offset fire, except in special cases. The fibreglass-hulled SEPTAR targets are transitted to the range area with onboard crews. The crew then transfers to a range boat and the unmanned SEPTAR enters the exercise area via radio control.

Harpoonex CPW-4

Harpoonex CPW-4 (ComPatWing 4) missions were executed by VP-91 'Black Cats', VP-62 'Broadarrows', VP-4 'Skinny Dragons' and VP-69 'Totems'. Several sorties were flown and scenarios involved simulated mining runs (Minex), dropping two Mk 46 torpedoes (Torpex), the Harpoon launches (Harpoonex), and mock ASW against American submarines.

VP-91 was called upon first to find the elusive Mk 30 Mod 1 underwater target in the range. The 'Black Cats' P-3C Update III entered the range area looking for trouble. Sonobuoys were dispensed at altitudes near 300 ft (91 m) AGL and at 225 kt (258 mph; 415 km/h). The Sensor 1 and 2 operators began receiving acoustic information on the Mk 30. The crews kept a watchful eye for the various clues and began strategically placing sonobuoys that began the process of elimination for pinpointing the target. After working the target hard for a while, the crew became confident of its location. Buoyant smoke markers were dispensed to mark the approximate location for visual reference. Vectors were given to the pilot, a final run was made, and the weapons bay was quickly opened, exposing the duo of Mk 46 torpedoes. "Now, now, now!" was called by the TACCO, and on the final "now" the torpedo was dropped. Once the torpedoes were dropped, the weapons bay was quickly closed.

Sensors 1 and 2 soon afterward reported that the Mk 30 had altered course. After another series of sonobuoys, a second run – the same result. Two kills. The VP-91 Orion then climbed to a higher altitude, allowing the VP-62 aircraft to move in to the area. The process began all over again and the Mk 30 was located and destroyed. The VP-4 P-3C, also with a Harpoon still attached to the wing, repeated the sequence a third time and the underwater target succumbed once more.

Next came the long-awaited Harpoon launch, for which a different range area was utilised. VP-91 was called in first and a couple of practice runs were made with the ISAR radar. "Green Range" was called, which means there were no contacts in the range area except the target. On the final run, "Clear to Fire" was

sounded and the launch commenced. A brief flame, then smoke, exited the Harpoon rocket motor and the missile dropped quickly from the starboard outboard pylon. The ATM-84D dropped straight down toward the Pacific and began its sea-skimming profile toward the well-locked-on SEPTAR.

HACLS launch

Next was VP-62's turn. Its launch was the first by a non-test crew/aircraft to use the HACLS integrated into the main onboard computer system. Hitherto, the HACLS system has been a stand-alone system, not fully integrated into the P-3's sensor suite of radar, acoustics, ESM etc. This situation is changing as HACLS and the Harpoon launch become more integrated and automated. For example, information from the various crew station no longer has to be fed into the system by the TACCO, but can be fed directly to the HACLS and the missile.

For their 'conventional' Harpoon shoots, VP-4 and VP-91 achieved similarly accurate results in their attack on the QST-35.

The Minex portion followed the initial ATM-84 launches. This involved a low-level high-speed run over a range bay as the P-3Cs made a simulated mine drop over the area. The aim is to drop a straight line of mines at a depth of approximately 300 ft (91 m). Rolling in from an IP the Orion must maintain a straight-and-level course while factoring in altitude, air speed, wind direction and the critical timing of weapons release to/from an unbroken line.

'Sinkex'

VP-4, VP-91 and VP-62 Orions all fired ATM-84D's telemetry rounds (without warheads), but VP-69 'Totems' got the real thing. Orion crews probably only get to fire a real Harpoon once in their lifetimes. For this crew the date was 9 April 1997 at PMRF Barking Sands. The target was a decommis-

VP-4 (left), based at NAS Barbers Point, was one of the squadrons which participated in the 'Sinkex' phase of Harpoonex CPW-4, dropping Mk 82 bombs. VP-47 (below), another Barbers Point resident, also took part in 'Sinkex', but one of its Orions made an AGM-65 Maverick firing, as well as bomb drops, against the target vessel.

Left: A VP-65 Orion is seen here climbing away from its home at NAS Point Mugu. VP-65 is one of four VPs attached to Reserve Patrol Wing Pacific (the others being VP-69, 91 and 94).

sioned destroyer, the ex-USS *Edwards*, that was towed to the range and strapped down (anchored). The exercise was dubbed 'Sinkex', and participants also included Canadian navy vessels, VP-1 'Screaming Eagles', VP-4 'Skinny Dragons', VP-47 'Golden Swordsmen' and VP-69 'Totems'. VP-1 made the first shot at the doomed vessel using a live Maverick missile, which was a direct hit. Then both VP-4 and VP-47 attacked and dropped four tons of Mk 82s on the ex-warship. Next came VP-69 with a live AGM-84D, which was promptly delivered to the centre of the hull with a direct hit. The target was also peppered by Canadian warships using 120 rounds of both 57-mm and 76-mm high explosive. The poor *Edwards* finally succumbed to the onslaught, and will be born again in the form of a reef.

Although not every Harpoonex Harpoon scored a direct hit, all three ATM-84s were deemed to be close enough to be called good

hits due to their close proximity to the target reflector. The range helicopters recorded the shots, as did sensors on the targets that give proximity feedback. The VP-62 P-3C was equipped with the older radar and the VP-91 Orion had the ISAR. When comparing the Harpoon runs at the QST-35 remotely controlled boat target, it was discovered that the ISAR bird had a good radar lock well before the other P-3.

Once all six torpedoes had been dropped, a Barking Sands-based SH-3 Sea King picked up the torpedoes. After use, an onboard timer releases weights on the practice torpedo, allowing it to float to the surface for recovery.

As with all exercises, not everything went perfectly, but that is the value of training. All the experiences were shared and discussed so that improvements and ideas can be implemented later. This exercise gave the P-3 crews the opportunity to experience actual weapons delivery and launches so that if they are ever called upon to serve in a conflict, they will be more prepared and know what to expect.

After the shoot, P-3C aircraft commander, Lieutenant Commander Horst Brauchler of VP-62, reflected, "Yesterday we spent two to three hours briefing for the Harpoon shoot. Items discussed were to ensure that the range will be clear, that the targets will be ready, and that it will be safe to launch. Today we went in to do our Harpoon launch at 3,000 ft (914 m) and 300 kt (344 mph; 554 km/h) true air speed, but there were clouds at our altitude. We then dropped down below the layer to 2,000 ft (609 m) and co-ordinated with the crew and range. Prior to the launch we did an ASW sortie against an underwater Mk 30 target, and dropped a pair of Mk 46 torpedoes. One item that would be very helpful for our community would be to have all P-3s modified with a GPS. Our older inertials tend to drift due to the number of hours that you are out there in your

aircraft, and ultimately you can be miles off. The GPS narrows it down to pinpoint accuracy, and by today's standards the inertials are effectively obsolete. GPS is the way to go."

AWC Don Henderson, a VP-62 Sensor 3 operator, said, "First we did the ASW exercise portion, utilised MAD, found the target. I kept my eye on the TACCO scope, and backed up the TACCO when required. I offered my input and it is the TACCO's decision to decide which information to use. After we dropped our torpedoes, we transitioned out of ASW portion and various things quickly popped up. You have to be flexible, which we demonstrated very well. The Harpoon shoot came next and my primary function was to identify the target. I marked the QST-35 target position, and provided the target information to the TACCO. The TACCO then got a solution, fired the Harpoon, and we peeled off, continually scanning for traffic. Overall, everything went well and we showed a lot of flexibility. We did a lot of different things in a short period of time and that's what it is all about."

The future of the P-3

Lieutenant Commander Scott Anderson of Nav Air works on the engineering side and is an avionics systems project officer (ASPO) on the P-3. The job is very involved, since the P-3 is a weapons/sensors platform. When asked about the P-3, Lieutenant Commander Anderson stated, "Our job is driven by fleet requirements and Congressional mandates, and then we incorporate the system capabilities into the aircraft. Last year we were involved with the integration of the SLAM avionics into the Orion, which involved a datalink guidance system. All P-3C Update IIIs will eventually be modified via an upgrade programme (AIP), and modifications include Maverick and SLAM capability plus the addition of the ISAR radar. There is a Congressional mandate (FAA nav requirement) that will result in the GPS being added to all P-3s. From the mission standpoint, the mission of the P-3 has evolved to include the ASUW (Anti-Surface Warfare) – that means

In Cold War days Orion crews were among the very few personnel who trained against their actual wartime adversaries, every day. They are now faced with maintaining those ASW skills while adapting to new, and still emerging, roles.

the weapons and sensor systems need to be upgraded accordingly. Weapons systems such as online Harpoon capabilities, Maverick, and SLAM are examples.

"Sensor system changes include upgrades to the EW, ESM and radar (ISAR), and system capabilities need to be target-discriminating. We are in the process of also upgrading the infra-red detecting system, and other programmes are cockpit modernisation and instrument place-ment, which involve glass flight displays. Workload sharing, where one operator can be sitting at one station and do the functions of another, is being explored. An example would be cross-training the navigator and TACCO to be able to help with the other's function. Other enhancements are always being explored, the P-3 is a great aircraft, and will be around for years to come."

The role of the Reserve

Harpoonex underlined the importance of the Navy Reserve P-3C squadrons to any future battle plan. Typical of such units is VP-65, which is based at NAS Point Mugu, California. Known as the 'Tridents', VP-65 is assigned to Commander, Patrol Wing Four. The unit operates world-wide, performs a variety of missions, has a full wartime complement of aircraft, and the skilled officers and enlisted personnel required to man them.

The VP-65 XO, Commander Phil Winters, summed the role of his squadron and the Reserve Orions with the following, "VP-65, like any patrol squadron, is a self-contained, deployable, go-anywhere, do-anything unit. We perform many diverse missions. We do ASW, ASUW, counter-narcotics, mining, bombing, reconnaissance, and SAR. We are often doing our different missions, in different parts of the world, simultaneously. There are a lot of moving parts! And, it takes a great deal of team work and co-ordination to execute well. We pride ourselves on keeping all of our parts moving in sync and executing well. It's very gratifying for everyone in 'Team Trident' – aircrew, maintenance, and administration – to see all their hard work pay off with the successful accomplishment of our missions."

Lieutenant Commanders Dave Eguchi and Grady Howe, who head up the VP-65 training department, had the following to note about the 'Tridents' and training. "Reserve squadrons capitalise on a unique synergy. TARs (active duty) and selected Reservists combine a tradi-tional Navy perspective with a variety of approaches to problem-solving from the civilian world. The result is a DoD benchmark for cost-effective normal operational readiness. It's quite a challenge to co-ordinate personnel availability and training requirements with only 60-odd training days spread throughout the year. The payoff for the Navy in meeting that challenge is a mission-ready squadron at a reduced cost in comparison to our active duty counterparts."

Another VP-65 P-3C pilot and mission commander, Lieutenant Commander Mike Norman, said, "The advent of speciality systems combined with upgraded weapons complements

and capabilities have ensured the Orion's continued popularity with warfare commanders and theatre commanders-in-chief, Navy-wide. Reserve VP squadrons have become the bench-mark for implementation of the Navy's plan to mask the historically recognisable division between active-duty and Reserve components. This theme of integration (referred to as 'One Navy') has been utilised as the standard business practice of the typical P-3 Reserve squadron for years. Maintaining pace with previous standards of excellence, today's Reserve crew finds itself in virtually every international hot spot, flying with the same level of mission responsibility and productivity as their active-duty counterparts.

"Effective employment of the 'Hunter' requires a unique orchestration of 10 tactical crew members, working in concert toward a common mission objective. This temperamental lesson in group dynamics is often made to look easy by our Reservists because of the superior level of training attained by flying with the same tactical nucleus for sometimes up to 10 or more consecutive years. This base of experience is an immeasurable, yet quintessential element of sustenance for the continued maintenance of a solid naval air force, specifically when one considers the ramifications of a 'right sizing' period, and the concessions made therein."

VP-65 Orion pilot Lieutenant Commander Will Oxx, who is renowned as the VP commu-nity's conventional weapons expert, stated, "To combat the growing number of diesel submarines operating in shallow littoral waters, my crew developed new conventional weapons delivery tactics. We've been the first P-3 ever seen on many live ranges around the country, and we've dropped more bombs than anyone in our community. Practice makes perfect – and we don't miss.

"I really enjoy being part of the VP-65 Trident team. Camaraderie is a big reason; another is that the P-3's so much fun to fly! The P-3 continues to fly essential missions around the world. Orion aircraft have been outfitted with a variety of new sensors and updated equipment which have dramatically expanded its mission capabilities. Because this platform continues to grow to meet the needs in our new world, the P-3 is one of the first assets for which naval commanders call during a crisis. With its long range, it can provide a rapid response worldwide on short notice. My crew has been training for seven years now. We've been working as a team for so long that we've become quite a close-knit family. We set new records everywhere we go."

Ted Carlson

Panavia Tornado Variant Briefing
Part Two: *Air Defence Variant*

Above: These Tornado F.Mk 3s wear the 'fighting cock' badge plus the black and white checkerboards of No. 43 Squadron, based at RAF Leuchars in Scotland. Both are carrying ACMI instrumentation pods and camouflaged (Tornado GR.Mk 1-style) 330-Imp gal (1500-litre) fuel tanks.

Left: Trial drops of inert SkyFlash missiles from the Tornado ADV began in March 1981 (more than two years after live guided firings began from RAF Phantoms) and guided live firings began in February 1985. This No. 111 Sqn Tornado is seen making a live SkyFlash firing during a missile practice camp. Note the fully-extended Frazer Nash launching rams.

The Tornado ADV was designed to defend Britain against unescorted Soviet bombers – chiefly the Tu-22M – which were seen as a major threat to targets in the UK, and to its maritime assets. This mission demanded an aircraft with a powerful radar, high transit speed and healthy range. As a result, the Tornado F.Mk 3 is perhaps an over-specialised aircraft intended for too narrow a role. Still, it remains the UK's front-line fighter/interceptor and its crews have established a reputation for skilful flying and innovative tactics.

The RAF's requirement for the Tornado ADV was outlined in Air Staff Target 395 in 1971, although the original requirement for the IDS (dating from 1968) had been drawn up with an air defence version in mind. It was the needs of a potential fighter Tornado which led to the RAF's insistence on Mach 2 performance capability for the IDS, for example. The fighter Tornado was intended first and foremost as a long-range interceptor,

loitering on CAP between 300 and 400 miles (186 and 248 km) from base (or further), searching huge sectors of sky with its own onboard sensors (and reacting to information provided by ground radars and AWACS). It would then launch its missiles at multiple incoming low-level targets, head-on, while they were still well outside visual range. Moreover, it would have to be able to do this over the sea, in the worst weather. The Controller (Aircraft) at

the time referred to the proposed Tornado fighter as a 'battleship of the air', and ACM Sir Neil Cameron was happy to describe it in similar terms in 1977: "I would call the air defence Tornado a bomber destroyer." This was not intended as a criticism, since he also said that the aircraft offered "a tremendously improved capability to intercept enemy aircraft approaching this country or the naval forces or shipping around this country." The conversion of Tornado from bomber to fighter was a particularly ambitious aim, since the baseline Tornado IDS was optimised for high speed at low level, and considerations of agility, range at altitude and endurance were of no more than secondary interest. The Tornado was also a heavy aircraft, and this made it inevitable that the fighter variant would never be a featherweight. Despite its relatively compact dimensions, a fully laden Tornado F.Mk 3 is heavier than a wartime Sunderland flying-boat.

In many respects, with an initial requirement for 165 interceptors, the RAF might have been better advised to buy an off-the-shelf interceptor, or even to develop a dedicated fighter from first principles. With this in mind the RAF was directed to look at the latest American teen-series fighters, to see if they could meet the RAF's requirement at lower cost, or exceed it at the same unit cost. The possibility of acquiring the Grumman F-14 was examined, but this aircraft was too expensive with its AWG-9/

AIM-54 Phoenix weapons system, and without it did not offer much improvement over the RAF's existing F-4 Phantoms. The aircraft was said to cost 50 per cent more than the ADV, and the AIM-54s were 300 per cent more expensive than SkyFlash rounds. Moreover, when the F-14 was examined, the US Navy was suffering what Group Captain Mike Elsam (then serving with the RAF's Operational Requirements Branch) described as "appalling problems with reliability and maintainability. We would not have bought it on that score alone. On those counts the F-14 never even got in the shuffle." The single-engined, single-seat F-16 was obviously a superb clear-air dogfighter, but was equally clearly unsuitable for the RAF's intended mission. In 1976, the RAF was simply not interested in the short term in acquiring a dogfight-capable aircraft, and in the longer term one was being developed anyway. This was the aircraft being developed as a battle-field support follow-on for the Jaguar and Harrier to meet AST 403, which was also intended to function as an 'agile, eyeball, dogfighter'. Similarly, the RAF looked at the F-15, and was impressed by its aerodynamic qualities and performance. But fighter-versus-fighter combat was not considered to be a high priority and the Eagle's single-seat configuration was not considered to be compatible with the RAF's air defence responsibilities, while the RAF also had reservations about the performance of the AN/APG-63 radar. A two-seat F-15 was a more attractive option, especially when it was thought that the USAF might buy Tornado IDS to meet its Enhanced Tactical Fighter requirement.

On the other hand, anything that threatened the ADV was seen by many as being an unremittingly bad thing, since the increase in unit cost of the IDS might have led to German withdrawal from the entire programme. Moreover, some were optimistic about the ADV, and there were reports that Germany might later buy ADVs as F-4 replacements.

When the ADV later ran into problems and delays, the F-15 was again examined as a possible stopgap. It was again ruled out by its single-seat configuration, limited radar capability and unsatisfactory ECCM, which offered no advantage over the proposed Tornado ADV, while having the disadvantage of providing no British jobs and of using up scarce foreign currency reserves. The F-15 made a final appearance in the Tornado ADV story in the late 1970s, when the US government proposed leasing Britain four squadrons of F-15s (about 80 aircraft) during the period 1981-85 as a stopgap to fill the perceived shortfall in UK air defence, voicing a supposed concern over the lack of air defence assets to protect their bases in Britain. Britain rejected the offer of leased F-15s, seeing it as an ill-disguised Trojan Horse intended to lead to the cancellation of the ADV and to an RAF F-15 buy.

When the decision to launch the ADV was made (in about 1969) it was not possible to see the full extent of the compromises which would be necessary, since the Tornado IDS itself was still far from flight. The idea of a dual-role air superiority interceptor and ground attack/strike aircraft was, in any case, neither new nor controversial. Following the cancellation of the TSR.2, the new Labour government had endorsed two collaborative projects with France. The first of these was the Jaguar and the second was the unimaginatively titled AFVG (Anglo-French Variable Geometry).

Although it never flew, the AFVG was seen as a Lightning and Mirage III replacement in the

Rolling away from a tanker after refuelling, for the benefit of the camera, this aircraft wears the double eagle badge of No. 11 Squadron. This unit is still dedicated to NATO's Supreme Allied Commander Atlantic, for maritime air defence.

Above: This atmospheric view of a No. 56(R) Squadron F.Mk 3 was taken in the early hours of the morning, at RAF Leeming. The squadron is today based at RAF Coningsby. No. 56(Reserve) Squadron is the RAF's F.Mk 3 operational conversion unit (though it does not have that official title) and is now also involved in training crews for the Italian air force.

Left: This classic view of one of the RAF's initial Tornado F.Mk 2s was taken from the rear ramp of an RAF Hercules. The first F.Mk 2 flew in 1984 and all served with No. 229 OCU as trainers. By 1988 they had been withdrawn to make way for the F.Mk 3.

in March 1969, Belgium, Canada and the Netherlands had dropped out of the project. The aircraft continued in two forms, a two-seater with top-grade all-weather avionics (the Panavia 200) and a daylight-only single-seater (the Panavia 100). Even at this stage, the UK MoD issued AST 395, covering an interceptor derivative of the Panavia 200, which would have a new advanced radar and SkyFlash missiles. It was originally thought that they would be carried underwing, though it soon became apparent that, to reduce drag, a semi-submerged arrangement below the fuselage would be better. Unfortunately, this would necessitate a slight fuselage stretch, though Britain was unwilling to impose such a lengthening on the IDS variant having just criticised its partners for sticking to national requirements which had compromised the basic design of the airframe. The low-drag missile carriage allowed the ADV to promise better performance than the F-4 it would replace, and increased internal fuel capacity by 10 per cent.

Strike credentials assured

The Luftwaffe and Italian air force finally adopted the two-seat configuration in about 1970, when the Italians finally accepted CAS and interdiction as their primary roles. The baseline MRCA seemed to have finally lost its pretensions of also being an air-to-air fighter, although Panavia later announced the development of Radpac, a radar package which would have given the basic IDS additional air-to-air capability with improved air-to-air tracking and compatibility with BVR missiles like the AIM-7, made possible by the addition of Doppler processing and an air-to-air target illuminator – such as proposed to Canada in 1978.

Although the baseline Tornado became

air defence role, as well as a Canberra/Buccaneer/Phantom replacement in the strike role. Moreover, when the AFVG died, the British part of the team formed the core of the MRCA project. In the beginning the MRCA was seen as a genuinely multi-role aircraft and not merely as the role-flexible ground attack/strike/reconnaissance aircraft it actually became. Indeed, the MRCA was initially seen

in two guises, as a single-seat F-104G replacement for Germany, Italy, the Netherlands and Canada, and as a two-seat pure strike aircraft for Britain and the German navy. During the early years MBB even pressed for a single-engined MRCA. Canada and the Netherlands demanded high specific excess power and agility figures in order to fulfil air superiority missions.

By the time the MRCA design was finalised

Above: In 1989 Tornado F.Mk 3s from No. 229 OCU made an unprecedented squadron exchange with the JA 37 Viggens of F13 Wing, Flygvapnet, based at Norrköping. Both units have now ceased to exist. However, at that time the aircraft of No. 229 OCU had adopted the lion badge and red chevrons of No. 65 Squadron, the OCU's wartime 'shadow' identity – while still retaining the OCU badge on the fin. The F.Mk 3 and the JA 37 fulfil a broadly similar role, and were developed at roughly the same time.

Right: This formation of No. 29 Sqn F.Mk 3 and camouflaged No. II(AC) Sqn GR.Mk 1A highlights the differences between the pugnacious IDS and the sleek Tornado ADV.

steadily more orientated towards the ground attack and interdiction roles, the British Air Staff and its Operational Requirements Branch began to seriously study the possibility of producing a dedicated interceptor version of the MRCA, and examined such an aircraft against the possible alternatives, which were seen as the F-14, F-15 and F-16, and the French Avion de Combat Futur, which much later became the Mirage 2000. After these aircraft were finally rejected, it was announced that 165 of the 385 Tornados on order for the RAF would be of the ADV version. Full-scale development of the ADV was launched on 4 March 1976 (authorisation followed one day later), and an Instruction to Proceed (ITP) with the manufacture of two ADV prototypes was issued to BAe at Warton on 11 March 1977. They were retrospectively added to the first Tornado production batch, replacing planned IDS production aircraft on the line. A third ADV prototype was added soon afterwards.

Unlike its NATO allies, Britain felt that it had little need to oppose fast, agile fighter threats at relatively short range. Instead, the primary threat facing Britain was one of multiple element formations of cruise missile-carrying long-range bombers capable of flying down through the Greenland-Iceland-UK gap from bases in the North Cape or Kola

Peninsula. They were likely to have heavy EW/ECM support. NATO's reliance on Britain as an 'aircraft-carrier' off the coast of Europe, and as a potential airhead for the reinforcement of NATO during wartime, made its air defence crucially important.

Britain began to build up a new air defence system, increasing the size and capability of its inflight-refuelling tanker force, establishing an airborne early warning force, and revolutionising the ground-based radar network. The heart of any air defence system lies in the fighters which provide the necessary punch. Neither the RAF's ageing Lightnings or newer Phantoms

had the range, endurance or combat persistence to cope with the perceived threat. What the RAF needed was a long-range, long-endurance, BVR missile-equipped interceptor capable of patrolling and guarding the huge UK Air Defence Region (UK ADR). It was anticipated that such an aircraft would be able to detect and engage a number of targets in all weathers, from maximum stand-off range. Air Staff Requirement 395 was drawn up around just such an aircraft.

Some critics have suggested that even the limited task of destroying formations of bombers at beyond visual range was quite beyond the Tornado ADV. They submit that the aircraft's

Taxiing out at CFB Cold Lake in 1994, these No. 29 Squadron Tornados are about to depart for another Maple Flag combat training sortie. F.Mk 3s, and their crews, are regular participants in several North American exercises, where their superior tactics and training have made their mark.

Above: Until Italy accepted a 'bridging loan' of F.Mk 3s from the RAF, the Royal Saudi Air Force was the only other Tornado ADV operator. The Saudi purchase of 24 ADVs was made in the mid-1980s, at a time when the USA was reluctant to augment the small batch of F-15Cs delivered to the Arab state in 1981. A follow-on order for Tornado ADVs was announced in 1989, but never made, and, following Iraq's 1990 invasion of Kuwait, Saudi Arabia's F-15 inventory was substantially expanded.

Left: This No. 229 OCU Tornado was the RAF's designated F.Mk 3 display aircraft for 1990 and is seen here practising its routine in Cyprus.

Opposite page: Coningsby-based No. 56(R) Sqn maintains the famous traditions of the 'Firebirds', always one of the premier RAF fighter squadrons.

reliance on semi-active radar homing missiles limited its ability to destroy more than one target, since it effectively had to follow its weapon towards the hostile aircraft until impact, by which time it would probably be too close to the enemy formation to take another BVR shot. Moreover, critics point out that at such close range the Tornado ADV might find itself within visual range of a Sukhoi Su-27 or MiG-31, or already under attack from a Russian BVR missile. At the time, though, the Tornado ADV seemed like an excellent solution to the problem posed by the Soviet bomber threat, and there were many who were pleasantly surprised by the aircraft's agility and performance. Moreover, the Su-27 and MiG-31 were not then known to exist as threat aircraft. RAF fighter pilots found

that the Tornado ADV could out-scissors a Hawker Hunter, out-accelerate a Lightning and comprehensively 'wax' a Phantom, fast or slow, high or low. Even today, RAF Tornado ADVs perform well enough in exercises, using AWACs, JTIDs, their two-man crew and good tactics to maintain situational awareness and to defeat better-armed and more agile opponents.

Foxhunter radar for the ADV

The first and most critical change to the basic Tornado was the provision of a new dedicated fighter radar. This was the newly developed GEC Marconi AI-24 Foxhunter, a frequency-modulated interrupted continuous wave (FMICW) set operating in the 3-cm I-band. Marconi-Elliott (with Ferranti as a major sub-

contractor) received a contract to develop the radar in 1976, building on existing radars which had been flying in experimental and trials aircraft for years. The radar consisted of eight (not 12, as often stated) liquid-cooled LRUs clustered around a central transmitter. The front-end was predominantly analog, with a coherent travelling wave tube transmitter giving high power over a range of bandwidths. The conventional twist-cassegrain antenna was light and simple, and gave greater consistency and lower sidelobes than the new planar arrays which were in vogue with the latest teen-series US fighters. The radar incorporated a J-band illuminator for SkyFlash or similar semi-active radar homing missiles. A modern pulse-Doppler radar was not used, the choice being a compromise based on the performance required.

High PRFs were used to maximise detection

This No. 11 Sqn aircraft was the personal mount of the squadron boss, Wing Commander David Hamilton. The black fin echoed similar markings carried by the squadron's Lightning F.Mk 6s during their final days of operations in 1988.

The RAF's acquisition of the Sentry AEW.Mk 1, which entered service in 1991, finally allowed the Tornado force to exploit and expand a modern, integrated air defence AEW&C system. The belated addition of improved datalink systems and better BVR missiles for the F.Mk 3 will help further bridge the gap before the arrival of the EF2000.

range, while low PRFs were used against targets with little Doppler shift (e.g., tailchase targets). The radar incorporated sophisticated track-while-scan capabilities, and was extremely user-friendly, with its synthetic symbology clearly displayed and easy to manipulate. A built-in processor suppressed ground clutter and the radar also incorporated an integrated Cossor IFF-3500 interrogator, whose dipole antennas were mounted on the surface of the main reflector. The new radar necessitated the provision of a new cold air unit to cool it, and a pop-up ram air turbine (RAT) was provided to power essential emergency systems for use in the event of a high-altitude engine flameout, in place of the one-shot battery fitted to the IDS.

The Tornado ADV was originally envisaged as having an electro-optical Visual Augmentation System, which would have given the crew a TV picture of the target sufficient for positive identification in time to allow a front hemisphere

missile shot by day, or in a starlight-only night. The equipment would also permit an interceptor to safely shadow a target by night, or to make passive, emission-free intercepts in some circumstances. In late 1978 Marconi Avionics received a contract to develop the equipment, which was to be expanded from existing low-light-level TV systems. The VAS was to have been carried on a retractable mounting just in front of the cockpit, and was intended to be steerable. Quite what happened to the VAS (which never reached service) remains a mystery. The deletion of this feature was reportedly more due to cost than technical performance. At around the same time, the RAF was officially optimistic that Tornado ADV crews would have a helmet-mounted sight, but this optimism proved sadly misplaced, and RAF fighter pilots will have to wait for Eurofighter before they gain a piece of equipment which their Russian counterparts (and even Israeli and

South African pilots) take for granted. The non-appearance of a helmet sight was due to the importance placed on BVR operations, and the relative unimportance of short-range capability in the ADV.

SkyFlash primary armament

The new radar was designed to be compatible with BAe's SkyFlash missile, a British derivative of the AIM-7E-2 Sparrow which used an externally identical airframe, but with an improved seeker and fuse. At one stage it was felt that the Tornado's primary weapon would actually be the AIM-7E-2 Sparrow, but this missile's known susceptibility to ECM was considered to be a major drawback, and the decision was taken to develop an indigenous derivative of the weapon. This was designed to combine the Sparrow's proven airframe, rocket motor and warhead with a new Marconi radar seeker and a new proximity fuse developed by EMI. BAe also developed new guidance and control systems, with new autopilot, actuators and power supplies. It was intended that these new items would improve accuracy, reliability, discrimination between targets and ground clutter, and would provide the ability to target a

RAF Tornados, along with other NATO aircraft and those from non-NATO European air forces, make regular detachments to the instrumented North Sea Air Combat Range, which is owned and operated by British Aerospace.

Right: This fully-armed Tornado, equipped with extra ALE-44 chaff/flare dispensers, is seen on patrol over Saudi Arabia during Operation Desert Shield. The F.Mk 3s later had to give up their larger 'Hindenburger' fuel tanks to the GR.Mk 1 force when the fighting started.

Below: A No. 25 Sqn F.Mk 3 makes a dusk departure from its home base at RAF Leeming.

single aircraft in a tightly-packed formation.

The SkyFlash was developed from 1969, ordered in 1973 and entered service in 1978 as a weapon for the RAF's McDonnell Douglas F-4 Phantoms. A range of 31 miles (50 km) against targets flying at down to 250 ft (76 m) is claimed. A fire-and-forget version of the missile, the SkyFlash 2, using mid-course inertial guidance and an active radar terminal guidance unit, was specifically developed for the Tornado ADV, but this weapon was abandoned before it could enter production, and the RAF's Tornados entered service with the SkyFlash 1 developed for the Phantoms which they replaced.

Although the SkyFlash missile armament was originally to have been carried on pylon-mounted launch rails under the wings, this would have represented an unacceptable high-drag solution, and would also have increased frontal radar cross-section to an unacceptable level. Instead, the Tornado ADV's fuselage was stretched slightly (providing space for avionics

and a small 165-Imp gal/750-litre increase in internal fuel capacity in a new Tank Zero immediately behind the cockpit), while staggered low-drag missile recesses were let into the lower fuselage, in which the front pair of missiles was semi-submerged. The rear pair of missiles was carried with only their upper wings and fins recessed. Separation of the weapons from their missile recess was achieved by the use of Frazer Nash pyrotechnic rams which forced the missiles down and away from the aircraft's belly, applying a four-ton force to each missile.

Short-range missiles, new avionics

For short-range engagements, the Tornado ADV relies on four AIM-9 Sidewinders. It was once expected that the aircraft would eventually carry the (AIM-132) ASRAAM, but when this missile was eventually ordered (many years later) by the MoD it was to equip the Harrier GR.Mk 7 and the Eurofighter, and not the Tornado F.Mk 3. ASRAAM compatibility is

now to be conferred on the Tornado F.Mk 3 in its ongoing mid-life upgrade – the Capability Sustainment Programme.

The port internal cannon was removed in the ADV to make way for avionics and the submerged inflight-refuelling probe and its associated 'pipework'. Even with the one remaining internal cannon, the Tornado F.Mk 2 packed a heavier punch than the Phantom which it replaced. The weapon was of 27-mm calibre, and was fixed in a rigid internal mounting, making it considerably more accurate than the podded cannon carried by the RAF's F-4.

The fighter variant had a very different avionics and instrument fit to that of the IDS. The Tornado ADV was given double the original IDS's computer power, going from 32k to 64k, and also introduced a GEC-Marconi TACAN, Cossor ILS and IFF, though these were also being incorporated in IDS aircraft, as was the revised communications suite. The latter consisted of a GEC-Plessey VHF/UHF, Rohde and Schwarz HF/SSB, and SIT emergency UHF, with a Comms Control Unit by Ultra and an Epsilon CVR. As well as lacking the IDS's Texas Instruments TFR, GEC-Marconi LRMTS and Lital Secondary Attitude and Heading Reference System, the Tornado ADV also lacked the Decca 72 Doppler of the bomber. The provision of IFF was essential, of course, but caused delays, since NATO was then caught in a major impasse over what the

This No. 11 Sqn Tornado was one of those stationed at Gioia del Colle, in Italy, as part of the RAF's contribution to Operation Deny Flight. No. 11 Sqn was the first RAF squadron to arrive at 'Joya', on 19 April 1993, and immediately began flying night sorties, every night, for three weeks.

next generation IFF should be. The US wanted to stick with a D-band (1-2 GHz) system (since it already operated a large number of D-band IFF-equipped aircraft), while most European nations favoured an E/F-band (2-4 GHz) system. Eventually, the participating nations agreed on a D-band IFF system which incorporated a radar mode, allowing a radar pulse to interrogate the IFF transponder, and not just a dedicated interrogator.

The ADV cockpits have both similarities to and differences from the IDS. Front cockpits are remarkably similar, though the ADV lacks the moving map and TFR E-scope displays of the IDS and instead has a CRT head-down display screen on which the pilot can view an intercept display, or any display being viewed on the navigator's TV Tabs, using a left/right selector switch. The rear cockpits are also similar, with a centrally-mounted hand controller and two CRT displays (known as TV Tabs) on each side

of the main panel. The IDS has a combined moving map and radar display between them, but it is not fitted in the ADV's rear cockpit. The IDS navigator's wet-film display recorder was replaced by a displayed data video recorder in the ADV, and the backseater also had a GEC Marconi FH 31A artificial horizon, which could also feed pitch and roll information to other systems. Trainer versions differ further, with the IDS rear cockpit losing one of the two TV Tabs, and the ADV simply having the left-hand TV Tab relocated to the centre of the panel.

New fuel systems

Although the Tornado's range was already quite respectable, the aircraft did receive a small increase in internal fuel capacity, bringing the total to 1,571 Imp gal (7143 litres). Since inflight refuelling would inevitably be a feature of the ADV's QRA and CAP roles, the Tornado IDS's external refuelling-probe was

Wearing the red Maltese cross of No. 1435 Flight, this F.Mk 3 was one of four Tornados allocated to the unit charged with air defence of the Falkland Islands. It wears the traditional 'C' (for Charity) codes – the others being F/Faith, H/Hope and D/Despair. The names were inherited from the Gloster Gladiators which single-handedly defended Malta for a period during World War II.

replaced by a fully retractable internal probe. Replacing the bulky system of the Tornado IDS gave a significant reduction in drag, and an improvement in the aircraft's appearance.

The lengthened fuselage, together with the longer, more pointed radome, increased overall length, and the new fuselage's increased fineness ratio gave a significant reduction in drag at transonic speeds. Other minor aerodynamic changes included a lengthening of the fixed wing glove vanes on the intake sides, giving them greater leading-edge sweep than on the IDS. This compensated for the changed centre of gravity of the ADV. On the ADV the new wing gloves had a fixed leading edge, with the Krueger flaps of the IDS removed. They would have been considerably less effective on the more highly swept leading edge, and necessitated larger control inputs during slow speed handling. They have now been inhibited on the GR.Mk 1.

The new variant's handling was fine-tuned by reprogramming the GEC-Marconi Triplex fly-by-wire Command Stability Augmentation System/AFDS (APFD) to reduce stick forces and to increase roll rate. The autopilot software was also revised. A Spin Prevention and Incidence Limitation System (SPILS) was developed for all fighters, which protects the pilot against inadvertent departures from controlled flight. The stretching of the forward fuselage necessitated the moving of the pitch feel unit, and the opportunity was taken to adjust this to give considerably lighter stick forces and more 'fighter-like' handling.

Although it was designed to meet an RAF requirement, the Tornado ADV used a basic airframe constructed by all three partner nations, with the same broad workshare. BAe built ADV front and rear fuselages, MBB built the centres and Aeritalia the wings. All Tornado ADVs were assembled at Warton however.

Jon Lake

Crewmen take shelter (perhaps unadvisedly!) under a No. 43 Sqn Tornado F.Mk 3 during a thunderstorm at RAF Leuchars, in Scotland.

Tornado Variants: Tornado ADV

Tornado ADV prototypes

The three Tornado ADV prototypes were officially designated as F.Mk 2s, and differed little from the production F.Mk 2s which followed. All three aircraft were fully equipped with a comprehensive air-to-ground telemetry system, which allowed real-time analysis of test-point manoeuvres and clearance for the pilot to proceed to continue testing at more severe conditions of speed, altitude, attitude, roll rate, g or whatever. In previous test programmes aircraft had to land between sets of manoeuvres for exhaustive analysis of recorded data before being cleared to continue. Sortie lengths were extended by the regular use of inflight refuelling, and progress was generally smooth and quick.

The first of the three prototypes was ZA254, which was rolled out at Warton on 9 August 1979. It made its 1-hour 32-minute maiden flight on 27 October 1979 in the capable hands of Warton chief test pilot Dave Eagles, with ADV project navigator Roy Kenward acting as flight test observer, and reached Mach 1.25 on this flight. Mach 1.6 was reached during the second flight, and Mach 1.75 on the third. Initial flight test progress was extremely rapid. The aircraft exceeded Mach 1 during its first 1-hour 32-minute flight, and flew 8.5 hours in the five flights undertaken during the first week. They included a night landing and a dry inflight-refuelling prod, with a full wet contact on the third flight. The aircraft soon demonstrated more rapid acceleration than the IDS, although straight line speed was structurally limited to the same 800 kt IAS (915 mph; 1475 km/h) limit.

The first prototype was soon put to work flying more representative sortie profiles. In 1982, for example, the aircraft flew a simulated CAP 375 miles (604 km) from base, with a 2-hour 20-minute loiter on station. This was achieved carrying two of the small IDS 330-Imp gal (1500-litre) fuel tanks, and not the bigger 495-Imp gal (2250-litre) tanks developed especially for the ADV. The aircraft did not use inflight refuelling, and loitered in the vicinity of Warton for 15 minutes before landing with 5 per cent reserves remaining. A01 later conducted a number of SkyFlash missile firings, despite not being fitted with radar or full-standard avionics.

The second prototype, ZA267, was fitted with dual controls, but also had a representative main computer and rear cockpit displays. It made its first flight on 18 July 1980, and was subsequently used for a whole range of armament trials, including firing of the internal cannon and unguided launches of the SkyFlash missile. After making its maiden flight in a primer finish, it adopted the same white, black and grey finish as the first ADV. The initial SkyFlash trials necessitated the addition of prominent camera calibration markings, and proved the effectiveness of the revolutionary new Frazer Nash launchers developed for the ADV. These launchers each consisted of two cartridge-powered two-stage rams which impart sufficient velocity on the missile for it to clear the launch aircraft without exceeding its airframe limits, and in a relatively shallow installation. The two rams rigidly control the missile in pitch during launch, while spigots fore and aft prevent movement. A yoke on each rear ram prevents missile movement in roll. Initial cannon-firing trials revealed one of the first problems with the ADV. The distance between the gun muzzle and intake of the

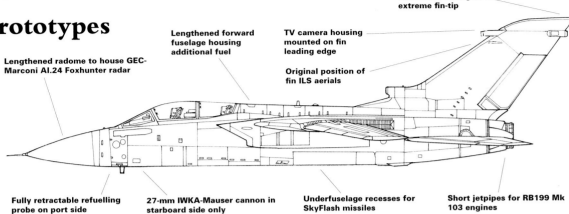

Lengthened radome to house GEC-Marconi AI.24 Foxhunter radar

Lengthened forward fuselage housing additional fuel

TV camera housing mounted on fin leading edge

Additional fairing at extreme fin-tip

Original position of fin ILS aerials

Fully retractable refuelling probe on port side

27-mm IWKA-Mauser cannon in starboard side only

Underfuselage recesses for SkyFlash missiles

Short jetpipes for RB199 Mk 103 engines

Above: Prototype A01 was painted in a black, grey and white scheme, which was distinctive and conspicuous in the air, but which avoided using non-operational, training-type colours.

Right: From their earliest days the prototype Tornado F.Mk 2s were routinely flown at high speeds, approaching Mach 2.

ADV was greater than on the IDS, and gun gas ingestion characteristics were thus different. In early firings, gun gases coated the optical device used to monitor turbine blade temperatures, and biased the engine controls dangerously. Gun firing had to be recleared, and the aircraft spent many hours firing the gun over Aberporth range, at various speeds and angles of attack.

The second aircraft was subsequently used for high-altitude zoom climb trials, and the results of them, together with computer simulations, revealed that the aircraft would be capable of attaining heights in excess of 70,000 ft (21340 m). It wore much the same grey and black colour scheme as the first prototype, and remains current at Boscombe Down.

The third F.Mk 2 prototype was ZA283, flown for the first time on 18 November 1980, and was intended as the radar development aircraft, although it initially flew with lead ballast. It was painted in an

overall grey scheme, similar to that applied to RAF Phantoms and Lightnings, and at last 'looked the part'. Radar was finally flown in the aircraft on 17 June 1981, having been delivered to Warton many months later than had been scheduled. Fortunately, the development radar sets were more reliable

than anticipated, and BAe was able to recover lost time by flying long-duration Foxhunter development sorties, with the Tornado and Lightning target accompanied by Buccaneer buddy refuelling tankers and with a second target waiting on the ground to take over if necessary. A03 switched to a

Above: A01 is seen here, unpainted, at the Warton factory, just prior to its roll-out in August 1979.

Right: Early artist's impressions of the ADV (this one dates from 1978) were a reasonable reflection of the 'real thing'.

B Model Foxhunter in March 1983. A02 began to fly with a B model radar fitted early in 1983.

In April 1983 the second prototype was retrofitted with increased thrust RB199 Mk 104 engines. They were the intended powerplant for the production Tornado ADV, and replaced the IDS-type Mk 103 used in the interim F.Mk 2s.

By the end of 1996, the second F.Mk 2 prototype was still leading an extremely active life at Boscombe Down as part of the Fixed Wing Test Squadron, while ZA254 was removed from storage at BAe's Warton plant for use as a gate guardian at RAF Coningsby. The third prototype is still available for trials.

This view of the third F.Mk 2 development aircraft was taken in 1990 when it was on charge with British Aerospace, where it remains.

Tornado F.Mk 2

The first 18 production Tornado ADVs for the RAF were delivered to an interim standard, without auto wing sweep (achievable through what should have been a simple software modification), with the ability to carry only two underwing Sidewinders, and still powered by IDS-type RB199 Mk 103 turbofans. They were rated at 9,656 lb st (42.95 kN) in dry power, and 16,920 lb st (75.27 kN) with full reheat. The aircraft also had only a single FIN 1010 INS fitted, even though it was realised that the aircraft really needed two, lacking the IDS's facility to make fixes using its attack radar. The first six (Batch 4, Block 8) were fitted with dual controls, and two of the remaining 12 (Batch 4 Block 9) were also twin-stickers. There was no change of designation for the two-seat aircraft, although they were unofficially referred to as F.Mk 2(T)s.

The first production F.Mk 2 was ZD899, but ZD900 made the first flight, in March 1984. Production F.Mk 2s differed from the prototypes in having no forward RWR fin fairing (used in the prototypes for a test camera), the forward RWR antennas being housed instead in the wing glove fairings.

Although not officially confirmed at the time, it has been widely reported that most of the F.Mk 2s were actually delivered without radar, leading to mocking references to 'Blue Circle' (a famous British cement company, whose name echoed the colour-based codenames applied to British weapons and avionics during the 1950s and 1960s – in fact, the ballast used was not cement but steel bars).

The ADV's Foxhunter radar was delayed by a multitude of technical problems, and by the RAF 'moving the goalposts', demanding progressive improvements in capability beyond that detailed in the initial contract and specification (such as a tailchase capability). Shortcomings from the original specification included unacceptably large sidelobes (which brought increased detectability, and vulnerability to countermeasures) and a severe shortfall in multi-target tracking capability. Technical problems with the AI.24 were unexpected and unwelcome. The radar had been flying in an MoD(PE) Canberra since 1975, and had proved reliable and impressive in that (somewhat limited) environment.

It was not until 17 June 1981 that ZA283 became the first Tornado to fly with the new radar. Test versions of the radar had flown previously in Canberra and Buccaneer testbeds. ZA283 (the third of the three F.Mk 2 prototypes) remained the only radar-equipped Tornado ADV for some time, flying with B series radar (the third incarnation flown on ZA283) in March 1983. The first of 20 pre-production sets was delivered in July 1983, but radars were not fitted on the Warton production line until mid-1985, by which time the radar was four years late and more than 50 per cent over budget. Tornado F.Mk 2s were delivered to No. 229 OCU at Coningsby between 5 November 1984 and October 1985.

All F.Mk 2s are understood to have eventually flown with PP radar fitted, allowing a limited degree of realistic role training. Few aircraft arrived on the unit with radar, however. The aircraft had sufficient combat capability to allow the unit to be

Annotations
Eight of 18 aircraft completed as twin-stickers

Forward-facing RWR antennas in wing glove fairing

Repositioned fin ILS antennas

Aircraft initially delivered with steel ballast in place of radar

Early-style fin base profile

Sidewinder launch rails on inboard side of wing pylon only

RB199 Mk 103 engines retained

declared to NATO as an emergency air defence unit in May 1985. In December 1986 the declaration was increased in scope and the unit took up the shadow squadron identity of No. 65 Squadron. This milestone was achieved with all 18 instructor crews trained, as the first crews of No. 29 Squadron arrived to begin conversion. The OCU thus found itself in the unusual position of being assigned a reserve role before any front-line squadrons had formed. The first F.Mk 3s had arrived at Coningsby in July 1986, and some F.Mk 2s had already been retired to storage, without training a single student.

The 16 F.Mk 2s which had served with No. 229 OCU were placed in storage at RAF St Athan with only 250 flying hours each, on average. They did have relatively high fatigue indices, due to the nature of the training they had been forced to conduct and to much of the flying being undertaken without underwing fuel tanks. Without radar, there was a concentration on air combat manoeuvring, and this naturally consumed more fatigue than high-level supersonic intercepts. The last F.Mk 2 left No. 229 OCU in January 1988. A handful of aircraft continued in productive service, nonetheless. ZD899 was retained at Warton as a test and trials airframe (after service at Boscombe Down), while ZD900 continued to be used by the A & AEE (later the DTEO) at Boscombe Down. From the ex-No. 229 OCU pool, ZD935 went to the ETPS at Boscombe Down, and ZD902 went to the RAE (later DRA) at Farnborough, where it later became the TIARA testbed. ZD939

had escaped from storage at St Athan to become a ground instructional airframe with the Saudi Support Unit at Warton by October 1991, and ZD937 had been relegated to BDR training by September 1993. The ETPS aircraft, ZD935, was relegated to ground instructional duties at Coningsby by October the same year.

It had once been hoped that the F.Mk 2s would be brought up to F.Mk 2A standards, identical to the F.Mk 3 except for their less powerful engines. The disbandment of No. 23 Squadron and the entry into service of the eight F.Mk 3s originally ordered by Oman led to a reduced requirement for Tornado ADVs, however, and the aircraft remained in storage. Hopes that the low-houred F.Mk 2s might be brought up to F.Mk 3 standards (or sold for export, perhaps to Malaysia) were finally dashed

This aircraft is one of the 16 F.Mk 2s briefly operated by No. 229 OCU, at RAF Coningsby, between November 1984 and August 1986.

when the RAF decided to scrap 12 of the stored F.Mk 2s in 1993. Fortunately, this plan was not implemented, and the aircraft's centre-sections were instead used in the repair of some of the 18 F.Mk 3s allegedly damaged by a civilian maintenance contractor (Airwork) at St Athan during 1993. All of the stored aircraft, plus the instructional airframes at Warton and Coningsby, and even ZD900, the flyer with Boscombe Down's DTEO Fixed Wing Test Squadron, are involved in the repair programme, which will leave ZD899 and ZD902 as the only flying F.Mk 2s.

Tornado F.Mk 2A

The Tornado F.Mk 2A designation was originally reserved as a designation for the F.Mk 2s following their planned upgrade to virtual F.Mk 3 standards. They were to have received later-standard radars, Auto Wing Sweep (AWS, also known as MDS), a second INS, provision for four Sidewinders and a new computer. Everything, in fact, except the F.Mk 3's more powerful engines. In the event, with the end of the Cold War, it was decided not to upgrade the aircraft for a return to service, and they remained in storage. Plans to export the

aircraft came to nothing, and a handful trickled into service with test and experimental units. Eventually, a decision was made to scrap 12 of the F.Mk 2s for spares recovery, but before it could be implemented the aircraft were reprieved, as donors for the repair of 18 F.Mk 3s allegedly damaged by a contractor. Sixteen F.Mk 2s gave up their centre fuselages.

The F.Mk 2A designation has since been applied (perhaps unofficially) to the TIARA testbed, which is described in greater detail below.

Tornado F.Mk 3

The interim F.Mk 2 was replaced on the production line by the F.Mk 3, which introduced a host of improvements. The most obvious, and arguably the most important, was the incorporation of the new RB199 Mk 104 engine. This had a 14-in (36-cm) extension to the afterburner section and used a DECU 500 digital engine control unit. The DECU 500, developed by Lucas Aerospace and Rolls-Royce, was the world's first full-authority digital engine control (FADEC) unit and gave precise computer control of the engines, while also offering improved fault diagnosis and engine monitoring. These modifications gave a 10 per cent increase in combat thrust, and reduced afterburning fuel consumption by 4 per cent. The new engine installation was obvious externally because the trailing edge of the fin below the rudder was extended aft, following the line of the rudder trailing edge down to the jetpipes. On early aircraft it cut forward in a scallop.

The F.Mk 3 was also fitted with a second FIN 1010 three-axis digital INS. The two INSs monitor each other, and monitor altitude information on the HUD. If the INS detects a difference in data, the HUD 'occults', switching off and then back on every minute. The F.Mk 3 was fitted with an Automatic Manoeuvre Device System (AMDS) which automatically deployed flaps and slats according to wing sweep, deploying both when manoeuvring with 25° of sweep, and slats only with the wings at 45°. Neither leading- nor trailing-edge devices could be deployed with the wing more fully swept.

The F.Mk 3 was supposed to have been fitted with auto wing sweep (actually not used at squadron level), which would have scheduled the wing to one of four pre-set positions, according to speed. Sweep of 25° would be selected at speeds up to Mach 0.73, 45° for speeds up to Mach 0.88, and 58° for speeds up to Mach 0.95. Beyond Mach 0.95, the wing would be swept back through 67°.

The power of the Tornado F.Mk 3's punch has been increased through provision for two extra AIM-9s, bringing the total to four. The inboard underwing pylons had extra stub pylons added to the outboard faces, to augment those on the inboard faces. The F.Mk 3 had a new main computer, a 128-K Litef Spirit III with twice as much computing power as the F.Mk 2.

Although covered by a single service designation, the different batches of RAF Tornado F.Mk 3s have differed from each other to a quite considerable degree, particularly in equipment fit and above all in radar standard and capability. IDS aircraft were assigned to units mainly on the basis of their batch number, but ADVs have had to be assigned according to block number within an individual batch. Squadrons have been forced to swap aircraft *en masse* as they have taken up new responsibilities, or undertaken different detachments.

The single crucial difference between aircraft from different blocks lies in radar standard although, as earlier radars have been upgraded, the differences have reduced or in some cases disappeared.

The first AI24 Foxhunter radar sets delivered were well below even the RAF's original specification, and were known as Type W (or W standard) radars. Although the W standard radar was below specification, early Tornado F.Mk 3 crews were publicly enthusiastic about the new radar's resistance to jamming, its look-down performance and multi-target track-while-scan abilities. This may have indicated that the RAF's specification was over-ambitious, or may simply indicate that even the below-spec Foxhunter marked a considerable improvement over the F-4M's radar, and over the ageing AIRPASS radar of the Lightning. Radar development flying continued apace at Warton, and up to four Lightning targets were used in the multi-target testing of the radar which began in

The GEC-Marconi Ariel Towed Radar Decoy is now operational on the RAF's F.Mk 3s. The TRD is fitted to a modified BOZ pod, which is itself carried on new outer pylons.

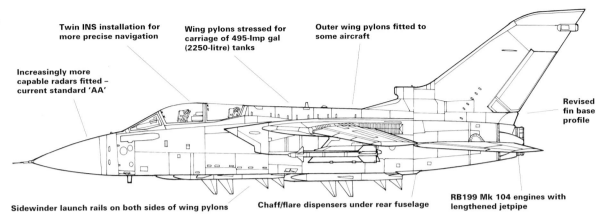

Twin INS installation for more precise navigation

Wing pylons stressed for carriage of 495-Imp gal (2250-litre) tanks

Outer wing pylons fitted to some aircraft

Increasingly more capable radars fitted – current standard 'AA'

Revised fin base profile

Sidewinder launch rails on both sides of wing pylons

Chaff/flare dispensers under rear fuselage

RB199 Mk 104 engines with lengthened jetpipe

Above: This photograph highlights the differences between the basic F.Mk 3s (of No. 5 Sqn) that were rushed to Saudi Arabia on 11 August 1990, after Iraq's invasion of Kuwait, and the aircraft that replaced them on 29/30 August. The aircraft in the foreground has the Stage One Plus 'war mods' including twin ALE-40(V) dispensers and RAM on the wings and tailplane.

Right: This 'Desert Eagles' F.Mk 3 is carrying a full load of SkyFlash and AIM-9M missiles, along with a Phimat chaff pod – unusually positioned under the starboard main pylon, instead of fuel tanks.

1983. The Lightnings were used for their greater speed and manoeuvrability, thereby making the intercept geometry more difficult for the Tornado.

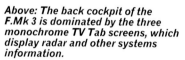

Left: This is the front cockpit of an RAF Tornado F.Mk 3 in basic configuration. It does not have the improved centre stick controls to manage weapons and radar.

Above: The back cockpit of the F.Mk 3 is dominated by the three monochrome TV Tab screens, which display radar and other systems information.

Seventy Type W radars were produced for the first 62 ADVs (those from Batch 4 and some of those from Batch 5, which is to say all of the 18 production F.Mk 2s and the first 44 F.Mk 3s). Forty-four of the Type W radars (presumably those fitted to the F.Mk 3s) were subsequently upgraded to Type Z standards, in a programme which began in 1988.

The next 80 RAF Tornado ADVs received Type Z (or Z standard) radars, which had increased tracking capability and increased range, and effectively met the RAF's original specification before additional levels of capability were requested. Most of the original Type W radars were brought up to Z standard from 1988, and all the Z standard sets (including those which had begun life as Type W radars) were themselves subsequently brought up to the definitive Stage One standard.

The last 46 RAF Tornado F.Mk 3s and the 24 aircraft delivered to Saudi Arabia were fitted with the new Stage One radar, manufactured from September 1988, with revised cooling and new software. The aircraft also gained a new F/A-18-type stick-top, giving improved HOTAS operation, as part of the Stage One upgrade. This put the weapons selection switches onto the stick (guns-Sidewinder-SkyFlash), as well as the radar air-to-air override control. The last eight production ADVs, originally intended for Oman but delivered to the RAF as F.Mk 3s, were similarly equipped. The aircraft with Stage One radar fitted on the line were initially delivered to the squadrons at Leuchars, and the last aircraft to be upgraded were those at Leeming.

An interim modification state, known as Stage One Plus, was hurriedly rushed into service on those aircraft deployed to the Persian Gulf in 1990 for participation in Operation Desert Storm. The Stage One Plus upgrade combined a series of modifications intended to enhance the Tornado F.Mk 3's combat capability and survivability, together with modifications which allowed the aircraft to operate in the Gulf's harsh climatic conditions.

The Foxhunter radar was upgraded to AA standard, with improved cooling and revised software which gave much enhanced ECCM and close-combat capability. The Tornado's high PRF radar is ideally suited to the long-range stand-off engagement of enemy bombers, but is not optimised for close-in dogfight-type engagements. Marconi reportedly began working on a Medium PRF version of Foxhunter to remedy this deficiency, but the Type AA radar was a useful interim step. Improvements were made to the Hermes RHWR, with improved software to recognise all potential threats and all in-theatre friendly forces. Have Quick secure voice radios were also added. Unfortunately, this was not sufficient to allow complete interoperability with the USAF's F-15Cs and the US Navy's F-14s, which had advanced IFF and secure communications equipment. The risk of blue-on-blue engagements led to the decision to use the F.Mk 3s only over friendly territory, and not well forward over Iraq itself. Two Tracor AN/ALE-40V flare dispensers (each with 15 cartridges) were scabbed on below the engine access doors on the lower fuselage, canted slightly outboard, away from the aircraft centreline, but were subsequently replaced by Vinten Vicon 78 dispensers before the fighting began. The modification of engine access doors was undertaken at RAF St Athan, with doors being flown directly from and to Leeming by Chinook helicopter. Another modification was the installation of nickel-

chrome tailplane leading edges, to replace the standard aluminium leading edges which proved prone to pitting and even burning through when enveloped by a Sidewinder rocket motor's launch plume. During the deployment (about two thirds of the way through No. 11 Squadron's detachment), provision was made for the carriage of Philips-MATRA Phimat chaff dispensers on the underwing hardpoint, in place of a fuel tank (usually the starboard tank). The Phimat could physically fit onto the underwing pylon's inboard Sidewinder stub pylons, but prevented full flap deployment. Even on the outboard stub pylon, flap clearance is rather limited. In the Gulf War, only a single Phimat was usually carried, on the starboard outer missile pylon, but over Bosnia a pair of Phimats has been seen, mounted on the outboard stub pylons, Sidewinders inboard. Frontal RCS was reduced by the addition of strips of RAM (Radar Absorbent Material) on the leading edges of the wings, fin, tailplanes and weapons pylons, and on the inner faces of the engine intakes. During the Gulf War the F.Mk 3s were modified to allow the use of night-vision goggles by their crews, and were sometimes flown by crews wearing AR5 nuclear/biological/chemical respirators. Operational capability was further enhanced by the use of AIM-9M Sidewinders specially purchased from the USA. The AIM-9M's WGU-4A/B seeker offered better target discrimination in the Gulf, and the Mk 36 Mod 11 rocket motor improved performance.

Tornado IDS aircraft in the Gulf War carried the larger, supersonic 495-Imp gal (2250-litre) ADV fuel tanks, and ADVs frequently carried the smaller, subsonic 330-Imp gal (1500-litre) tanks usually associated with the IDS. With them fitted, the ADVs had a manoeuvring limit of 5g, whereas with the larger tanks fitted the aircraft was limited to only 2.75g.

The retuning of engine limiters (to allow higher turbine gas temperatures, although the variable monitored was turbine blade temperature) gave a 5 per cent boost in maximum dry and maximum reheat thrust (for limited periods) through actuation of a 'Combat Boost' switch. This was located on the engine control panel, on the pilot's right-hand console. The basic thrust limits of 9,105 lb st (40.5 kN) (16,523 lb st/73.5 kN in reheat) were achieved in normal stator temperature limits of 1290°-1300° C (2,354-2,372° F), and these limits were increased by 20°C (68° F). The extra thrust obviously had some implications for combat

These No. 5 Squadron aircraft are completely clean except for a single ACMI pod each, carried to starboard. The 'flatness' of the Tornado underside is accentuated in this lighting.

This line of 'Tonkas' is seen at RAF Akrotiri in April 1992. They are Stage One Plus aircraft with obvious additional RAM coatings on the wings, wing gloves and fin.

performance, but was useful in the high temperatures encountered in the Gulf. The aircraft deployed to the Gulf had their air conditioning systems uprated to reduce humidity during start-up, and cockpit canopies were modified to prevent heat buckling and to allow the canopy to lock and unlock properly. Hot weather tyres, with different ply ratings for heavy weights and high temperatures, were also fitted.

All of the Gulf War modifications affecting the radar and main computer software were adopted post-war, while the tyre, canopy and air conditioning modifications were already fitted to Saudi aircraft. The unused auto wing sweep system was disconnected as part of the Stage One Plus upgrade.

Aircraft in RAF service are routinely subjected to a steady trickle of minor modifications and improvements which do not necessarily bring about any change in designation or appearance, and which may not be part of any larger 'package' of modifications. In order to reduce fatigue, it was once proposed that Tornado ADVs would be fitted with simple 175-lb (80-kg) weights in each wingtip to reduce the upward-bending moment on the wings. The modifications were considered but not adopted, because the benefits were not considered to be all that great. This will also be reduced through the incorporation of a 'wing fuel hold fuel management system' which delays emptying wing fuel, reducing the contents of the fuselage fuel tanks first, leaving the wings heavy.

Quite soon after the Gulf War, the Tracor AN/ALE-40 chaff/flare dispensers allocated for use by the F.Mk 3 fleet were replaced by Vinten Vicon 78 Series 210 dispensers (which had been used during the war by aircraft in-theatre), mounted in a similar under-nacelle location. The RAF has subsequently standardised on the Vicon 78 Series 400. Tornados operating over Bosnia carried a similar selection of stores to those that had flown in Operation Desert Storm. The smaller 330-Imp gal (1500-litre) IDS tanks were carried underwing, with Phimat chaff dispensers (outboard) and AIM-9M Sidewinders (inboard) on the stub pylons. The aircraft tended to carry four SkyFlash, but sometimes only two, one forward to port and the other in the rear starboard position.

Stage One Plus F.Mk 3 aircraft flying over Bosnia found themselves operating in a sophisticated SAM threat environment, which soon revealed some shortcomings in the aircraft's defensive equipment suite. Two F.Mk 3s were fired at by an SA-2 and an SA-6 on 24 November 1995, for instance. By the summer of 1995, Leeming-based F.Mk 3s were being sighted with the outboard underwing hardpoints reactivated and carrying IDS-type outer wing pylons. They were first fitted during mid-1994, and were carried by F.Mk 3s deployed from Leeming in November 1994. It soon became clear that they were intended to carry a modified BOZ chaff/flare dispenser pod airframe used as a housing for a Marconi Ariel towed radar decoy under the port wing, with a standard BOZ pod or a MATRA Phimat to starboard.

The GEC-Marconi Radar and Defence Systems Ariel towed radar decoy (TRD, inevitably pronounced as 'turd') was first deployed operationally aboard BAe Nimrods during the Gulf War. In 1995 the UK's Statement on the Defence Estimates acknowledged that the system had been "successfully embodied on Tornado F.Mk 3 aircraft operating over Bosnia."

The TRD is designed to be a decoy, presenting enemy SAM radars with an alternative target far from the aircraft towing it. The TRD is said to be more effective than using ejected decoys or chaff (which rapidly produce a Doppler mismatch with the fast-moving target) and more robust than the use of cross-polar jamming. There are actually two types of Ariel TRD, both designed to operate in the E-J bands. One is a high-power, autonomous, datalinked decoy, and the other uses EW equipment in

These SkyFlash missiles are the Improved SkyFlash model, carried during Operation Deny Flight operations. They are recognisable by their white-painted fin bases and the lack of the rocket motor safe/arming key.

The Celsius Tech BOL integral chaff/flare dispenser and launcher pylon now can be carried by the F.Mk 3. The rear of the BOL pylon carries the countermeasures, while the bulbous nose contains missile seeker-head coolant.

To carry the Ariel Towed Radar Decoy, F.Mk 3s have been fitted with GR.Mk 1-style outer pylons. TRD introduction was delayed from 1994 to 1995, but has now been used over Bosnia and in Red Flag exercises.

The RAF uses a mix of AIM-9L and AIM-9M Sidewinders carried on standard LAU-7 launchers, although a new launcher is now being introduced. These live 'Lima' Sidewinders are seen here on a No. 1435 Flt QRA aircraft.

British-built Vinten Vicon 78 Series 210 chaff/flare dispensers have replaced the US-supplied Tracor ALE-40(V) dispensers fitted during Operation Desert Shield. The pods are fitted to the engine bay doors.

The Philips-MATRA Phimat pod was the F.Mk 3's primary chaff dispensing system. As the Swedish-built BOL pylons are introduced they will become less common but are still used as counterbalances for the TRD.

the towing aircraft, transmitting signals from this equipment, acting as a towed, 'slave' jammer. It is uncertain which type is used by RAF Tornado F.Mk 3s.

Work on the TRD began in 1986, and low-power and inert airframes were first towed by a BAe Jetstream. More powerful testbeds were towed from a Buccaneer at speeds of up to 570 kt (650 mph; 1045 km/h) and in turns of up to 4.5*g* in 1988, when the first supersonic tows were made. In 1989 the BAe EAP was used for further

supersonic trials. Tornado trials are believed to have begun during 1994.

The aircraft's main computer was reportedly given an additional new processor by 1995, allowing the introduction of new clearer displays (new symbology and new presentation, not new screens) which began trials. Most vitally, the new single board main computer gave improved speed and power, giving full functionality during simultaneous use of the Stage Two radar and JTIDS. The planned introduction of a

new processor will bring all surviving RAF Tornado F.Mk 3 radars to Stage Two (AB) standard (also known as Stage 2G), allowing automatic target acquisition and tracking, and discrimination of head-on targets through analysis of first- and second-stage compressor discs. Modification kits were to have been delivered in 1991, but there have been delays. Automatic wing sweep (supposed to have been incorporated in production F.Mk 3s) may finally appear in the Stage Two aircraft, along with JTIDS.

Tornado Variants: Tornado ADV

Left: *Seen refuelling for a Deny Flight CAP, this F.Mk 3 is carrying the standard Bosnia loadout of twin AIM-9, Phimat and SkyFlash.*

Below left: *This F.Mk 3 landing at Coningsby provides a good view of its all-moving tailplane and flaps.*

the bipartite Memorandum of Understanding signed on 18 March 1994, the 24 aircraft will remain RAF property, subject to immediate recall if required. The RAF, for its part, will provide all necessary training, logistic and technical support to the AMI throughout the period of the lease.

Factors influencing Italy's choice of leased Tornado F.Mk 3s included the country's existing Tornado IDS maintenance infrastructure; the compatibility of the Tornado ADV with the indigenous Selenia Aspide was also quoted by some sources as being a factor. In fact, Aspide is not expected to be integrated with the Italian F.Mk 3s, and the AMI has leased 96 SkyFlash missiles to go with its airframes. Because the AMI has never operated a two-seat air defence aircraft, the Tornado F.Mk 3s (understood to be known simply as Tornado ADVs to their new operators) will be flown by two pilots, with some trained pilots acting as WSOs in the backseat. The initial backseaters will transition to the front seat after three years, having maintained flying currency on MB-339s attached to the stormo for the purpose. Their experience of operating the BVR weapons system will make them particularly useful when they eventually come to convert to Eurofighter. One existing Tornado backseater (not a trained pilot) was retrained as an ADV WSO at Coningsby in the first course of Italian aircrew. The Italian ground and aircrew were trained at the RAF's Tornado OCU, No. 56(R) Squadron at RAF Coningsby. Most were former F-104G/S pilots, although a handful had experience flying the IDS.

The Italian aircraft were drawn from a number of production blocks but all had already been modified to Stage One standard. Before delivery they were modified, at Italian expense, to Stage One Plus standards, with AA standard radar, NVGs, modified RHWR, chaff/flare dispensers and Have Quick II secure voice radios. None had served in the Gulf and none had been used in Operation Deny Flight.

The first Italian Tornado was formally handed over at RAF Coningsby in July 1995, and with the rest of the first batch of Italian Tornado F.Mk 3s was delivered to Gioia del Colle, where they re-equipped the 36° Stormo's 12° Gruppo. The second batch will be delivered between January and July 1997 and will then go to the 37° Stormo's 18° Gruppo at Trapani/53° Stormo's 21° Gruppo at Cameri.

AMI code/serial	RAF serial
36-01/MM55056	ZE202
36-02/MM7203	ZE761
36-03/MM55057	ZE837
36-05/MM7204	ZE730
36-06/MM7205	ZE787
36-07/MM7206	ZE760
36-10/MM7207	ZE762
36-12/MM7202	ZE832
36-13/MM7209	ZE835
36-14/MM7210	ZE836
36-16/MM7211	ZE792

One additional RAF F.Mk 3 was painted up in Italian markings as the spare aircraft for the ceremonial handover, and subsequently participated in the IAT at Fairford in 1994.

36-12/'MM'	ZE340

The Tornado F.Mk 3 production batches and blocks are detailed below, for completeness.

Batch 5 Block 10

Batch 5 Block 10 included 18 RAF F.Mk 3 aircraft (ZE154-168, ZE199-201), including six twin-stickers (ZE154, ZE157, ZE160, ZE163, ZE166 and ZE199, AT009-AT014, plane sets 486, 500, 513, 529, 542, and 552). The operational aircraft (AS011-AS022, plane sets 493, 497, 505, 509, 519, 524, 532, 538, 545, 549, 555, 559) were randomly interspersed with the trainers and Batch 5 IDSs, and all Block 10 ADVs were delivered with W Standard radar.

Even before the first flight of the ADV prototype, it was announced that the aircraft would be equipped with an "on-line, netted data ECM-resistant datalink system." In fact it was many years before any Tornado carried a datalink, even as a trials fit. JTIDS (Joint Tactical Information Distribution System, 'Jay-tids') was designed as a tactical datalink which would allow fighter, AWACS and other aircraft to share up-to-the-minute tactical information. The use of JTIDS by the Tornado F.Mk 3 would compensate for any deficiencies in onboard radar or primary missile armament range, by allowing the aircraft to make use of the much greater radar capability of the RAF's newly acquired Sentry AEW.Mk 1 AWACS. This would also help the Tornado crew maintain better situational awareness. The second production F.Mk 3 was held back on the production line (for 10 months) and had a JTIDS terminal installed when it made its maiden flight on 16 October 1986. The aircraft subsequently deployed to MCAS Yuma, Arizona, for trials, becoming the first ADV to cross the Atlantic, supported by one of the RAF's new TriStar tankers. On its return to the UK the aircraft became the first British fighter to make an unrefuelled Atlantic crossing.

The Tornado F.Mk 3 OEU conducted JTIDS service trials, including a major test on 27 October 1993 during which data was transferred back and forth between two F.Mk 3s, two RAF Boeing Sentries and a pair of French E-3F Sentries. Following further interoperability trials in the USA (at Mountain Home AFB, Idaho during July 1994) in conjunction with USAF F-15Cs, Nos 5 and 29 Squadrons at Coningsby were issued with Block 15/16 Stage One aircraft retrofitted with JTIDS datalink equipment (NATO Link 16). No. 111 Squadron also has JTIDS installed. All RAF ADVs will be fitted for JTIDs, but not all will have the equipment installed, since it will be moved around as required while the RAF waits for the yet-to-be defined NATO Multifunction Information Distribution System. JTIDS already provides a significant improvement in capability, giving the crew enhanced situational awareness and allowing the Tornado to operate effectively in a radar-silent mode, using a Sentry radar picture. The introduction of AMRAAM will perhaps allow targets to be engaged without using the Tornado's onboard radar.

Although the Stage Two modifications will make the Tornado F.Mk 3 an extremely effective interceptor, it is a sad fact that the aircraft remains less capable than had once been planned. As mentioned previously, the aircraft had originally been intended to have a Visual Augmentation System (VAS) for long-range visual identification of targets. This would have consisted of an image-intensifying electro-optical sensor giving a highly magnified TV picture of the target, even in starlight-only conditions. The Tornado ADV also remains less well-armed than was hoped. Even before the F.Mk 3 entered service, many analysts were looking forward to the integration of the AIM-120 AMRAAM on the Tornado ADV. The AIM-120 ran into many difficulties and delays, and its fire-and-forget capability has been found to be more limited than expected. In many scenarios, the missile is to all intents and purposes little more capable than the SkyFlash, since the launch aircraft still has to maintain the target aircraft within its radar scan while the missile is in flight, although it does not force the crew to keep the radar locked on to the target until missile impact. It remains some way from RAF service; the indigenous Active SkyFlash has been cancelled, as was the Anglo-Swedish SkyFlash 90. AMRAAM itself was cancelled insofar as the Tornado was concerned in 1992, but procurement was subsequently revived as part of the Tornado F.Mk 3 CSP (described below). In terms of its missile armament, the Tornado F.Mk 3 is little better than the F-4M Phantom FGR.Mk 2s which it replaced, although the firing envelope is equivalent to the full carriage envelope, much wider than the F-4's missile launch envelope.

The delays to Eurofighter, and the slippage in its service entry date, prompted Italy to take advantage of the RAF's supposed surplus number of Tornado F.Mk 3s. These aircraft were theoretically made available by the disbandment of No. 23 Squadron, although the extended grounding of 18 aircraft damaged during servicing and a fleet-wide shortage of RB199 engines caused by delays in overhauls actually left the RAF with a shortage of serviceable aircraft. A large number of aircraft in storage might have yielded greater flexibility and would have allowed the RAF's squadrons to run on longer themselves by spreading flying hours over a larger number of airframes.

Nevertheless, Italy has been able to sign a five-year no-cost lease (with the option of a five-year extension) on 24 Tornado ADVs. The deal was signed on 17 November 1993, after Italy examined offers of up to 70 leased F-16s or F-15s, either of which might have led to purchase and thereby threatened Eurofighter procurement. Under

Batch 5 Block 11

Batch 5 Block 11 included 34 RAF F.Mk 3 aircraft (ZE202-210, ZE250-258, ZE287-296 and ZE338-343), including 22 operational aircraft (AS023-044, plane sets 565, 569, 574, 576, 583, 586, 593, 595, 602, 605, 610, 612, 617, 619, 624, 626, 631, 633, 638, 641, 645, 647) and 12 twin-stickers (ZE202, ZE205, ZE208, ZE250, ZE253, ZE256, ZE287, ZE290, ZE293, ZE296, ZE340, ZE343, AT015-026, plane sets 562, 571, 581, 590, 600, 607, 614, 622, 629, 636, 643, 649). Z standard radar.

Batch 6 Block 12

46 F.Mk 3 aircraft (ZE728-737, ZE755-764, ZE785-794, ZE808-812, ZE830-839, ZE858), included 39 operational aircraft (AS045-083) and seven twin-stickers (ZE728, ZE735, ZE759, ZE786, ZE793, ZE830, and ZE837, AT027-033, plane sets 652, 666, 679, 693, 705, 718, 730). Z standard radar.

Batch 6 Block 13

Fighter Tornados within Batch 6 Block 13 consisted of 22 RAF F.Mk 3 aircraft (ZE862, ZE887-889, ZE907-908, 911, 934, 936, 941-

Italy opted to accept a leased batch of ex-RAF Tornados, to act as a stopgap for its air defence force, before the first deliveries of EF2000.

942, 961-969, 982-983), included 12 operational (AS092, 093, 098, 101, 106, 111, 114, 115, 120, 121, 122 and 123, plane sets 753, 757, 765, 772, 781, 790, 794, 796, 802, 803, 804 and 805) and 10 twin-stickers (ZE862, ZE908, ZE934, ZE941, ZE963, ZE964, ZE965, ZE966, ZE967 and ZE968, AT034-043, plane sets 742, 755, 766, 778, 788, 797, 798, 799, 800 and 801). Stage One radar. AS084-090, 091, 094-100, 102-105, 107-113 were diverted to RSAF with new variant identities. AT039 and AS116-AS119 were reallocated identities AT039-043 to replace the Saudi two-seaters.

Batch 7 Block 14

Seven RAF F.Mk 3 aircraft (ZG728, ZG730-735, AS124-130), with no twin-stickers, were included in Batch 7 Block 14. They were plane sets 834, 838, 841, 845, 850, 855 and 859. Stage One radar.

Batch 7 Block 15

Seventeen RAF F.Mk 3 aircraft (ZG751, 753, 755, 757, 768, 770, 772, 774, 776, 778, 780, 793, ZG795-799, AS131-147, plane sets 863, 872, 877, 882, 886, 891, 899, 904, 908, 910, 912, 915, 917, 918, 919, 920 and 921), with no twin-stickers. The Block 15 aircraft were the first to be equipped with JTIDS, and had Stage One radar.

Batch 7 Block 16

Block 16 included eight RAF F.Mk 3 aircraft (ZH552-559, AT44-AT51, plane sets 922-929), all twin-stickers. They were the aircraft originally built for Oman (as KT001-KT008), and were Stage One radar-equipped. ZH559, the last RAF Tornado F.Mk 3, was delivered to No. 56(R) Squadron on 24 March 1993.

Tornado F.Mk 3 (repaired aircraft)

When it became necessary to increase the Fatigue Index of the Tornado F.Mk 3, the necessary airframe modifications (25 FI) were contracted out to industry. An initial batch of 15 aircraft was successfully modified by BAe, but the contract for a subsequent batch of 18 aircraft was won by Airwork services, whose £7 million tender was £4 million lower than BAe's.

The first four aircraft (ZE292, ZE295, ZE343 and ZE728) were returned to service following modification, and pilots reported some handling peculiarities; RAF engineers soon found the cause to be longeron distortion. The longerons had reportedly been distorted when inappropriate tools (pneumatic guns) were used to remove the light alloy collars which covered fasteners connecting panels to the longerons. The remaining 14 aircraft undergoing modification by Airwork at St Athan were inspected, and 12 were found to be severely damaged, with two more having suffered lighter damage. The contract was immediately cancelled and work on the aircraft was halted while options were explored. The four 'finished' aircraft were returned to St Athan.

At one stage it was felt that the 12 most severely damaged aircraft would have to be returned to Panavia in Germany for a centre fuselage rebuild, and during 1994 it was announced that 14 of the aircraft would be prematurely scrapped. In the event, it was decided to repair the aircraft, rebuilding the most severely damaged by using the centre-

sections from 16 of the 18 surviving stored and flying Tornado F.Mk 2s. Since it had already been decided to scrap most of these aircraft, it represented a remarkably cost-effective solution, and was made possible by some flexible and incisive thinking within the RAF and MoD, and by BAe's willingness and ability to do the work as required.

BAe was awarded a contract to undertake a trial rebuild of ZE154, using the centre-section of F.Mk 2 ZD901. Both aircraft were removed from storage at St Athan and were trucked to Warton on 24 October 1994. The rebuild was successful and ZE294 was next to be repaired, using the centre-section of ZD906. All 16 of the worst damaged F.Mk 3s will receive new centre-sections from the F.Mk 2s and will be returned to service. The two more lightly damaged aircraft were simply repaired and returned to their units.

Concern about the extent of the damage caused to the F.Mk 3s intensified following the loss of one of the aircraft on its first post-rebuild test flight on 28 September 1996. The aircraft crashed into the sea off Blackpool, narrowly failing to return to Warton. The BAe test crew escaped unharmed, but the aircraft was lost. Although there was no evidence that the accident bore any relation to the damage allegedly caused by Airwork, or to the subsequent repair, stories in the media highlighted concerns that there could have been a link.

The unfortunate story was concluded in

March 1997, when it was announced that Bricom (Airwork's parent company at the time of the alleged damage) would pay the MoD £5 million in compensation for 16 aircraft damaged at St Athan. The cost of the BAe repairs has not been revealed, but the £5 million figure places a very low value on the F.Mk 2s which donated their centre-sections to the programme (which could have otherwise been sold abroad or returned to service).

F.Mk 3 serial	F.Mk 2 centre-section used
ZE154	ZD901
ZE251	ZD936
ZE254	ZD941
ZE255	ZD932
ZE258	ZD905
ZE288	ZD940

ZE292	ZD939
ZE294	ZD906
ZE295	ZD938
ZE343	ZD900
ZE728	ZD903
ZE729	ZD933
ZE736	ZD937
ZE759	ZD904
ZE786	ZD934
ZE793	ZD935

The 25 FI modification programme was reinstated by the RAF using service personnel, and on 16 September 1994 the RAF was formally awarded the contract to modify the next batch of aircraft.

Wearing the marks of No. 43 Squadron, this F.Mk 3 was the lead-ship to be redelivered to the RAF after a major overhaul and rebuild at the hands of British Aerospace.

Tornado ADV (export)

Oman: The first customer for the Tornado outside the three partner nations was almost the Sultanate of Oman, which ordered eight Tornado ADVs on 14 August 1985. They were for delivery by 1987, and the £250 million price tag included training, support and SkyFlash missiles. It was hoped that these aircraft would replace the SEPECAT Jaguars then in use in the air defence role, freeing up the Jaguars to replace the Al Quwwat al Jawwiya al Sultanat Oman's ground attack Hawker Hunters. Deliveries were originally scheduled to begin in 1988, but were put back to 1992, before the order was subsequently cancelled in favour of an order for the much less capable BAe Hawk 200. The Omani aircraft were eventually delivered to the RAF as F.Mk 3s, wearing the serials ZH552 to ZH559.

Saudi Arabia: The second order for the Tornado ADV came on 26 September 1985, when Saudi Arabia ordered a massive package of BAe aircraft under the Al

This pair of unarmed Tornado ADVs, of No. 29 Sqn RSAF, were among the very first to be delivered in February 1989. The Saudi Tornado ADV force is based at Dhahran.

Yamamah programme. This included 48 Tornado IDS strike aircraft, 30 Pilatus PC-9s, 30 BAe Hawk Mk 65s, two Jetstream

navigator trainers and 24 Tornado ADVs. The 24 Tornado ADVs were drawn from the RAF's aircraft built in Batch 6, with six aircraft completed as twin-stickers (though planned as standard operational aircraft for the RAF). The 24 aircraft were replaced in RAF service in later batches. The Saudi

ADVs were all Batch 6, Block 13 aircraft.

The aircraft delivered to the RSAF were respectively plane sets 737, 739, 740, 744, 746, 747, 749, 751, 758, 760, 761, 763, 768, 770, 773, 775, 777, 780, 782, 784, 785, 787, 791 and 793 (see table for individual identities). The twin-stickers replaced RAF

The sale of Tornados to Saudi Arabia was seen as a major success for British industry. A much-touted second batch of deliveries (Al Yamamah II) never materialised.

aircraft planned to be operational aircraft. Saudi serials were not allocated in strict RAF serial order, as detailed.

The aircraft were delivered from 9 February 1989, arriving at Dhahran to re-equip No. 29 Squadron on 20 March 1989. Formation of No. 34 Squadron was eventually abandoned in 1993. The Saudi aircraft differed little from contemporary RAF F.Mk 3s and were actually the first production ADVs to be fitted with the Stage One Foxhunter radar. The aircraft wore much the same basic colour scheme (with Saudi national markings and RSAF titles) and carried much the same stores. Weapons supplied included BAe SkyFlash and AIM-9L Sidewinder missiles, and the aircraft tended to fly with the big 'Hindenburger' fuel tanks.

A second arms package was agreed in July 1988 as Al Yamamah II, and was to have included 36 Tornado ADVs and 12 IDSs. By the time the contract was signed in May 1993, the order had been changed to cover the supply of 48 IDSs, with no ADVs. It has been suggested that Saudi Arabia was not entirely satisfied with the ADV's ability to meet its unique requirement, and that as an air defence aircraft it was rendered surplus to requirements by massive deliveries of F-15 Eagles. It was even reported that the ADVs already in service might be rebuilt or converted to a SEAD or maritime strike configuration.

Jordan: Another potential ADV customer was Jordan. After the USA shelved the Northrop F-20 Tigershark, Jordan approached Saudi Arabia with a request that it should order between eight and 10 extra ADVs for subsequent transfer to the Royal Jordanian air force. The UK refused such an indirect deal, although Jordanian pilots evaluated the Tornado while the prospect of a direct sale was explored. Jordan's interest later switched to the IDS (which see).

RAF variant	RAF serial	New variant	RSAF serial	RAF variant	RAF serial	New variant	RSAF serial
AS084	ZE859	DS01	2905	AS099	ZE909	DT05	3451 later 2913
AS085	ZE860	DS02	2906	AS100	ZE910	DT06	3452 later 2914
AS086	ZE861	DT01	2901	AS102	ZE912	DS09	3453 later 2915
AS087	ZE882	DT02	2902	AS103	ZE913	DS010	3454 later 2916
AS088	ZE883	DT03	2903	AS104	ZE914	DS011	3455 later 2917
AS089	ZE884	DT04	2904	AS105	ZE935	DS012	3456 later 2918
AS090	ZE885	DS03	2907	AS107	ZE937	DS013	3457 later 2919
AS091	ZE886	DS04	2908	AS108	ZE938	DS014	3458 later 2920
AS094	ZE890	DS05	2909	AS109	ZE939	DS015	3459 later 2921
AS095	ZE891	DS06	2910	AS110	ZE940	DS016	3460 later 2922
AS096	ZE905	DS07	2911	AS112	ZE943	DS018	3461 later 2923
AS097	ZE906	DS08	2912	AS113	ZE960	DS018	3462 later 2924

Tornado F.Mk 3 Capability Sustainment Programme

The emergence of new threats like the Su-27 underlined the limitations inherent in the ADV's original concept, as a pure BVR bomber destroyer, while continuing dissatisfaction with the aircraft's radar and high-altitude performance led to studies into various upgrades. Replacement of the troublesome Foxhunter by the AN/APG-65 was proposed, and re-engining was also considered. The RB199 engine had been optimised for low-level flight, and at low altitudes offered relatively high thrust with low specific fuel consumption, but it was far from being a true fighter engine, and thrust fell off markedly at higher altitudes. This proved to be an irritation in the Tornado F.Mk 3, whose pilots often found themselves embarrassed by a lack of thrust at high altitude. Even when inflight refuelling, F.Mk 3 pilots often had to 'plug-in' afterburner at some heights. The ADV's lack of high-altitude 'grunt' had an impact on tactics, forcing the aircraft to fly CAPs at lower altitudes than were ideal and which perhaps had been routine in Lightning days. Ideal loiter heights for the ADV were between 20,000 and 25,000 ft (6097 and 7621 m), for instance. Fuel consumption also increased dramatically at the higher cruising speeds associated with the fighter role, and this had driven the many attempts to reduce drag in the aircraft.

The Eurojet EJ200 engine developed for Eurofighter was designed from the start for all-altitude use, and to be installationally interchangeable with the RB199. This allowed the Tornado engine to serve as an interim Eurofighter prototype powerplant, and offered the possibility of re-engining the Tornado itself. An AN/APG-65-equipped, EJ200 ADV upgrade was reported to have been briefly considered during 1988. This extra thrust would have radically transformed the Tornado ADV's acceleration, climb rate and sustained turn performance, though the aircraft's outright straight line speed was not thrust limited even with the RB199. Unfortunately, the upgrade would not have produced an aircraft as effective as Eurofighter (calculated as being 2.35 times that of the modified ADV) and the cost of a retrofit for those ADVs which would survive to augment EF2000 ruled it out.

Continuing delays to the Eurofighter, whose service entry date has already slipped beyond 2000, have necessitated a modest upgrade to the RAF's F.Mk 3s, however. Some of the British Secretary of State for Defence's key advisers urged a purchase of F-16s as a stopgap, instead of refurbishing the Tornados; although this proposal attracted some support, it was soon rejected, and a limited Tornado F.Mk 3 upgrade is now certain, if still not entirely defined. The F-16 would have given RAF pilots vital experience of a modern, agile single-seat fighter, but indirect costs would have been considerable since the aircraft was not compatible with existing RAF inflight-refuelling aircraft, flying clothing, helmets and logistics/maintenance infrastructure. More seriously, the acquisition of the aircraft would have given the RAF a fighter just capable enough to raise questions as to the need for the Eurofighter itself. A Tornado upgrade would have none of these disadvantages.

On 5 March 1996 it was announced that BAe would be prime contractor in a £125 million upgrade to about 100 RAF ADVs to extend their service lives to 2010. At this early stage it was expected only that the upgrade would include the provision of AMRAAM and ASRAAM compatibility, and radar enhancements to permit simultaneous engagement of multiple targets. The inclusion of AMRAAM and ASRAAM marked an about-face, since procurement of these missiles for the ADV had been cancelled as recently as 1992, on economic grounds. The experience of Tornado ADV aircrew fighting against USAF F-15 and F-16 pilots armed with AMRAAM, and of simulated engagements with AMRAAM-armed German F-4F ICE fighters in exercises, may have served to underline the inadequacies of SkyFlash. It is also becoming increasingly likely that the Russian equivalent to AMRAAM (the R-77 AA-12 'Adder') will soon be in front-line service with a number of potentially hostile MiG-29 operators. Some sources even credit this missile with a longer range (and greater 'fire-and-forget' capability) than AMRAAM itself, let alone SkyFlash. Additional new AIM-120 missiles will not actually be procured, however, since the Tornado will take AMRAAMs procured for the Royal Navy's Sea Harrier F/A-2s, and ASRAAMs purchased for the Harrier GR.Mk 7.

Some of the modifications generally ascribed to the upgrade were in fact already underway, including the provision of JTIDS and the Marconi Ariel TRD, and some of the changes to the main computer and cockpit displays. The upgrade will include the installation of a single, dual-redundant Mil Std 1553B databus, and the main computer will provide enhanced aiming cues to the crew and act as a bus controller. AIM-9/ASRAAM pylons and launch rails will be modified to incorporate Celsius Tech BOL-304 chaff dispensers and Vinten flare dispensers.

The precise number of aircraft covered by the upgrade remains uncertain, with some reports suggesting that the number upgraded will be only sufficient to equip "two squadrons...sufficient to fulfil the needs of a rapid-reaction force."

The cost of Eurofighter has made it by no means certain that enough aircraft will be procured to fully replace the ADV, and it is quite possible that a significant number of Tornado fighters will be expected to serve for some years to come.

Tornado Integrated Avionics Research Aircraft (TIARA)

The availability of surplus Tornado F.Mk 2 airframes came as a welcome boon to Britain's aeronautical research and experimental establishments. Two F.Mk 2s (the first and second production aircraft) had been delivered to the Aeroplane and Armament Experimental Establishment for trials, and remained at Boscombe Down with the Fixed Wing Test Squadron. One of these aircraft later went back to BAe.

With ex-No. 229 OCU F.Mk 2s available from late 1986, two different agencies took aircraft from storage at St Athan. The Empire Test Pilot's School used twin-sticker ZD935 from 1988 until February 1990, when it returned to St Athan. Another twin-sticker, ZD902, was delivered to Farnborough in 1988, where it was used for air defence equipment and avionics trials. It returned to St Athan for conversion to virtual F.Mk 3 standard, albeit without the Mk 104 engines or auto wing sweep. The aircraft's reliance on the Mk 103 engine is not ideal, since the newer engine would improve maintainability and reduce operating costs, while also offering an improvement in performance. The aircraft received 5 FI modifications, strengthening panels near the wing box, during its three-month stay at St Athan.

On its return it became the Tornado Integrated Avionics Research Aircraft (TIARA), tasked with flying a variety of project support and research tasks, not always in support of a particular programme, but exploring and developing general concepts which would be applicable across a range of future aircraft projects. The MoD was considered to be the prime customer for the aircraft from the beginning, but the project team also hoped to collaborate with industry on a number of ventures, and began 'marketing' the aircraft to potential customers and collaborators by displaying it at the 1994 Farnborough air show. The aircraft was mocked-up with various sensors and equipment but the aircraft did not actually make its first flight in TIARA configuration until 18 October 1995, a flight which doubled as the aircraft's delivery to its new base at Boscombe Down.

One of the most important areas examined by TIARA is sensor fusion, and the project team envisage adding different equipment and avionics items to a fairly ambitious and comprehensive core fit, which was built up gradually from 1988. This is based around four Mil Std 1553 databuses, one dedicated to the radar running at 250 Hz, and three running at 50 Hz.

The fact that ZD902 was a dual control aircraft was vitally important, allowing the rear cockpit to be kept 'standard' for the safety pilot. The front cockpit was extensively modified and re-equipped as the 'experimental station', representing a generic future single-seat fighter cockpit. The front cockpit thus has three Smiths 6¼ x 6¼ in (15.9 x 15.9 cm) raster cursive shadow mask CRT colour MFDs below a Smiths wide angle holographic Z-HUD. This covers 30° in azimuth and 22° in elevation, and is broadly representative of the current state of the art in HUD design.

The aircraft uses an F/A-18 stick-top, and has a Sea Harrier throttle as a hand controller. It is fitted with comprehensive telemetry equipment, and has provision for video recorders for the HUD, the MFDs, the FLIR (when carried) and for a panoramic over-the-shoulder view of the cockpit. There are head trackers in both cockpits to allow head steering of seekers or sensors.

One of the first items of equipment flown aboard TIARA was the GEC-Marconi FIRSTSIGHT IRST. This advanced air-to-air infra-red sensor was developed specifically for the application, to act as a technology demonstrator and development tool, providing high-quality digital imagery to allow the development of future IRST algorithms and hardware. The equipment gathers IR energy through a 150-mm (5.9-in) diameter dome on the top of the Tornado nose, through a Zinc Sulphide window. This is then reflected down to the thermal imaging sub-system (based on a TICM Class II Miniscanner operating in the 8-12 μm band, similar to that used by the FLIR of the Harrier GR.Mk 7) via a stabilised mirror which steadies the image in elevation and azimuth, with stabilisation in rotation provided by a prism. The mirror could also be used to steer the system's line of sight across the entire field of regard of the equipment. The sensor image is digitised by the thermal imager and then passed to a signal processing sub-system. It flew in October 1996, and was the first British airborne IRST.

Initially flown without radar, TIARA later received a Blue Vixen radar, chosen for its availability and its multi-mode capabilities, which made it an ideal complement to other air-to-air and air-to-ground sensors and avionics for sensor fusion work.

Among the projects to be undertaken by TIARA is an in-house funded direct voice input programme, initially with a 200-300 word vocabulary; high-speed RHAWS work; and work involving helmet-mounted target designators, sights and displays, including the GEC Advanced Integrated Avionic Helmet. The aircraft can be fitted with an interchangeable GEC IRST or a steerable FLIR. In its definitive configuration, TIARA

will almost certainly fly with captive ASRAAM seeker heads fitted to the inboard underwing pylons.

It is uncertain if the TIARA Tornado will receive JTIDS, although it remains an option, and there is some hope that the outboard underwing pylons will be reactivated to allow the carriage of stores, including towed radar decoys.

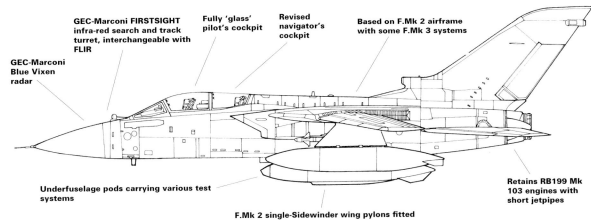

Labels on diagram:
- GEC-Marconi FIRSTSIGHT infra-red search and track turret, interchangeable with FLIR
- Fully 'glass' pilot's cockpit
- Revised navigator's cockpit
- Based on F.Mk 2 airframe with some F.Mk 3 systems
- GEC-Marconi Blue Vixen radar
- Underfuselage pods carrying various test systems
- Retains RB199 Mk 103 engines with short jetpipes
- F.Mk 2 single-Sidewinder wing pylons fitted

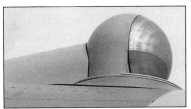

The FIRSTSIGHT IRST is one of the most important of the TIARA's new sensors now under development.

Different equipment can be flown inside underfuselage pods based on standard flight-cleared fuel tanks.

Below: The TIARA is seen here taxiing out at Boscombe Down for IRST trials. It also carries FLIR sensors in the modified fuel tanks.

The TIARA front cockpit (right) has been extensively modified with three new colour MFDs with soft keys, a holographic HUD and HOTAS controls. The rear cockpit (above) has only been slightly altered.

Super Tornado

The Super Tornado (or Tornado International) was an unbuilt project based on the longer, higher fuel capacity fuselage of the Tornado ADV, but with an additional ground attack capability. The aircraft remained in essence an ADV, and was not actually optimised for the strike, attack and maritime strike roles, although it was to have been cleared for the carriage of bombs, ALARM missiles and Sea Eagle, which of course necessitated some cockpit changes. The new variant had few disadvantages by comparison with the standard IDS, and many advantages. At one stage, some thought it likely that the Super Tornado might be selected to meet the

RAF's long-term requirement for a Buccaneer replacement, though the aircraft was primarily offered to export customers, including Japan. The Super Tornado was studied in 1987, and was never openly marketed. No details were officially released, although customer information was prepared, with an ADV prototype flying sorties with all four underwing pylons activated for brochure photography. The programme was stopped in 1988, as it was felt that the type offered only a small potential for increased sales and yet demanded a significant level of investment, which could not be justified in order to chase the limited market opportunity.

Tornado J

The Tornado J was proposed in 1987 as a solution to the JASDF's requirement for a new maritime strike aircraft to replace the Mitsubishi F-1. The aircraft was proposed after it became apparent that the baseline

Tornado IDS lacked sufficient range to meet the Japanese requirement and was intended to make the Tornado more attractive to the Japanese in some other respects. Thus Tornado J was to have been jointly developed by Panavia and Japan's own aircraft industry. The aircraft would have been based on the lengthened ADV

airframe, but incorporated features from the IDS and ECR. Metal was never cut on the Tornado J, though the third ADV prototype had its outboard underwing pylons reactivated to allow demonstration flights and to facilitate publicity photographs – which have never been released.

LVJ Tornado

The LVJ (Luftverteidigungs-Jäger) Tornado was the last attempt to design a Tornado derivative to meet the Luftwaffe's requirement for a new fighter, which eventually led to participation in the quadrinational Eurofighter. The aircraft was essentially a Tornado ADV-type fuselage married to a new compound delta low-set wing, with a short-coupled canard high on the side of the intake. The canard foreplane was added to increase lift, and to generate pitch instability, but was never intended for pitch control. The design was studied in 1980, but was quickly abandoned due to its inadequate performance. Cost savings were relatively insignificant, and the aircraft held out little hope of matching even existing aircraft like the F/A-18.

German Air Force Air Defence Tornado

Germany considered using the Tornado to meet its requirement for a fighter on several occasions, initially exploring the possibility of a rearmed but otherwise unmodified IDS. After examining the basic ADV (known in Germany as the ADV 075) in 1974-75, Germany examined the possibility of acquiring a single-seat Tornado derivative,

perhaps with a fixed wing, and with certain new technologies for service in the air defence role, the GAFAD Tornado. The aircraft was held to have insufficient performance and the idea was not pursued, although Tornado Commonality Concepts continued to be studied with the aim of attaining maximum sub-system

commonality and to minimise development and production costs. By 1980, a Tornado derivative with a fixed, carbon-fibre forward-swept wing was under investigation. The forward-swept wing offered reduced drag at transonic speeds, and high transonic lift coefficient, though transonic performance was not critical to the German fighter role.

South America

Part Two: *Argentina, Bolivia, Chile, Paraguay and Uruguay*

The southern region of South America was home to one of the continent's longest-standing disputes: that between Argentina and Chile. Both nations are today on the verge of a significant expansion of their combat air power. They, in turn, are surrounded by three of the region's most peaceful nations: Bolivia, Paraguay and Uruguay. Of these, only Paraguay maintains an air force that is any more than a quaint antique. All three are more concerned with maintaining an internal air transport infrastructure, with a limited ability to protect their borders from smuggling.

Argentina

Throughout its history, one of Argentina's characteristics has been the nature of the country's decisions: independent of the influence of major countries. This nation of 2.7 million km² (1.042 million sq miles), having a population of 35 million people with predominantly European roots, was previously considered by other Latin American countries as the model to follow. However, a period of political instability darkened the country's bright future. In 1983, though, Argentina returned to democratic rule, spurring a vast reform of the republic from a social to an economic orientation. Territorial and border disputes – mainly with Chile – gave way to political alliances – especially with Brazil – to an unprecedented level. Argentina is the leading proponent for the consolidation of the MERCOSUR block, integrated with Uruguay and Paraguay and

having Chile as an associated country. The nature of the constitution of binational military structures with Brazil is currently under discussion, following a positive experience of joint manoeuvres and personnel exchanges. In the international scene, Argentina is probably the US's most reliable South American partner after a series of political movements that ranged from intervention in Operation Desert Storm to strong support for the economic blockade of Cuba. The Clinton administration rewarded this conduct by lifting all arms restrictions on sales to Argentina and offering the same status enjoyed by NATO members or close allies such as Israel or Japan. Although the country's situation has improved notably in the last five years, the reduction of regional conflicts coupled with limited defence expenditures have forced a reduction of military structures.

Fuerza Aérea Argentina

The Fuerza Aérea Argentina was born as an independent force on 4 February 1945, receiving all personnel and assets from the Ejército Argentino. Most of this equipment was outdated, comprising a combat force of Curtiss 75 Hawk fighters and Martin 139 bombers. After a couple of years the Fuerza Aérea assembled the strongest air arm in the area, with British support. The gems were the 100 Gloster Meteor F.Mk IVs and the 45-strong bomber fleet of Avro Lancasters/Lincolns. Over the following years, the United States became the primary military source and Meteors, Lincolns and Prentices give way to Sabres, Skyhawks and Mentors. However, Argentina's request for more advanced equipment in the late 1960s was rejected by the US, and the country turned to European sources. The Fuerza Aérea Argentina, through its controlled Fabrica Militar de Aviones, pushed the development of aircraft to meet its specific requirements, such as the IA-50 Guaraní light transport, the IA-58 Pucará attack/armed reconnaissance turboprop and the IA-63 jet trainer. At

the time of the 1982 Falklands War, BAC Canberras and the Mirage family fleet, plus the locally built IA-58 Pucará, were among the combatants. After a traumatic post-war period, the Fuerza Aérea is showing the first signs of a rational recovery.

Chain of command

The Fuerza Aérea Argentina is a dependant of the Ministerio de Defensa and is headquartered at Edificio Condor in the Capital Federal district. All operational aircraft – known also as Sistema de Armas, or weapon systems – are controlled by the Comando de Operaciones Aéreas through the Grupos Aéreos of the Brigadas Aéreas. All training assets are the responsibility of the Comando de Instrucción, whose major components are the Escuela de Aviación Militar (EAM) for pilots and the Escuela de Suboficiales (ESFA) for petty officers. Technical support and maintenance facilities are provided by the Comando de Material, organised into three major workshops: Area

Material Córdoba, Area Material Rio Cuarto and Area Material Quilmes. Control of civil and commercial aviation is also assigned to the Fuerza Aérea, which established the Comando de Regiones Aéreas to manage such activities as air traffic control, airport management and security and civil aviation training.

Mirage and Dagger force

In the second half of the 1960s, the backbone of the Argentine AF comprised two squadrons of A-4P Skyhawks, one of F-86F-40 Sabres and another squadron for light attack with Morane MS-760 Sabres, plus a handful of Gloster Meteor F.Mk 4s. The Fuerza Aérea only received true supersonic fighters after the purchase of 10 Mirage IIIEAs and two Mirage IIIDAs, under a FF123 million contract signed on 14 July 1970. These aircraft were delivered during 1971 to the newly activated Grupo Aéreo 8 de Caza Interceptión based at BAM Mariano Moreno. The Mirages also introduced the first Argentine AAMs, the radar-guided MATRA 530. Another seven Mirage IIIEAs and two more Mirage IIIDAs were delivered between 1977 and 1980; they are characterised by having two extra wing hardpoints for MATRA 550 Magic AAMs.

Disputes about the possession of several islands in the Beagle Channel area prompted the Argentine and Chilean authorities to reinforce their military structures in anticipation of border clashes. Under a secretive programme codenamed Dagger, the Fuerza Aérea purchased 26 Israeli-built IAI Neshers and activated Grupo Aéreo 6 in only four months. Although the conflict was resolved by peaceful agreement, another batch of 13 Neshers (including two two-seaters) arrived by mid-1981, enabling the activation of a second squadron in the strong Grupo 6. Dagger squadrons played an important role during the Falklands War, at the cost of 11 aircraft destroyed in combat. To fill the gap, the Fuerza Aérea procured more fighters using its Peruvian/Israeli connection. A total of 19 re-engined Mirage IIICJs and three Mirage IIIBJs was delivered between December 1982 and March 1983, and were assigned to Escuadrón 55 of Grupo Aéreo 4 de Caza. Several aircraft were diverted to another young unit, Escuadrón 10 at BAM Rio Gallegos.

Despite reports to the contrary, the Fuerza Aérea did not purchase Peruvian Mirages to cover wartime losses. The 10 Mirage 5s were obtained for US$50 million under a contract signed on 14 December 1981. After a brief period with VI Brigada Aérea, the Mirage 5Ps were transferred during 1987 to Escuadrón Aéreo 10 at BAM Rio Gallegos. The complete Mirage 5P fleet was modernised by a local company – Aerocuat S.A. – which added an RWR system, VLF/Omega navigation system and Dagger noses. These Mirages were rewired to accept Fuerza Aérea standard weapons, like the IAI Shafrir AAM. At the end of this programme the aircraft were redesignated Mirage 5PA 'Mara'.

In the face of budget restrictions, the Fuerza Aérea was forced to consolidate its units, while at the same time, older models were withdrawn

The FAA's Mirage III fleet is consolidated at *BAM* Tandil, with *Grupo 6*. Air defence aircraft are operated by *Escuadrón I*. Several camouflage schemes were trialled on the Mirage IIIEAs (above) but an overall toned-down grey scheme was selected (below). Training is undertaken on Mirage IIIDAs and the similar two-seat Dagger Bs (left).

Left: *Escuadrón II* of *Grupo 6* operates the ground-attack force of 20 upgraded 'Finger' Dagger As (seen here) alongside nine Mirage 'Maras' (upgraded ex-Peruvian air force Mirage 5Ps).

Twelve A-4P/C Skyhawks are active with *Grupo Aéreo 5* at *BAM General Pringles*. By the end of 1998 they will have been joined by the FAA's newly-acquired A-4ARs (much upgraded ex-US A-4Ms).

from service. Thus Escuadrón 55 was deactivated when its Mirage IIICJ fleet was grounded because it was expensive to maintain. The proud Grupo Aéreo 8 was disbanded and its diminished line-up of Mirage IIIs became one squadron of Grupo Aéreo 6. This traumatic process was completed when the Mirage 'Maras' left Base Aérea Militar Rio Gallegos by late 1996, completing the disbandment of the Grupo Aéreo 10 de Caza. The Mirage family fleet is now consolidated at Base Aérea Militar Tandil, where Grupo Aéreo 6 is based. Escuadrón I operates the surviving 12 Mirage IIIEAs plus two Mirage IIIDAs for the air-to-air role; Escuadrón II is the fighter-bomber unit with 20 IAI Fingers and nine Mirage 'Maras'. The CEASO flying test unit uses a single Mirage IIICJ from Rio Cuarto air force workshop and is considering the reactivation of one or two Mirage IIIBJs for its use.

Skyhawk force

Only a mixed fleet of 12 A-4P/C Skyhawks is still flying with Grupo Aéreo 5 at BAM General Pringles. They are the remains of a powerful force of 50 A-4P Skyhawks delivered from 1966 and 25 A-4C Skyhawks purchased in the 1970s. The A-4Ps, basically an A-4B airframe with updated avionics, spoilers and zero-hour engines, operated with Grupo Aéreo 5, and the standard A-4C flew with Grupo Aéreo 4 at Mendoza. Both units were active in the Falklands War and were responsible for sinking HMS *Coventry*, HMS *Antelope* and RFA *Sir Galahad* – but at the cost of 19 aircraft lost. After the war, by December 1983, Escuadrón I of Grupo Aéreo 4 was disbanded and all Skyhawks were consolidated into Grupo Aéreo 5. During 1984, under programme Halcón, a total of 12 A-4P/Cs received 30-mm DEFA 553A-4s and other minor improvements.

The Fuerza Aérea considered several options to replace its aged Skyhawks. Among them Argentine AF pilots evaluated the A-7, ex-Jordanian F-5As and the Chengdu J-7/F-7, but the replacement arrived in the form of another Skyhawk variant. In May 1991, the FAA requested the provision of a batch of surplus Lockheed Martin F-16As, but the US rejected this request. Instead, up to 54 A-4M Skyhawks were offered under an initial US$94.5 million contract. By April 1993 the release of 32 A-4Ms and four OA-4Ms was announced, starting a controversial project which came under intense British scrutiny. Under the Fighting Hawk Programme, signed in August 1994, the Fuerza Aérea was allowed to integrate a downgraded Westinghouse AN/APG-66 multi-mode radar, called ARG-l.

Although initially the Argentines showed a preference for the US Navy/Smith Industries as the contractor team for the upgrade programme, Lockheed Martin finally won the US$285 million contract. It includes the complete overhaul and upgrade of 36 aircraft fitted with zero-time J52-P-408 engines, eight spare engines, 200,000 20-mm rounds and spares to support the operation of the aircraft for two years, plus training and logistic support.

At one time, McDonnell Douglas approached the Argentine government with an offer of 23 surplus (Kuwaiti) A-4KU Skyhawks. A mission headed by Brigadier Jorge Giannatasio selected airframes with a minimum remaining life of 60 per cent, among them ex-USMC A-4Ms in storage at AMARC. On 1 August 1995 the first aircraft

left Davis-Monthan AFB for LMAS facilities in Ontario, where half of the fleet will be overhauled. The balance will be modified at Lockheed Aircraft Argentina S.A. – LMSA. The extensive rework performed under the Fighting Hawk programme extended the aircraft's service lives to 2015. The first six A-4ARs are scheduled for delivery on 10 August 1997, with 10 more before the end of the year, enabling the activation of one squadron. Grupo Aéreo 5 will receive its full complement during 1998.

Finally, after lengthy negotiations, in May 1997 the US lifted its last restrictions, enabling the transfer of standard AN/APG-66 radars to the Fuerza Aérea, which is now seeking advanced air-to-air and air-to-surface weapons. It was recently announced that the US military aid package for Argentina includes the transfer of eight additional Skyhawks for training purposes, plus another 11 to be used as spares sources.

Pucará force

The FMA IA-58 Pucará is the other major combat type in Argentine markings and made its service debut in the 1970s. Two squadrons were equipped primarily for armed reconnaissance and ground strike support with Grupo Aéreo 3 de Ataque, based at Reconquista. Thanks to their rugged design and STOL characteristics, the Pucarás frequently are deployed to several BAMDOs (Base Aérea Militar de Despliegue Operativo, or FOLs – Forward Operating Locations), some of which are sections of highways in the Patagonia area. Wartime experience gave way to specific roles for the Pucarás, such as helicopter hunter and photo-reconnaissance. For the last task several IA-58A Pucarás were adapted to operate the Halcón del Sur RPV system. The IA-58A is used as a launcher and control platform for the Quimar MQ-2 Bigua, the local designation for the Italian Meteor Andromeda system.

Until late 1990, Escuadrón IV de Ataque of Grupo Aéreo 9 operated the IA-58A from Comodoro Rivadavia, from where it performed maritime reconnaissance duties. This squadron was selected as the recipient of the strong IA-58C version. The Pucará Charlie evolved as a single-seater model, fitted with nose-mounted 30-mm DEFA gun and capable of carrying MATRA 550 Magic AAMs plus an advanced EW system. Plans to convert up to 15 standard Pucarás were cancelled due to a shrinking budget; Escuadrón IV was disbanded and all Pucarás are now concentrated in two squadrons at BAM Reconquista.

Half a dozen of the venerable BAC Canberra B.Mk 62s/T.Mk 64s are still in flying condition with Grupo Aéreo 2. Despite its outdated design and reports of its imminent retirement, the Canberra has been retained by the FAA in service for new roles. Although no information has been released, there are indications that they have been locally modified to perform long-range reconnaissance and EW missions from BAM General Urquiza, Paraná.

Training assets

The training of future Argentine pilots is undertaken at the Córdoba home of the Escuela de Aviación Militar (EAM) of the Grupo Aéreo Escuela. The young officers must complete the one-year basic training course, known as Curso de Aviador Militar (CAM), before earning their wings. The primary trainer has been the Beech

T-34A Mentor since the early 1960s. The idea to replace the locally assembled Mentors with SIAI SF.260s was abandoned in favour of a modernisation programme, which includes the provision of new engine. The first aircraft (serialled E-060) was received on 9 May 1997 and a total of 30 Mentors will be modernised by LMSA. Advanced training was performed with the FMA-built MS.760A Paris, until its transfer to Grupo Aéreo 4 during 1985. The EMB-312A Tucano was selected as replacement, and between June 1987 and August 1988 the EAM received a total of 30 aircraft.

Those pilots selected for combat roles continue their training with the Escuela de Caza at BAM El Plumerillo, home of Grupo Aéreo 4 de Caza. Escuadrón II undertakes the first stage with its armed MS.760As. Twenty aircraft are still active in the dual role of advanced training and light attack, but their days are limited since the model will be withdrawn from service by late 1998. Escuadrón I, which concludes the training of fighter pilots, is the only operator of the FMA IA-63 Pampa. Both aircraft types are used for combat tactics, instrument and formation training, as well as gunnery practice. After completion of the CAM – Curso de Aviadores de Combate – combat pilots started their operational career with the Pucarás of Grupo Aéreo 3 de Ataque.

Transport crews are assigned to Escuadrón VII of Grupo Aéreo 9. Its DHC-6 Twin Otters are used for multi-engine training conversion, also known as Curso de Estandarizacion de Procedimientos para Pilotos de Transporte (CEPTA), which normally takes a year. Although most of the training is performed in Patagonia, an area characterised by strong winds and bad weather, the unit has attained an outstanding safety record. Helicopter training is the responsibility of Grupo Aéreo 7 de Helicópteros. Rotary wing crews follows the Curso de Estandarizacion de Procedimientos Aéreos para Helicópteros (CEPAH), flying the RACA-built Hughes 500Ds of Escuadrón I. This squadron also maintains a detachment of helicopters in Chipre in support of the UN peacekeeping mission.

The Instituto Nacional de Aviación Civil (INAC), based at Moron Airport, is the civil aviation flying school but is under control of the Fuerza Aérea Argentina through its Comando de Regiones Aéreas. Currently, students can choose from five different courses, with specific aircraft assigned: Commercial Licence with Chincul/Piper PA-28-236 Dakota IV and PA-28RT Arrow IV; 1st Class Commercial Licence with Chincul/Piper PA-34-220T Seneca III; Instructor Licence with Cessna A182J/K/L; Agricultural Pilot with the unique two-seater Chincul/Piper PA-25-235 Pawnee; and Commercial Helicopter Licence using RACA-built Hughes 500D. All of these aircraft fly with Fuerza Aérea markings and serials although they are not operational.

Transport and support assets

The Fuerza Aérea maintains a substantial transport element, most of which is concentrated in Grupo Aéreo 1 de Transporte based at BAM El Palomar. Long-range, heavy transport and air refuelling is performed by the Hercules fleet of Escuadrón I. The initial fleet of eight C-130Hs and two KC-130Hs suffered two losses (TC-62 destroyed in Tucuman by terrorist sabotage on 28 August 1975, and TC-63 destroyed in action on

bove and right: All operational *FAA Pucarás fly with two
quadrons of Grupo 3. The camouflaged aircraft seen here is
rrying the Halcón del Sur RPV, based on the Italian Mirach.*

bove and right: The 'fighter school' at Escuadrón II, Grupo
éreo 4, BAM El Plumerillo, still uses the FMA-built MS.760A
aris for advanced/weapons training. Argentina is the last
ilitary operator of the Paris, which first flew in 1954.*

Above: The EMB-312A Tucano
erves with the Escuela de
viación Militar and is a likely
eplacement for the last MS.760s.*

Right: Twelve IA-63 Pampas
are in service with
Escuadrón I of Grupo 4 at
BAM El Plumerillo.*

*Escuadrón V of Grupo Aéreo 1 de Transporte
operates the FAA's single VIP-configured Boeing
757-23A, alongside several Boeing 707s.*

*A single Lockheed L-100-30 Hercules is flown by
Escuadrón 1, Grupo Aéreo 1. It wears a civilian
scheme for service with LADE.*

*Grupos Aéreos 1 and 9 operate a mix of Fokker
F27 Mk 600s and military-spec Fokker Troopships
(F27 Mk 400Ms) on transport duties.*

*Escuadrón II of Grupo Aéreo 1 de Transporte
operates a pair of Fokker F28 Mk 1000s as
passenger transports. They fly chiefly for the
Escuadrón de Aviones Presidenciales.*

*Lineas Aéreas del Estado (LADE) is the
paramilitary transport arm of the FAA, which
draws on Grupo Aéreo 1 for its resources. It
currently operates four Fokker F28 Mk 1000Cs.*

*The vintage FMA IA-50 Guaraní II still survives in
service with Escuadrón III, Grupo Aéreo 2, as a
photographic survey aircraft. The Guaraní II first
flew in April 1963.*

1 June 1982). Reinforcements came during December 1982 in the shape of a single L-100-30 Hercules operated in civil markings, plus five ex-USAF C-130Bs. Logistic support during operational squadron deployments, regular Antarctic transport flights (or LAN – Vuelos Logísticos Antarticos), paratroop transport and aerial refuelling for both navy and air force fighters demand a high activity level of this relatively small fleet.

Escuadrón II flies four Fokker F28 Mk 1000C Fellowships mainly as personnel transport and normally under charter contract to commercial operators. Escuadrón IV has a line-up of three Fokker F27 Mk 400M Troopships and three F27 Mk 600 Friendships, which are shared with Lineas Aéreas del Estado (LADE), flying scheduled low-fare under-developed routes. Escuadrón V, activated during the 1980s, flies four Boeing 707-372C/3387B/389Bs for a variety of roles, including long-range transport, photographic reconnaissance and Elint tasks. After losing two aircraft in recent years (T-96 in Brazil on 31 March 1993 and LV-LGP/TC-92 at Ezeiza on 23 October 1996), the Fuerza Aérea is considering reinforcing its Boeing 707 strength with another aircraft in cargo configuration. Funds are available to convert one aircraft (probably the 707-387B T-95) as tanker.

Grupo Aéreo 9 de Transporte is headquartered at BAM Comodoro Rivadavia, and its flights are closely associated with LADE activities. Escuadrón VI flies two Fokker F27 Mk 400M Troopships and two F27 Mk 600 Friendships. Escuadrón VII complements its role of multi-engine school with passenger transport, SAR and Antarctic operations. Normally a couple of DHC-6 Twin Otters fitted with skies and extra fuel tanks are detached at BAM Marambio in the Antarctic, to support scientific activities.

The locally designed, twin-engined transport FMA IA-50 Guaraní II is coming to the end of its service life. Twenty examples were delivered for transport duties from 1968 to Escuadrón III of Grupo Aéreo 1 at BAM El Palomar, which is now under the control of Grupo Aéreo 2. Another four Guaraní IIs specially configured as photographic platforms were added. The Comando de Operaciones Aéreas and the Escuela de Aviación Militar have their own Guaraní as staff transports. Many aircraft were considered as potential replacements, among them the BAe Jetstream 31 and the Raytheon/Beechcraft C-12, but no decision has been made. Also based at

Paraná is Grupo Aéreo 1 Aerofotogrametrico with three Learjet 35As for aerial photo and another two for navaid checks.

The bulk of the helicopter fleet of the Fuerza Aérea is concentrated at Grupo Aéreo 7 de Helicópteros. As stated previously, Escuadrón I operates most of the 18-strong fleet of Hughes 500D/Es. This small helicopter is used not just for training, but is fitted with rocket launchers, 12.7-mm machine-guns and devices for nocturnal operations. Only two Bell UH-1Ds and five Bell 212 IFRs are assigned to Escuadrón II for transport and SAR duties. This squadron will receive eight additional UH-1Hs from US surplus stocks by late 1997, and the FAA is trying to obtain at least another four Bell UH-1Ns or Bell 212s, mainly for air/sea rescue duties. Heavylift is supplied by the surviving two Boeing Vertol Model 308 Chinooks of Escuadrón III, which also has a single VIP-configured Sikorsky S-61R.

Since 1996 the Fuerza Aérea has been heavily involved in fire-fighting duties over the Patagonia National Parks, using both Chinooks and Bell 212s as fire-fighters. After a series of demonstrations performed in May 1997, Argentina is seriously considering the purchase of an initial fleet of three/four Canadair CL-415s.

Although a helicopter unit, Grupo Aéreo 7 operates half a dozen Rockwell 500U Shrikes for liaison duties. Escuadrón III of Grupo Aéreo 4 is a specialised helicopter unit, flying SA 315B Lamas into the rugged and dangerous Andean mountains. Every Grupo Aéreo maintains its own Escuadrilla de Servicios (a base flight) for general duties, the composition of which varies from one unit to another. It normally includes a trio of DINFIA-built Cessna A-182s (as in Grupos 3, 4 and 5) or Rockwell 500Us (Grupo 6, BAM Rio Gallegos), FMA IA-50 Guaranís (Grupo Aéreo Escuela) or a single Hughes 500 (Grupo 6, Grupo Aéreo Escuela). The Fuerza Aérea also maintains a glider fleet of Let L-13 Blaniks, Grob G.113 Twin Astir, Grob Standard Astir II and SZD-30 Pirat II, distributed between the Escuela de Aviación Militar and Grupos Aéreos 4, 5 and 6.

The Escuadrón de Aviones Presidenciales is a squadron based at Aeroparque Jorge Newbery and specialises in VVIP transport duties. Head of the fleet is a brand new Boeing 757-23ER for Presidential use, with two Fokker F28 Mk 1000s plus single examples of the Sikorsky S-70A and Sikorsky S-76. The Fellowships could be converted in an emergency to medevac transports.

Fuerza Aérea Argentina

Comando de Operaciones Aéreas

I Brigada Aérea, BAM El Palomar (Buenos Aires)

Grupo Aéreo I de Transporte

Escuadrón I	Lockheed C-130B/H, KC-130H, L-100-30
Escuadrón II	Fokker F28 Mk 1000
Escuadrón IV	Fokker F27 Mk 400M/600
Escuadrón V	Boeing 707-372C/387B/389B

II Brigada Aérea, BAM General Urquiza (Paraná)

Grupo Aéreo 2 de Bombardeo

Escuadrón I	BAC Canberra B.Mk 62/T.Mk 64
Escuadrón II	Learjet 35A
Escuadrón III	FMA IA-50 Guaraní II

III Brigada Aérea, BAM Reconquista

Grupo Aéreo 3 de Ataque

Escuadrón I	FMA IA-58A Pucará
Escuadrón II	FMA IA-58A Pucará

IV Brigada Aérea, BAM El Plumerillo (Mendoza)

Grupo Aéreo 4 de Caza

Escuadrón I	FMA IA-63 Pampa
Escuadrón II	Morane MS.760A Paris
Escuadrón III	SA 315C Lama

V Brigada Aérea, BAM General Pringles (Villa Reynolds)

Grupo Aéreo 5 de Ataque

Escuadrón I	O/A-4AR Skyhawk II (1997)
Escuadrón II	O/A-4AR Skyhawk II (1998)

VI Brigada Aérea, BAM Tandil

Grupo Aéreo 6 de Caza

Escuadrón I	Mirage IIIEA/DA
Escuadrón II	IAI Finger, Mirage 5PA

VII Brigada Aérea, BAM Mariano Moreno

Grupo Aéreo 7 de Helicópteros

Escuadrón I	RACA Hughes 369HE/500D/E
Escuadrón II	Bell UH-1D/212
Escuadrón III	Boeing Vertol 308 Chinook, Sikorsky S-61R, Rockwell 500U Shrike

IX Brigada Aérea, BAM Comodoro Rivadavia

Grupo Aéreo 9 de Transporte

Escuadrón VI	Fokker F27 Mk 400M/600
Escuadrón VII	DHC-6-200 Twin Otter

Comando de Regiones Aéreas
Instituto Nacional de Aviación Civil, Moron Airport (Buenos Aires)

Piper PA-28 Arrow IV/Dakota, Piper PA-25 Pawnee, Piper PA-34 Seneca, Cessna A182, RACA Hughes 500D

Comando de la Aviación Naval Argentina

Flight operations of the Armada Argentina started in 1918, when a naval aviation detachment based at San Fernando was officially activated, with two Macchi M-7 seaplane fighters, two Macchi M-9 seaplane bombers and a single Curtiss Seagull. Puerto Belgrano Naval Base (Buenos Aires) became the home of the Escuela de Aviación Naval. The Argentine navy's strong influence not only prevented the dissolution of its aviation branch – as happened in other countries – but it pushed its naval aviation to become the leading service in all of Latin America. It was the first to operate in the Antarctic, the first to introduce helicopters (1946), the first to use combat jets (F9F Panther and TF-9 Cougar), the first to

operate from aircraft-carriers in 1958 and the first naval aviation in the world to sink a major combat unit with a single ASM during 1982.

The Comando de la Aviación Naval Argentina (COAN) is in the midst of a restructuring process which, due to budgetary restrictions, is not straightforward. Under directives of the Estado Mayor General de la Armada, the Aviación Naval is consolidating its squadrons at two bases – Comandante Espora and Almirante Zar. This means that at least three naval air stations will be closed in the coming years. With available funds at their lowest in history, the Aviación Naval is concentrating its resources to improve maritime capabilities, sustaining projects like Tata and

Cormoran, but placing on standby replacement of the EMB-326GB or the Etendard upgrade.

The Aviación Naval Argentina is organised into three Fuerzas Aeronavales, each of which is divided in a variable number of Escuadras Aeronavales. The smallest operational unit is the Escuadrilla Aeronaval, which uses aircraft to accomplish a primary róle. Normally, two Escuadrillas comprise one Escuadra Aeronaval.

Fuerza Aeronaval Nº 1

The Fuerza Aeronaval Nº 1 (FAE 1), based at Base Aeronaval Punta Indio (Veronica – Buenos Aires), has been responsible for training naval personnel since 29 October 1929 when the

Above and above left: The FAA operates a mix of Learjet 35s on VIP transport and photographic survey missions. They fly with Escuadrón II, Grupo 2, at Paraná.

FAA DHC-6 Twin Otters are used primarily on LADE services linking remote locations in the vast Patagonian region, where there is no commercial air service.

Above: The FAA still possesses approximately 90 T-34As, with 30 undergoing a life extension programme.

Below: Some of the Hughes 500s attached to Escuadrón 1, Grupo 7 operate in 'Avispa' gunship configuration.

Below: A single example of the Sikorsky S-70A is now in service with the Escuadrón de Aviones Presidenciales.

Above: Each example of the FAA Twin Otter fleet is regularly rotated through Antarctic service at the Vice Comodoro Matambio air base.

Right: The FAA Chinooks are all commercial Boeing Vertol Model 308 aircraft.

Below: The FAA and the army still operate the Aérospatiale SA 315B/C Lama.

Left: Escuadrón II of Grupo 7 operates a few Bell 212s (seen here) and UH-1Hs.

INAC (the FAA-supervised national civil aviation training service) uses a mix of Chincul-built Piper designs such as the PA-34-220T (left) and the PA-28-236 Dakota IV (above).

One of the most unusual types in the FAA inventory is the Chincul/Piper PA-25 Pawnee agricultural aircraft, which is operated as a dual-control trainer. Chincul has assembled over 140.

Escuela de Aviación Naval (ESAN) was reformed as a land-based training school. After an introductory course on sailplanes and Boeing N2S Kaydets, student pilots begin basic and elementary training in the Beech T-34C.1 Turbo Mentor, which requires 190-200 hours. The first batch of eight Turbo Mentors arrived at Punta Indio on 15 June 1978, replacing T-28S Fennecs. The ESAN received a total of 15 Turbo Mentors, which reached the 75,000-flying hours mark on 18 October 1995.

Operational training is accomplished by 1º Escuadrilla Aeronaval de Ataque, equipped with 10 EMBRAER-built EMB-326GB Xavantes. Initially the Aviación Naval purchased eight Italian-built MB.326GB Pelicanos during 1970, for the dual role of advanced training/light strike and photo-reconnaissance. In 1980, a fleet of 10 Aermacchi MB.339AA armed jet trainers was obtained to replace the older MB.326GB. Some MB.339s were destroyed in the Falklands War and the survivors were grounded due to lack of spares for their Rolls-Royce Viper Mk 632-43 engines. As a stopgap measure, a batch of 11 EMB-326GB Xavantes was purchased by late 1982. At the same time, a navalised version of the IA-63 Pampa was considered to be the most likely candidate for the 1st Attack Squadron. That project came to an abrupt end after the decision to halt the IA-63 production line, which forced naval aviation to keep the aged Xavantes in service. Standard weapons carried by the little EMB-326GB include Mk 82 bombs, rockets, 0.5-in machine-gun pods, the Pescador ASM, plus the Vinten photo-pod. The planned redeployment of the 1º Esc Aeronaval de Ataque from Punta Indio to Comandante Espora NAS is scheduled for 1998.

Fuerza Aeronaval Nº 2

FAE 2 is in charge of all aircraft assets that formerly comprised the Grupo Aeronaval Embarcado (GAE), or the aircraft-carrier component. The ARA *Independencia* (V-l) (ex-HMS *Warrior*), operative since 1958, was replaced by the ARA *25 de Mayo* (V-2) (ex-HrMs *Karel Doorman*) in the late 1960s because the latter's angled deck was more suited for fast jet operations. These aircraft arrived in 1971 when a batch of 16 upgraded A-4Qs was delivered for the 3º Escuadrilla Aeronaval de Caza y Ataque. With its complement of A-4Qs crewed by well trained pilots, the ARA *25 de Mayo* gave the Armada Argentina an unmatched power over regional navies. This substantial advantage was increased again with the introduction of Exocet-armed AMD/BA Super Etendards in 1982. The 50-year-old carrier is in need of a huge and expensive refit to extend its life (although for no more than a decade), and consequently in May 1997 the Armada Argentina made the drastic decision to deactivate its only carrier. This leaves the FAE 2 at Base Aeronaval Comandante Espora (Bahia Blanca – Buenos Aires) without its major seaborne platform. Carrier qualification is maintained via the use of the Brazilian light carrier Nael *Minas Gerais* (A-11) during the annual Bilateral and Fraterno exercises.

The Escuadra Aeronaval Nº 2 has the primary role of anti-submarine warfare, using both fixed-wing aircraft and helicopters. Currently the Escuadrilla Aeronaval Antisubmarina is the last Latin American operator of the Grumman Tracker. This association dates to 1961 when six over-hauled S-2A Trackers were obtained from the US Navy. Years later a single S-2F arrived, followed by six S-2Es and most recently by three S-2Gs. A total of six S-2E/G airframes was selected for conversion under the Tata programme, which involves re-engining with 1,645-shp (1227-kW) TPE331-15 turboprops. Four Trackers are flying in the new S-2T standard and the conversion programme performed by Taller Aeronaval Central (TAC) will be completed in the first half of 1998. The next phase involves the replacement of some outdated sensors, particularly the AN/APS-88A search radar.

Additional ASW capabilities are provided by the Sea Kings of the 2º Escuadrilla Aeronaval de Helicópteros. The flight line includes five Sikorsky-built S-61Ds equivalent to USN SH-3D standard, which are locally designated SH-3, and two Agusta-built AS-61D.4s or PH-3s (with the same SH-3H systems) equipped with SMA APS-705 radars. These helicopters operate from the four 'Argentina'-class destroyers and from ARA *Almirante Irizar* (Q-4), an icebreaker. The Argentine navy is negotiating the provision of a number of second-hand SH-3Hs from the US Navy. Initially, the talks included an extra batch of six to eight bare Sea Kings to be used as troop transports on behalf of the Infanteria de Marina, but the plans were dropped, since the Argentine marines favoured the simpler Bell UH-1H for its first helicopter battalion.

The Escuadra Aeronaval Nº 3's squadrons are completely equipped with French-built aircraft, the most noteworthy type being the AMD/BA Super Etendard. Eleven of the 14 delivered remain on squadron strength, although normally six are in flying condition. There is not enough cash to implement the Super Etendards' mid-life update programme, so the rumoured transfer of extra aircraft from the French Aéronavale is not true. Most recently, during the joint naval manoeuvres completed during 1996, the Super Etendards undertook operations from the Brazilian carrier, including the first catapult launches. Despite budget constraints, live weapons training is sustained to maintain the operational level of the Exocet/Super Etendard duo. In the last exercise performed in the third quarter of 1996, a single AM-39 hit was enough to sink a 'Gearing'-class destroyer near Puerto Belgrano.

The 1º Escuadrilla Aeronaval de Helicópteros, a long-time operator of the multifaceted SA 316B Alouette III, in March 1996 added a new type to its inventory: the Eurocopter AS 555SN. The first group of four Fennecs shared the same Alouette hangar and most of their roles. The radar-equipped AS 555SN is better adapted to naval roles aboard the MEKO 360 destroyers and the smaller MEKO 140 corvettes. The Fennecs were the result of a naval aviation requirement for a shipboard helicopter to take the place of the Westland Sea Lynx order, which was blocked after the Falklands War. The Eurocopter AS 565SA Panther was selected; however, funding was sufficient to purchase only the cheaper Fennec. The total requirement is for eight helicopters without weapon systems. The Aviación Naval is using its own technical skills to add limited combat capabilities to the Fennecs, with provisions to carry AS12 missiles and Whitehead A.244S anti-submarine torpedoes.

Half a dozen of the 14 SA 316B Alouettes still active fill a variety of roles: anti-surface attack, troop transport, gunship, observation, SAR, medevac and training. The small Alouette joined the operational tour of destroyer units to such remote places as the Persian Gulf and South African waters in March 1997. Since there is an insufficient number of Fennecs, and the Alouettes are well maintained, the latter will be retained in service for many years.

Fuerza Aeronaval Nº 3

Since its activation in the mid-1950s, the Fuerza Aeronaval Nº 3 has been dedicated to transport roles, initially with a mixed fleet of Beechcraft C-45/D-18S, Douglas C-47 and Douglas C-54. The FAE 3 is a good example of the rationalisation and change of roles in the Aviación Naval. Until late 1994 the Escuadra Aeronaval Nº 5 was composed of two transport squadrons, both based at Base Aeronaval Ezeiza, home of the FAE 3. The 1º Escuadrilla Aeronaval de Sostén Logístico Móvil was disbanded and its cargo/passenger Lockheed L-188PF Electras were transferred to another unit. Thus, the three Fokker F28 Mk 3000s from the 2º Escuadrilla Aeronaval de Sostén Logístico Móvil are still fulfiling the transport role the unit has had since its inception in 1977. In the near future, though, the unit will be redeployed to Base Aeronaval Almirante Zar, ending Base Aeronaval Ezeiza activity. The F28 Mk 3000s are regularly used on scheduled logistic flights between Buenos Aires and Base Aeronaval Ushuaia, with stopovers at Trelew, Rio Grande and Rio Gallegos. They also support the operational deployment of other naval units, carrying personnel, cargo or spares to distant places like US, England, France and Kuwait. Among its secondary roles, the 2nd Transport Squadron undertakes maritime surveillance and Antarctic observation flights.

The Escuadra Aeronaval Nº 6 at Base Aeronaval Almirante Zar (Trelew-Chubut) is the only one to experience an expansion. Its most important squadron, the Escuadrilla Aeronaval de Exploración, has a nominal strength of five L-188 Electras that have been locally converted to maritime patrol aircraft. The Armada Argentina – a long-time operator of Lockheed P2Vs – has since the mid-1970s been very interested in obtaining a batch of P-3 Orions, but due to political considerations only obtained four SP-2H Neptunes from the US as an interim solution.

Negotiations to purchase four to six Breguet Atlantic NGs fitted with AM39 Exocets were very near completion by early 1982, but further talks were blocked by the post-war embargo. To meet urgent requirements, the Armada Argentina launched an emergency project with Israeli assistance. A total of five L-188 Electras was obtained on the international civil market in 1982/83. The basic conversion of the aircraft included the installation of one SMA APS-705 surface search radar, which required a large ventral radome ahead of the wing leading edge. A total of four Electras was modified, with some equipment differences between them. One of the aircraft received a single point IFR kit and another an APU installed in the rear cargo position. One, named the Electra Wave, became a flying platform for an advanced Elint system. This aircraft is easily recognised by its two side conformal antennas in the rear fuselage and by the radome fitted over the cockpit. It is known that the Electra Wave uses an IAI Sigint 240 system but all missions of

Above and right: The Argentine navy's potent Super Etendard force is operated by 2º Escuadrilla Aeronaval de Caza y Ataque of Escuadra Aeronaval 3, based at Bahia Blanca.

Above: The Escuadrilla Aeronaval Antisubmarina, of EAE 2, operates S-2T Trackers, fitted with TPE331 turboprops.

Right: Fast jet training for the navy is undertaken by the EMB-326GBs of Escuadra Aeronaval 4.

Above: The Escuela de Aviación Naval flies Beech B-34Cs (seen here) and Fairchild/Pilatus PC-6s.

Right: One of the navy's most precious assets is its specially modified (by IAI) Electra Wave Sigint aircraft.

Left: 2º Escuadrilla Aeronaval de Sostén Logístico Móvil operates the F28 Mk 3000.

Radar-equipped AS 555SN Fennecs (right) serve with 1º Escuadrilla Aeronaval de Helicópteros. The same unit operates gunship-configured Alouette IIIs (below).

Left: Remarkably, the navy still uses Boeing N2S Kaydets as basic trainers.

this aircraft are classified. One of the Electrons – the name applied to the Electras modified for maritime patrol – was lost on landing at Trelew, but the squadron has gained the Electras of 1º Escuadrilla Aeronaval de Sostén Logístico Móvil. Although the Electras performed well in their missions over the sea, their most important contribution was to maintain trained flying crews for the P-3 Orions.

The Escuadrilla Aeronaval de Exploración will soon be re-equipped with six P-3Bs, from late production batches, from ex-US Navy stocks. The first pair will arrive in the last quarter of 1997, with deliveries of the remaining four during 1998, bringing the Electra's operations to an end. There is a chance that one of the P-3Bs will be modified to serve as an Elint platform with the IAI Sigint system.

From late May 1986 the Escuadrilla Aeronaval de Vigilancia Maritima has been based at Trelew. It may appear to be the youngest unit in naval aviation, but it is the continuation of the Escuadrilla Aeronaval de Reconocimiento from which it received its seven Beechcraft B200 Super King Airs. Those aircraft are now undergoing conversion by the Arsenal Aeronaval Nº 2. The first feasibility studies into converting the standard passenger-configured Super King Airs to a Beech 200T Maritime standard were conducted in the early 1990s. The Cormoran Programme has encountered several problems, but the first example (serialled 6-P-48) was finally delivered to the squadron in May 1997. The most obvious change is the installation of one Bendix King RDR-1500 surface search radar in a ventral radome, a photo-reconnaissance kit and a ventral hatch. The Cormoran-modified aircraft are used for coastal patrol, fishery surveillance, pollution control and SAR. Development is not complete, as the installation of a FLIR and wingtip ESM antennas is still under consideration. The surviving photographic B80 Queen Airs of the disbanded Escuadrilla Aeronaval de Reconocimiento were deactivated and sold on the civil market.

Comando de Aviación Naval Argentina

Fuerza Aeronaval Nº 1, BA Punta Indio (Veronica)

Escuadra Aeronaval Nº 1
Escuela de Aviación Naval   Beech T-34C.1, Fairchild PC-6B2/H2

Escuadra Aeronaval Nº 4
1º Escuadrilla Aeronaval de Ataque   EMBRAER EMB-326GB

Fuerza Aeronaval Nº 2, BA Comandante Espora (Bahia Blanca)

Escuadra Aeronaval 2
Escuadrilla Aeronaval Antisubmarina   Grumman S-2T
2º Escuadrilla Aeronaval de Helicópteros   Sikorsky/ Agusta A/SH-3D/H

Escuadra Aeronaval 3
2º Escuadrilla Aeronaval de Caza y Ataque   Super Etendard
1º Escuadrilla Aeronaval de Helicópteros   SA 316B Alouette III, AS 555SN Fennec

Fuerza Aeronaval Nº 3, BA ViceAlmirante Zar (Trelew)

Escuadra Aeronaval 6
Escuadrilla Aeronaval de Exploración   L-188 Electra (P-3B Orion)
Escuadrilla Aeronaval de Vigilancia Maritima   Beech 200 Super King Air/Petrel
2º Escuadrilla Aeronaval de Sostén Logístico Móvil   Fokker F28 Mk 3000

Comando de Aviación del Ejército

When the Air Force achieved its independence, the Ejército Argentino lost all aircraft assets and personnel. Army flying activities resumed in 1956 with the reception of six locally built IA-20 El Boyeros for artillery spotting. By 17 November 1959 the Agrupación de Aviación Nº 1 had been created to undertake light transport, observation and liaison duties. By then, the new army aviation had a growing fleet which included Piper L-21Bs, Cessna 180s and Cessna 310s, and 12 Douglas C-47s (purchased on the Brazilian civil market) for parachute transport. Bowing to political pressure, the Army transferred this valuable fleet of Dakotas to the Fuerza Aérea.

Despite strong opposition, the Ejército obtained an increasing number of aircraft such as Cessna U-17, Piper PA-23 Apache/Aztec, Piper PA-31 Navajo, Bell OH-13H, Hiller FH-1100 and others. During 1975, army aviation was involved in counter-insurgency operations in the northern province of Tucuman, where a Marxist guerrilla group operated. The Equipo de Combate Condor (Condor Combat Team) was activated, including a flight of armed Bell UH-1H Hueys and a fixed-wing flight with light planes. The use of aircraft was the decisive factor in defeating the terrorist group, but one UH-1H Huey, one Piper L-21B and one de Havilland Canada DHC-6 Twin Otter were destroyed due to ground fire.

To support its ground forces during the Falklands War, the Aviación del Ejército deployed its Batallón de Aviación 601 to the Falklands Islands and to nearby continental bases. A total of 46 helicopters was used during the war, including 10 civilian machines with military crews. The Huey and Puma losses were heavy, in addition to the loss of the only two CH-47C Chinooks. The wartime effort and these losses limited flying activity for many subsequent years.

Current structure

Today all the operational elements of the Aviación del Ejército are under control of the Agrupación Aviación de Ejército 601 headquartered at Campo de Mayo Army Aviation Airfield. This group is organised into four specialised squadrons. The Escuadrón de Aviación de Exploración y Reconocimiento 601 is the youngest, having been activated in late 1993 after the delivery of two OV-1D Mohawks on 24 December 1992. Twenty-three OV-1Ds were obtained in several batches, plus several Motorola AN/APS-94F SLAR kits. The Mohawks were fitted locally with GPS, video recorders and FLIR systems. Development of a weapon system is under way, with naval aviation assistance. In addition to army manoeuvres, the Mohawks also participated in joint army/navy amphibious exercises. It was reported that another 11 OV-1Ds are ready for transfer to the Argentine army, but the present number already exceeds its needs. A pressing problem is the limited number of flying crews available to operate this complex aircraft.

As in many countries, the Bell UH-1H is the workhorse helicopter of the Argentine army. In February 1970 four brand new UH-1Hs were received, used mainly to train pilots and ground crews. They were followed by another eight in

June 1973 and seven more between October and November 1974. Initially, from March 1971, the Hueys were assigned to A Company of the 601st Aviation Battalion. Currently, most of the UH-1Hs are in service with Grupo de Helicópteros de Asalto 601, sharing the transport role with the AS 332B Pumas and the last SA 330 Puma. The Super Pumas are detached during the summer months to the Argentine navy's icebreaker ARA *Almirante Irízar* (Q-42) to support the Antarctic operation. Another Huey operator is Escuadrón de Aviación de Exploración y Ataque 602, activated in December 1986; it operates them as gunships, in addition to the armed Agusta A 109A Hirundos. Six delivered by late 1979 are still in service, and recently have been modified to carry the locally designed ATGW CITEFA Mathogo and 105-mm CITEFA Yaguarete rocket launchers. From civil sources, army aviation obtained six Bell 205A-1s and another six surplus US Army UH-1H Hueys, which allowed the distribution of helicopters between several army corps flight detachments. Under US military aid programmes at least six additional UH-1Hs could be delivered in the near future. There is no information available regarding the proposed transfer of six to eight AH-1S Cobras from retired US Army stocks – they would be the only dedicated combat helicopters in South America, apart from Peru's Mil Mi-25s.

Transport and training

Escuadrón de Aviación de Apoyo 603 is tasked with logistic support and operates a mixed fixed-wing fleet. Troop and cargo transport is performed by a trio of Alenia G222s active since 1977, plus two DHC-6-300 Twin Otters and a single CASA C.212-200 Aviocar that are also available. Three Fairchild SA-226AT Merlin IVs are configured as medevac transports, and four Fairchild SA-226T Merlin IIIs are used as staff transports. The squadron's complement also includes most of the eight Cessna T-207As and one surviving Cessna U-17A-CE.

A large proportion of army aviation pilots come from the civil field and have their own Commercial Pilot licence. After a brief stage with the Escuela para Apoyo de Combate General Lemos, where they receive military instruction, the new sub-lieutenants enter the Escuela de Aviación de Ejército, also based at Campo de Mayo airfield. All personnel follow an intensive training course on the Cessna T-41D Mescalero, which has two external stores stations. The Escuela also has some dual-command OV-1Ds for advanced training, using high-visibility orange drop tanks as recognition markings. Those pilots who select helicopters will be trained on the Hiller UH-12E.4. Eight Soloy/Hiller conversions were completed during November 1983, replacing the previous fleet of three Bell TH-13T, three OH-13S and two OH-13H Sioux used as trainers. Argentine army aviation is the only Latin American military aviation service with active-duty female pilots, one of whom flies Bell UH-1Hs.

Survey and liaison

The Instituto Geográfico Militar has single examples of the Beech 65 Queen Air and Cessna

Left: Under the Cormoran programme, navy Beech 200 Super King Airs were modified for maritime reconnaissance with Bendix-King RDR-1500 search radars and other airframe changes.

Above: A mix of Agusta- and Sikorsky-built SH-3D/Hs serve with FAE 2 at Bahia Blanca.

bove and right: Argentina's acquisition of ex-US Army V-1D Mohawks in 1992/93 transformed the capabilities of the Comando de Aviación del Ejército.

Left: Escuadrón de Aviación de Exploración y Ataque 602 operates Agusta A 109s in gunship configuration, alongside Bell UH-1Hs, from its base at Campo de Mayo.

Above: The Hiller UH-12E-4 is still used by the army aviation school at Campo de Mayo.

For high-speed VIP transport duties the Ejército operates a single Sabre 75A business jet.

Three Fairchild Merlin IIIs are each allocated to army units at Santa Fe, Córdoba and Buenos Aires.

The larger Fairchild Merlin IVAs are all allocated to Escuadrón de Aviación de Apoyo 603.

This Cessna 500 Citation I operates alongside the Sabre 75A as part of Escuadrón de Aviación de Apoyo 603 at Buenos Aires/Campo de Mayo.

Escuadrón de Aviación de Apoyo 603 operates a wide range of transport types including the Cessna U-27, DHC-6-300, CASA C.212 (seen here) and G222.

Cessna U-207s serve with Secciones Aviaciones de Ejército 4 and 5. They are used, with the Merlin IIIAs, for army liaison and staff transport.

500 Citation, modified for aerial photography and flying with army aviation markings.

Corps-level helicopters

Every large battlefield unit (known as an Army Corps) has a flight used mostly for staff transport. Fixed-wing aircraft are on loan from Escuadrón de Aviación de Apoyo 603. II Army Corps has a detachment of Bell UH-1Hs with Sección Aviación 12, while Sección Aviación 2 normally uses a Merlin III based at Rosario. III Army Corps has one Merlin III and one Cessna 207 based at the Escuela de Aviación Militar (Córdoba) for Sección Aviación 4. Based at Mendoza AFB are two SA 315B Lamas of Sección Aviación 8 on behalf of IV Army Corps. The largest field unit is V Army Corps, headquartered at Bahía Blanca. Sección Aviación 5 is based at Comandante Espora NAS with the usual Cessna 207/Merlin flight for staff transport. The following units (all under command of V Army Corps) have helicopter flights: Vl Infantry Brigade is assigned Sección Aviación 6 with SA 315B Lamas; IX Infantry Brigade, Sección Aviación 9 with UH-1Hs; and XI Mechanised Brigade, Sección Aviación 11 with UH-1Hs.

For every major ground unit based in Patagonia, the army has a well-equipped airfield complete with paved runway, such as Río Mayo, Puerto Deseado, Puerto Santa Cruz and others.

Comando de Aviación del Ejército

Agrupación Aviación de Ejército 601, Campo de Mayo (Buenos Aires)

Grupo de Helicópteros de Asalto 601
Bell UH-1H, Bell 205A.1, SA 330L Puma, AS 332B Super Puma

Escuadrón de Aviación de Exploración y Ataque 602
Augusta A 109A, Bell UH-1H

Escuadrón de Aviación de Exploración y Reconocimiento 601
Grumman OV-1D

Escuadrón de Aviación de Apoyo 603
Cessna U-207, Merlin IV, DHC-6-300, CASA C.212, Sabre 75, Alenia G222

Escuela de Aviación de Ejército, Campo de Mayo (Buenos Aires)
Hiller UH-12E.4, Cessna T-41D, Grumman OV-1D

Instituto Geográfico Militar, Campo de Mayo (Buenos Aires)
Beech 65, Cessna 500 Citation

Sección Aviación de Ejército 2, Rosario (Santa Fe)
Merlin IIIA

Sección Aviación de Ejército 4, Córdoba
Cessna U-207, Merlin IIIA

Sección Aviación de Ejército 5, Bahia Blanca (Buenos Aires)
Cessna U-207, Merlin IIIA

Sección Aviación de Ejército 6, Neuquen
SA 315B Lama

Sección Aviación de Ejército 8, Mendoza
SA 315B Lama

Sección Aviación de Ejército 9, Comodoro Rivadavia (Chubut)
Bell UH-1H

Sección Aviación de Ejército 11, Rio Gallegos (Santa Cruz)
Bell UH-1H

Sección Aviación de Ejército 12, Resistencia (Chaco)
Bell UH-1H

Internal Security Forces

The Argentine services that provide internal security and border control have a paramilitary structure. These well-equipped forces – the Gendarmeria Nacional and the Prefectura Naval Argentina – are under the control of the Minister of Public Affairs, and both operate their own unarmed aircraft. The Federal Police, also under the control of the same ministry, has a helicopter fleet of MBB BO 105Cs, Eurocopter BK 117s and AS 365C Dauphins, plus a Cessna 500 Citation, all based in the Capital Federal District. The Policia Bonaerense (Buenos Aires State Police) flying service includes more than 50 aircraft and helicopters, among them MBB BO 105CBS and Robinson R22 Beta/Mariner (which could be replaced with Bell 206 JetRangers) and light aircraft including the Piper PA-28 Lance and PA-42 Cheyenne 400LS.

Servicio de Aviación de Prefectura Naval Argentina

The Prefectura Naval Argentina (formerly the Prefectura General Maritima), the oldest Argentine force, is responsible for control and security of naval traffic on large rivers, lakes and territorial waters up to 200 nm (230 miles; 370 km) from the coast. First steps toward having its own aviation service were made during 1947, when a small group of officers completed the naval aviator course, flying the Boeing N2S Kaydet and North American SNJ of the Argentine navy.

On 7 September 1951 the Division Aviación was activated officially, with three Grumman JRF Goose amphibians for fishery control, based at Aeroparque Jorge Newbery. Scarce resources limited the flying activity. Around 1957 the service purchased four brand new Nord Norécrins and moved its operational base to Don Torcuato airfield in the Buenos Aires area. Other types delivered were two de Havilland DH-104 Doves, one Cessna T-50 Bobcat for training and a single Sikorsky S-51 for SAR duties. During 1962 the service changed its structure and name to become the Servicio de Aviación. Two former Aerolineas Argentinas Douglas DC-3s replaced the Doves, and five Bell 47G/Js were purchased. Five Short SC-7 Skyvan 3Ms and six Hughes 500Cs arrived in the 1970s.

The Prefectura Naval currently has three aviation detachments to facilitate the control of traffic in the 200-nm limit as well as to support SAR and oil pollution control activities. The main base is Estación Aérea San Fernando, inaugurated during September 1996, which houses the two Schweizer 300Cs and two Piper PA-28-181 Warriors used for training by the Centro de Extensión Profesional Aeronáutica. The nucleus of the Spanish-supplied CASA Aviocar fleet is also based there, including two CASA C.212-300s (standard cargo version) and three specialised CASA C.212-300 Patrulleros (for maritime patrol).

Patrol helicopter fleet

The helicopter fleet has been reduced but includes two recently upgraded Aérospatiale (Eurocopter) SA 330L Pumas and three Eurocopter AS 365M2 Dauphins. Limited funds prevent the purchase of sufficient helicopters for use aboard the five large oceanic patrol corvettes. Estación Aérea Comodoro Rivadavia was established in 1990 with a detachment of two CASA C.212s, and Estación Aérea Mar del Plata, activated during 1996, usually has a Puma or Dauphin assigned.

Departamento de Aviación de Gendarmeria Nacional

This large ground force of more than 40,000 troops is grouped into units deployed along the borders, and into a few rapid deployment infantry companies. On 8 October 1955 the Dirección de Aeronáutica of the Gendarmeria (by that time under the control of the Ejército Argentino) was established, with three FMA IA-20 El Boyero light observation aircraft. They were followed some months later by three Macchi MB-308s and one Max Holste MH-1521 Broussard, for use at Formosa, Misiones and Salta in the northern frontier. During the 1960s, the renamed División de Transportes Aéreos obtained three Fairchild FH-1100s and two Bell 47G-3Bs, complemented by five Cessna 182Hs and two Cessna 337 Skymasters.

Today, the Departamento de Aviación has its headquarters at Campo de Mayo Army Airfield, where the administrative, logistic and maintenance facilities are based. A fleet of five Pilatus PC-6B2/H2 Turbo Porters is normally deployed to the south for liaison, observation and light transport. The fixed-wing fleet also includes several ex-Argentine army Piper L-21Bs and Cessna U-206 Skywagons. In recent years, the Gendarmeria has been involved in anti-drug operations along the sensitive borders with Bolivia and Paraguay. To reinforce the activity of ground forces (known as Escuadrones), the helicopter force is assigned on demand; it has a strength of five RACA-built Hughes 500C/Ds, one Helibras HB-350 Esquilo and six SA 315B Lamas. Due to these types' limited cargo capacity, the Gendarmeria Nacional reportedly will receive a batch of UH-1Hs to be used in anti-narcotic actions.

Jorge Felix Nunez Padin

Above: The Ejército operates both SA 330L Pumas and AS 332B Super Pumas (seen here).

Below: T-41Ds are used for basic training by the army at Campo de Mayo.

Below: Argentina's Prefectura Naval (which equates to a coast guard) operates three Eurocopter AS 365M2 Dauphins.

Above: Two smartly-painted DHC-6-300 Twin Otters operate as part of the army's Escuadrón de Aviación de Apoyo 603.

Left: Alongside its Dauphins, the Prefectura Naval also operates SA 330L Pumas which have been fitted with radar and flotation gear.

Two standard CASA C.212-300 transports are in Prefectura Naval service, alongside Patrullero maritime surveillance versions with radar.

The Servicio de Aviación de Prefectura Naval Argentina uses two PA-28-181 Warriors for flying training duties.

The Piper PA-23, like many other Piper types, is built under licence in Argentina by Chincul. This PA-23 serves with the Prefectura Naval.

Two float-equipped Schweizer 300Cs serve with the Prefectura Naval for basic rotary-wing pilot training.

Above: Five RACA-built Hughes 500C/Ds fly as part of the police air service, based at Campo de Mayo.

Left: The largest type in the Gendarmeria Nacional inventory is the PC-6B Turbo Porter.

Bolivia

Bolivia was so-named after Simon Bolivar following the war of liberation in 1825, and is a relatively poor country in central South America, with an area of 1.098 million km² (424,188 sq miles). Land-locked, it shares its borders with Chile, Peru, Brazil, Paraguay and Argentina. It is well provided with natural resources, notably copper, lead, tin, silver and tungsten, natural gas and oil. The revenue from these resources has yet to make an incisive increase in overall wealth, and the still unexploited terrain relies heavily on the internal air network.

Fuerza Aérea Boliviana

The air force, Fuerza Aérea Boliviana (FAB), has been severely restricted by a limited budget. Most of its funding supports transport and helicopter resources, while the 'sharp end' – anti-narcotics and COIN tasks – has been little improved. This said, however, US aid in support of the anti-drug operations led to the delivery of 16 Bell UH-1Hs, 10 in late 1987 and six more in 1990. A similar arrangement regarding the FAB's C-130As occurred in mid-1988 when six ex-USAF examples were received, followed by two more in 1990. The United States also agreed to overhaul the air arm's Lockheed AT-33As.

The current structure dates to 1941 when the Italian Military Mission was replaced by one from the United States. At that time, the country was divided into four Regiones Aéreas, each of which had a Grupo Aéreo with two seven-aircraft Escuadrillas. They were 1 Region Aérea at Air Base El Alto, La Paz; 2 Region Aérea, El Trompillo, Santa Cruz; 3 Region Aérea, La Florida, Sucre; and 4 Region Aérea, El Tejar.

Organisation and headquarters

Today this has been slightly restructured into three Brigadas Aéreas. Of these, I° Brigada Aérea is still located at El Alto, La Paz. II° Brigada Aérea is at Cochabamba, Colcapiru, and III° Brigada Aérea is at El Trompillo, Santa Cruz. Within these regional areas are 11 operational Grupos and the Collegio Militar de Aviación. Base Aérea 'General Jorge Jordan', El Alto, is the principal air base close to the seat of government and major city of La Paz. Here the bulk of the transport system can be found, much of which is operated by the Transporte Aéreo Militar (TAM) which also retains the FAB title of Grupo Aéreo de Transporte 71.

Equipped with a mixture of assorted Lockheed Hercules, Fokker F27 Friendships, IAI Aravas, Rockwell Commanders, CASA C.212 Aviocars and other minor types, the unit is tasked with support of the interior and out-based units. The Transporte Aéreo Boliviano (TAB), a pseudo-civilian operation, is also attached to GAdT 71.

La Paz itself is situated 12,000 ft (3658 m) above sea level in the Andes, with the airfield situated on a plateau 1,640 ft (500 m) higher. The 'hot-and-high' conditions present unique operating problems. The location does provide its own security, though, and to some degree negates the necessity of having an air defence system.

However, with a requirement to support the army in anti-guerrilla activity and to interdict the smuggling of illicit drugs, the FAB does need some front-line capacity. To undertake the COIN role, the FAB utilises a number of Canadair-built AT-33As. These first-generation jets were initially acquired in 1973 when 15 examples were delivered from surplus Canadian air force stocks, although one of these was lost during the delivery flight. Used to supplement the nine F-86F Sabres supplied by Venezuela, these early jets have survived to become the only 'high-performance' aircraft in the FAB inventory.

The surviving AT-33As were supplemented by additional deliveries, and are assigned to Escuadrón 310 under Grupo Aéreo de Caza 31 at El Alto, with an operating detachment at El Trompillo under Grupo de Caza 32, and Grupo Aérea de Caza 33 at Cochabamba. Another five were received in 1977 in an exchange by North West Industries for the last six airworthy P-51D Mustangs. Later in 1985 an additional 18 former French T-33ANs were acquired in a $6.2 million contract.

Rotary-wing operations are conducted principally by Grupo Aéreo 51, which is equipped with the Bell UH-1H, Hughes 369 and Aérospatiale SA 315B/HB 314 Lama. Located at the former international airport of El Trompillo, Santa Cruz, having relocated recently from Base Aérea de Colcapiru, Cochabamba, they support army, navy and air force requirements. Also at El Trompillo is the FAB's only surviving airworthy Douglas C-47 Dakota, FAB 1038, which is a Basler Turbo BT-67 conversion delivered in 1991 and sports the civilian TAM 38 registration. This aircraft is tasked primarily in anti-narcotics related operations.

Training and helicopter operations

Also at El Trompillo is the College of Military Aviation (COLMILAV) with its variety of Cessna aircraft, many of which have been acquired following confiscation in drug-related prosecutions. Pilot primary training is now carried out at Santa Rosa, the school having relocated there in 1982. The two flying units, Escuadrón Primario and Escuadrón Básico, originally utilised the 22 Pilatus PC.7s alongside a handful of T-28 and T-6G aircraft. The former were reassigned to COIN operations, having been superseded by 15 T-23 Uirapurus donated by Brazil.

With the bulk of the helicopter assets having vacated Cochabamba, Grupo Aéreo Mixto is left with a small search and rescue detachment of SA 315B Lamas, together with the survivors of the 16 Pilatus PC.6B Turbo-Porters procured for COIN operations. They will be supported by the PC.7 once they have been converted to this task.

The FAB has a number of other operating locations, including Base Aérea de Rebore which is still thought to be home to the Grupo de Operaciones Aéreas Especiales. This unit had originally received the Hughes 369M, although whether they have relocated to within the structure of Grupo Aéreo 51 is unclear. This applies equally to Grupo Aéreo de Cobertura Nº 1 at El Tejar, as its former T-6Gs are thought to have been withdrawn. Conversion of the PC.7 to COIN operation will probably see a detachment here.

With a very limited defence budget, future procurement for the FAB lacks any real commitment. Short of effective finance, many proposals including the 1970s order for 10 Hispano HA.220 close-support jets became another in a line of projected buys. Even when funds were supposedly assigned in 1980 for the acquisition of 24 fighters, when both the SEPECAT Jaguar and the IAI Kfir C2 were short-listed, this came to nothing. There is a real need to find a replacement for the AT-33A, and the latest proposal of 12 IA-63 Pampa jet trainers suitably enhanced for Bolivian operations seems a far more sensible solution. A decision will have to be taken shortly for a replacement, or the FAB will have to do without the capability altogether.

Fuerza Aérea Boliviana

1° Brigada Aérea –
Base Aérea 'General Walter Arze', El Alto, La Paz

Grupo Aéreo de Caza 31,
Base Aérea 'General Walter Arze', El Alto, La Paz

Escuadrón 310	Canadair AT-33AN
Escuadrón 311	Beech 55, Rockwell Commander 680,
	Sabreliner 60, Beech King Air 90/200C, Cessna 421, CASA C.212

Grupo Aéreo 71

Escuadrón 711	Lockheed C-130A/H Hercules
Escuadrón 712	Fokker F27 Friendship, Convair CV.580,
	IAI Arava, Lockheed L.188 Electra

Grupo Aéreo 91

Escuadrón 911	Gates Learjet 25D, Beech King Air 200

Servicio Nacional de Aerofotogrametrica

Gates Learjet 25D/35A, Cessna 402, Piper PA-23

Escuadrilla Ejecutiva

Sabreliner 60, Cessna 402B/421B, Piper PA-34 Seneca

11° Brigada Aérea – Base Aérea de Colcapiru, Cochabamba

Grupo Aéreo Mixto

Aérospatiale SA 315B Lama, HB 315B Gavião, Pilatus PC.6B Turbo-Porter

Grupo Aéreo de Caza 33 – Base Aérea 'Jorge Wilsterman'

Grupo Aéreo de Operaciones Aéreas Especiales, Rebore

Hughes 369M

Grupo Aéreo 61

Escuadrón 611	SIAI-Marchetti SF.260CB, Pilatus PC-6B

Grupo Aéreo 62, Riberalta

Escuadrón 621	Various transports

Grupo Aéreo 72

Escuadrón 721	Basler BT-67 Turbo-Dakota

III° Brigada Aérea –
Base Aérea El Trompillo, Santa Cruz de la Sierra

Grupo Aéreo de Caza 32

Escuadrón 310 (det)	Canadair AT-33AN
Escuadrón 321	Beech 36, Beech 58

Collegio Militar de Aviación –
Base Aérea El Trompillo, Santa Cruz de la Sierra

Base Aérea Santa Rosa

Escuadrón Primario Aerotec A.122 Uirapuru, Aerotec A.132B Tanagra
Escuadrón Básico   Aerotec A.122 Uirapuru, Cessna 152, Pilatus PC.7

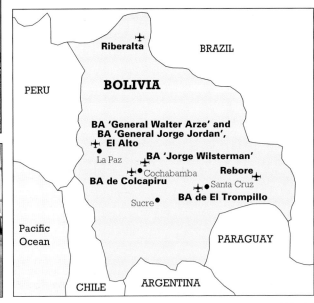

Above: Ancient T-33ANs are Bolivia's 'front-line' combat type.

Right: PC-7s are tasked with training duties at Santa Cruz de la Sierra.

Below: This C-130A serves with Escuadrón 1 of Grupo 71.

Right: IAI Aravas operate as part of Transporte Aéreo Militar (TAM) – or Grupo 71 – based at La Paz.

Below: Bolivia took delivery of T-23 (A-122) Urupurus from Brazil. They serve as basic trainers.

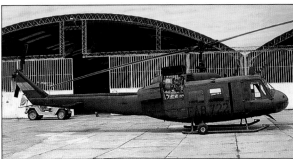

Above: Basler BT-67 Turbo Dakotas serve with Grupo Aéreo 72.

Right: Thirty-two UH-1Hs are now in FAB service.

Below: Escuadrón 712 operates F27s alongside its CV 580 and L.188.

This Sabreliner 60 serves as a Presidential transport with the FAB's Escuadrilla Ejecutiva, based alongside Grupo Aéreo de Caza 31 at El Alto, La Paz.

Escuadrón 911, part of Grupo Aéreo 91, operates this Learjet 25D and a Beech King Air 200. The FAB also operates photo-survey Learjet 25Ds and 35As.

Escuadrón 311 operates the Rockwell Commander 680, Beech King Air 90 and 200 Super King Air, CASA C.212 and this Beech 55 Baron.

Armada

Being land-locked, Bolivia has very limited needs to patrol its rivers and lakes. In most areas the Armada Boliviano relies on support from the air force. Its sole Cessna 402C patrol/communication aircraft is kept at El Alto, La Paz.

Ejército Boliviano

Bolivian army aviation maintains a few communication and support aircraft from the FAB facility at El Alto, La Paz. For all other operations it relies on FAB assets for support, although it has

one transport, a CASA C.212 (EB-002). The Aviocar's sister aircraft, EB-50, was lost in an accident on 21 April 1995, as was a Beech King Air 200, EB-002, on 26 November the same year.

Carabinero Boliviano

For most operations the Bolivian police (Carabinero Boliviano) relies on FAB aviation assets for support and transport. It does maintain one Cessna 421B, CB-001, for communication duties.

Carabinero Boliviano

CASA C.212 Aviocar, Beech King Air C90/200

Ejército Boliviano

Base Aérea 'General Jorge Jordan', El Alto, La Paz
CASA C.212 Aviocar, Beech King Air C90/200

Peter R. Foster

Chile

Although only the seventh largest country in South America, in terms of area, Chile is one of the traditional 'big four' powers in the region, the others being Argentina, Brazil and Peru. Its armed forces, which have been resoundingly victorious in the few foreign wars in which they have engaged since the country's independence, have the proud motto "always victorious; never vanquished" and through training missions have exercised considerable influence on those of

many other countries in the region. The Chilean air force is the world's fourth oldest independent military air arm – a status of which it is justifiably proud – the original air arms of the army and navy having been merged as the Fuerza Aérea de Chile in March 1930. The navy re-established its own aviation arm in 1953, followed by the army in 1970. The paramilitary national police force, the Carabineros de Chile, now also operates a number of both fixed- and rotary-winged aircraft.

Fuerza Aérea de Chile

The FACH, which numbers approximately 13,000 men and women, operates about 320 fixed- and rotary-winged aircraft, and is organised into three functional commands – Combat, Personnel, and Logistics.

Combat Command controls the five air brigades and the five wings which operate most of the flying equipment of the FACH. They are deployed between a total of 13 groups (squadrons). There is reasonable AEW radar cover over most of the country but this extends effectively beyond the country's land frontiers only in the extreme north and south, due to the physical barrier of the Andes to the east. The recent acquisition of a Phalcon AEW aircraft (modified from a former LAN-Chile Boeing 707 by IAI and designated Condor in Chilean service) will go some way to remedy this deficiency. This aircraft was used to monitor French nuclear testing in the Pacific during the early part of 1996.

The Brigada Aérea (Air Brigade), which consists of two or more Grupos (squadrons), is the main operational formation of the FACH, the Ala Base (Base Wing) being primarily an administrative and logistic support unit which is generally concentrated at a single base. Each wing includes a liaison flight, equipped with assorted light aircraft and helicopters, plus an anti-aircraft artillery group. There is also an anti-aircraft artillery regiment at La Colina, near Santiago, which serves primarily as an administrative headquarters and training school for the five dispersed A/A artillery groups. Each wing also has an elec-

tronic communications group, and the groups attached to the 1st and 4th Wings (31st and 34th) also include an electronic warfare element.

Air Brigade I (HQ Los Condores, Iquique) covers the northern part of the country, from the Peruvian frontier to the Huasco River in southern Atacama Province, and controls the 4th Wing, at Los Condores. This brigade consists of the 1st (Attack/Training) and the 2nd (Reconnaissance and Photographic) Squadrons. The 1st Squadron, which serves as a combined light strike and operational training unit, is equipped with ENAER T-36 trainers and A-36 light strike aircraft. The 2nd Squadron, formerly based at Los Cerrillos, Santiago, is a special unit operating the single survivor of two Canberra PR.Mk 9s and five modified Beech 99As, primarily in Elint/Sigint roles. The 1st Wing also includes the 11th Cerro Moreno Liaison Flight which operates a single DHC-6, two Piper PA-28s and three SA 315B helicopters; the 21st A/A Artillery Group; and the 31st Electronic Communications Group.

Air Brigade II (HQ Los Cerrillos, Santiago) covers the region southward from Huasco to the Bío-Bío River, combining the 9th, 10th and 11th Squadrons, and consists of the 2nd Wing, also embracing the two Learjet 35As of the Aerial Photogrammetric Service. The 9th Squadron, formerly a fighter unit based at Antofagasta and stood down approximately a decade ago, was reactivated at Los Cerrillos in 1993 and is now the major helicopter element of the FACH, equipped with 16 Bell UH-1Hs, six MBB BO 105s

and a single BK 117. The 10th (Transport) Squadron, based at Comandante Arturo Merino Benitez International Airport, Pudahuel, Santiago, is the main transport unit of the FACH and is equipped with four Lockheed C-130Bs and two Hs; three Boeing 707s, of which two have been modified to KC-137 standard for inflight refuelling (for which all the first-line combat aircraft of the FACH are now equipped); and a fourth Boeing 707, modified to Phalcon AEW standards by IAI. A single Boeing 737-300, a Gulfstream III and a Beech Super King Air 200 are on order for the Presidential Flight which previously operated one of the existing Boeing 707s. The 11th (Training) Squadron, at Los Cerrillos, which is primarily a refresher training unit for personnel currently assigned to non-flying duties, is equipped with ENAER T-35 Pilláns. It also controls both the Piper PA-28 Dakotas of the Air Force Specialists' School and the five Extra 300s of the 'Halcones' aerobatic team. The 2nd Wing also includes the 12th Liaison Flight with two DHC-6s, a Beech King Air 100, three Beech 99As and a Piper PA-28; the un-numbered and un-named air force paratroop battalion and anti-aircraft artillery regiment; the 22nd A/A Artillery Group; and the 32nd Electronic Communications Group.

Air Brigade III (HQ El Tepual Military Air Base, Puerto Montt), covers the region between the Bío-Bío River and Cerro San Valentín, in southern Aysén Province and consists of the 3rd and 5th Squadrons, also comprising the 5th Wing, at Puerto Montt. The 3rd (Attack) Squadron is a light strike unit, equipped with CASA/ENAER A-36Bs and based at Temuco, and the 5th (Communications) Squadron is a light transport unit, equipped with four CASA C.212s and based at Puerto Montt. The 5th Wing also comprises the 15th Liaison Flight, with five ENAER T-35Bs and two BO 105 helicopters; the 25th A/A Artillery Group; and the 35th Electronic Communications Group.

Air Brigade IV (HQ 'Carlos Ibánez' Military Air Base, Punta Arenas) covers the region south from Cerro San Valentín to Cape Horn and is made up of the 4th, 6th and 12th Squadrons, all based at Punta Arenas. It also includes the 3rd Wing. The 4th (Fighter) Squadron operates 15 Dassault Mirage 50CHs, DCHs and FCHs which have been upgraded to Pantera standards, plus five unmodified ex-Belgian Mirage 5s that also will be eventually upgraded. The 6th (Special

146

*bove: The solitary aircraft operated
 the Bolivian naval air arm is this
essna 402C, based at El Alto, La Paz.*

*Right: This is the ill-fated Ejército
Boliviano CASA C.212 Aviocar which
crashed in April 1995.*

*hile's F-5Es
ight) have been
bstantially
pgraded by IAI to
igre IV standard,
ding new radar,
datalink and
eapons such as
e Python IV
AM. They make
very potent
ombat force. F-5Fs
re used for
aining.*

*hile's Mirage
C/FC fighters
ight) and 50DC
ainers (below)
ave been
pgraded to
antera standard
rough the
ddition of Elta
/M-2001B
nging radar (in
n extended nose),
ew HUD, INS and
vionics, Chilean-
uilt RWR and
haff/flare
ispensers, and
R probes. The
anteras serve
ith Grupo 4.*

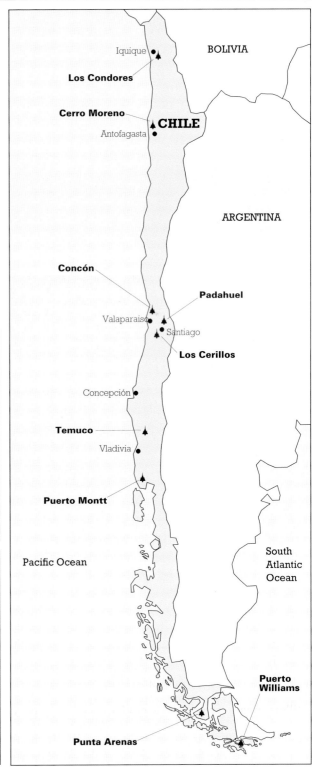

BOLIVIA

Iquique
Los Condores

Cerro Moreno
▲ CHILE
Antofagasta

ARGENTINA

Concón

Padahuel

Valaparaiso
Santiago

Los Cerillos

Concepción

Temuco

Vladivia

Puerto Montt

Pacific Ocean

South
Atlantic
Ocean

Puerto
Williams

Punta Arenas

Operations) Squadron is equipped with four armed DHC-6s, and the 12th (Attack) Squadron operates Cessna A-37Bs in the light strike role. These latter aircraft will be replaced by Beech/Pilatus PC.9s. The Fourth Brigade also controls the 19th (Antarctic Exploration) Squadron which is based at 'Teniente Marsh' Military Air Base in the Chilean Antarctic territory, where it operates single examples of the DHC-6, BO 105 and Bell UH-1H. The 3rd Wing also includes the 23rd A/A Artillery Group and the 33rd Electronic Communications Group.

Air Brigade V, which was formed only at the end of 1995, is based at Cerro Moreno, Antofagasta. This is the main fighter unit of the FACH, originally forming part of Air Brigade I, and comprises the 7th and 8th Squadrons and the 1st Wing. The 7th (Fighter) Squadron is equipped with Northrop F-5E (12) and Fs (three). They have been upgraded to Tigre standards and are presumably to be joined by the mysterious additional F-5Es believed to have been acquired from Honduras. The 8th (Fighter) Squadron, which until recently operated the remaining Hunter FGA.Mk 9s, FGA./FR.Mk 71s and T.Mk 72s of the 32 which formerly equipped both the 8th and 9th Squadrons, has recently re-equipping with 15 ex-Belgian Mirage/MirSIP 5BAs that have been upgraded to Elkan standards. The 4th Wing also includes the 14th Los Condores Liaison Flight, equipped with a single DHC-6 Twin Otter and two SA 315B Lama helicopters; the 24th A/A Artillery Group; and the 34th Electronic Communications Group.

Logistics Command controls the non-flying supply and maintenance wings, both also with their headquarters at El Bosque.

Air Force Personnel Command controls the Escuela de Aviación Capitán Avalos (Air Force College), the Specialists' School, the Academia de Guerra Aérea (Air Force Staff College) and the Academia Politécnica Aérea (Air Force Technical School). All are located at El Bosque, Santiago.

The Escuela de Aviación Capitán Avalos is at El Bosque, Santiago, and its flying elements are equipped with Cessna T-37B and Cs, and ENAER T-35 Pilláns, without any squadron organisation. The school offers a basic three-year course to officer cadets, followed by two years of specialised training before commissioning, in the rank of second lieutenant. This is carried out either in operational units, in the case of flying officers, or at the Academia Politécnica Aérea, in the case of technical officers. The completion of the course of the Academia de Guerra Aérea is a prerequisite for appointments to the Air General Staff or for promotion to rank beyond that of major. The Academia Politécnica Aérea also provides a two-year course for NCOs and is equipped with Cessna T-41s and Piper PA-28 Dakotas.

Operational environment

The FACH has contributed to United Nations peace-keeping operations, most recently in the Middle East in the aftermath of the 1991 Gulf War, where it still maintains a helicopter unit with five aircraft from the 9th Group at Los Cerrillos and about 50 personnel.

Chile's traditional external threats come from Argentina and Peru. The most recent tension with Argentina, during the late 1970s/early 1980s, found Chile at a considerable material disadvantage due to the embargo enforced by

most arms-manufacturing countries against its contemporary military government, which had overthrown the democratically elected but highly undemocratic Marxist regime of Salvador Allende in 1973. Chile's active support for Britain in the Falklands War of 1982 should therefore have come as no surprise, and Argentina's subsequent defeat paved the way for the Beagle Channel Treaty of 1984, which resolved the most recent difficulties between these two traditional enemies.

A contemporaneous threat from Peru was also very real, the more so as Peru might have been expected to take advantage of any conflict between Chile and Argentina to launch a strike from the north. After the defeat of its major potential ally, Peru alone did not dare to try conclusions with Chile. Today, although traditional enmities have not been removed, neither Argentina nor Peru poses any immediate threat to Chile and the current atmosphere is one of *détente* between the three countries.

Chilean aeronautical industry

As a result of the arms embargo, Chile was forced to develop its defence industry. It is therefore now largely self-sufficient in the production of trainer and light strike aircraft. Local industry, with Israeli assistance, has developed considerable expertise in the upgrading of existing aircraft and the prolongation of their useful lives.

Starting from almost nothing, in 1981, the Air Force Maintenance Wing began the development of a variant of the Piper 236 Dakota light aircraft, as a replacement for the Beech T-34. This emerged as the T-35 Pillán two-seater primary trainer and in 1984 the Empresa Nacional de Aeronáutica de Chile (ENAER) was set up to handle this project. Approximately 80 examples of this aircraft were delivered to the FACH and just under 60 are still in service. Ten were also sold to Panama and 15 to Paraguay; 40 were built under licence in Spain, for the Spanish air force, as the Tamíz. Ultimately, it is proposed to build up to 120 examples of the turbo-prop variant, so far displayed only in prototype form, as replacements for the existing piston-engined version. A version of the Spanish CASA C.101 Aviojet was developed as the T-36 Halcón. Although this type was intended to replace the Cessna T-37 and A-37 in the advanced-training (T-36) and light-strike (A-36) roles, the rather unwelcome gift of additional quantities of extremely second-hand and relatively useless examples of both of these types from the United States in 1994 undermined this programme. However, 38 examples of the A-36 and T-36 remain in service, the A-36s having undergone a communications, avionics and sensor systems upgrade. A radar-equipped maritime strike version, designated A-36M and armed with the British Aerospace Sea Eagle air-to-surface missile, was also developed but to date has only flown in prototype form.

Upgrade programmes

In 1985, with the assistance of Israel Aircraft Industries, ENAER commenced the modernisation of the Chilean air force's Mirage 50s to a configuration resembling that of the IAI Kfir, the upgraded aircraft being known as the Pantera. A comparable upgrade was subsequently carried out on the air force's Northrop F-5 Tigers, which were then known as Tigres. Most of the Mirage 5s, recently purchased from Belgium, have also

already undergone a degree of modernisation as the Elkan, which nevertheless leaves them short of the ENAER/IAI Pantera upgrade.

The existing fleet of F-5s is also being augmented. Originally this was believed to be by the transfer of the 12 examples of this aircraft operated by the Honduran air force and which, after the relative pacification of the Central American region, were deemed by the United States to upset the local balance of air power. Although several F-5s of apparently Honduran origin were delivered to Chile during the early months of 1996, at least six aircraft of this type were still noted to be in Honduran service during the following September. A possibility is that Honduras yielded partially to US pressure and sold half its F-5 inventory to Chile, but the matter remains shrouded in mystery.

Future fighters

Piecemeal acquisitions of Mirage 5s and F-5s notwithstanding, the withdrawal in 1995 of the last of the much-loved Hawker Hunters, which had formed the backbone of the Chilean air force's fighter-bomber force for three decades, left a vacuum in its combat aircraft inventory. Argentina's recent acquisition of A-4 Skyhawks is considered by the Chileans to have seriously upset the regional air power balance, although these aircraft are not in the same class as either the Mirage 5, the Mirage 50 or the F-5.

The FACH is therefore actively shopping for a standard combat aircraft to take it into the 21st century. The United States, in an apparent reversal of its traditional policy of refusing to sell modern defence equipment to its southern neighbours, is currently offering a squadron or two of F-16s or even F/A-18s to Chile. The FACH now appears to have chosen the Pilatus/Beech PC.9, the winner of the JPATS competition in the US, as the potential replacement for both the Cessna T-37 and A-37. But, memories of the recent US arms boycott continue to rankle. Almost a quarter of a century of reliable service by the Mirage 50, recently reinforced by the Mirage 5, presents a convincing argument in favour of the Mirage 2000 as Chile's next generation of combat aircraft, but the choice may fall on the more advanced Swedish JAS 39 Gripen. Air Force Commander-in-Chief Fernando Rojas Vender appears unequivocally to have thrown his weight behind the Gripen, contrary to Defence Minister Edmundo Pérez Yoma who remains a protagonist of the F-16.

Fuerza Aérea de Chile

UNIT	TYPE	BASE
Grupo 1	ENAER A-36, T-36 Halcón	Los Condores, Iquique
Grupo 2	Canberra PR.Mk 9, Beech 99A	Los Condores, Iquique
Grupo 3	CASA/ENAER A-36B	Temuco
Grupo 4	Mirage 50CH/DCH/FCH Pantera, Mirage 5	Punta Arenas
Grupo 5	CASA C.212	Puerto Montt
Grupo 6	DHC-6 (armed)	Punta Arenas
Grupo 7	Northrop F-5E/F Tigre	Cerro Moreno, Antofagasta
Grupo 8	Mirage/MIRSIP 5BA Elkan	Cerro Moreno, Antofagasta
Grupo 9	Bell UH-1H, MBB BO 105, BK 117	Los Cerrillos, Santiago
Grupo 10	C-130B/H, 707/KC-137, Boeing/IAI Phalcon	Pudahuel, Santiago
Grupo 11	ENAER T-35 Pillán, Piper PA-28 Dakota	Los Cerrillos, Santiago
Grupo 12	Cessna A-37B (Beech/Pilatus PC.9)	Punta Arenas
Grupo 19	DHC-6, MBB BO 105, Bell UH-1H	'Teniente Marsh' Military Air Base, Antarctica

Above: Armed A-36 Halcóns fly COIN missions with Grupo 3, based at BAM Maguéhue, Temuco, as part of 3 Brigada Aérea.

Right: Grupo 10, part of Ala 2, at BAM Los Cerrillos, maintains the FACH's C-130B/H fleet.

Right: A small number of SA 315B Lamas remain in service with the Esc de Enlace, based with Grupo 1 at BAM Los Condores.

Below: BO 105s serve with Grupos 5, 10 and 19. The FACH operates a mix of BO 105CBS and CB-4 aircraft.

Above: Chile's unique Condor/Phalcon AEW/Elint platform flies with Grupo 10, part of Ala 2, 2 Brigada Aérea.

Below: Locally-built ENAER T-35A/B Pillán trainers fly with the Esc Básica at BAM El Bosque, Santiago.

Specially-modified Beech 99A Petrel aircraft fly Sigint/Elint missions as part of the Esc de Guerra Electrónica, Grupo 2, Ala 2, BAM Los Cerillos.

Short-nosed DHC-6-100s are flown by the Esc de Enlace (liaison squadron) at BAM Cerro Moreno and the survey unit at Grupo 2, BAM Los Cerillos.

UH-1Hs fly as part of Grupo 6, Ala 3, based at BAM 'Carlos Ibánez', Puenta Arenas and are sometimes detached to King George Island Antarctic base.

Left: The BO 105CB-4s of Grupo 19 are based at BAA 'Teniente Rodolfo Marsh Martin', on King George Island.

Above: Cessna T-37B/Cs serve with the Esc Avanzada (advanced training flight), BAM El Bosque.

Above: Fourteen ENAER PA-28-236 Dakotas serve with the Esc de Enlace, Ala 4.

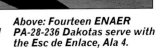

Aviación del Ejército de Chile

The aviation element of the 57,000-strong Chilean army consists mainly of the 1st 'Independencia' Aviation Brigade, which was promoted from regimental to brigade status at the beginning of 1996 and is based at Rancagua, near Santiago. It deploys approximately 90 aircraft, most of which are concentrated within the brigade. Others are deployed on an *ad hoc* basis in accordance with operational requirements, in support of five

of the army's seven divisions. Existing sub-units are the Sección de Aviación de Ejército 1 (Antofagasta); Sección de Aviación de Ejército 3 (Temuco); Sección de Aviación de Ejército 4 (Aerodromo Las Marias, Valdivia); Sección de Aviación de Ejército 6 (Arica); and Sección de Aviación de Ejército 7 (Las Bandurrias, Coyhaique), all of which are subordinate to divisions bearing the same numerical designation.

Aviación del Ejército de Chile

CASA CN.235	transport	3
CASA C.212 Aviocar	utility/transport	6
Cessna Citation II	VIP transport	1
Piper Navajo	communications	4
Cessna 337	AOP	3
Cessna R172K	liaison/training	16
MDH/Hughes 530F	attack helicopter	5
Aérospatiale SA 330 Puma	transport helicopter	14
Aérospatiale AS 332 Super Puma	transport helicopter	3
Aérospatiale SA 315B Lama	utility helicopter	16
Bell 206	utility helicopter	2
Bell UH-1H	utility helicopter	3
Enstrom 280FX	utility helicopter	15

Aviación Naval Chilena

The Chilean navy is traditionally Latin America's best in qualitative terms, even though in size it now lags behind the navies of Argentina, Brazil and Peru. It includes two helicopter-carrying destroyers, each equipped to handle and support two AS 332 Super Pumas or AS 532 Cougars; two other helicopter-capable destroyers and four helicopter-capable frigates. Several auxiliary, logistic support and amphibious vessels can also accommodate and/or support helicopters.

Chilean naval aviation accounts for a modest 600 or so from a total naval manpower of the order of 24,000, operating approximately 50 aircraft. It is organised into two groups, based at Concón and Puerto Williams, each comprising elements of its four operational squadrons. They are (General Purpose) Squadron VG-1, which is equipped with CASA C.212s and EMBRAER EMB-110CNs (three and three examples respectively, for transport and communications tasks); (Attack Helicopter) Squadron VA-1, equipped with AS 332 Super Pumas and AS 532 Cougars (four of each type tasked with ASW duties); (General Purpose Helicopter) Squadron VH-1 with MBB BO 105s (eight in service) which are replacing the surviving Bell 206Bs (six still in service); and (Maritime Reconnaissance) Squadron VP-1 with Lockheed P-3A Orions (eight), EMBRAER 111ANs (six) and Dassault-Breguet Falcon 20/200s (two). Training Squadron VT-1 is equipped with Pilatus PC.7s (10 aircraft),

which can also double in the light strike role.

The principal naval air base is at Concón, 12 miles (20 km) to the north of Vina del Mar, with minor bases at Punta Arenas and Puerto Williams. Having won the battle with the air force for the control of all military aircraft (both fixed- and rotary-winged) which operate over the sea, the Chilean navy would like to operate a small number of Sea Harriers; more realistically, the

formation of a fixed-wing combat squadron of about 20 navalised CASA/ENAER A-36M Halcón aircraft is envisaged when finances permit.

Aviación Naval Chilena

UNIT	TYPE	BASE
Squadron VG-1	CASA C.212 Aviocar, EMB-110CN	Concón
Squadron VA-1	AS 332 Super Puma, AS 532 Cougar	Concón
Squadron VH-1	MBB BO 105, Bell 206B	Concón
Squadron VP-1	Lockheed P-3 Orion	Concón
Squadron VT-1	Pilatus PC.7	Concón

Prefectura Aérea de los Carabineros de Chile

Since 1927 all law enforcement agencies in Chile have been incorporated into a single force – the Carabineros de Chile – which has a paramilitary organisation and forms a potential reserve for the army. In addition to normal police functions, the Carabineros are also responsible for customs control, and provide the Presidential Guard. The Air Police, which ranks as a separate prefecture within the overall structure of the 32,000-strong Carabineros, operates 20 to 30 fixed- and rotary-winged aircraft. They include MBB (Eurocopter) BO 105C, CB and LS and Bell 206L3 helicopters, Swearingen SA-226TC Metro and Piper Navajo twin-engined and single-engined Cessna 182Q,

206 and 210M Centurion II aircraft. There is no known subordinate group or squadron organisation.

Prefectura Aérea de los Carabineros de Chile

Swearingen SA-226TC Metro	communications	4
Piper Navajo	communications	4
Cessna 182Q	liaison	4
Cessna 206	liaison	2
Cessna 210M Centurion II	liaison	2
MBB BO 105	utility helicopter	8
Bell 206L3	utility helicopter	2

Adrian J. English

Paraguay

A landlocked, predominantly agricultural country, Paraguay gained its independence from Spain on 14 May 1811 and has retained its sovereignty in spite of a number of attempts by its neighbours to annex part – if not all – of its lands. External troubles have left Paraguay untouched since the early part of this century. A period of recurring

internal social disturbances in the early 1950s led to the introduction of a military government. Since then, a number of exiled groups have attempted to stage *coup d'états*, but with little success. The country subsequently returned to a bicameral parliament with a Senate and a Chamber of Deputies.

Fuerza Aérea Paraguaya

With nearly 40 years of relative tranquillity, there is little argument for maintaining a substantial air force. However, with an area of 406752 km² (157,056 sq miles) – much of it marsh and lakes in the east, with the arid plain of the Chaco

Boreal to the west – air transport is an integral part of the country's communication system.

The Fuerza Aérea Paraguaya (FAP) was formed in 1927 as part of the army. Then known as the Fuerzas Aéreas del Ejército Nacional Paraguayo,

its headquarters and flying school were at Campo Grande, 15 km (9 miles) from the capital Asunción. 1946 saw the first major change to affect Paraguayan military aviation when the Fuerza Aérea Paraguaya became an independent service in its own right. In spite of this, re-equipment was slow and restricted. Today, the FAP remains primarily a transport and communications force.

FAP Headquarters remains at its original home of BAM Nhu Guazu, Campo Grande. The flying elements under the control of 1 Brigada Aérea currently are commanded by General de Division D Cesar Rafael Cramer Espinola. Subordinate to 1 Brigada Aérea are five Grupos, each having a number of Escuadrones.

The combat element of the FAP is Grupo Aerotáctico (GAT) located at Asunción-Silvo Pettirossi International Airport, on the opposite side of the main road to Campo Grande. Within this Grupo there are three Escuadrones. The 1º Escuadrón de Caza 'Guaraní' is equipped with the EMBRAER-Macchi EMB-326GB Xavante

Three Cessna L-19A Bird Dogs serve as tugs for the various gliders and sailplanes in service with the Esc de Planeadores and Esc de Alta Acrobacia of Grupo 11, BAM Los Cerillos.

In addition to the FACH's Petrel aircraft, three Beech 99As are used for communications/ transport tasks as part of Grupo 10 alongside its Boeing 707s, 757 and Lockheed C-130s.

The FACH has recently acquired higher-powered CASA C.212-300 Aviocars to operate alongside the C.212-100s that have been in service since 1994.

Left: Registered to the Corporación de Fomento, this Cessna 650 Citation III is FACH-tasked.

Right: Grupo 6, based at Punta Arenas, flies DHC-6-300s (as does Grupo 5) configured for Antarctic operations.

Below left: Enstrom 280FX helicopters serve with the army aviation flying training school.

Left: SA 330F/L Pumas serve with the Ejército, along with AS 332B/M1s.

Above: Army aviation operates this Chincul PA-31.

Left: Five MD 530Fs, delivered in 1990, form the Ejército's sole combat helicopter capability.

Above: Three CN.235M-100 transports operate with the army's six smaller CASA C.212-100s.

Above: VT-1 of the Chilean naval air command operates 10 PC-7 Turbo Trainers from BAN Vina del Mar.

HA-1 operates the navy's six AS 532SC Cougars/ Super Pumas which are regularly detached aboard the navy's larger warships.

Radar-equipped EMB-111CN Bandeirantes are used for maritime patrol duties by VC-1. Three were delivered in 1976.

VP-1 flies a single Dassault Falcon 200 on patrol duties alongside its P-3 Orions and EMB-111ANs. The unit also has three UP-3A Orions.

Three CASA C.212-100 Aviocars were delivered to the navy in 1978 and serve alongside three EMB-110CN transports with VC-1.

From its main base at Tobalaba (Santiago), the Chilean military police air unit flies a mix of BK 117B-1s (left), B206B JetRangers (above), Cessna U206G Stationairs and BO 105s.

151

and is tasked in the COIN/attack role. The Escuadrón is further divided into two Escuadrillas, 'Orion' and 'Centauro'.

Paraguay first showed interest in the Xavante during 1977 as a replacement for its AT-6Gs. However, the US offered six Cessna A-37Bs and the Xavantes were shelved. Ultimately, though, the Cessnas were never delivered and nine AT-26s (1001-1009) were ordered in April 1979. Deliveries commenced on 7 May 1980. Factory fresh, they were the first jet aircraft to be operated by the FAP. One aircraft (1008) was lost on 9 September 1980, barely four months after arrival, but additional funding was found for an attrition replacement. Although still current in the inventory, at least three further aircraft have been lost: 1002 on 23 April 1985 near Cacupe, 1003 in 1988 and 1001 in 1990.

Operations and maintenance are conducted from Asunción although the Escuadrón detaches to both Ciudad del Este and Concepción, where a new facility was opened in December 1996.

The 2º Escuadrón de Caza 'Indios', and its attendant Escuadrillas 'Taurus' and 'Scorpio', were equipped with six Lockheed AT-33As that were donated by Taiwan in 1990/91. The aircraft (1020-1025) began operations on 20 August 1991 and had led a trouble-free existence until the loss of 1020 in 1996. Following this the aircraft were grounded, and it is expected that the unit will re-equip with 12 former Taiwanese F-5E/Fs during 1997. Once converted, the 2º Escuadrón de Caza will relocate to Concepción.

The 3º Escuadrón de Caza, 'Moros', operates the EMBRAER T-27 Tucano in the COIN role. Once again, severe funding shortages saw the aircraft grounded in late 1996 while awaiting Martin-Baker seat overhaul. During this period the two subordinate Escuadrillas, 'Gamma' and 'Omega', were reduced to operating ENAER T-35B Pillán aircraft to maintain flight currency.

Six EMB-312A Tucanos (1051-1056) were delivered on 6 November 1987. Attrition has accounted for two aircraft, 1054 and 1056, but funding has precluded any replacements. Although based at Asunción, deployments are often made to Ciudad del Este.

Sharing the Asunción-Silvo Pettirossi facility are the heavier transport assets of both Grupo Aéreo de Transport Especiales (GATE) and Grupo de Transport Aéreo (GdTA). The latter is the direct descendent of the Transporte Aéreo Militar (TAM) that was formed in 1954 to operate flights to remote areas of the country. The unit is today equipped with two airworthy C-47s and four CASA C.212s.

The other transport and communications element, GATE, has a number of major responsibilities. Its primary function is the support of the Presidential and government aircraft such as a single Boeing 707-321B (FAP 01), a DHC-6 Twin Otter 200 (FAP-02), a civilian-registered Cessna Citation 550 (ZP-TYO) and a Beech King Air 90 (ZP-TJW). On top of this, it provides communication and liaison flying for the air force with a collection of Beech, Piper and Cessna types, some of which it took over from Lineas Aéreas de Transporte Nacional (LATN) in 1989 when that company went into liquidation.

BAM Nhu Guazu, Campo Grande, with its grass runway, provides a home for the remainder of the FAP's assets. It is here that all instruction is carried out, including that of technical training. Training on flying assets is conducted under the auspices of Grupo Aéreo de Instrucción (GAI). Students begin their *ab initio* training of 30-40 hours on the three surviving Aerotec A-122 Uirapurus or T-23s (0010/12/14) which were acquired from Brazil. Initially, eight were reported as having been transferred in 1975 followed by an additional six in 1986. They supported a number of Neiva T-25s (believed to be five) which were acquired from Chile in 1983 and which have subsequently been replaced by the ENAER T-35.

Twelve ECH-51A/B Pilláns were received from an original order for 15. One aircraft, 0111 c/n 213, was lost in an accident on 27 November 1992 but was subsequently replaced by aircraft c/n 196 which took up the vacant serial. Students undertake another 120 hours of flying training on the Pillán with Escuadrilla 'Antares' before moving to the tactical phase, which is conducted by GAT with 80-90 hours on the T-27 Tucano.

The unit also retains two airworthy T-6G Texans which it uses for display flying.

Campo Grande houses all of the FAP helicopter assets. Grupo Aéreo de Helicópteros (GAH) undertakes both the training and opera-

tional role. On strength it currently has three Helibras HB 350B Esquilos from four delivered in 1985 and two Bell UH-1Hs received in 1996 as a gift from Taiwan. The Esquilos are assigned serials H-025/027, although the latter still retains the H-001 it operated while in use as part of the Presidential Flight.

Although not directly a part of GAH, the unit also provides a home for the white-painted Presidential Agusta A 109-II (H-001) and three ageing Bell UH-1Bs (PR-H003/4/5) supplied by the US for anti-narcotics operations.

Fuerza Aérea Paraguaya

Ministerio de Defensa Nacional, Asunción
1 Brigada Aérea – Campo Grande

Grupo Aerotáctico (GAT) – Asunción-Silvo Pettirossi IAP
1º Escuadrón de Caza 'Guaraní'

Escuadrilla 'Orion'	EMB-326GB Xavante
Escuadrilla 'Centauro'	EMB-326GB Xavante

2º Escuadrón de Caza 'Indios'

Escuadrilla 'Taurus'	Lockheed AT-33A
Escuadrilla 'Scorpio'	Lockheed AT-33A

Both Escuadrillas are scheduled to transition to the Northrop F-5E/F Tiger II during 1997 and relocate to BAM Concepción

3º Escuadrón de Caza 'Moros'

Escuadrilla 'Gamma'	EMB-312 T-27 Tucano
Escuadrilla 'Omega'	EMB-312 T-27 Tucano

Both Escuadrillas currently use ECH-51A/B Pilláns while the T-27s are unserviceable

Grupo Aéreo de Transporte Especiales (GATE) –
Asunción-Silvo Pettirossi IAP

Escuadrilla Presidencial	Boeing 707-321B, DHC-6 Twin Otter, Cessna Citation 550, Beech King Air 90
Escuadrilla	Cessna 402B, Cessna 185, Cessna U206 Stationair, Cessna 210 Centurion, Piper PA-23 Apache, Piper PA-32R Lance

Grupo de Transporte Aéreo (GdTA) –
Asunción-Silvo Pettirossi IAP

Transporte Aéreo Militar	Douglas C-47/DC.3, CASA C.212-200

Grupo Aéreo de Helicópteros –
BAM Nhu Guazu, Campo Grande

Escuadrón	Helibras HB 350B Esquilo, Bell UH-1B/H Iroquois
Escuadrón Presidencial	Agusta A 109A-II

Grupo Aéreo de Instrucción – BAM Nhu Guazu, Campo Grande

Escuadrón	Aerotec A-122 Uirapuru
Escuadrón 'Antares'	ENAER T-34A/B Pillán, North American T-6G

Aviación de la Armada Nacional Paraguaya

The service was formed as the Servicio de Aeronáutica de la Marina (Naval Air Service) in 1927 during the period of the French Military mission at Campo Grande, and shared the army's MS.139 basic trainers. Later it received a number of flying-boats for operation off the Paraná-Paraguay River system and surrounding lakes. The service was absorbed into the Army Air Force before the outbreak of World War II.

Re-established in the mid-1960s, the naval air service exists to provide aerial patrol of Paraguay's river systems and a limited amount of communication flying in support of its outlying patrol stations.

The service has only two principal operating locations: Asunción-Silvo Pettirossi IAP, where the fixed-wing element can be found; and Sajonia Naval Aviation Base, where the rotary-wing element is stationed. Total assets are thought to

amount to only six fixed-wing examples: two Cessna 150Ms (122/124), one Cessna U.206A (132), two Cessna 310s (142/144) and a single Cessna 401B (146). The four helicopters comprise a pair of Helibras HB 350B Esquilos and single examples of Hiller UH-12E Raven and Bell OH-13H Sioux.

Aviación de la Armada Nacional

Fixed-Wing Element – Asunción-Silvo Pettirossi IAP
Cessna 150M, Cessna U206A Stationair, Cessna 310, Cessna 401B

Helicopter Element, Sajonia Naval Aviation Base
Helibras HB 350B Esquilo, Hiller UH-12E Raven, Bell OH-13H Sioux

Arma Aérea del Ejército Paraguayo

Following the separation of the Fuerza Aérea Paraguaya from the army in 1946, the army's aerial requirements have in most cases been met by the FAP. A few aircraft were obtained for artillery spotting duties, including two Hiller UH-12Es donated by Chile in July 1980 and three Brazilian-supplied Neiva 56B Paulistinhas (E.01, E.03

and E.05). More recently, the army has acquired a few liaison aircraft including a Beech Baron (TE-02), Cessna 310 (TE-03) and a Cessna 206 (TE-04), all of which operate from within the FAP facility at Asunción-Silvo Pettirossi IAP. Maintenance is carried out by FAP technicians.

Peter R. Foster

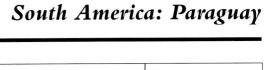

Top: Two flights of the 2º Escuadrón de Caza operate the AT-33A. The 'T-birds' were delivered in 1990.

Above: Two flights of 1º Escuadrón de Caza operate the FAP's EMB-326GBs.

Left: The two component flights of 3º Escuadrón de Caza operate the FAP's EMB-312 Tucanos.

Above: Three HB 350B Esquilos were acquired in 1985 and serve with the Grupo Aéreo de Helicópteros.

Right: Both T-6G Texans and T-35A/B Pilláns serve with the GAI at Campo Grande.

Above right: Three C-47As, dating back to 1950, still serve with the GdTA/TAM.

In 1975 Brazil delivered four Aerotec A-122 Uirapuru basic trainers which now serve with the Grupo Aéreo de Instrucción, at BAM Nhu Guazu.

The FAP has a small helicopter fleet. The most important type in service is the UH-1H, two of which were donated by Taiwan in 1996.

Paraguay took delivery of four CASA C.212-100s in 1984. Today they operate with the surviving C-47s as part of the Grupo de Transporte Aéreo.

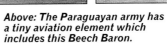

Left: A single Agusta A 109A serves with the Grupo Aéreo de Helicópteros, at Campo Grande.

Above: The Paraguayan army has a tiny aviation element which includes this Beech Baron.

The Paraguayan naval air arm is only slightly larger than the army's and includes this Cessna 150M.

153

Uruguay

Although strategically placed at the mouth of the River Plata, Uruguay is under no illusion that its position of importance is well appreciated by its two very powerful neighbours, Brazil and Argentina. The country is aware that if either had designs on Uruguay's or the other's territory, Uruguay's low-lying fertile plains would become a major battleground. It is impossible for a country the size of Uruguay to support armed forces that

would be capable of staving off an all-out attack from either of its neighbours, and with that in mind its best defence lays in the diplomatic approach and neutral stance that it takes. Arising from this, Uruguay currently enjoys very good relations with all of its neighbours, but still finds sufficient means within its budget to provide the country with a credible air arm to meet any counter-insurgency threat.

Fuerza Aérea Uruguaya

FAU history dates back to March 1913 when the Minister for War and Navy issued a request for military aviators. The Escuela Militar de Aviación was formed on 20 November 1916. Limited finances saw only gradual increases in equipment but, during World War II following Uruguay's decision to make a number of air bases available to the US government, it received aircraft under the lend-lease arrangement. Today, the FAU is structured to provide an offensive arm that is tasked with border patrol and to counter the country becoming a route for the narcotics trade. The transport and communications arm predominantly supports outlying settlements in the north and west, military objectives in the border areas, and Uruguay's Antarctic commitment.

With around 3,000 personnel, the FAU is organised into three major commands. Comando AeroTáctico (CAT, Tactical Air Command) is responsible for all operational flying, with four squadrons and a tactics conversion unit; Comando Aéreo de Entrenamiento (CADE, Air Training Command) is responsible for the Escuela Militar de Aeronáutica (AF Academy Basic Flying Squadron), Escuela Técnica de Aeronáutica (Technical Training School) and Escuela de Comando y Estado-Mayor (Command and Staff College); and finally, the Comando Aéreo de Material (CAM, Air Material Command) is responsible for maintenance, supply, communications and airfields.

The offensive element of the FAU is formed around Brigada Aérea II which is located at Base Aérea Nº 2 General Urquiza, Durazno-Santa Bernadina, 120 km (75 miles) north of Montevideo. There are two primary operating units assigned to Brigada II: Grupo de Aviación 2-Ataque (Pucará), and Grupo de Aviación 2-Caza (A-37B).

The Pucará was ordered in November 1980 with four examples (220-225) being delivered in the following August and the remaining two in October. Unfortunately, one example, 225, was lost on 22 July 1993, killing both crew. It was hoped that sufficient funds could be found in the 1996 budget for the purchase of three additional examples, but this unfortunately did not come to fruition. Instead, one of the remaining airframes has had to be cannibalised to keep the others flying. Regular exchanges take place with a sister unit in Argentina.

Joining the Pucarás at Durazno are Cessna A-37B Dragonflys of Grupo de Aviación 2-Caza. Larger than its sister squadron, GdA-2 was, until June 1996, also equipped with the Lockheed AT/T-33A,

but the shortage of spares and the cost of maintenance forced their retirement.

The A-37Bs were ordered from new in 1975 and eight (270-277/FMS 75-00410-417) were delivered on 16 December 1976. The Dragonfly has given sterling service over the past 20 years although losses have accounted for at least two aircraft. These, 270 and 276, collided during a routine training mission on 7 October 1987. 271 and 272 have also been conspicuous by their absence, suggesting that they, too, might have been casualties at some time.

Introduction of NVGs and compatible instrumentation has given the unit a day/night ability that is especially important in its anti-narcotic operations. The FAU received an important top-up of eight additional jets from surplus US ANG stocks. The first two, (278/279), were received on 11 February 1988 as attrition replacements for the two lost in the accident the previous October. They were followed on 18 March 1989 by another six (280 to 285).

The unit at this period operated the survivors of eight AT-33As which had been delivered in two batches, four (201-204) on 20 October 1956 and four (205-208) on 23 June 1969. They had initially been procured as introduction trainers to the Lockheed F-80C and later as a replacement. 1989 had also seen the supply of five surplus USAF T-33As, three of which (209-211) were placed in service while the remaining two were retained for spares reclamation. Retired in June 1996, they are currently awaiting disposal.

In support of Brigada II the unit has a small liaison flight comprising three Cessna 185s or U-17As, a single Cessna 206 (744), and a Piper PA-18 Cub (730). The air force procured eight Cessna U-17As, one (750/65-10852) being received on 30 July 1965 followed by four more (751-754/65-12734-37) in the following September and three RU-17As (755-757) on 12 April 1966. It is thought that only four now remain operational.

Providing a dual function at Durazno are the Pilatus PC.7U turbo-trainers. Now designated AT-92, the six aircraft (301-306) were received on 26 February 1993 to initially provide advanced fixed-wing training. They appear to have also taken on a more offensive COIN role to assist the FAU's dwindling assets. The aircraft still undertake their primary function within the Centro de Instrucción y Entrenamiento de Vuelo Avanzado (CIEVA), where students undertake a 120-hour, approximately two-year course before

receiving their operational posting. There are plans to streamline the course length to one year, which is considered to be both cost-effective and a better training package.

The AT-92s are not best suited to the COIN role in their present configuration as they are not fitted with ejection seats. This was ably demonstrated on 8 April 1994 when aircraft 304 suffered a horrific crash, with the loss of both crew. It was thought that if the aircraft been fitted with ejection seats then the crew would have survived. The aircraft itself was returned to Pilatus and was rebuilt, eventually being redelivered to FAU charge in October 1996.

The transport, helicopter and communication elements are collectively assigned to Brigada Aérea I at Base Aérea Nº 1, Capitán Boise Lanza, Montevideo-Carrasco International Airport. Originally assigned Grupos de Aviación 3, 4, 5 and 6, the Brigada was restructured in the mid-1990s with the fixed-wing assets operating under the auspices of Grupo de Aviación Nº 3 (Transporte) and the rotary wing with Grupo de Aviación Nº 5 (Busqueda y Rescate).

The three grouped transport squadrons are still operated autonomously within a flight structure. The three flights operate the Lockheed C-130B (three of which were received from surplus USAF stocks), three CASA C.212 Aviocars, a single Fokker F27 Mk 100 and three EMB-110C Bandeirantes.

The Hercules are used heavily in Antarctic resupply support flights. Two are retained in an airworthy condition: 591 which was received on 22 May 1992, and 592 on 18 August 1992. The third aircraft, 593, arrived at Carrasco on 18 April 1994 and has never flown in FAU markings, having been cannibalised for spares. Like all FAU transport assets, the operational pair operates the a duel military/civil identification of CX-BQW and CX-BQX, respectively.

The three CASA C.212s are from an original batch of five (530-534), received by the FAU in late 1981/early 1982. Budget constraints forced the sale of aircraft 530/CX-BOF and 534, the long-nosed SAR variant, back to the manufacturer in Spain. The others maintain the resupply routes in and around the country as part of the military airline Transporte Aéreo Militar Uruguayo (TAMU). The most heavily worked transport aircraft are, however, the Brazilian-built EMB-110C Bandeirantes. Received on 13 January 1976, the first five aircraft (580-58) were originally assigned to Grupo de Aviación 6 before consolidation. They were joined by a sixth aircraft, 585/CX-BKF, on 18 August 1978 following the loss of aircraft 584 on 22 June 1977. One of the Bandeirantes, 585/CX-BKF, is an EMB-110B1 variant and is equipped for photo-mapping.

The sole surviving Friendship is used on TAMU flights to neighbouring countries. The airline was formed in 1961 for internal operation but was later expanded with flights to Argentina, Bolivia, Brazil and Paraguay. It was on one of these flights that Fairchild-Hiller FH-227D 571/CX-BHY was lost in a crash at Los Andes on 13 October 1972, in which more than 15 people died. The two other FH-227Ds have been withdrawn: 570 following a crash landing at Carrasco, and 572 when its hours ran out. The latter is possibly heading for preservation. The second F27 Mk 100 (560) is still extant but currently serves as a spares source.

South America: Uruguay

Until recently Grupo de Aviación 2-Caza, of Brigada Aérea II, operated a combined force of A-37B Dragonflys (above) and AT-33As (left). The AT-33s were retired from use at the end of 1996. The A-37s remain in use at Durazno.

Above: FAU Fokker F27 Mk 400s and Fairchild FH 227Ds serve with Grupo 4.

Below: Early model Bell 204s have been superseded by a small number of UH-1Hs.

Uruguay took delivery of six IA 58A Pucarás in 1981. Today they operate as Grupo de Aviación 1-Ataque (attached to Brigada Aérea II), based at BA 2 General Urquiza, Durazno-Santa Bernadina.

The United States delivered two surplus C-130B Hercules to the FAU in 1992. They serve as part of Grupo de Aviación 4, alongside F27s/FH 227s.

Uruguay acquired six PC-7s in 1992. They have been modified to carry weapons and now serve with Brigada Aérea II, and with a training unit.

Uruguay's two Bell 212s were delivered in 1981. This aircraft is tasked with Antarctic support missions, while the other is used as a VIP transport.

The FAU's small transport helicopter fleet of UH-1Hs will be substantially boosted when its new (ex-RAF) Wessex HC.Mk 2s enter service.

The FAU uses EMB-110C Bandeirantes for transport tasks and EMB-110B1s for photo survey duties with Grupo 6, at BA 1.

Beech T-34A/B Mentors serve alongside the Cessna T-41Ds and PC-7s of the EMA (Escuela Militar de Aeronáutica), at Pando.

This Piper PA-18 Cub is one of a selection of light aircraft attached to Brigada Aérea II for liaison and communications flying.

Grupo de Aviación 5 maintains the rotary-wing assets, comprising two Bell 212s and three Bell UH-1Hs and six, ex-RAF Westland Wessex HC.Mk 2s (from the disbanded No. 28 Sqn, in Hong Kong). The six Wessexes were handed over, at Kai Tak, on 3 June 1997. The Bell 212s were received on 14 January 1981. One, 030/CX-BPM served as the Presidential transport. The other, 031/CX-BPN, was painted in a red/white scheme for Antarctic operations and is air-freighted to the region for 'summer' operations once a year. These helicopters are worked very hard and both are due for replacement.

Tactical taskings are assigned to the three ex-US Army Bell UH-1Hs (050-052) and are being supplemented by the Wessexes. The addition of the Wessex will give Grupo 5 more flexibility. It is planned to have several Wessexes out-based to more northerly locations, including Durazno, where they will be better placed to give aid and support to the civilian population.

A mixture of communication aircraft can also be found at Carrasco, including a Rockwell 680 Aero Commander (501), a Cessna 182D (740), a Cessna 206 (744) and a Cessna 210 (746), all of which have been acquired through confiscation. They are used by BA 1 for communication flying and probably by the Instituto de Adiestramiento Aeronáutico under the Dirección General de Aviación Civil from Aerodromo 'Angel S. Adami', Melilla. This is a civilian flying training school of the Uruguayan Aviation Authority but has instructor pilots assigned from the FAU. Many of its aircraft are on the civilian register, although a few, including a Cessna 310L (542), retain their military identity. This also applies to one of the two airworthy Beech Queen Airs, 540/CX-BPB; the other, 541/CX-BKP, is used by the Air Force Academy at Pando. A third example, 546/CX-BOX, is a spares ship.

The Air Force Academy is located a few miles to the north of Carrasco at Aeropuerto Militar General Artigas, Pando where the Escuela Militar de Aeronáutica undertakes flying tuition. As with most flying schools, the Academy begins with between 150 and 180 applicants and finishes with around 15 who undertake the final flying phase.

Wastage runs at around 15-20 per cent, which is considered acceptable. The unit has 15 instructor pilots, all of whom have undertaken at least one operational tour, and is equipped with six Cessna 172s or T-41Ds and 12 Beech T-34A/Bs. Students undertake a four-year course that include academics. Screening takes place on the T-41D, with the T-34 Mentor being used for the bulk of the 100 hours basic tuition before students move to the advanced flying phase on the Pilatus PC.7U at Durazno.

Five of the Cessna T-41Ds (600-604), were received on 24 November 1969, with two more following on 16 March 1971 (605) and 3 July 1971 (606), although the former was later lost in a crash. The Mentor did not arrive until 1977. The first example, T-34A (650), was a gift from Chile and serves with the Comando Aéreo de Mantenimiento at Carrasco. It was followed by 30 surplus ex-US Navy T-34Bs in 1977, of which 25 were used in FAU service (with serials 660-684) and the remainder for spares. Chile then donated four more aircraft on 17 July 1980. Three T-34Bs became 685-687 and the T-34A was assigned 651, before being passed to the Uruguayan navy as 261. They ultimately replaced the T-6 in both the basic flying training role at Pando and the advanced training role then performed by Grupo de Aviación Nº 1.

On 24 April 1991 Uruguay received as a gift from Spain 17 former Spanish air force T-34A Mentors. They were not introduced into service immediately, although they were assigned the serial range 630-646. To date, only 10 are believed to have taken up FAU markings (632-636/643-646), while the other airframes remain stored at Carrasco.

As stated earlier, funding for the FAU is still very limited and although a number of pressing decisions need to be made, it is likely that the air force will have to soldier on with its current inventory. Priority, as far as the budget goes, is to maintain the Antarctic operation that will probably see the introduction of a new helicopter in the near future. The arrival of the former RAF Wessex HC.Mk 2s has given an added edge to the country's SAR capability, with some of the

operating costs probably being offset against other government departments. The remainder will be used up in maintenance costs, leaving little or none for additional procurement or attrition replacement.

With the reliable but old Cessna A-37B needing an effective replacement, the United States may offer an equipment life-line in support of anti-narcotic operations. Whether the desires of the air force for a more capable aircraft will be met is open to question, but there is certainly enough third-generation US hardware available to provide a very necessary upgrade, not only to Uruguay but to other similarly situated countries.

Fuerza Aérea Uruguaya

Comando Aerotáctico

Brigada Aérea I –
BA Nº 1 'Capitán Boise Lanza', Montevideo-Carrasco

Grupo de Aviación 3	CASA C.212, Lockheed C-130B Hercules, EMB-110 Bandeirante, Fokker 100 Friendship
Grupo de Aviación 5	Bell 212, UH-1H Iroquois, Westland Wessex HC.Mk 2

Brigada Aérea II –
BA Nº 2 'General Urquiza', Durazno-Santa Bernadina

Grupo de Aviación 1-Ataque	FMA IA-58 Pucará
Grupo de Aviación 2-Caza	Cessna A-37B Dragonfly
Grupo de Aviación-CIEVA	Pilatus PC-7 (AT-92)
Grupo de Aviación	Cessna U/RU-17A, PA-18, Cessna 206

Comando Aéreo de Entrenamiento
EMA, Aeropuerto Militar General Artigas, Pando

Escuela Primario	Cessna T-41D
Escuela Básico	Beech T-34A/B Mentor, Beech Queen Air

CIEVA, BA Nº 2 'General Urquiza', Durazno-Santa Bernadina
Centro de Instrucción y Entrenamiento de Vuelo Avanzado

Pilatus PC-7 (AT-92)

Comando Aéreo de Mantenimiento
Brigada de Mantenimiento y Abastecimiento,
Montevideo-Carrasco

Rockwell 680 Aero Commander, Beech T-34A Mentor, Cessna 182D, 210

Dirección General de Aviación Civil
Instituto de Adiestramiento Aeronáutico
Aerodromo 'Angel S. Adami', Melilla

Beech Queen Air, Cessna 310L, Cessna 182D

Aviación Naval Uruguaya

The Uruguayan Naval Air Arm was formed on 7 February 1925. The current naval air station at Laguna del Sauce was not constructed until 1945 and was activated as Base Aeronaval Nº 2 in September 1947. Reorganisation in 1951 saw the service's name change to Aviación Naval.

Helicopters first arrived in 1955 with the delivery of two Bell 47Gs (A-001/002), and a military agreement with the USA resulted in the supply of three S-2A Trackers (851-853) in March 1965. They equipped Escuadrón Antisubmarino y Exploración and were later supplemented in 1982/83 by three upgraded S-2G models (854-856). The S-2Gs were finally retired in 1994, which left a single Beech 200T (871) fitted with APS-128 search radar as the only ASW asset. This and a pair of Piper PA-34-200Ts (210/211) carry out coastal patrols, and the two Senecas also provide advanced twin-engined training.

In 1979 Argentina presented Uruguay with nine T-28P Fennecs. They provided the force

with an attack capability but only four were put into front-line operation, a number further reduced to two in 1988 following the loss of one example and the sale to Canada of another. The remaining two were retained until the retirement of the S-2G Trackers, when they were placed into storage, but re-entered service in mid-1997.

Three Sikorsky CH-34Js (delivered in 1972) were flown by Escuadrón de Helicópteros until retirement in 1988,when two were exchanged in a deal with Bristow Helicopters for three Westland Wessex 60s.

The three 'new' Wessexes (063-065) were delivered in August 1991 and May 1994, two (063/065) having previously seen service with the Ghana air force. They and two 'new' Bell 47G-3Bs now equip the squadron.

Training of naval pilots is still carried out with four Beech T-34s of the Escuela de Aviación Naval. The T-34s comprise two T-34C Turbo Mentors (271-272), the third (270), procured in

May 1981, having been lost in a fatal crash on 22 March 1982. The other two are T-34B 260 and former FAU T-34A 261 (upgraded with the injection system of the B model).

Three Cessna 182s (754-756) are used for support and liaison duties. The base at Laguna del Sauce has recently undergone an important upgrade while development of the airport takes place. This has resulted in the Grupo de Escuela being relocated from the main airfield facility closer to the Base Aérea 2, with improvement in taxiways, hangars and airfield support.

Aviación Naval Uruguaya

Inspección General de Marina

Grupo de Escuadrones –
BA 2 'Captain Curbelo', Laguna del Sauce

Escuadrón Antisubmarino y Exploración	Beech 200T Super King Air
Escuadrón de Helicópteros	Westland Wessex 60, Bell 47G-3B1/2
Escuadrón de Entrenamiento Avanzado	(Sud) T-28 Fennec, Piper PA-34T-200 Seneca, Cessna 182H/J/K

Grupo de Escuela –
'Mayo Villagram', BA 2 'Captain Curbelo', Laguna del Sauce

Escuela de Aviación Naval	T-34B Mentor, T-34C Turbo Mentor

This Cessna Model 185/U-17 is another of Brigada Aérea II's 'hack fleet', which also includes RU-17s and a single Cessna 206.

Uruguay's T-41s come in camouflaged (flying with the BMA at Montevideo-Carrasco) and red and white (flying with the EMA) colour schemes.

The Instituto de Adiestramiento Aeronáutico, based at Melilla, operates this Beech Queen Air along with examples of the Cessna 310 and Cessna 182.

AU C.212-200 Aviocars operate in camouflaged and 'civilian' schemes. The Aviocars fly with Grupo 3.

Above: A single 1955-vintage Bell 476G5 survives in navy service for liaison and training tasks.

Below: Since 1992 the navy has flown two Westland Wessex Mk 60s as part of the Esc de Helicópteros.

Above: The Aviación Naval Uruguaya operates this Beech 200T on maritime patrol duties.

Right: Uruguay's S-2G Trackers may now all be in storage.

Below: The navy's T-28 Fennecs were withdrawn in the late 1980s but some were believed to have been placed back in service by mid-1997.

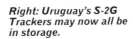

A single Piper PA-34-200 Seneca serves with the Aviación Naval's Esc de Entrenamiento Avanzado (advanced training squadron).

Four T-34A/B Mentors and two T-34C Turbo Mentors were acquired in 1981 and serve with the Escuela de Aviación Naval, at Laguna del Sauce.

All Aviación Naval aircraft, including this Cessna 182 (one of three currently in service), are based at BA 2 'Capitán Curbelo', Laguna del Sauce.

Picture acknowledgments

Front cover: Randy Jolly. **4:** Robert Hewson, Aero Vodochody. **5:** Malcolm Nason, Henry B. Ham, Dylan Eklund, Gilles Auliard. **6:** Bruno Cowet, Chris Schmidt. **7:** Lockheed Martin, K. Dimitropoulos. **8:** Yefim Gordon, René van Woezik. **9:** Tim Senior, Chris Schmidt, Dylan Eklund. **10:** Yaso Niwa, Nathan Leong. **11:** Peter R. Foster, RNZAF (two). **12:** Greg L. Davis, René van Woezik, Aldo Ciarini. **13:** Greg L. Davis (four). **14:** Mike Reyno, Mike Kopack. **15:** Jamie Hunter (two), Nigel Pittaway. **16:** McDonnell Douglas (two), Henry B. Ham. **17:** McDonnell Douglas, Robin Poldermann, Jamie Hunter. **18:** Yefim Gordon (two). **19:** Yefim Gordon, Artur Sarkisyan/VPK-MAPO. **20:** Yefim Gordon, Robert Hewson (two). **21:** Yefim Gordon (three), Robert Hewson. **22:** Luigno Caliaro (three). **23:** Northrop Grumman. **24:** Jamie Hunter (five). **25:** US Navy via Jamie Hunter. **26:** Richard A. Cooper (three), Jamie Hunter. **27:** US Navy via Jamie Hunter (two). **28:** Richard A. Cooper, Jamie Hunter (two). **29:** David Donald (two), Robert Hewson (two), József Gál. **30:** Mark Knight. **31:** Mark Knight, Cpl John Cassidy/Strike Command. **32:** Mark Knight, David Donald. **33:** David Donald (five). **34:** David Donald (two), Mark Knight. **35:** Geoff Lee/BAe, Mark Knight (two). **36:** Mark Knight (two). **38:** No. II(AC) Sqn (two), Chris Lofting, Mark Knight. **39:** Mark Knight (two). **40:** David Donald (six). **41:** Cpl John Cassidy/Strike Command, Lindsay Peacock, David Donald. **42:** Lindsay Peacock, David Donald (six). **43:** Cpl John Cassidy/Strike Command (two), Lindsay Peacock. **44:** No. 39 (1 PRU) Sqn (three), David Donald (two), Cpl John Cassidy/Strike Command. **45:** Lindsay Peacock, David Donald, DERA via Falcon Aviation. **46:** Bill Sweetman. **47:** USAF. **48:** Northrop Grumman. **49:** Ted Carlson/Fotodynamics, Northrop Grumman. **51:** USAF. **52:** Northrop Grumman (two), Bill Krause. **53:** USAF, Anthony D. Chong (two). **54:** Northrop Grumman, USAF/Bill Krause. **55:** Northrop Grumman. **56:** USAF, Northrop Grumman. **57-58:** Northrop Grumman. **59:** USAF/Dave Strong, Northrop Grumman. **60:** Northrop Grumman, TSgt Gary Howard/163ARW via Ted Carlson/Fotodynamics. **61:** Northrop Grumman. **62:** USAF (two). **63:** USAF. **64:** Bill Sweetman, James Benson. **65:** USAF, Northrop Grumman. **66:** Northrop Grumman. **67:** Northrop Grumman. **68:** Anthony D. Chong (two). **69:** via Robert F. Dorr, Robert Hewson (two), Northrop Grumman. **77:** Warren Thompson (eleven), Northrop Grumman, Robert Hewson. **78:** USAF/SSgt Hamilton, USAF, USAF/Dave Strong. **79:** USAF, USAF/Davin Russell. **80-81:** USAF/Davin Russell. **82:** USAF. **83:** USAF/Bill Krause, USAF/Davin Russell (two). **84:** Northrop Grumman. **85:** USAF, USAF/Davin Russell. **86:** USAF (three). **87:** USAF, USAF/Bill Krause (two). **88:** Randy Jolly (two), Geoff Stockle. **89:** Ted Carlson/Fotodynamics. **90:** Northrop Grumman. **91:** Anthony D. Chong, Randy Jolly, Northrop Grumman. **92:** Northrop Grumman, Anthony D. Chong. **93:** USAF, Northrop Grumman. **94:** USAF (ten). **95:** USAF (two), Ted Carlson/Fotodynamics. **96:** Ted Carlson/Fotodynamics, Kaman. **97:** Kaman, Ted Carlson/Fotodynamics (two). **98:** Kaman (two). Terry Panopalis Collection, Skip Robinson via Robert F. Dorr. **99:** Kaman. **100:** Kaman. **102:** Kaman (three), Rick Mullen. **103:** Kaman (two). **104:** Ted Carlson/Fotodynamics. Kaman (two). **106-108:** Ted Carlson/Fotodynamics. **109:** Ted Carlson/Fotodynamics, PH1 M. Rinaldi via Carlson/Fotodynamics. **110-113:** Ted Carlson/Fotodynamics. **114:** Bob Archer, BAe. **115:** BAe, Kevin Wills. **116:** A.B. Ward, BAe. **117:** Peter Liander, MoD, A.B. Ward. **118:** Tony Paxton, Geoff Lee/BAe, Ian Black. **119:** Geoff Lee/BAe. **120:** via Andy Thomas, Ian Black. **121:** Tony Paxton, A.B. Ward (two). **122:** Ian Black (two). **123:** BAe (four). **124:** Ian Black, Stephen Kill. **125:** Ian Black (two). **126:** A.B. Ward (two), via Andy Thomas. **127:** A.B. Ward (five), David Donald, Tim Senior. **128:** Tim Ripley, Geoff Stockle. **129:** Aldo Ciarini, Tim Senior, Ian Black. **130:** Ian Black. **131:** Falcon Aviation (five). **133:** Jorge Felix Nunez Padin (six). **134:** Jorge Felix Nunez Padin (five), Patrick Laureau (five), René L. Uithoven, Robin Poldermann. **137:** Jorge Felix Nunez Padin (thirteen). **139:** Jorge Felix Nunez Padin (nine), Patrick Laureau. **141:** Jorge Felix Nunez Padin (six), Cees-Jan van der Ende and Roland van Maarseveen (six). **143:** Cees-Jan van der Ende and Roland van Maarseveen (six), Jorge Felix Nunez Padin (three), Aldo Ciarini, CASA via Jül Montez. **145:** Gerry Manning (four), Alan Key (seven). **147:** Alan Key (three), Patrick Laureau (three), Patrick Laureau (five). **149:** Patrick Laureau (nine), Hendrik J. van Broekhuizen (three), Denis Hughes. **151:** Hendrik J. van Broekhuizen (two), Patrick Laureau (three), Denis Hughes (two), Baldur Sveinsson (two). **153:** Peter R. Foster (eleven), Denis Hughes. **155:** Andreas L. Mata (four), Peter R. Foster (eight). **157:** Peter R. Foster (nine), Patrick Laureau (two), Denis Hughes.